is a good BOOK

To Gabe
From Uncle Leo + Aunt Dori
Merry Christmas 2013
We love you bunches!

Tyndale House Publishers, Inc., Carol Stream, Illinois 60188

THE ONE YEAR®

DEVOS for ANIMAL LOVERS

Cool Things Animals Show Us about Our Creator

Dandi Daley Mackall

Visit Tyndale's exciting Web site at www.tyndale.com.

The One Year Devos for Animal Lovers: Cool Things Animals Show Us about Our Creator

Designed by Jacqueline L. Nuñez

Edited by Stephanie Voiland

For manufacturing information regarding this product, please call 1-800-323-9400.

ISBN 978-1-4143-3171-3

Printed in the United States of America

16 15 14 13 12 11 10
7 6 5 4 3 2 1

INTRODUCTION
ALL GOD'S CREATURES

God could have made the world without animals. Or God could have settled on one animal—a cow, maybe. Or one type of fish—an angelfish, or a shark.

Do we really need a couple hundred breeds of dogs and nearly that many horse breeds? Was it necessary for cats to come in different colors and fur patterns or for birds to be able to sing their own unique songs?

Our Creator, in his infinite wisdom, kindness, creativity, and love, has filled the world with so many different kinds of creatures that scientists can't even agree how many types of animals exist on earth. And more species are being discovered all the time.

Each animal has a purpose in the world—to spread pollen, to dig, to fill a spot in the food chain, to keep the environment balanced . . . and to teach us about God, the Creator.

If you're reading this book, you probably consider yourself an animal lover, so you've experienced for yourself how important animals are—not only to the world, but to you. Most pets show us unconditional love, gratitude, joy, generosity, compassion, and creativity—all the qualities we'd like to see in our friends, and in ourselves.

It's no accident that creation reflects the Creator. Animals can give us insights into who God is and how God works. Nobody who owns a loving dog can doubt the kindness of God. The sight of a horse galloping, the touch of a cat's soft fur, the sound of a goose honking—they all point to a God we want to get to know better.

As you read this book, you'll discover more about the animals you already love . . . and more about the loving God who created them.

Estimates of the number of animal species range from a few million to nearly a billion. Every time you see an animal—even a bird or a bug—you can talk to God about his amazing creation. (That's praise!)

> *God said, "Let the earth produce every sort of animal . . . livestock, small animals that scurry along the ground, and wild animals." And that is what happened. God made all sorts of wild animals, livestock, and small animals, each able to produce offspring of the same kind. And God saw that it was good.*
>
> **GENESIS 1:24-25**

ON PURPOSE

Bees know what they're all about. Worker bees have one mission in life: to serve the queen. Everything a worker bee does is on purpose, even though she might live for only six or eight weeks.

As soon as a worker honeybee is an adult, she will spend her first week cleaning the hive. The next week she might take over feeding the queen's babies. During week three the worker builds the wax cells of the hive. The fourth week she's put on guard duty. And finally she gets to fly off to flowers and collect pollen.

A worker bee makes about 10 trips a day back and forth to the hive, visiting as many as 1,000 flowers each trip. And that's what the bee will do until she dies.

What's your purpose in life? To get rich? To go to college? To move out of the house? To get married? To become a doctor? Those ambitions may be good ones, but they're not really *purpose*. A purpose should last you your whole life. If your purpose is to go to college and you get there, then what?

You need to know why you're here on earth. You need a purpose that everything you do can fit into. All your decisions can be checked against that purpose before you take another step. Those honeybees make their trips, take the pollen, and work their whole lives for one purpose: to serve the queen bee.

We serve a great King. Knowing and serving God gives us a purpose that explains why we're here. The psalmist wrote, "Whom have I in heaven but you? I desire you more than anything on earth" (Psalm 73:25). That's a good place to start for the new year. Desire God—to know him, to enjoy him, and to serve him.

> *O people, the Lord has told you what is good, and this is what he requires of you: to do what is right, to love mercy, and to walk humbly with your God.*
> **MICAH 6:8**

With back-and-forth trips from flowers to the hive, the total distance honeybees travel to produce a pound of honey is equal to traveling around the world twice.

• • •

TODAY: Talk to God about the things you want out of life. What do you want your life to look like in 10 years? in 20 years? Write down your overall purpose in life and tuck it in a safe place where you can check in from time to time and see how you're doing.

A cat can't see what's under its nose. Whiskers and smell help keep cats from bumping into things.

• • •

TODAY: Ask God to remove your spiritual blind spots. Keep your eyes open for people who are hurting. Then see what you can do to help.

BLIND SPOTS

Don't you love the big, beautiful, soulful eyes of a horse? Horses have the largest eyes of any land mammal. Those giant eyes are set on the sides of their heads, which means they can see almost all the way around them, in nearly a complete circle. While horses graze in the pasture, they're able to keep an eye out for predators and danger on all sides—without interrupting lunch.

But horses can't see *all* the way around, only about 340 degrees out of 360. If you're standing directly in front of a horse, or directly behind (not a good idea, by the way), the horse won't see you. You'll be in the animal's blind spots.

You have blind spots too, and they're bigger than a horse's blind spots. Look straight ahead and see how far behind and to the sides you can see without turning your head. Even when you turn your head, you can't see much behind you, right?

When it comes to spiritual things, we all have blind spots. We say or do things that are wrong, but we may not *see* what we've done. You make a joke at someone's expense, teasing about a bad haircut or laughing because your friend is overweight or short or dressed funny. You might not realize that what you're doing is hurting someone else. *Blind spots.*

How can we miss seeing how depressed a friend is? how much pain our own brother or sister is in? how much pressure our parents are under? *Blind spots.*

So how do we get rid of spiritual blind spots? We can listen to God, who talks to us through his creation, in prayer, and through his Word. Have you ever read a passage in the Bible and felt the words were written for you? God's words have the power to open your "blind" eyes. His Spirit can break through any blind spot and help you see clearly.

The word of God is alive and powerful. It is sharper than the sharpest two-edged sword, cutting between soul and spirit, between joint and marrow. It exposes our innermost thoughts and desires.

HEBREWS 4:12

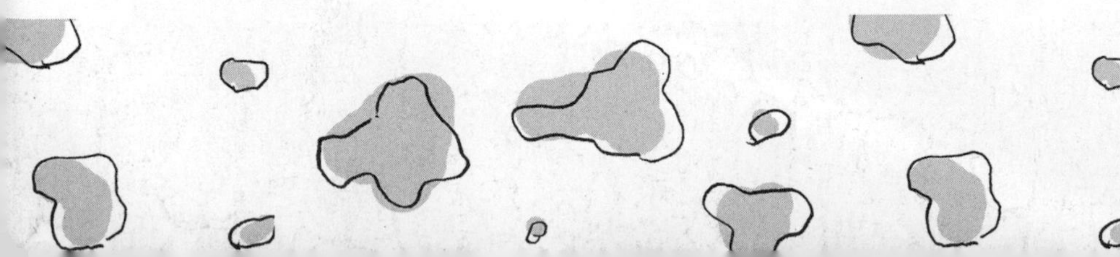

CATNAPS

Cats sleep more than any pet on the planet. The average cat sleeps away two-thirds to three-quarters of its life. Still, cats have been big favorites throughout history. Four thousand years ago in Egypt, the penalty for killing a cat—whether you meant to or not—was death. Some cats were mummified after death, like the pharaohs, and placed in tombs with saucers of milk.

Even though cats sleep a lot, they only allow themselves to fall into a deep sleep for three or four hours a day. The rest of the day, cats enjoy catnaps.

A catnap is a state of light sleep. While napping, a cat can still hear the slightest sound and be ready to jump up at a second's notice. Cats have a third eyelid, a thin membrane that slides across the cat's eye, underneath the regular eyelid, when a cat is in deep sleep. When Kitty is just napping, he keeps the third eyelid rolled up and out of the way. He's staying tuned in to the world around him. That's the great thing about a catnap: the cat is still alert.

Nobody can think about God every second of every day, right? Ordinary things like school and dinner, or playing football or riding a horse, or even talking with parents and friends—they all require our attention too.

But even when life gets busy, you can still stay tuned to God. You can keep your soul's "third eyelid" open and ready to respond. Don't let yourself sink into spiritual deep sleep times, when you wouldn't hear God if the earth shook and your name flashed in neon lights. Instead, be easy to wake up, prepared to give God your full attention.

Stay tuned in to God, sensitive to his whispers.

I stay awake through the night, thinking about your promise.
PSALM 119:148

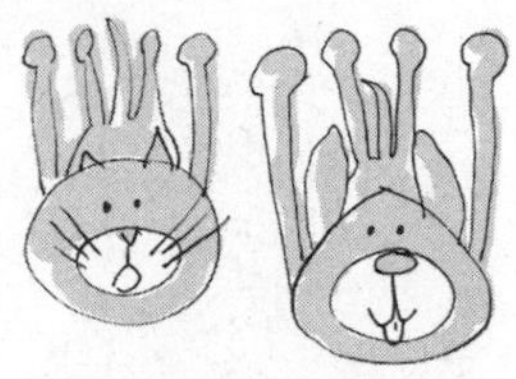

In the 1600s, heavy rains flooded the streets of London, England. Scores of dogs and cats and other creatures got caught up in the rapid currents of water and drowned. Their bodies floated in the floodwaters, making it look like it had rained cats and dogs. And so the expression "raining cats and dogs" was born.

• • •

TODAY: Think of three things you'll be doing today that will require a lot of thought (like taking a killer test or playing ball or reading). Make it a point to check in with God during those busy activities.

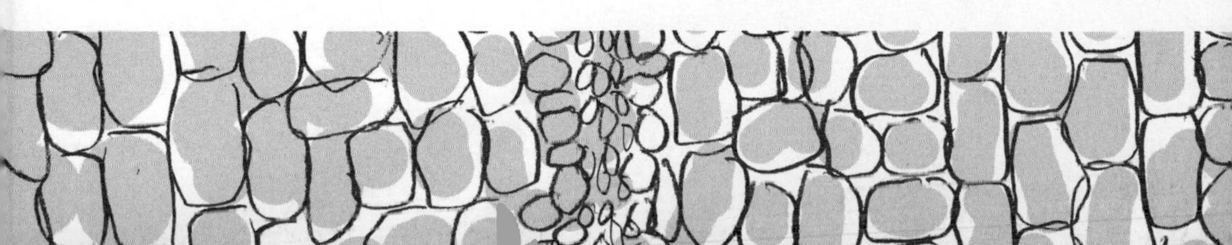

WHO'S TOP DOG?

Every pack of dogs in the wild has a leader, called the alpha dog. Usually a female, the alpha dog will nip dogs that get out of line or stray too far from the group. She gets to eat first and lead the way. It may look like the alpha dog is just plain bossy.

But the other dogs know they're better off with the alpha in charge. She'll make smart decisions for the good of the pack.

Our pets need a leader too, even if they're not out in the wild. And if you don't claim the alpha role, your dog will. Here's what that scenario may look like:

Your dog takes *you* on walks, instead of the other way around.

Your dog "marks its territory" on the living room rug.

Doggie is free to do whatever it wants, including chewing on Mom's slippers.

Your commands to "Stop barking!" or "Come!" are ignored.

Life is chaotic when the wrong alpha tries to lead the pack.

You may have heard Christ referred to as the Alpha and the Omega, the beginning and the end. Christ is the best alpha anyone—any pack, any church, any individual—could ever have. He leads with love and wisdom, and he makes decisions that take us to the best places.

Before you jump into a new group of friends, talk to your Leader. Talk to Christ about every decision. When you find yourself in trouble or you get off track, turn to Christ and follow him back to safety.

Life goes more smoothly when you quit trying to be "top dog."

Christ is also the head of the church, which is his body. He is the beginning, supreme over all who rise from the dead. So he is first in everything.
COLOSSIANS 1:18

Most dogs have at least 100 different expressions, thanks to their expressive ears. But many people think pit bulls and bulldogs have only about 10 facial expressions. Maybe that's why they're so misunderstood by other dogs, who figure that with those mugs, the dogs must be looking for a fight.

• • •

TODAY: As you go through your regular routine today, pay attention to anything you do or anyplace you go where you just might be taking over as the alpha. Talk to God about it, and make way for the real Top Dog.

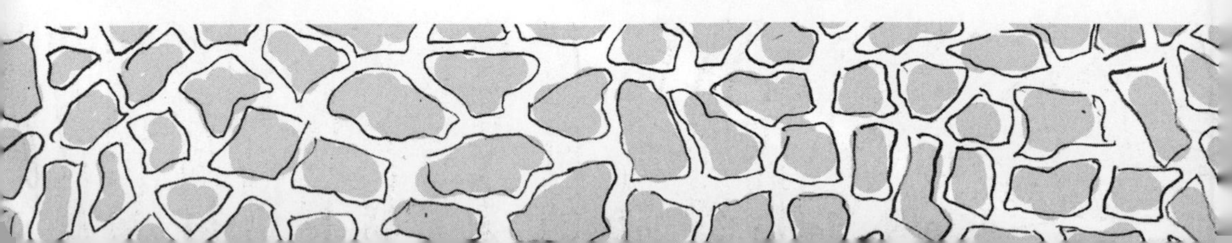

TO LIFE!

The life span of animals runs the gamut, from mere hours to hundreds of years. Some mayflies don't survive even 24 hours as adults. The gastrotrich, a multicelled water creature, lives about three days. Aphids live about a month.

Lice (those nasty creatures that make elementary schoolkids scratch their heads in wonder) manage to mate and lay eggs in their one-month life span. If you knock them off your head, though, they'll die in two days.

On the other hand, a queen termite may live from 15 to 50 years. Parakeets average about 12 years, while parrots live about 40 to 100 years. Horses average between 20 and 30 years, but elephants live to be 60 or so. Guppies have a life span of 5 years, carp 30, and whales 50.

The prize for the longest life span has generally gone to the giant tortoise, which averages 177 years and has been known to reach 200. But the rougheye rockfish and a clam called the ocean quahog may have lived even longer than that.

Ever heard the term *life expectancy*? As humans, we generally figure we'll live on earth for about 80 years. But Isaiah 40:7 warns, "The grass withers and the flowers fade beneath the breath of the Lord. And so it is with people."

We can talk averages, but nobody knows how long we'll live. And nobody lives forever . . . at least not on earth.

But that's okay. No matter how long we're expected to live on earth, we have the promise that we'll live with God in heaven forever if we believe in God's Son.

How do you know what your life will be like tomorrow? Your life is like the morning fog—it's here a little while, then it's gone.
JAMES 4:14

You can tell a whale's age by counting the number of rings in its waxlike earplugs (don't try this at home).

• • •

TODAY: Ask (and answer) that old question: If you died today, do you know that you'd go to heaven? There's no in-between—it's yes or no. Your answer doesn't depend on how good you've been on earth (thank goodness!), but on how perfect Christ is and if you've put your trust in him.

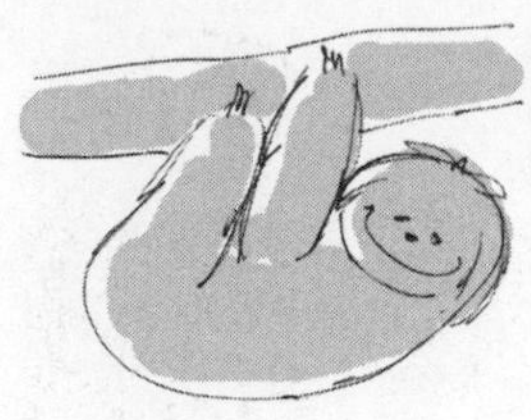

SLOTH

If you could have a sloth for a pet, it would be pretty boring. These furry, long-armed, chubby creatures don't do much. Sloths hang out in Central and South America, dangling upside down from high branches.

And they sleep. Sloths have two speeds: sleeping and almost sleeping. About 20 hours of their day are spent in true sleep.

Just how lazy is a sloth? The sloth is so lazy, algae grows on it!

Just how slow is a sloth? It moves at the speed of 6 feet per minute, although it can get up to 12 feet per minute if it's being chased (and probably caught).

The early church came up with a list of the "seven deadly sins," and sloth was on that list.

Have you ever charted how much of your day is spent sloth-style? Take an average Saturday or a day off in the summer. You start out with 24 hours, the same as every other person on the planet. That's fair. But then what?

Time is a gift. Psalm 118:24 says, "This is the day the Lord has made. We will rejoice and be glad in it." God made all 24 hours, and you get to spend them every single day. So how do you spend your hours? Massive doses of television, computer games, and slothlike sleep?

Or are you making each day count? Are you doing things like volunteering for community and church outreaches, and helping people God puts in your path (including your parents and siblings)?

Life isn't all that long (even though time crawls when you're in math class). If you want to make your time on this planet count, now's a good time to start.

Teach us to realize the brevity of life, so that we may grow in wisdom.
PSALM 90:12

APPROXIMATE ANIMAL SPEEDS

Cheetah: 70 mph
Pronghorn antelope: 60 mph
Lion: 50 mph
Gazelle: 50 mph
Coyote: 43 mph
Zebra: 40 mph
Sloth: slower than 1/10 of a mph

• • •

TODAY: For three days in a row, keep a record of how you spend your 24 hours. Make a chart that accounts for every 30-minute time period of the day. Then analyze the results and see if you're satisfied with where the time goes.

A WAY OUT

When you think about it, it's amazing that all small animals don't get wiped out by big ones. But when God created animals, he built in special features to help them escape.

What's an opossum supposed to do when it's about to be run down by a giant dog? Stop, drop, and play dead. "Playing opossum" takes all of the fun out of the chase for the dog, and the opossum lives to sneak away after the dog gives up. The tiger moth does the same thing, only better. When the moth falls over and plays dead, the predator sees the bright orange on its underside, a color that signals: "I taste bad, dude!" The hognose snake, one of the least attractive snakes you'll ever meet, plays dead too. It rolls over onto its back and keeps its mouth wide open. If you turn it over, it will flop back and keep playing dead.

Lizards scurry away from danger in a zigzag pattern. If they're unlucky enough to be caught by, say, a coyote, most lizards can break off their tails in the middle and leave the tail behind as a decoy. Sometimes the piece of tail keeps wiggling, and the coyote starts chasing it, leaving the lucky lizard a way of escape. (And a new tail will grow back in no time.)

Have you ever done something wrong—something you didn't really want to do, but you felt like you just couldn't help yourself? Maybe you went along with your buddies when they cheated on a big test. Maybe you broke your parents' house rule about which Internet sites to visit because you didn't want to be the only one left out. You might have said or thought: "I had to do it." "I didn't have a choice." "I just couldn't stop myself." "There was no way out."

The truth is, there's always a way out. God wired you so you're always able to escape a tempting situation. And God controls the circumstances so you're not tempted in ways you're not equipped to handle.

> *The temptations in your life are no different from what others experience. And God is faithful. He will not allow the temptation to be more than you can stand. When you are tempted, he will show you a way out so that you can endure.*
>
> **1 CORINTHIANS 10:13**

It might seem like an impossible task for a baby bird to hatch through the wall of an egg, but baby birds are equipped with two secret weapons: an "egg tooth" on the tip of the beak and a pipping muscle in the neck that lets the newborn force its way out.

• • •

TODAY: As you go through the day, jot down every temptation you run into. Also, make note of your "escape route." Thank God for always giving you a way out.

Moths sleep in the day, and butterflies sleep at night. It's one way to tell them apart.

• • •

TODAY: Remind yourself at every step today: *God is watching over me.* If you need to give yourself a visual cue, try the old tie-a-string-around-your-finger trick. Or maybe just wear a ring you don't usually wear. Then when you see it, remember.

GODLY INSOMNIA

If you could choose a bear or an ant as your "watchdog," which would you pick?

Don't be too quick to decide on that bear. It'll hole up in a cave to hibernate away the winter. Most ants, on the other hand, don't sleep. They could watch out for you night and day.

Or what about these other watchdog possibilities? An albatross can sleep while it flies. The sooty tern may fly for several years with only a few seconds of sleep during flight. Seals sleep only 90 seconds at a time.

You might consider a "watch duck." At night, a flock of ducks will form a circle on the water. Ducks on the outside of the circle sleep with one eye open. Ducks on the inside get to shut both eyes.

Fish sleep with their eyes open, but they don't have a choice. They don't have eyelids.

Some animals, like horses and giraffes, sleep standing up, ready to run if necessary. Still, a horse that feels safe and secure might conk out on its side a couple of hours at night. And giraffes may cheat and lean against a tree.

A "watch goat" might be a good investment. Goats rest about eight hours a day, but they don't sleep and they don't close their eyes.

But you already have something better than a watch goat, a watch duck, or a watch giraffe. You have something—Someone—much better. The God who created the universe watches over you night and day. And God never sleeps.

God sees everything that happens to you. There's no place you can go without his protection. Knowing that God is watching over you, guarding you, shouldn't make you careless or naive though. Part of God's protection involves your built-in sensors that detect trouble and your conscience that should kick in and tell you to stay out of trouble.

Be thankful that God never sleeps.

He will not let you stumble; the one who watches over you will not slumber.
PSALM 121:3

DON'T FORGET TO SHARE

Honey ants really know how to share. They store food for the whole colony in case of emergency. First, a honey ant eats all the honey it can hold, turning itself into a giant (okay, giant for an ant) ball of ant that can barely move. When times get tough in the winter and the colony runs out of honey, it's time for the honey ant to share. This generous, chubby ant spits up the stored honey and shares with its buddies.

Some vampire bats are good at sharing too. One species of small vampire bat has to eat every single night to stay alive. On a bad night when there's simply no blood to be had by the little vampire, another bat may vomit blood to share. Sweet!

If birds have built nests in the eaves or on the windowsills of your home, you might have noticed that it's not always the same bird that returns to the nest the following year. It seems like they're following Peter's advice in 1 Peter 4:9: "Cheerfully share your home with those who need a meal or a place to stay."

Sharing is one of the first things parents teach their children. And it's one of the hardest lessons for a toddler to learn. If you have a little brother or sister, you've probably heard him or her scream, "Mine!" And you've probably shouted it yourself when someone invaded your room and your stuff.

We're not born good sharers. But God tells us we need to share, to follow Christ's example. Jesus shared everything he had, including his life. And when you do share, God can change you from the inside so you'll want to share. Christ in you will help you do it, and his Spirit will even make you feel good about it.

All the believers met together in one place and shared everything they had. They sold their property and possessions and shared the money with those in need. They worshiped together at the Temple each day, met in homes for the Lord's Supper, and shared their meals with great joy and generosity.

ACTS 2:44-46

Believe it or not, sharks share. (Say that three times fast.) A little fish called the shark sucker, or remora, attaches itself to the belly of a shark and tags along, scarfing up leftovers from the shark's meals.

• • •

TODAY: Make a list of the things you don't like to share with your siblings or friends. Talk to God about why it's so hard to part with each item on your list. Then offer to share at least one of those items with someone else.

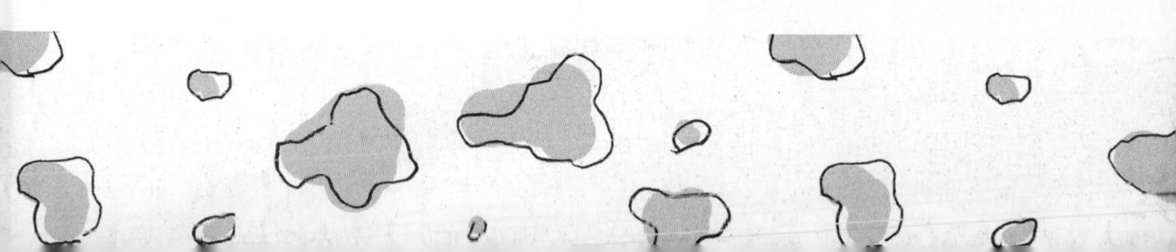

Some 3,500 years ago, Egyptians made fish glue by boiling the skins or bones of fish. In the Middle Ages, monks used to grind gold and mix it with fish glue to gild illuminated manuscripts. This glue was also used to mend stringed instruments called lutes.

• • •

TODAY: Talk to God about your relationship with him. It's a fact that God has you in a tight grip, glued securely so you won't be snatched away. That's worth giving thanks for. But are you taking advantage of your closeness to God? How many times do you think about God during the day? How often do you sense God's presence?

STICK LIKE GLUE

Some animals know a lot about glue. Take barnacles, for instance. Barnacles are little crustaceans, which makes them cousins to the crab. These little shelled creatures glue themselves to a rock, a piece of wood, or a ship, and they stick like glue to that surface for the rest of their lives. The "glue" used by barnacles is stronger than any human-made glue.

Ever heard of rabbit-skin glue? People used to make all kinds of glue from animals (without the animals' permission, mind you). The Renaissance painters used rabbit-skin glue as an ingredient in their plaster to cover a canvas before painting with oils.

For thousands of years, people used animal glues when working with wood. Some glues were developed by boiling the skins and hooves of horses and cattle. That's just wrong. Today most glues, like Elmer's glue, are man-made, but animal-hide glues are still used to repair certain antiques and musical instruments.

Glue can be a good thing, depending on where it comes from. The good news is that when we become part of the family of God, Jesus promises that we will stick to him like glue. He told his disciples that nobody could pull them away from him.

We're in the hand of Christ, and he's in the hands of his Father. That's a grip nobody can unglue.

Even you can't unglue your relationship to the Father.

> *[Jesus said,] "I give them eternal life, and they will never perish. No one can snatch them away from me, for my Father has given them to me, and he is more powerful than anyone else. No one can snatch them from the Father's hand. The Father and I are one."*
> **JOHN 10:28-30**

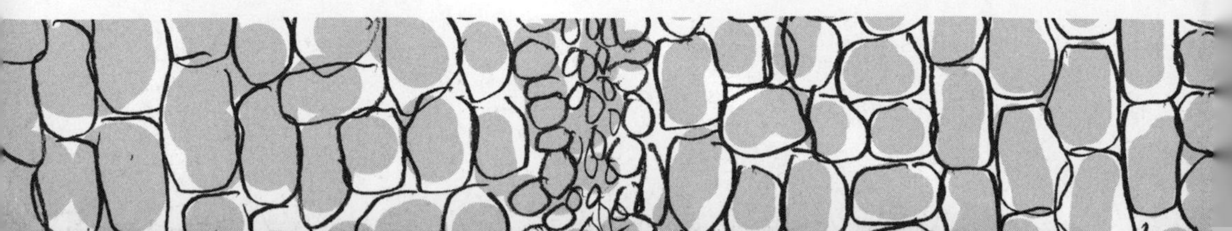

THE IMPORTANCE OF SHEDDING YOUR SKIN

Have you ever run across a snake skin? You can usually find a skin in one whole piece, turned inside out. Snakes crawl out of the old skin, shedding it because it's worn out or too small.

Baby snakes have to shed their skins soon after they're born because they quickly outgrow the old skin. During the first year, some snakes might shed up to seven times. Growing snakes have to keep shedding their entire lives.

Did you know that people shed too? Your skin gets worn down and wrinkly, so you need new cells to replace the old ones. You can't leave your skin in one piece and slip into new skin, but you do shed. You just do it bit by bit, with a little skin dropping off every day.

If you stay out in the sun all day, you'll have proof of shedding. (But it's not good for you.) Sunburn makes our skin wear out and shed faster.

Spiritually, we do a kind of shedding too. When we believe in Christ, we get a new nature. We put on the new and cast off the old. Galatians 6:15 says, "What counts is whether we have been transformed into a new creation."

But this process isn't a onetime thing—we have to keep growing and "shedding" our old selves. For the rest of our lives, we should become more like Christ. Have you noticed that you don't get angry as quickly as you used to? Is it a bit easier to forgive a friend and to understand and have compassion? If you haven't "shed your skin" for a while, maybe you need to kick-start your growth. Set a time to read the Bible every day. Get into the habit of praying when you walk to school or before you go to sleep.

It's not always easy shedding your skin. But God promises that one day you will get to ditch that whole body of yours, skin and all, and put on a brand-new heavenly version.

> *We grow weary in our present bodies, and we long to put on our heavenly bodies like new clothing.*
> **2 CORINTHIANS 5:2**

Snakes shed their skin because snake skin isn't elastic. It can't stretch with the slithering creature as it grows.

• • •

TODAY: Look back over the past year of your life with Christ. Have you changed? Can you think of specific evidence to show that you're growing in Christ? Are you kinder to others, closer to Christ, more patient than you were 12 months ago? Take steps to make sure you keep shedding spiritually for the next 12 months. Write down a plan of Bible study, church involvement, prayer, and outreach.

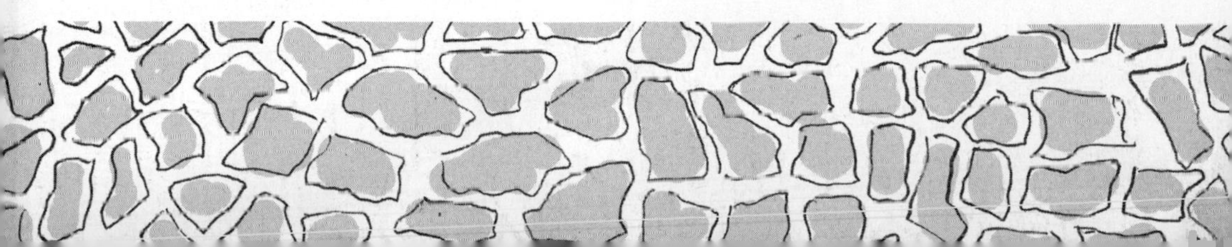

LAUGH, KOOKABURRA!

Remember that old song about a kookaburra sitting in an old gum tree, the "merry king of the bush is he"? You had to beg the bird to "laugh, kookaburra! Laugh, kookaburra!" until the silly song got stuck in your head, right?

There really is such a thing as a kookaburra—a type of kingfisher that lives in Australia and New Guinea. And it does laugh . . . kind of. The bird lets out a crazy call that sounds like a hysterical human cackle.

A single bird begins with a gurgling, low giggle sound that turns into hilarious laughter and soon draws in other kookaburras, which throw their heads back and join in.

One species of spotted hyenas is called the laughing hyena, but there's not much funny about these meat eaters. They make their weird gurgling, cry-laugh noise when they're on the prowl for dead animals they can rip to pieces and devour.

It's open to debate whether or not animals laugh, but there's no doubt that some animals enjoy our laughter. Horses, for example, love laughter. Some trainers use laughter to help gentle wild horses and get them used to human company.

How often do you laugh? Are you free to laugh at yourself and at the day's events, or are you too caught up in what people might think about you? A good sense of humor is a gift—to yourself and to others—as long as you're laughing at the right things.

Laughter can be as cruel and deadly as a hyena's war cry if the laughter is mean-spirited. Laughing at other people or making fun of them just isn't funny.

You are the best target for your laughter. If you drop your books when you open your locker or if you trip on a chair leg coming into class, laugh it off instead of getting upset.

Laugh! After all, if you know Christ and have a great friendship with God, you have a lot to be happy about.

Always be full of joy in the Lord. I say it again—rejoice!
PHILIPPIANS 4:4

Kookaburras eat mice, rats, crabs, insects, and a few reptiles, like squirmy snakes and leathery lizards—and they still manage to laugh.

• • •

TODAY: When you're all alone, try laughing out loud. Think of all God's given you, including a world of amazing animals, and laugh for joy!

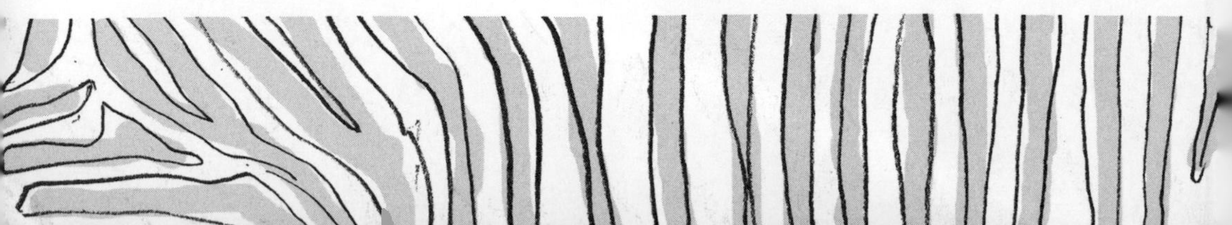

KEEPING YOUR FOCUS

Rabbits need to be able to hear their enemies coming and get a quick head start because foxes and coyotes can run down a poor rabbit with no problem. That's why God gave rabbits such big ears. The ears on a lop-eared rabbit can be as long as the rabbit itself—around 14 inches. Their big ears help them focus sound and sharpen their hearing so they can get a jump start on outrunning coyotes, foxes, and wildcats.

A rabbit's curved ears funnel sound in a similar way to how we cup a hand behind our ears and say, "Huh?"

It's a no-brainer that we should want our focus to be on Jesus. So what are you doing to improve your focus? Cupping your hand behind your ear probably won't help. But there are other things you can do. The apostle Paul told Timothy to focus on reading the Bible, encouraging believers, and teaching others about Jesus.

If you spend all day on your phone or online, don't be surprised if your focus slips away from God and soon all you think about is what other people think of you. If you eat, sleep, and dream soccer or art or music, guess where your focus is?

Focusing on God doesn't mean you give up doing everything else. If you love baseball, then of course you're going to think about it a lot. Just don't leave God out. Thank him for baseball.

If you love God, you'll find yourself thinking about him and all he has done for you. Knowing God better leads to loving him more because of who he is. You just can't help yourself.

Until I get there, focus on reading the Scriptures to the church, encouraging the believers, and teaching them.
1 TIMOTHY 4:13

Here's how focused an archerfish is on getting its next meal: This fish eyes an unsuspecting insect high above the water—usually one that's sitting on the leaf of an overhanging tree about five feet away. The fish adjusts its aim and then spits at the insect, knocking it off the leaf . . . just in time for dinner.

• • •

TODAY: For one whole day, keep track of what you think about—not every single thought, but your focus. Where do you spend most of your mental time and energy? That's your focus. If it's not on God, maybe it's time to rethink. What's getting the best of your mind?

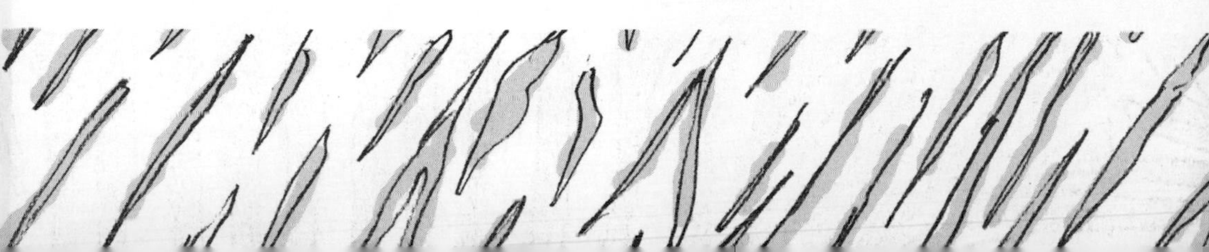

HANG IN THERE!

"If you can't stand the heat, get out of the kitchen."

—PRESIDENT HARRY S. TRUMAN

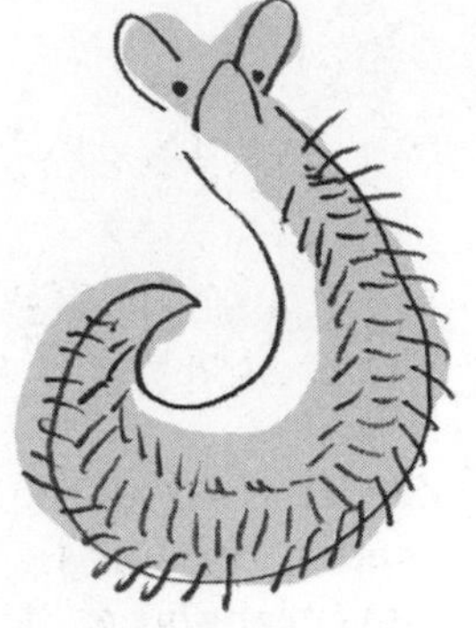

The Pompeii worm is known as the hottest animal on earth. It can survive temperatures as hot as 194 degrees Fahrenheit. It can handle multiple extreme temperatures at the same time, with one end soaking in 194-degree water, while the other end is in 72-degree water.

• • •

TODAY: Catch yourself every time you complain today. Ask a good friend to elbow you every time he or she hears you complain. When you feel a complaint coming on, douse it with a good dose of gratitude and thank God for one blessing in your life.

Harry S. Truman became president when Franklin D. Roosevelt died near the end of World War II. The guy knew about heat. It was Truman who made the final decision to release the atomic bombs on Japan and force an end to the war.

Pompeii worms know about heat too. They live in the hottest places in the world—in geysers with temperatures that could melt an ordinary worm, in volcanic mountain ranges, and in the deep sea near hydrothermal vents where the temperature is hot enough to boil water and the pressures get so great that you'd be crushed to death there.

But do you hear *them* complaining?

How much complaining do you do in an average week? Do you gripe about too much homework? about a teacher who is too tough? about kids at school who are mean? about a best friend who isn't loyal? about too many chores? about not having enough money? about too many rules? The list could go on and on. . . .

We complain about heat in the summer and cold in the winter, bad calls at the game, boring teachers, the cafeteria lunch menu. Everybody does it, so what's the big deal?

The big deal is that complaining isn't just tossing out meaningless words that fill air space. When God led the people of Israel out of Egypt, their gratitude lasted only until the next complaint. They complained about being hungry, and God fed them. Then they complained about being thirsty, so God produced water. But the complaints kept coming, and God considered their complaints as gripes about him, not about Moses or their circumstances.

When we complain, it's actually God we're griping against. Constant complaining proves that we're not grateful for all the blessings God has already given us.

Moses and Aaron said . . . "In the morning you will see the glory of the Lord, because he has heard your complaints, which are against him, not against us. What have we done that you should complain about us?"

EXODUS 16:6-7

PUTTING THE "GOLD" IN GOLDFISH

What's not to love about a goldfish? With their built-in glow, it's just part of the nature of these beautiful golden fish to sparkle before our eyes . . . or is it?

Did you know that if you deny a goldfish light, it will stop being so golden? Keep the fish outside in a pond, with plenty of sunshine, and it'll be just fine. The fish will stay bright and glowingly gold. But if you put the same fish in dim light, the poor thing will turn drab and dull.

What's the moral of the goldfish story? Stay in the light. Jesus is the Light of the World, and all we have to do to keep from becoming dull and lifeless is stay close to him. We can reflect his light, doing what he would do, making the right choices, and showing others what it looks like to live for him.

So how can you stay in the light?

God is the one who gets the credit for making us like Christ, but there are things you can do to make your relationship with Christ stronger. Get involved in your church. Volunteer for outreach programs. Find ways to help in your community. Talk to God all throughout the day, not just at the "Now I lay me down to sleep" times. Spend most of your time with friends who want to stay in the light too.

The truth is, since God wants you to stay in the center of his will, he helps you stay in the light. And even if you do wander so far away from the light that you start feeling drab and dull, you can always swim back. The Light will be waiting for you.

> *If we are living in the light, as God is in the light, then we have fellowship with each other, and the blood of Jesus, his Son, cleanses us from all sin.*
> **1 JOHN 1:7**

Goldfish belong to the carp family and can grow as big as two feet long and weigh nearly 10 pounds. Although the oldest known goldfish lived to be 45 years old, most pet varieties live five or six years. But if you won a goldfish at the county fair, you can count on it lasting about 24 hours.

• • •

TODAY: Think of two things you can do—two changes you can make to your normal daily routine—to help you draw closer to God. For example, set aside time to read the Bible. Talk to God all throughout the day.

Be extra cautious around bats. If you spot a bat in your bedroom, you might need a rabies vaccination.

• • •

TODAY: Think about any "biting and devouring" you've observed lately. Have you been part of it? Did you watch silently or laugh along? Talk to God about strategies for stopping those put-downs and negative comments.

BITING THE HAND THAT FEEDS YOU

Most bites to humans are caused by pets. Dog bites are the most frequent, followed by cat bites. Although more dogs bite than cats, cat bites have a higher risk of getting infected because those long, sharp cat teeth deliver deeper puncture wounds.

Wild animals, such as skunks, raccoons, and bats, bite thousands of people every year. That's when you have to think about the possibility of rabies. Rabies is a rare but deadly disease spread through the saliva of a rabid animal.

Beware of animals that are acting weird or that go out of their way to bite for no reason. A raccoon that's active during the day is also suspect. If you're bitten by a wild or stray animal, you need to call the animal control authorities. Have someone try to keep an eye on the animal until authorities get there, but stay away from it.

Proverbs 30 warns about people who curse their fathers and don't thank their mothers. It says these people have "teeth like swords and fangs like knives" (Proverbs 30:14). Our words can bite and wound. You may not even realize how much your careless comment or put-down hurts your family member. But bites do hurt.

Paul cautioned the Galatians that they had the power to destroy one another. He said that if they were always biting and devouring one another, they'd better be careful.

Our words can be used to snap at each other, destroying friendships, families, youth groups, and whole classes. At first, word wars can seem funny. Someone slams you, and you and your buddies slam back. Everybody laughs. But harmful words stick and spread, like a bad infection. Before you know it, the comments aren't one bit funny, and you've made a bunch of enemies.

Beware of biting!

If you are always biting and devouring one another, watch out! Beware of destroying one another.
GALATIANS 5:15

THE LAW OF THE JUNGLE

Everybody knows that the lion is king of the jungle. Weighing in at around 500 pounds, wearing a full and hairy mane, and possessing a roar that will stop a wolf's howling and a hyena's laughter, the lion deserves the title of king.

Few animals are dumb enough to challenge the lion. They know that the law of the jungle puts him first, with every other creature falling lower in the food chain. And life in the jungle runs much more smoothly when the pride, or group of lions, submits to the king.

The jungle isn't the only place where communities have laws or rules of survival. Prairie dogs have a "law of the prairie." They're social animals, living in families, neighborhoods, and colonies, and they look out for each other. When one prairie dog takes its turn watching out for predators, it will stand up on its raised tunnel entrance and bark out a warning when danger is near. Working together, the whole community of prairie dogs ends up stronger.

We live in a community too. And we function best when we work in the community of believers, together following the Lion of Judah, which is one of Jesus' names in the Bible. Paul urged believers to work together for the Kingdom of God.

What part are you playing in God's Kingdom? Do you help your friends grow in Christ? Do you talk about God openly and respectfully, no matter where you are? Do you encourage your family to do things that help draw you closer together and closer to Christ?

We need each other. It's a jungle out there!

Look, the Lion of the tribe of Judah, the heir to David's throne, has won the victory.
REVELATION 5:5

A lot of jungles and animal habitats are in danger from too much hunting and too little concern about the animals as more buildings go up. As a result, lions no longer roam North and South America or Europe, and prairie dog colonies are much smaller than they used to be.

• • •

TODAY: Talk to God (the King) about three people—one person in your family, one person who's already part of the Kingdom, and one person who doesn't know Christ yet. Ask God to show you the best ways you can support each person. See if there's something you can do today . . . and then do it!

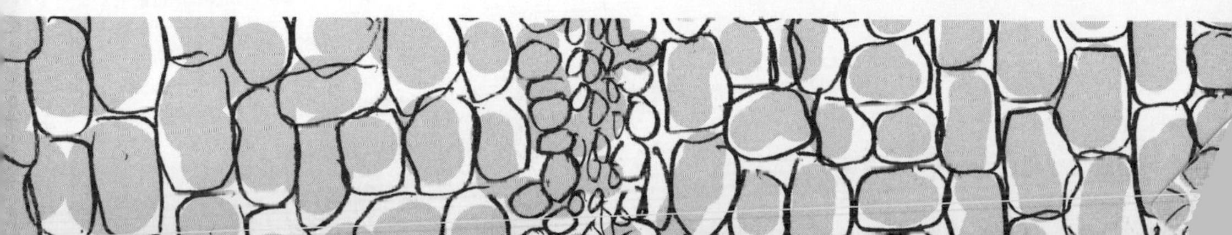

18 January

Cows' knees bend funny. A cow can climb up the stairs but not down.

• • •

TODAY: Write down what you'd like your life to look like in 10 years. Do you think your current path is leading there? Ask God to show you the steps to take to be the person you want to be. Listen to that internal compass!

A COW'S COMPASS

Scientists have recently discovered that cows have a strange type of internal compass. It's a little like those built-in GPS devices used for navigating in cars. When cows are outside in a pasture, most of the time they'll end up facing north or south, as if drawn by the earth's magnetic poles. No one is entirely sure why.

But cows aren't the only ones with a built-in compass. Each year when the weather turns cold, usually around October, western monarch butterflies fly in huge butterfly clouds to "Butterfly Town, USA," the nickname for Pacific Grove, California. Eastern monarchs find their way from the East Coast of the United States to central Mexico, migrating 2,000 miles or more.

The millions of monarchs that migrate every fall often stop at the same rest spots year after year. And the most amazing thing is that the butterflies flying to Mexico on the identical route of their ancestors have never even been to Mexico—they just have something wired into their DNA that tells them where they need to go.

If God can guide cows and butterflies, he can guide you, too. Your own journey has already required thousands of decisions: *Should I listen to my parents? Should I peek at that person's quiz answer? Will I forgive that person for what she said?*

If God's Spirit is inside you, you can rely on God's guidance. Pay attention to your own "internal compass," your conscience. And read the Bible, since the map for most of your life is laid out in the Scriptures. Finally, pray.

Ask God for guidance, and you'll get it.

The Lord says, "I will guide you along the best pathway for your life. I will advise you and watch over you."
PSALM 32:8

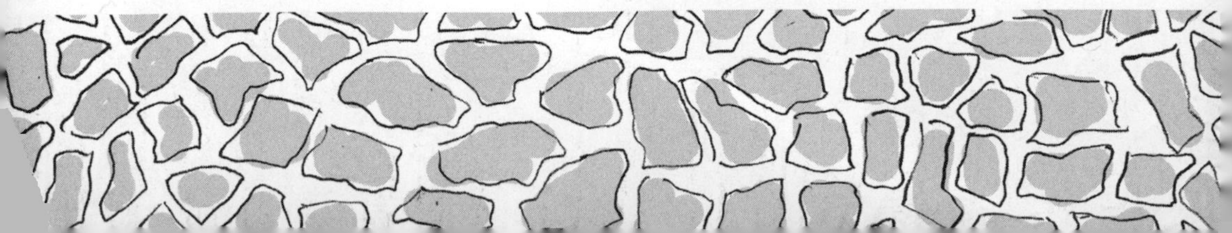

FEET FIRST

With their strong backs and rippling neck muscles, horses may seem hardy and tough, and in some ways they are. It's amazing to watch racehorses in the Kentucky Derby run all out at speeds up to 40 miles per hour. Those Thoroughbreds have well-muscled legs and strong lungs that can make them champions.

And yet a tiny crack in a hoof can destroy a great racehorse's career. Or worse. Owners and trainers who ignore the importance of a horse's hoof may end up paying a terrible price when that million-dollar racehorse ends up lame.

Feet are important to other animals too. Camels can walk across sand that most animals would sink in. That's because their hooves have two big "toes" that are covered with tough, leathery pads. But if the camel's feet are bad, even its humps won't help it make its way through the desert.

Sometimes what seems like the least important part of an animal is actually the most important. The same goes for people in the body of Christ. We're all needed—not just the pastor or teacher or solo singer. We're equally important in the body of Christ.

Do you feel like a foot sometimes—not very important, a little ignored, maybe even stepped on? Do you assume your friends, your youth group, your church, your family could get along fine without you? Wrong! They need you. There's a role only you can play.

And that goes both ways: you need other people too. Your group needs the friendly talkers, but also the "uncool" kids on the fringes of your Sunday school class, the quiet kids, the people whose gifts are more undercover. No matter what part of the body of Christ you represent, you are needed.

> *The body has many different parts, not just one part. If the foot says, "I am not a part of the body because I am not a hand," that does not make it any less a part of the body. . . . In fact, some parts of the body that seem weakest and least important are actually the most necessary. . . . All of you together are Christ's body, and each of you is a part of it.*
>
> **1 CORINTHIANS 12:14-15, 22, 27**

A horse's hoof is so vital to its health that its hooves should be cleaned out every day—and more often if the horse is ridden. The V on the underside of horse's hoof is called the frog and must be carefully cleaned.

• • •

TODAY: Thank God for making you part of the body of Christ. Then prayerfully list five things you know people need you for . . . and five things you need other people for.

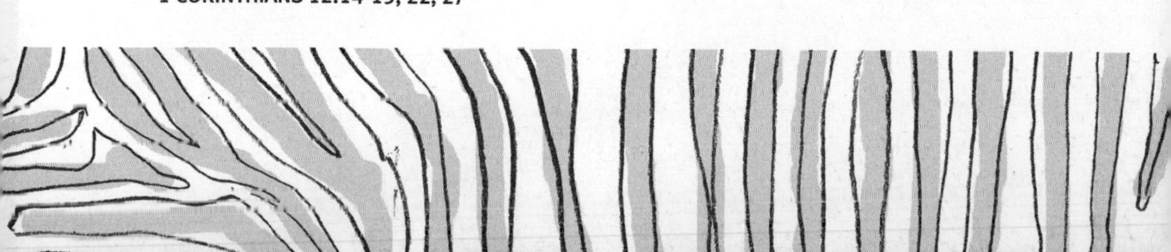

Pigs don't sweat—or at least they don't sweat enough for it to affect their body temperature. That's why they like to wallow in the mud to cool off. So the next time someone says you "sweat like a pig," just say thanks.

• • •

TODAY: Make a list of the things you worry about from the minute you wake to the minute you go to sleep. Talk to God about each item. Circle any worry you honestly believe your heavenly Father doesn't already know about. Underline any item you think is too big for the Creator of the universe to handle. (Not sure? Look at Matthew 6:32 again. God knows *all* your needs, even better than you do.)

NO SWEAT!

When animals get too hot, they have different ways of cooling off. Snakes and lizards and frogs just have to find shade or water or maybe a place to burrow out of the sun.

But mammals like monkeys, rabbits, dogs, cats, and cows have a different cooling system: they sweat. The evaporation of the water creates "air-conditioning." Horses, apes, and humans have the pleasure of sweating all over, starting with under the arms (as if you didn't know).

Cows sweat through their noses. Dogs and cats sweat through their feet, but they need more cooling than those sweat glands can provide. So dogs pant, and water from the tongue evaporates and cools them off. Cats are too sophisticated to pant, so they lick their paws and chest.

Whales, even though they're mammals, don't sweat or pant, but then they do have cool water all around them.

What kinds of things cause you to sweat? Homework? Tests? Family problems? Money? Popularity (or the lack of it)? Do you worry about not having the right clothes, the right look, or the right friends? Have you done something you don't think you can tell anyone about?

Take a deep breath and remember that you are a child of the Creator of the universe. You're family. You'll never be alone because God, your heavenly Father, is looking out for you. There's nothing that can happen to you and nothing you can do that will take that away. God cares about every little thing that happens to you, and he loves you more than you can imagine.

So . . . no sweat, right?

Don't worry about these things, saying, "What will we eat? What will we drink? What will we wear?" These things dominate the thoughts of unbelievers, but your heavenly Father already knows all your needs.
MATTHEW 6:31-32

MAN'S BEST FRIEND

There's a reason people call dogs "man's best friend." You understand if you've spent much time around dogs. Dogs love their owners, and they don't mind showing it.

Some nursing homes have discovered that bringing in a dog or having a house pet can lower residents' blood pressure and promote a sense of well-being. There's something soothing about having a dog in the house.

Dogs have been important to people for a long time. When archaeologists dug up the ancient ruins of Pompeii, a city buried by a volcano in AD 79, they found a dog lying across the body of a child, as if it were trying to protect him.

After a rough day at school, when it feels like the whole world is against you, there's nothing better than cuddling up with your dog. Dogs want to be close to you. You can plop onto the floor, and your dog will curl up next to you. Good dogs love the nearness of their masters. And good masters long to be close to their dogs.

God longs for closeness with us too. Do you long to be close to God? Or do you pray only when you need something? What if your dog came around you only when it needed to go outside or wanted something to eat? You'd feel more like a hired caretaker than a best friend.

It's amazing that the God of the universe wants to be with us. But that's the way it is. And yet we can get so busy that we don't appreciate God's presence and friendship.

God wants to be your best friend. How about spending more time with the Master?

> *I long, yes, I faint with longing to enter the courts of the Lord. With my whole being, body and soul, I will shout joyfully to the living God.*
> **PSALM 84:2**

The "dog days of summer" have nothing to do with dogs. People used to think that Sirius, the "Dog Star," was responsible for heating up Rome in the summer by adding its heat to the sun. So they called the time between July 3 and August 11 "the days of the dog."

• • •

TODAY: Carve out at least 10 minutes today when you can curl up with God. Imagine climbing onto God's lap and just sitting there, enjoying his company.

A little bird called the Clark's nutcracker has the elephant beat when it comes to remembering. As it prepares for winter, each nutcracker stashes some 25,000 pine seeds in about 5,000 hiding places. These hiding spots span an area of several miles through the Rocky Mountains. Six to nine months later, the bird can find every seed, even if the hiding place is buried under snow.

• • •

TODAY: Start a memory book and record what God has done for you. Include the big things, like dying for you and loving you and giving you your family. And include the "little" blessings, like sunlight through tree branches, a warm blanket, and cold ice cream on a hot day.

A MEMORY LIKE AN ELEPHANT

An elephant never forgets, right?

Not exactly. But elephants do have great memories when it comes to storing important information. They have big brains, and although it's hard to measure the memory span of an elephant, the animal is clearly no dumbo.

Elephants learn from their experiences and store memories, calling them up when they need to. If an elephant runs into danger in a certain place, years later it won't want to return there. Elephants remember good feeding sites and watering holes. Circus elephants can remember voice and gesture commands. They recognize humans and other elephants they haven't seen for decades.

Over 100 times in the Scriptures we're commanded to remember. *Remember* your Creator. *Remember* God's miracles. *Remember* God's blessings. At the Last Supper, Jesus told the disciples to break the bread as a way to remember him.

God made us, so he knows how easily we forget. After Moses led the Israelites out of slavery in Egypt, they cheered for God and for Moses. A couple of days later they were already grumbling about food, water, the desert, Moses, and God. They acted as if they'd forgotten all God's miracles, including the parting of the Red Sea.

It's easy for us to forget answered prayers, blessings, and times when God was especially near to us. Maybe that's why God commands us to remember. Praising God helps us remember how great he is and how many blessings we've been given. If we're really grateful, we'll remember. And if we remember, we'll be grateful.

Let all that I am praise the LORD; may I never forget the good things he does for me.
PSALM 103:2

SING!

Ever wonder why birds sing? They wake us up in the morning and lull us to sleep at night. A second after a storm passes, birds are out there singing again as if nothing had ever stopped them.

From the first robins of spring to the yellow-throated warblers, bluebirds, cuckoos, nightingales, and even crows, the calls and songs of birds reach to every corner of the earth.

Birds seem to be born with the ability to sing, learning specific songs from listening to adults so that by six weeks, they can sing their mother's tunes. Robins and meadowlarks have 50 different songs. The red-eyed vireo sings nonstop in the forests of South America, belting out over 20,000 songs in 10 hours.

If their surroundings get too loud, birds will sing louder. The European nightingale has been singing louder and louder each year as cities have grown noisier and noisier. Ducks in the city quack faster and louder than country ducks, which quack with a slower drawl.

There's something about music that can reach deep into the soul. Just like birds, people all over the world sing. And the best kind of singing comes from a heart that overflows with joy and gratitude for what God has done.

Even if you're not a great singer, you can still sing. Sing when you're happy, and sing when you're down. You may not sell out any concert halls, but you can make a joyful noise to the Lord! If a bird sings in the forest (or if you sing in the shower) and nobody's around, God still hears.

> *We were filled with laughter, and we sang for joy. And the other nations said, "What amazing things the Lord has done for them." Yes, the Lord has done amazing things for us! What joy!*
>
> **PSALM 126:2-3**

Birds aren't the only singers in nature. Blue whales really belt out their songs. A blue whale can hear another whale's song from up to 528 miles away.

• • •

TODAY: Declare this week "singing week." Sing in the shower, around the house, in the car, at church, and anywhere else you can pull it off. Do an experiment: start humming a tune—for example, "Amazing Grace"—and see if eventually someone else picks up the refrain and hums the same tune. It's catching.

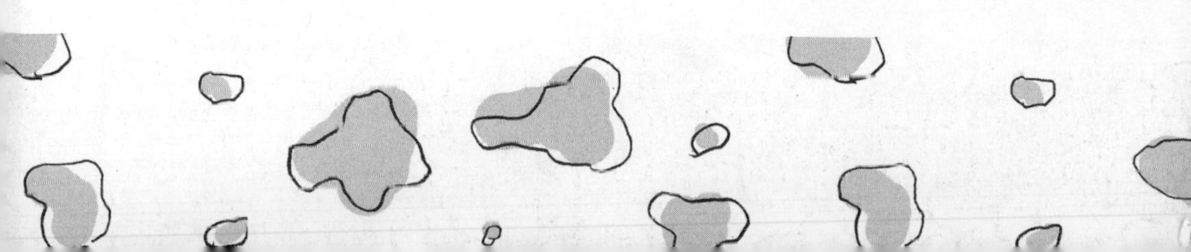

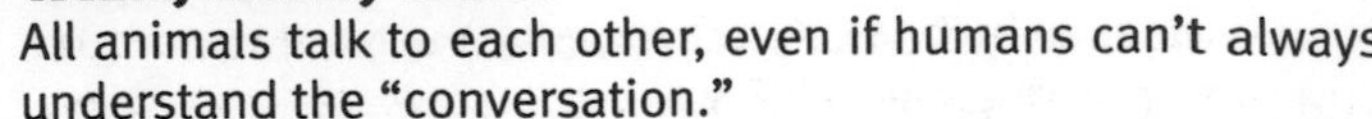

24 January

TALK, TALK, TALK

All animals talk to each other, even if humans can't always understand the "conversation."

Monkeys gibber.
Elephants trumpet.
Peacocks scream.
Bulls bellow.
Giraffes bleat.
Cats mew.
Pigeons coo.
Snakes hiss.
Raccoons chitter.
Magpies chatter.
Falcons chant.
Owls screech.
Cattle low.
Turkeys gobble.
Chickens cluck.
Horses neigh.
Donkeys bray.
Wolves howl.

How well do you communicate with the people around you? Sure, you might spend hours on your cell phone and computer, logging countless time texting and e-mailing. Technology has made it easy to communicate, right?

Or has it?

How well do you really connect with your friends, as opposed to just listening to yourself talk? Are you able to communicate through spoken words and gestures? Can you read expressions and understand what's behind someone else's words?

It's important to look beyond your friends' words. Ask them questions and listen to their answers. As Christians, we need to be able to communicate with people who don't know Christ. When Paul visited Athens, he connected with the non-believers there by finding a way to relate to them. He pointed out one of their altars with the inscription, "To an Unknown God." From there, he was able to introduce them to God the Father by asking them questions and listening to their answers. Then he led them to Christ. That's communication.

This God, whom you worship without knowing, is the one I'm telling you about.
ACTS 17:23

Parrots are the only animals that can speak with words people recognize as human speech. They can do this because their throats are designed to make many different sounds, including the sounds humans make.

• • •

TODAY: Choose one person to have a face-to-face talk with today. Ask that person at least five questions about himself or herself, and listen prayerfully to the answers.

SPEAK TO ME

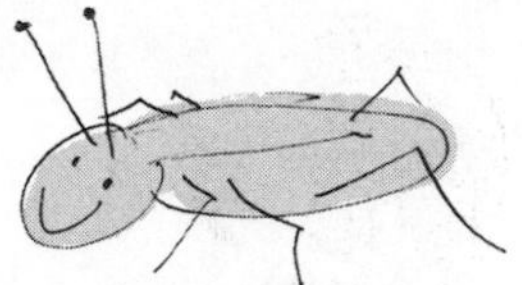

Communication in the world of animals doesn't always equal what we consider speech. For example, crickets don't have vocal cords, so they rub their wings or legs together to make their familiar summer-night sounds.

Bees go way beyond buzzing. When they find yummy nectar, they perform amazing bee dances, using air waves to signal other bees to come running. They can communicate through dance where their friends should go, how far away the nectar is, and what food will be there.

Ants, wasps, and other social insects can touch each other with feelers that communicate all kinds of information for their well-run communities: "Enemies are approaching." "Your turn." "This way!" Porpoises, sea lions, dolphins, whales, seals, rodents, and bats can communicate through sonic and ultrasonic sound waves.

Thumping works for certain animals, like the wallaby and the kangaroo. Frogs and toads, which can make plenty of noise in other ways, can also thump to connect with their fellow amphibians. A species of mole rats in Israel can communicate by head-thumping, banging their heads on their underground tunnels in rhythms that carry long distances.

How do you communicate with God? Still saying the "Now I lay me down to sleep" prayer? Nothing wrong with that, as long as the words haven't lost their meaning for you.

Maybe you've moved on to the nighttime listing of friends and relatives you ask God to bless. That's fine too, if you're connecting with God and not just mindlessly checking off names.

Prayer can be reciting the Lord's Prayer, a fantastic prayer that includes every major aspect of our relationship with God. But prayer is listening, too. And spilling our hearts to God. And confessing. And celebrating. And praising. And reading God's words in the Scripture. And seeing and appreciating a starry night or a friend's smile.

God is everywhere, and he invites us to communicate with him all day long in every way.

> *All Israel brought up the Ark of the Lord's Covenant with shouts of joy, the blowing of rams' horns and trumpets, the crashing of cymbals, and loud playing on harps and lyres.*
>
> **1 CHRONICLES 15:28**

Crickets chirp faster the warmer it gets. Count the number of chirps in 15 seconds and add 37. That equals the temperature outside.

• • •

TODAY: Try communicating with God in three different ways today. Here are some ideas to get you started: Read and pray over a psalm. Sing, dance, and shout your praise to God (when you're by yourself). Scout for signs of the Creator during the day.

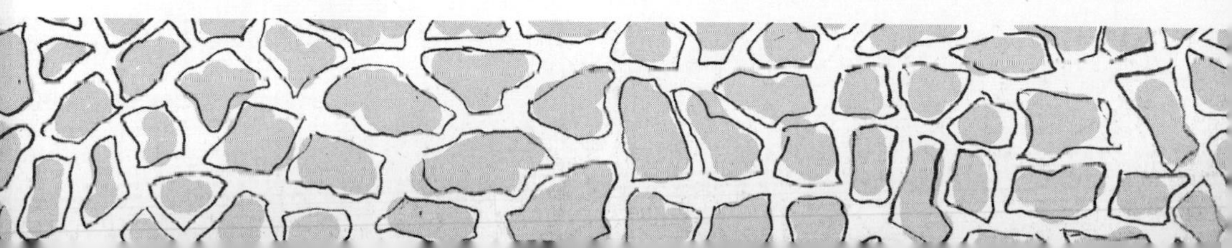

If a horse bucks when you're in the saddle, the best thing you can do is to pull up on the reins and try to get the horse's head up.

• • •

TODAY: Talk to God about things that have been bugging you lately. Ask God to point out anything you need to confess, and then ask for his forgiveness in those areas, thanking him that he always forgives.

BURR UNDER YOUR SADDLE?

Most people who ride horses a lot have at least one burr-under-the-saddle story.

A girl saddles her horse as usual and sets out for a leisurely ride through the pasture. Only this time her usually trustworthy horse shies at the slightest noise, switches its tail in anger, and tosses its head. Sooner or later, the horse catches the rider off guard and bucks her to the ground.

Or a family on vacation decides to go on a trail ride. The wrangler gives Dad, who never rides, the calmest horse in the stable, guaranteed to put up with any rider. Halfway out on the trail, the "calmest" horse acts up, takes the bit in its mouth, and tears back to the barn, with Dad hanging on for dear life.

An accomplished equestrian practices all year for the big show-jumping event, only to have her horse totally mess up on the field. For some reason the horse lacks concentration and focus.

No one, not even these poor horses, knows why they're acting up . . . until somebody checks under the saddle blanket and finds a prickly burr.

If even a tiny burr gets stuck to the blanket and rubs against the horse's back, that irritation may eventually cause a blowup.

We get burrs under our saddles too. We might do something wrong and try to forget about it. But sin doesn't just go away on its own. It stays there, irritating, rubbing deeper, keeping us from focusing on anything else. Nagging worries can rub us the wrong way too, if we don't turn the anxious thoughts over to God.

If you're crabby or unsettled and have that nagging feeling that something's wrong, talk to God about it. To take care of a horse with a burr, you just pick out the burr. To take care of your own "burr," you need to confess the sin to God and let him take it away.

Search me, O God, and know my heart; test me and know my anxious thoughts. Point out anything in me that offends you, and lead me along the path of everlasting life.

PSALM 139:23-24

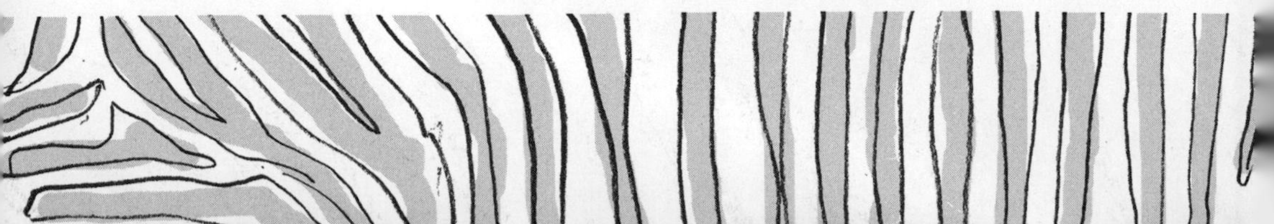

FAMILY RULES

Did you ever get a puppy, but then have to wait to bring it home? The best time for a new dog to join a human family is when it's about eight to twelve weeks old.

For one thing, a puppy needs to stay with its mother and nurse until about eight weeks. But there are other reasons to leave a puppy with its dog family for a while. That puppy has a lot to learn from its dog relatives about what it means to be a dog.

Puppies need their parents and siblings to teach them the rules of good behavior. In the safe family setting, a pup can get disciplined when it acts up. It can learn from play-fighting with the other pups in the litter how far to go in play. Learning to relate inside its family is the best way for your puppy to learn to deal with the outside world of humans.

Believe it or not, your family is where you learn most of your skills for fitting in and getting along with your friends and classmates. Sometimes family and school seem like two separate worlds that have little to do with each other and often get in each other's way. Maybe your parents seem out of touch, and your brothers and sisters just don't measure up to your friends. You may even resent the time you're forced to spend with your family.

But God designed the family to be the most vital group you'll ever belong to on earth. And following your family's rules will eventually equip you for all the other groups you'll be part of for the rest of your life.

> *Honor your father and mother. Then you will live a long, full life in the land the Lord your God is giving you.*
> **EXODUS 20:12**

A male and female swan pair up for life, finding each other when they're two or three years old and starting their family a year or two later. A father swan is a cob. A mother swan is a pen. And a baby is a cygnet. Both parents take care of the cygnets, which sometimes get to ride on Mom's or Dad's back.

• • •

TODAY: Write down five good habits you've developed or social skills you possess because of your family and your family's rules. Thank your parents for that.

STAY IN TOUCH

Some animal herds stay together for life. A female elephant will remain with her mother, sisters, female cousins, and aunts as long as she lives. Elephants have discovered that staying in touch with their extended families works. They do much better by sticking together than they would on their own.

In herds that stick together for life, the animals take care of one another. If one elephant is injured, the whole herd will slow down and wait for it. When one member of the herd dies, they all grieve together.

When your grandparents and great-grandparents were growing up, extended families usually lived in the same city, on the same street, or even in the same house. Grandparents helped care for the young children. And eventually children helped care for the older generation. "Respect your elders" was understood and lived out.

Times change, but maybe not as much as you might imagine. Every generation feels like it "outgrows" the ways of the old fogies before them. *That was then, this is now*, they think. But the truth is, we all have a lot to learn from the generations before us. Your grandparents have lived through some of the same struggles you're going through now. They've made good decisions and bad ones, and their faith has been tested. They have stories to tell—great stories. Don't lose those stories. Ask your aunt how she fell in love with your uncle. Ask your uncle to tell you about the biggest problem he ever had and how he made it through. Talk to your grandparents about what life was like when they were your age.

You might live far away from your grandparents and other relatives, but like the elephants, you can still be part of that connected, supportive family group.

> *You must remain faithful to what you have been taught from the beginning. If you do, you will remain in fellowship with the Son and with the Father.*
>
> **1 JOHN 2:24**

Some groups of animals have interesting names: a *tiding* of magpies, a *brace* of ducks, a *murder* of crows, a *mischief* of rats, a *rafter* of turkeys, a *gang* of elks, a *skulk* of foxes, a jellyfish *smack*, a *shrewdness* of apes, an *unkindness* of ravens.

• • •

TODAY: List 10 differences between the world when your parents were kids and your world today. (Get your parents to help with the list.) Do any of these changes help you to follow God's best for you? Do any of these changes make it harder to follow him?

THE LIVING DEAD

When winter comes to the Arctic, the wood frog doesn't find warmer ground or dig for cover like the toad does. Unlike other frogs, it doesn't head for deeper water that won't freeze. Instead, the wood frog sticks around on the forest floor among the fallen leaves. When the temperature drops below freezing and the thermometer falls to 18 degrees, the wood frog turns into a frog popsicle as its fluids and tissues turn to ice. Even its eyeballs and brain freeze, causing some people to call wood frogs "the living dead."

The frogs aren't dead—they're just frozen. But in the winter, they might as well be dead, since that's how they act—doing nothing, feeling nothing.

We sometimes act like the living dead too. Our hearts can freeze . . . or at least grow cold enough that we act like zombies. We walk around without feeling sorry for the homeless, without caring when classmates get left out or put down at school. We might show up at church and youth group, but nothing ever really speaks to us or changes the way we feel and think.

Jesus warned the religious leaders of his day against becoming like whitewashed tombs: proper and flashy on the outside, but dirty and rotting inside. They pretended to be so good and spiritual in public, but their relationship with God in private was cold dead.

How warm and fresh is your relationship with God? Do you love spending time talking to God and reading the Bible? Do your thoughts about Jesus overflow into conversations with your friends? Are you struck by the beauty of God's creation each day?

Maybe it's time to thaw out. Look around at the world God has made. Read the letters in the New Testament as if they were written for you. (They were.) Find ways to let God use you to help people in need.

Outwardly you look like righteous people, but inwardly your hearts are filled with hypocrisy and lawlessness.
MATTHEW 23:28

At least five species of frogs can freeze solid during the winter and survive: the wood frog, the boreal chorus frog, the spring peeper, Cope's tree frog, and the gray tree frog, which actually turns blue when it freezes. Thanks to their internal "antifreeze," these frogs thaw in early spring and hop away happily ever after. (Who knows? Some may even turn into princes if kissed.)

• • •

TODAY: Check your spiritual temperature. If you're somewhere in the range of cold to freezing, talk to someone—a family member, a close friend, or a pastor. Ask how you can get involved in helping other people and in growing in your own relationship with Christ.

PUPPY LOVE

We all know what puppy love is. Two kids head over heels gaga about each other. They ache when they can't be together.

Real puppies are born with that kind of love . . . for their mothers.

Puppies start out life without sight, without hearing, and with only a tiny bit of their sense of smell. But they can feel pain, and they can sense warmth and comfort. The nearness of Mom is what keeps puppies alive.

Pups will do what it takes to stay close to their mother. If removed from her, they'll crawl around until they find her and then snuggle close for comfort.

"Puppy love" is the way we should feel about God. That's not to say you should stay at an immature level in your faith—it just means that no matter how old you are, you know you still need God every minute. You're head over heels in love with God, and God is always ready to comfort and protect you.

At the end of a rough day at school—maybe you failed your spelling test, had a fight with your best friend, tripped and fell on your face in the cafeteria, and ended up with a stack of homework—you need the warmth and comfort you can get only from a close friendship with God.

People who don't seek comfort in God's love tend to look for comfort in the wrong places—overeating, alcohol and drug addictions, sex, doing whatever it takes to be liked or noticed or considered popular. All those things might give you comfort . . . for a few minutes or hours. But in the end, they lead to pain and self-destruction.

God's comfort lasts, and it's always close to you. All you have to do is accept it.

All praise to God, the Father of our Lord Jesus Christ. God is our merciful Father and the source of all comfort.

2 CORINTHIANS 1:3

A puppy's eyes open at around 10 to 15 days, and its senses of hearing and smell start to develop then too. By four weeks, a puppy's vision is almost as good as the vision of an adult dog.

• • •

TODAY: Talk to God about the things that make you feel bad at school or at home. What do you do to feel better? Thank God for offering comfort to you all day, every day. Pour out your heart to him.

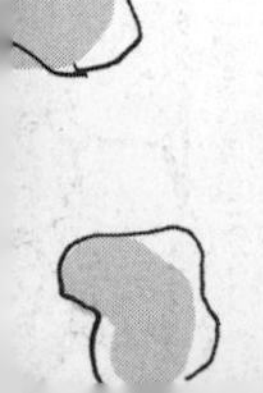
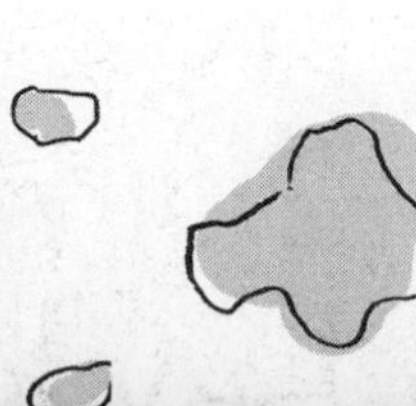
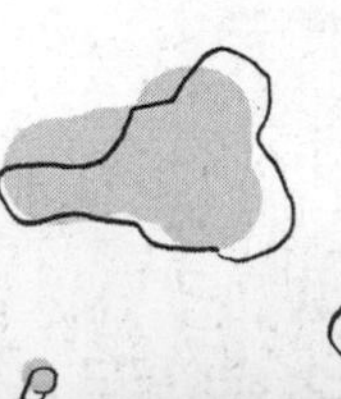

SWEET!

Dogs and cats have good taste—or at least a good sense of taste.

We humans have at least four types of taste buds on our tongues—sour, salty, bitter, and sweet. Some areas of the tongue are more sensitive to certain tastes. So we tend to taste sour food with the sides of the tongue, salty foods along the sides and at the tip of the tongue, and bitter food at the back of the tongue. Sweet tastes are sensed by taste buds at the tip of the tongue.

Dogs pick up sweet tastes a lot like we do. But instead of merely tasting sweetness on the tips of their tongues, dogs also taste sweet along the sides of the tongue. So dogs definitely have a "sweet tooth." In fact, dogs probably love sweet treats even more than we do. (Note: Don't give a dog chocolate, no matter how much it begs. Chocolate can be harmful for dogs.)

Cats are responsive to certain tastes and are extremely sensitive to the taste of water. But they don't share the sweet tooth of dogs and people. Since cats don't have taste buds that respond to sweets, you probably won't catch a cat begging for chocolate.

The Bible uses the term *sweet* to apply to people who do or say the right things. In Proverbs 16:24, Solomon wrote that "kind words are like honey—sweet to the soul and healthy for the body." If someone handed you a printout of all the words you spoke today, how many would be "sweet"—healthy to someone's body and soul? Did you encourage a shy classmate by telling him how much you got out of his history report? Did you compliment somebody on her new haircut?

If your whole school (and your family) decided to name a candy bar or an ice cream flavor after you, how sweet—or bitter—would the name be?

Imagine if every Christian lived in such a way that people were attracted to Jesus—as much as we're attracted to chocolate and ice cream. Sweet!

How sweet your words taste to me; they are sweeter than honey.
PSALM 119:103

Butterflies can distinguish between all different types of sugars we can't even taste. They are about 1,200 times more sensitive to sweets than we are.

• • •

TODAY: Every time your sweet tooth kicks in, ask God to make you "sweet" and to help you live a life that will attract other people to him.

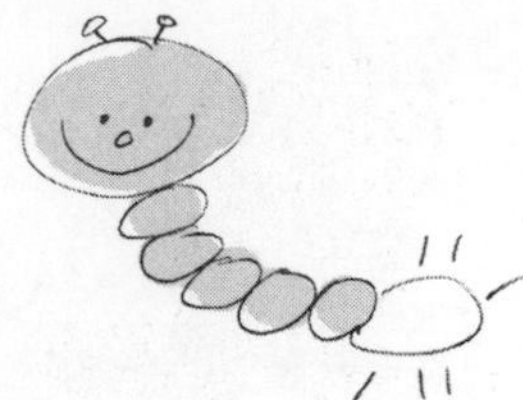

Adult glowworms rarely eat, but their little larvae are fierce, ravenous predators. Larvae find tiny slugs and snails, bite them, and inject poison that freezes the prey and liquefies it. Then the larvae suck the prey empty.

• • •

TODAY: List your five greatest temptations. Talk to God about each one. The next time you're faced with the temptation, rely on God's help. Stop, think, and pray before you say or do something you know you'll regret. Swallow the smart-mouthed comeback. Put down the brownie. Say no to that invitation. Ask for help.

GLOWWORMS

Despite their name, glowworms aren't really worms. They're actually beetles, with a membership in the insect family. These insects can put on a show at night that will put fireworks to shame.

Since male fireflies don't glow, it's the wingless adult female that earns the name glowworm. The glow comes from a chemical reaction that's so efficient, almost 100 percent of the energy turns to light, with no heat escape.

The best time to see the light show is between 10:00 and midnight on dry summer nights. Some glowworms light up to attract mates. Others glow to warn off enemies, like the toad, which reads the glow as a neon sign: *Poison!*

But some glowworms use their fluorescent color to tempt prey to come in. In the caves of Waitomo on the North Island of New Zealand, glowworms hang gummy threads from their bodies. When millions of these worms are strung up in the cave, they look like a glowing curtain. The glow attracts other insects that get stuck and then are eaten by the glowworms.

Glowing temptations are all around us. What tempts one person might not interest someone else. Your friend might want to smoke or drink, but you're not interested. Yet you might be tempted to brag or gossip or lie more than your friend is.

Whatever tempts you, God is stronger. And because Christ lives in you, you're stronger than that temptation, too. When the disciples asked Jesus to teach them how to pray, he included in his prayer a request for help in resisting temptation. He understands.

Don't let us yield to temptation, but rescue us from the evil one.

MATTHEW 6:13

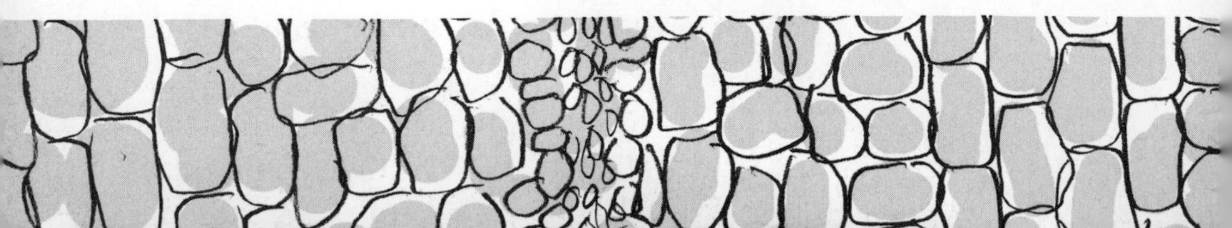

GROUNDHOG DAY

Every February 2, which is about halfway between winter solstice in December and the vernal equinox in March, we celebrate Groundhog Day. Actually, it's a little before sensible groundhogs end their hibernation and venture out into the world.

But on this day, Phil, the famous groundhog in Punxsutawney, Pennsylvania, is brought out to meet the public. If Phil sees his shadow, tradition and legend have it that we're in for six more weeks of winter. Frightened by his own shadow, Phil races back into his burrow for six more weeks of sleep. But if Phil doesn't see his shadow, we're supposed to get an early spring.

Does that sound logical to you? The truth is, Phil sees his shadow about 90 percent of the time, which makes him right most of the time. Why? Because Pennsylvania has long winters.

Groundhog Day is a fun tradition, and few people really believe that Phil's shadow is prophetic. But there are lots of traditions and fake prophecies people do believe. Some may have even landed in your e-mail in-box.

Have you ever gotten a message that tells you to send it on to a certain number of other people or you'll be sorry? How about the one that promises something great will happen to you if you send the message to everyone in your address book? Others warn you not to stop the blessing.

Maybe you send the message on. You don't believe it . . . but just in case, you hit that forward button.

Don't. Don't give in to the false threats or empty promises. Only God knows the future. He rains down his blessings on us. You don't need superstitious e-mails.

> *One day the Pharisees asked Jesus, "When will the Kingdom of God come?"*
>
> *Jesus replied, "The Kingdom of God can't be detected by visible signs. You won't be able to say, 'Here it is!' or 'It's over there!' For the Kingdom of God is already among you."*
>
> **LUKE 17:20-21**

What's the difference between a groundhog and a woodchuck (which would chuck wood if it could)? Nothing! It's the same animal.

• • •

TODAY: The next time you get a threatening message telling you that you *have* to send it on to nine other people or something bad will happen, hit that Delete button. God is in charge.

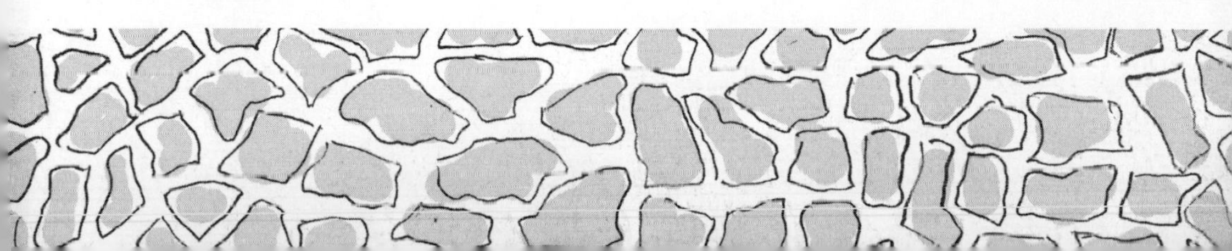

MY BAD

When you hang out with animals, accidents may happen. Horses don't mean to step on your foot, but it hurts when they do. They don't mean any harm when they switch their tails and catch your eye instead of a fly.

A puppy might think it's play-biting, but those puppy teeth can break skin and draw blood just the same.

A cat might consider your hand just another toy. So why not chew it? And since cats don't have other defenses, they might react with claws and teeth when they're scared . . . before they realize you're a friend, not a foe.

On the other hand, sometimes a horse kicks because it wants that rider off. Dogs might bite because they think you're going to take away their bone. Some cats scratch when they want to be left alone. And you're left hurting.

The same thing can happen with humans. You didn't mean to hurt your friend by leaving her out of the conversation at lunch. And she probably didn't mean to hurt you when she broke a confidence and spilled your secret. Your buddy wasn't out to get you when he didn't pick you first for his side. And you didn't mean anything by calling him that name.

But you're still left hurting.

Stupid (and not-so-stupid) things can separate good friends unless somebody steps up and apologizes. Why is it so hard to say you're sorry? Because "He started it!" Or "It wasn't my fault." Or "She's the one who needs to apologize first."

So what? You're *both* wrong once you let it affect your friendship. Why not be the more mature friend and apologize first? Yep—even if it wasn't all your fault. Apologizing defuses the whole situation. God doesn't care if you didn't start it—only that you finish it.

> *If you are presenting a sacrifice at the altar in the Temple and you suddenly remember that someone has something against you, leave your sacrifice there at the altar. Go and be reconciled to that person. Then come and offer your sacrifice to God.*
> **MATTHEW 5:23-24**

FAMOUS PEOPLE WHO "FELL" VICTIM TO HORSE ACCIDENTS:

William the Conqueror (fell off his horse during battle in 1087)

Genghis Khan (fell off his horse while hunting in 1227)

Isabella, Princess of Aragon (had an accident on her return from the Crusades in 1271)

Alexander III, King of Scotland (fell off his horse while riding in the dark in 1286)

• • •

TODAY: Apologize to at least one person, even if the problem wasn't your fault.

CAN YOU HEAR ME NOW?

Most animals have better hearing than humans do. Whales and dolphins have the greatest range of hearing—14 times greater than ours. Humans can hear frequencies up to 23,000 hertz, while dogs hear frequencies nearly twice that high and cats hear almost three times as high. Even cows and horses can hear up to about 35,000 hertz. Rats hear frequencies of 76,000, and mice hear up to 91,000.

Within each animal family, some hear better than others. Some of the dog breeds that have a tendency toward deafness are Akita, Doberman pinscher, bulldog, pit bull, cocker spaniel, foxhound, terrier, beagle, German shepherd, Saint Bernard, collie, schnauzer, husky, shih tzu, corgi, poodle, and dalmatian. Breeds with white pigmentation are more prone to deafness than others.

Most humans lose a certain degree of hearing as they get older. Your grandparents or great-grandparents might not hear what you say the first time.

But the Bible makes it clear that God hears every word we say. In fact, he hears it before we say it.

At times have you felt like your parents or teachers weren't really listening to you—like they'd already made up their minds? Or maybe you've been in a discussion when you wanted to say something but couldn't get a word in edgewise? It's frustrating not to be able to say what's on your mind.

Sometimes all you want is to be heard.

God hears.

You don't have to be in church or in prayer for him to hear you. You don't even have to make sense. God hangs on every word.

What a miracle that the God of the universe longs to hear from you!

Because he bends down to listen, I will pray as long as I have breath!
PSALM 116:2

Bees and wasps can't hear the way humans can (which is why they don't go away when you scream at them, and why they sting you, even though you've clearly asked them not to).

• • •

TODAY: All day long, say everything you want to say to God, knowing that he delights in listening to every word you think or speak.

Henry Blake, an English horseman and author, spent his life observing the messages horses send out. In his book *Talking with Horses*, he lists 47 messages and 54 "submessages" horses use to connect with each other and with humans.

• • •

TODAY: Keep reminding yourself all day long that the Holy Spirit lives inside you. Sense God's Spirit leading you, and make sure you follow that lead.

SIXTH SENSE?

When disaster strikes and a tsunami is about to hit, animals in the region appear to sense the coming danger long before humans do. Wild animals, from elephants to flamingos, try to escape to higher ground. Dogs bark and get restless. Birds fly off, and underground animals move as far from the disaster as they can get. Then people start speculating that the animals must have a "sixth sense," or psychic premonition.

But scientists say that animals' so-called sixth sense is really a supersensitivity of one or more of the five senses. Certain animals can feel the earth shake or smell the change in the atmosphere or hear shifts in the environment long before humans do.

Sometimes an animal is so in tune with a human that its intuition seems like a sixth sense. Good riders and horses work together and get to know each other's signals so well that they respond in sync. All the rider has to do is think about a lead change or a change in speed, and the horse senses it, likely picking up on a movement so tiny the rider doesn't even realize he or she is giving it.

When we come to Christ and accept Christ's forgiveness and resurrection, his Spirit—the Holy Spirit—comes to live inside of us. Instead of just handing us a list of rules to follow, God has given us the Spirit, who works in us from the inside out, making us want what God wants, changing us so that we're in sync with God.

We're guided from the inside—not by a sixth sense, but by something much better. We have the Spirit of the living God working in and through us so we can live in tune with God and respond to even his gentlest nudge.

> *When the Spirit of truth comes, he will guide you into all truth. He will not speak on his own but will tell you what he has heard. He will tell you about the future.*
> JOHN 16:13

HOME, SWEET HOME

Animals have come up with some pretty amazing places to call home. Some animals are master builders, fashioning fancy houses. Bees, wasps, and yellow jackets create wax inside their bodies, then use it to mold hives with room for the whole colony.

Prairie dogs dig burrows with passageways, private entrances and exits, and separate rooms for families. Rabbits live in communities, or warrens, underground.

Flamingos build mud nests on the edges of lakes and lagoons, while otters dig holes into riverbanks to create their dens, called holts.

Beaver lodges are amazing feats of engineering, constructed in pools of water after beavers build their dams. Their homes have underwater entrances, dry areas to sleep in, and rooms where they can store logs and food for the winter.

Bats hang out in caves, bears sleep in caves, and eels live in underwater caves. The Komodo dragon (a huge lizard) makes its own cave by dig, dig, digging.

There's comfort in knowing that no matter how bad things get, you can go home and curl up in your own bed. Home, sweet home.

But it's even cooler to realize that we have another home waiting for us. When Jesus told his disciples he'd be heading back to the Father soon, they were upset. But Jesus promised them that they'd be coming to his Father's home eventually. And in the meantime, he was going to get their rooms ready. "Don't let your hearts be troubled. Trust in God, and trust also in me. There is more than enough room in my Father's home" (John 14:1-2).

No home on earth will compare to what's waiting for us in heaven. And going to that home will be a real homecoming.

We are citizens of heaven, where the Lord Jesus Christ lives. And we are eagerly waiting for him to return as our Savior.

PHILIPPIANS 3:20

HERE ARE SOME NAMES OF ANIMAL HOUSES:

badger: sett
rabbit: warren
squirrel: drey
bat: roost
beaver: lodge
eagle: aerie
hare: form
otter: holt
snake: nest

• • •

TODAY: All day long, imagine that you need to pack, wrap up a few things, and then you're going home . . . to the room Jesus is fixing up for you. When you have your heavenly home in mind, how does your perspective on life here on earth change?

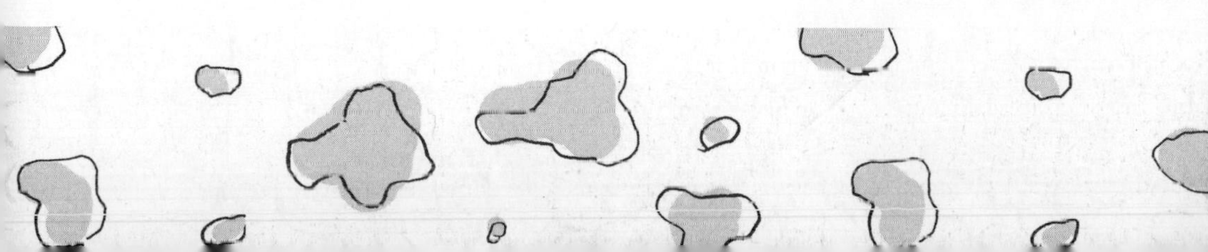

If you find a badger hole and want to know if a fox is sharing the sett, all you'd have to do is to sneak up and sniff around the entrance. You can't miss the strong, musty stench of a fox. (One thing to consider, though: badgers and foxes don't like nosy neighbors. . . .)

• • •

TODAY: Ask your parents or a teacher or a leader in your church what you can do to get involved in helping the homeless in your own town . . . and in the world.

A PLACE TO LAY YOUR HEAD

Foxes live in forests, deserts, farmlands, and even urban areas. Unlike wolves, which hang out in packs, a fox might settle with another fox or stay on its own. But wherever foxes go, they build homes, or dens. They might den underground, in caves, in hollow logs, or in piles of rock.

Some foxes take over the homes of other animals. If a fox decides to live in a badger's home (or sett), it may even peacefully coexist with its hostess.

In cities, foxes make their dens in abandoned buildings or in piles of rubble, or they might try to dig their way into a trailer.

Most animals in the wild have someplace to call home. Yet millions of people all over the world have to survive without a home.

Jesus didn't have his own home. He led his disciples through towns and villages, often going without sleep. When new believers wanted to tag along with Jesus, he let them know what they'd be getting themselves into. Jesus made it clear that, unlike foxes and birds, he didn't really have a home here on earth.

How amazing that Jesus would leave a spectacular home like heaven to come down to earth and be homeless!

No matter what kind of a home you live in, it probably beats a fox hole for warmth and comfort. The next time you complain about your bedroom or wish you had a bigger and better house, remember Jesus. And remember all the people in the world who have no place to lay their heads.

> *Jesus replied, "Foxes have dens to live in, and birds have nests, but the Son of Man has no place even to lay his head."*
> **LUKE 9:58**

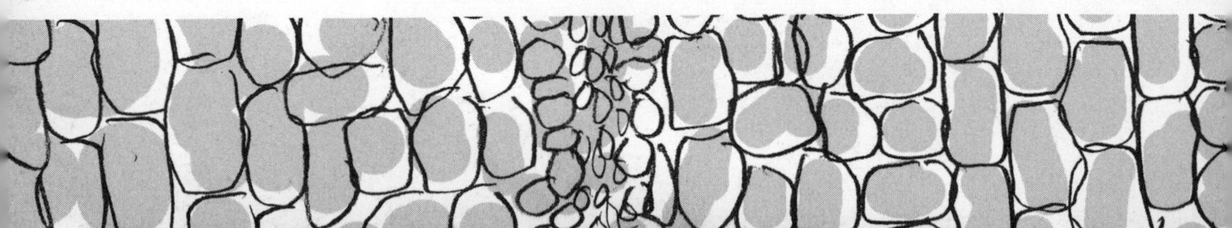

NO MORE CATERPILLAR PROBLEMS

The monarch butterfly is one of the most beautiful creatures in the world. It begins as a tiny egg laid on the underside of a milkweed plant. In three to six days, the egg hatches into a caterpillar you can barely see.

The caterpillar eats constantly for nine to fourteen days until it's full grown—about two inches long. A chrysalis forms around it, and it dangles from a tree in the cocoon. Inside the cocoon, an incredible transformation, or metamorphosis, is taking place, and after about a couple of weeks, out comes a delicate butterfly.

Imagine you're a creepy, crawly caterpillar, a wormlike creature that makes people shudder. Life doesn't get much lower than you are. You can't run away from birds or soar out of the reach of oncoming cars.

Then one day you end up in a tiny pod. Now you can't even crawl. You can't eat. You're useless. Until . . .

Suddenly the pod splits, and you're free. Really free! You have wings, so you flap them. And up you go, soaring on the wind. You can fly! You pass through an incredible world you had no idea existed. How could you have known about mountains and oceans, forests, sky, and stars? Your life was once limited to that milkweed plant and to your tiny cocoon . . . until now.

The world has opened for you. But not just for you. Others join you—as colorful and as fantastically beautiful as you are—all heading for the same place. And when you get there, you're part of something wonderful and unimaginable.

We can't imagine all that God has in store for us when we leave this life behind and exchange it for heaven. A caterpillar might think the cocoon is all there is . . . until it gets its wings.

It will happen in a moment, in the blink of an eye, when the last trumpet is blown. For when the trumpet sounds, those who have died will be raised to live forever. And we who are living will also be transformed.

1 CORINTHIANS 15:52

There are over 165,000 kinds of butterflies and moths, including painted ladies, mourning cloaks, question marks, cloudless sulphurs, common buckeyes, swallowtails, dogface butterflies, and Asian vampire moths.

• • •

TODAY: Think of 10 "caterpillar problems" you won't have in heaven. Thank God for the future he has planned for you!

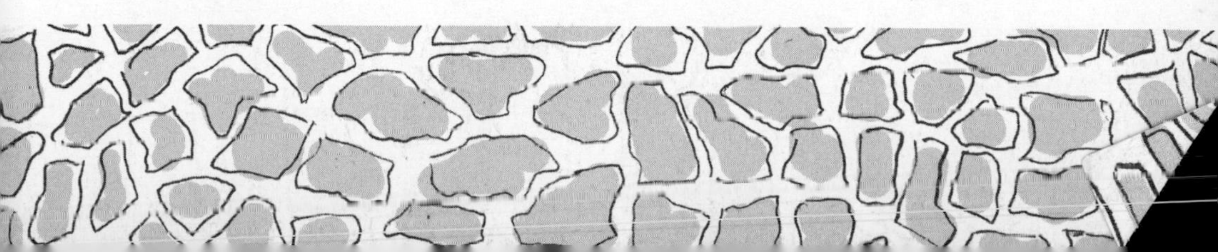

SOME ANIMALS HAVE UNIQUE GREETINGS:

Zebras might scratch each other's backs, or they could stand on hind legs and jump backward.
Emperor penguins touch beaks.
Elephants touch or shake trunks.
Japanese cranes dance.
Whales sing.

• • •

TODAY: Smile and say hi to five to ten people you usually just walk by. (It's okay if they don't smile and greet you back.)

GREETINGS

One of the best parts of having a dog is the greeting you get when you come home. No matter what has happened during the day, even if you forgot to tell your dog good-bye, your dog will be psyched to see you. And your pet won't be shy to show it—by barking or jumping up on you or panting or licking you . . . or all of the above.

Animals greet each other, too. A dog will sometimes say hey to another dog by barking and wagging its tail or by sniffing the other animal. Even coyotes and wolves exchange smelling rituals: sniffing backsides and faces, maybe waving their tails. Lions rub foreheads together. Lobsters wave.

How about you? Sniffing isn't really recommended as a great greeting. But why not be the first one to smile and say hi? What does that cost? You don't have to wait for the other guy to smile. And if he doesn't respond, even after you've said hi, so what? Don't let it get to you. Next time you see him, smile again.

The best smiles, of course, come from the inside. If you're walking with God, filled with God's Spirit, then you're smiling on the inside. And that should carry over to smiling on the outside. That doesn't mean you can't ever be sad, but beneath that sadness, you can have a sense of underlying joy.

Make people wonder, and even ask, what you're smiling about. You know how yucky it feels when someone isn't happy to see you. So work on being happy to see people—and showing it.

Can you imagine if everyone at school greeted each other the way your dog greets you?!

Greet each other with Christian love. Peace be with all of you who are in Christ.
1 PETER 5:14

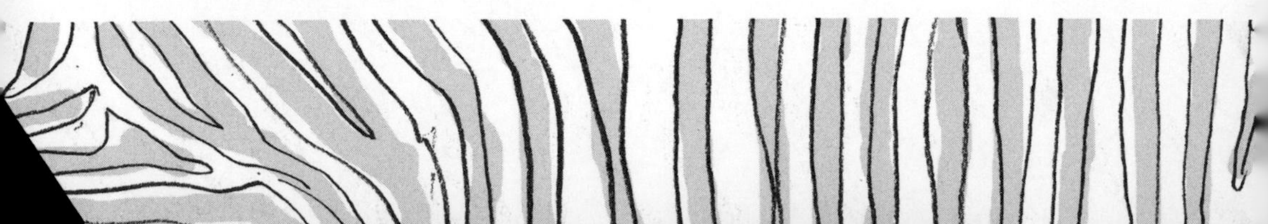

THE BOTTOM OF THE FOOD CHAIN

In the animal world, the food chain rules. Basically, it goes like this: giant fish eat big fish, which eat little fish, which eat tiny fish. Or think of it this way: if you eat hamburger, then you're higher on the food chain than cows.

Rabbits eat grass. Snakes eat rabbits. Owls eat snakes. Hawks eat owls.

A dragonfly might eat a mosquito. Then a fish eats the dragonfly. But the fish gets eaten by a bigger fish, which becomes dinner for a seal. And then along comes a great white shark. . . .

Some animals are lower on the food chain than others, but does that mean sharks are better than sunfish? Or that snakes are better than rabbits? Or that hawks are better than owls? No way! Most of us would take a rabbit over a snake any day. Besides, we need each animal in the food chain. The chain is only as strong as its weakest link. If snakes disappeared, the whole food system would be thrown out of whack. Rabbits and other creatures would run rampant, out of control.

Is there an invisible "food chain" at your school or in your neighborhood, with some kids lower and others higher? Are some people considered more popular and cooler to hang out with? Would you rather be seen with certain kids and not with others?

The different levels we create for people, putting some on lower or higher rungs, are pretty silly. We're all in the same chain. We've all sinned, and none of us come close to meeting God's standard for our lives. From God's perspective, we're all about the same level on the food chain.

Jesus chose mostly poor and uneducated followers. The rich people on the "top rungs" of society scolded him for eating with sinners and touching the untouchable.

Maybe it's time to reevaluate your own "food chain" and start seeing people the way God sees them. God values every person so much that he sent Jesus to earth to die for us—no matter where we fit on the popularity chain.

Everyone has sinned; we all fall short of God's glorious standard.
ROMANS 3:23

Humans eat about 1,500 insect species. About 500 species are eaten on purpose—fried grasshoppers, chocolate-covered ants, etc. The rest of the insects manage to slip into fruit, veggies, flour, and bread.

• • •

TODAY: Ask God to change the way you look at people you've considered lower on the "food chain" and higher on the "food chain." Think of a classmate or neighbor who is shy or unpopular and try to get to know that person better.

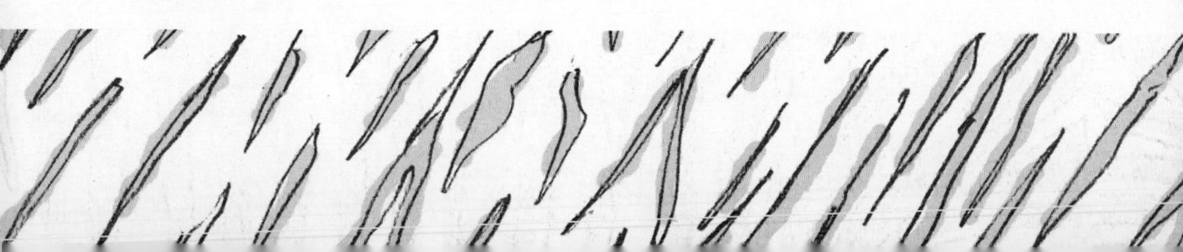

The blue whale mostly dines on krill, tiny shrimplike crustaceans that swim in the ocean. A blue whale might down as much as two tons of krill in a single dinner, which helps explain why the whale weighs about 150 tons.

• • •

TODAY: Be heads-up today and thank God for every bite of food you eat. Think about all that is needed to take care of you (such as housing, food, and clothes). Be grateful.

GOT YOU COVERED

When you think about it, it's amazing that baby animals survive in the wild. Like human babies, animals are born helpless. They depend on their parents for everything—food, warmth, protection, survival.

Fox cubs are born blind, and for the first few months of life, they are nearly defenseless. The delicate white-tailed fawn can't defend itself, so its mother tries to keep it away from predators by moving it to a new location a couple of times a day.

God has also given animals built-in defenses. For example, the white-tailed fawn has irregular white spots to help it blend in with its surroundings. For the first hours of life, a fawn is odorless—a huge protection against predators that rely on their sense of smell.

Unless humans or natural disasters destroy the animals' habitats, animals can usually find enough food. Have you ever seen baby birds in a nest? They cry, beaks open, while their parents do what it takes to fill those little bird bellies. They dig for worms and insects. (The early bird gets the worm, right?)

Even what animals eat will protect some of God's creatures. The postman caterpillar feeds on poisonous passionflower vines. The poison doesn't hurt it, but birds that eat the caterpillar will get sick, so they leave other postman caterpillars alone.

Speaking of caterpillars, those destined to become monarch butterflies have to eat 24 hours a day or they'll die. Now that's total dependence!

We are every bit as dependent on God as the weakest of baby animals. Yet even when we don't realize it, God takes care of us. He protects us and keeps us going, watches over us, and supplies all our needs.

The eyes of all look to you in hope; you give them their food as they need it. When you open your hand, you satisfy the hunger and thirst of every living thing.
PSALM 145:15-16

UNLIKELY PALS

Horses are relatively independent animals, but they crave constant companionship.

The best solution is to have another horse as a pasture buddy or stall buddy. Horses also form friendships with ponies, donkeys, and mules.

But other animals can make good, if unlikely, companions for horses—like barn dogs or barn cats. The right cat offers comfort by curling up on the horse's back. The right dog stands guard and sleeps outside a horse's stall. Goats can make great companions for horses too. Some horses become attached to cows and even chickens. Everybody needs a best friend—and sometimes there's no explaining why certain pals hit it off.

What do you look for in a best friend? Are all your buddies just like you? Same race? Same nationality? Same age? Same clothes and ways of thinking as you? If the answer to all those questions is yes, you might be limiting what you could be learning through relationships with a more diverse group of people.

What about that old neighbor who's always in his garden? Take the time to ask him about his past, and you could have the inside scoop on firsthand history. So what if your cousin is two years younger than you? She might end up being the loyal friend you don't have among your classmates. And don't count out siblings. You never know when a brother or sister might end up being a best friend.

Jesus hung out with all kinds of people—religious, nonreligious, rich, poor, people of many different races. He didn't limit himself to friendship with guys, either. Women followed him and became his friends too. Jesus was criticized for not picking the right friends, for spending time with the "wrong" people. But there were no limits to Jesus' friendship. That's good news for us—no matter who we are or where we come from, he wants to be our friend too.

There is no longer Jew or Gentile, slave or free, male and female. For you are all one in Christ Jesus.
GALATIANS 3:28

The giant land-bound rhinoceros and the little oxpecker bird are pretty unlikely pals, but they team up for a cool companionship. The oxpecker hangs out on the rhino's back and eats insects that land there, and the oxpecker warns the rhino when enemies come near, since the rhino can't see very well.

• • •

TODAY: List three people who are so different from you that you've never considered being friends with them. Start praying for them. What's one step you can take toward developing a friendship with each person?

If a horse doesn't get another horse to scratch its back, it will probably decide to roll in the dirt. If it's able to roll all the way over (instead of rolling in one direction, getting up, then rolling the other way), it probably means the horse is physically fit. Horse traders used to pay more for horses that could roll over all the way.

• • •

TODAY: List five ways that you might be able to motivate or help one of your friends. Prayerfully start the back-scratching.

MUTUAL BACK-SCRATCHING

Have you ever seen two horses scratch each other's backs? There's an art to it, as they line up side by side, facing opposite directions. Usually one horse gingerly starts the exchange, gently teeth-scratching an unreachable spot on its fellow horse's back or neck. If that goes well, the favor is returned. Then they move to other hard-to-reach areas—the withers, back, and rump.

Zebras go through a similar mutual back-scratching process. So do chimps, and they actually point to the spot they want another chimp to scratch.

It's a case of "I'll scratch your back; you scratch mine."

Do you and your friends help each other out? The Bible encourages us to look for ways to build one another up. If you know a friend is self-conscious and shy, maybe you can compliment her or include her in conversations when she's on the outskirts of the group.

If you have a buddy who's not athletic but likes sports, maybe you can work with him. Offer to show him a few pointers or practice together sometimes.

If you see someone who just can't get it in math class, offer to help. When others stand up for what's right, back them up. Tell them you admire them for it.

Unfortunately, the expression "I'll scratch your back; you scratch mine" has come to mean, "Okay. I'll scratch your back, but you'd better scratch mine, or it's no deal." It's great when something works two ways and both people benefit, but as Christians, we need to be willing to scratch others' backs, even if we don't get a back scratch in return.

Let us think of ways to motivate one another to acts of love and good works.
HEBREWS 10:24

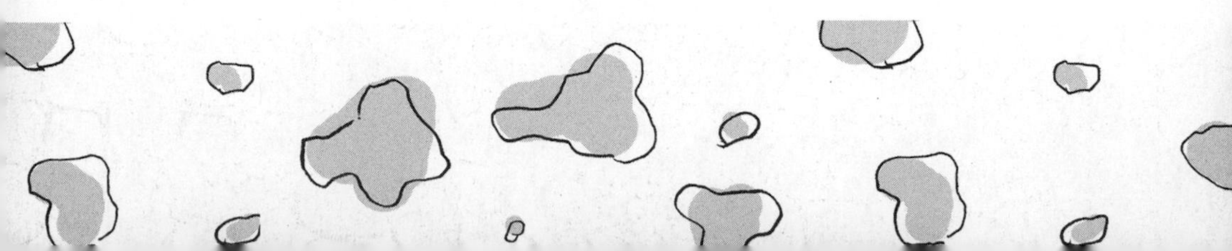

LOVE YOU, HONEY

Ever hear the old saying, "You can catch more flies with honey than with vinegar"? Although it's not clear why anybody would want to catch flies, the saying is probably true for other animals as well as flies: praise works better than punishment.

Horses respond well to praise. If you earn your horse's trust, it will try hard to please you.

Dogs, too, respond better to love and praise than they do to punishment. To housebreak puppies, people used to hit the poor pups with a rolled-up newspaper whenever they made a mistake. Most of the time the dogs had no idea why they were getting hit by their new owner. A better method is to praise puppies when they get it right—then they'll learn what they need to learn.

Our relationship with God should be based on love and trust, not fear of punishment. Christianity isn't just a set of rules we have to follow . . . or else. Christianity is a relationship with a living God who loves us and wants the best for us. When we understand how much God loves us, we'll naturally love him back.

The great thing about God is that the better we get to know him, the more we trust him. When you begin a new friendship with someone, you don't really know if you can trust this person or not. Maybe he or she is talking behind your back, for all you know. But with time, you discover that you can trust this new friend. Still, even with best friends, there are times when you'll let each other down. Nobody's 100 percent trustworthy—except God. God will never let you down. You can trust him completely.

Christ will make his home in your hearts as you trust in him. Your roots will grow down into God's love and keep you strong.
EPHESIANS 3:17

Even armadillos can be trained with positive reinforcement. Female armadillos give birth to identical infants of the same sex. Armadillos are the only animal known to get leprosy (or Hansen's disease).

• • •

TODAY: Tell God three things you've never told another living soul. It's okay—you can trust him.

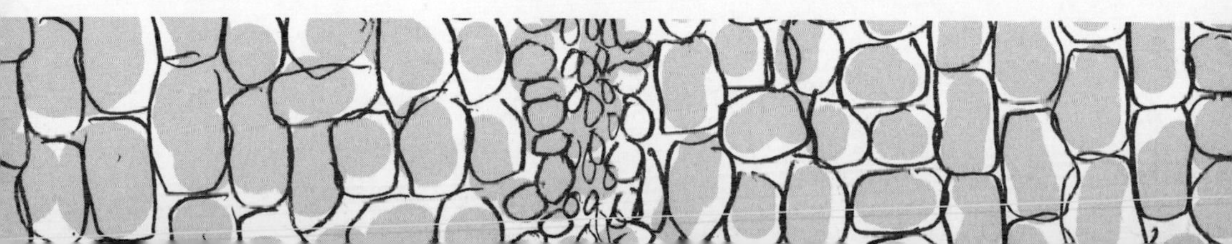

MINE, MINE, MINE!

Humans aren't the only ones who get into arguments and fights. Animal fights are pretty predictable, arising out of jealousy and squabbles over mates, territory, or food.

Male botflies protect the ridges over deserts because that's where they intend to mate. African weaver ants will kill and eat any intruders that so much as wander onto their land. Rhesus monkeys may fight for power, with two males that are lower in the hierarchy ganging up on the top male monkey. Birds called oystercatchers, which feed in flocks on mussel beds in the winter, may turn on each other when fighting for the same mussels.

Even domestic dogs end up in fights—sometimes over you. One dog thinks you're giving too much attention to its mate, and it doesn't like that. It may start with a low growl and a firm stare. The dog's body stiffens, and the fur around its neck and along its back stands up. Then if you're not careful, you'll have a dogfight on your hands.

James (the author of the New Testament book of James) wrote to the early believers that most of their quarrels came because they were jealous of what other people had. He told them to check their motives.

What do you fight about? If you're always bickering with your siblings, try to figure out why. Do you really think life is unfair at your house, or could you be jealous? Understanding your motives can help you get over a lot of squabbles.

If you're content and grateful for all God has given you, then you don't need to crave more. You don't have to feel left out if your friends all have the latest shoes and jackets or the best technology and electronics. It's okay.

Nothing to fight about.

What is causing the quarrels and fights among you? Don't they come from the evil desires at war within you?

JAMES 4:1

Sadly, some terrible "sports" involve making animals fight and then gambling over the outcome. Cockfighting is when two roosters are put into a pit to fight to the death. Special razor blades and curved ice picks are fitted into the roosters' legs to cut up their opponents. This cruel game has finally been banned in all 50 states, but it still goes on illegally. Dogfighting is a felony in all 50 states.

• • •

TODAY: Think about the last few arguments you've had. Write down the cause of each fight. Has jealousy been behind any of your problems? Turn over any feelings of jealousy to God, and ask him to give you a contented and thankful heart.

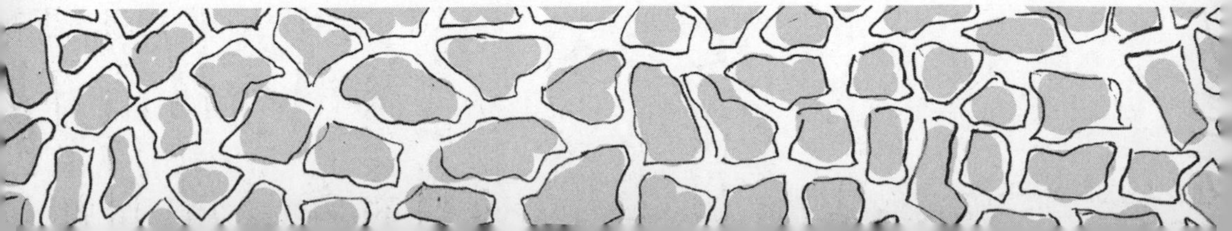

CHOOSING FRIENDS

Some people seem to be naturally good with animals. Dogs come to them, and horses see them as friends. Even cats curl up beside these animal lovers. Usually animals are attracted to what they sense in a person. If a person is calm and kind, then animals tend to give that person a chance to show that he or she is a friend, not an enemy.

But if someone doesn't like horses, a horse will pretty quickly pick up on that attitude. It may take longer for dogs, but eventually they learn who is going to treat them well and who is likely to mistreat them.

We need God's guidance when it comes to choosing our friends. It's easy to want to be with the popular group, even if we sense they may not be the best friends around. But you don't need to waste time trying to force yourself into a certain group. And it's not so smart to avoid people who may not be considered cool enough. If you do, you just might overlook someone with the potential to be a true friend.

If we stay in touch with God and talk to him about the people we meet, he can help us discern, or figure out, if a friendship is helping our faith or hurting it.

The same goes for relationships with the opposite sex. When those hormones kick in and crushes develop, logic sometimes takes a backseat. That's even more reason to keep your eyes open and your heart in tune with God.

Friendship and love shouldn't be blind to what the other person's actions are showing you. If a girl acts stuck-up, believe her. She's showing you who she is. If a guy does mean things, pay attention and ask yourself, and God, if this is somebody you need in your life.

Pray for everybody, but choose your friends wisely.

Solid food is for those who are mature, who through training have the skill to recognize the difference between right and wrong.
HEBREWS 5:14

Birds that feed on snakes and frogs can recognize poisonous snakes and poisonous frogs—through smell or sight—and stay away from them. They sense the difference between the good-for-you ones and the not-good-for-you varieties.

• • •

TODAY: Take a look at your relationships and ask God if you're in any relationship that's not healthy for you. Sense the danger, and do what it takes to get yourself out of that situation.

There's really no difference between a pigeon and a dove. We just like to call the smaller, white ones *doves* and the ones that sit around on statues in cities *pigeons*.

• • •

TODAY: Are there some areas of your life where you might be too worldly-wise? Are there some areas where you might need to get a clue? Ask God to help you walk that tricky line between having the shrewdness of a snake and the innocence of a dove.

SNAKES AND DOVES

Have you ever noticed that doves have a reputation of being good guys in the animal kingdom? The dove is a symbol of peace. Noah released a dove from the ark after the flood was over, and it came back with an olive branch when it found land. When Jesus was baptized, the Spirit came down in the form of a dove.

What we usually think of as doves are actually white rock pigeons. They do prefer staying out of conflict, finding seeds on bare ground, where there are enough seeds that they don't have to fight over food. They show up on farms where crops are doing well and water abounds.

In cities, doves, like gray pigeons, mainly live on handouts and leftovers. They're strong fliers with an instinct that leads them home. Doves can live for 15 years or so, even though they have few defenses, except to fly away from hawks and peregrine falcons.

Snakes, on the other hand, seem to know when danger is coming. Then they shrewdly stand their ground, ready to strike first when necessary. And most of them sneak up on their prey and strike without warning.

Jesus sent out his disciples with advice that might have confused them: "Be as shrewd as snakes and harmless as doves."

But it is, of course, great advice. While you're getting smarter and wiser in the ways people interact and the way the world works, you never want to lose your innocence. Do all you can to get along peacefully with classmates, teachers, and strangers. But don't be clueless when it comes to looking out and being safe.

Look, I am sending you out as sheep among wolves.
So be as shrewd as snakes and harmless as doves.
MATTHEW 10:16

MAKE PEACE

The bonobo is a certain species of primate that exists only on the south bank of the Congo River in Africa. Due to the loss of its natural habitat and extensive hunting, this animal is on the verge of extinction. One of the smallest apes, the bonobo used to be called a pygmy chimp.

In the bonobo society, females rule: their chimpanzee troops are led by females. Infants are carried around by their mothers for two years, and babies laugh when they're tickled by adults. Young bonobos stay close to Mom for several more years. The daughters eventually leave the troop in search of a group of their own to lead, but sons maintain a close relationship with Mom forever.

Yet one of the most amazing things about bonobos is that they're basically peaceful. Fights almost never break out. And when they do, they're resolved peacefully.

Jesus included peacemakers in the Beatitudes: "God blesses those who work for peace, for they will be called the children of God" (Matthew 5:9). It's hard enough not to be the one causing a fight or getting pulled into one. It takes even more courage to try to make peace.

Disagreements are bound to come up in any relationship. When arguments threaten the peace in your group of friends, can you step up and try to stop it? Sometimes you can call your buddies back to sense or calm the situation with humor. If you understand the problem, you might try to help your friends come up with a fair solution.

It's even harder to try to make peace when it's your group against another group. Your friends might accuse you of being disloyal or even call you a coward. But if you treat people fairly, you have a better chance of keeping the peace. The most effective time to be a peacemaker is before the war breaks out.

Those who are peacemakers will plant seeds of peace and reap a harvest of righteousness.
JAMES 3:18

Believe it or not, skunks are some of the most peace-loving, nonaggressive animals around. They only spray when frightened, and even then they do it as a last resort, after stamping their feet as a fair warning. But they're nearsighted, so to them you might resemble a scary predator. In that case, you'd better look out.

• • •

TODAY: Pray for peace—in your home, with your friends, at school, in the nation, and in the world.

ANIMALS MIGHT NOT HAVE A NAME FOR IT WHEN THEY VOMIT, BUT HERE ARE SOME WORDS HUMANS USE TO DESCRIBE IT:

barf, vomit, hurl, ralph, purge, puke, honk, spew, regurgitate, toss your cookies, lose your lunch, tango with the toilet, have a Technicolor yawn, revisit your breakfast, paint the town red . . . and green and orange, burp to the ninth power

• • •

TODAY: If you haven't been living all out for God, tell him you're sorry. Then find ways you can change things: Talk to a friend about your faith. Volunteer at a homeless shelter. Break a bad habit.

GROSS OUT!

Most animals, except horses and rats, can vomit. Horses have a band of smooth muscle around the esophagus, which means food can go down, but it can't be pushed back up.

Big deal, you say? Actually, it *is* a big deal. Horses can die because they're not able to vomit out something bad they've eaten by mistake.

Cats and dogs are among the lucky vomiters—cats especially, thanks to hair balls. Even long-necked giraffes can pull off a good vomit.

And so can people.

Believe it or not, so can God.

What would you think makes God want to hurl?

Lukewarm Christians—people who say they love him, but only live halfheartedly for him. That's what makes God sick.

Are you on fire for God? Or do you just go through the motions—attending church, maybe going to youth group—but never really connecting with God?

If God is God, and if you have Christ living inside of you, life shouldn't plug along in a lazy, empty way, day after meaningless day. If you knew that you only had a week on earth to help people come to Christ, wouldn't there be a sense of urgency to everything you do?

Wake up! Don't make God sick.

I know you inside and out, and find little to my liking. You're not cold, you're not hot—far better to be either cold or hot! You're stale. You're stagnant. You make me want to vomit.

REVELATION 3:15-16, ***THE MESSAGE***

GOLDEN RULE

Wolves live in packs led by an alpha pair, a male and a female boss. During their prime years, the leaders of the pack rule. If they share food equally and take good care of cubs and other pack members, they will have a long life as alpha pair.

But eventually the alpha pair has to retire and let other dominant wolves take over and lead the pack. That's where the Golden Rule comes into play: "Do to others as you would like them to do to you." Or "Treat people [or wolves] the way you'd like to be treated."

The way alpha wolves treat the pack is exactly how they'll be treated by the other wolves when they retire. If they abused the weaker members, they'll be abused themselves. But if they were kind, they'll be cared for kindly.

The Golden Rule is one of the first verses most kids learn. Yet Jesus said that this simple principle—treat others the way you'd like to be treated—sums up everything in the law and prophets.

Can you imagine what your school would look like if everyone followed that rule?

In a perfect world, we'd treat people well—smile, be nice, give them a compliment, offer to help them with their homework, include them when they look lonely—and we'd get that kindness back. It doesn't always work out that way though. This is earth, not heaven. But the rule is still "golden." There's no guarantee that you'll get kindness in return for kindness, but God still calls you to be kind. So if things feel unfair, it's going to be okay. God will pick up the slack. His kindness is enough.

> *Do to others whatever you would like them to do to you. This is the essence of all that is taught in the law and the prophets.*
> **MATTHEW 7:12**

An omega wolf is the low wolf on the totem pole in its pack. The other wolves may attack an omega to keep it from getting too close to the rest of the pack. The ranking of wolves in a pack goes from the alpha (top dog) to omega (at the bottom).

• • •

TODAY: Before you go to school, write down 10 things that you wish other people would say to you or do for you today. Do all 10 things for other people.

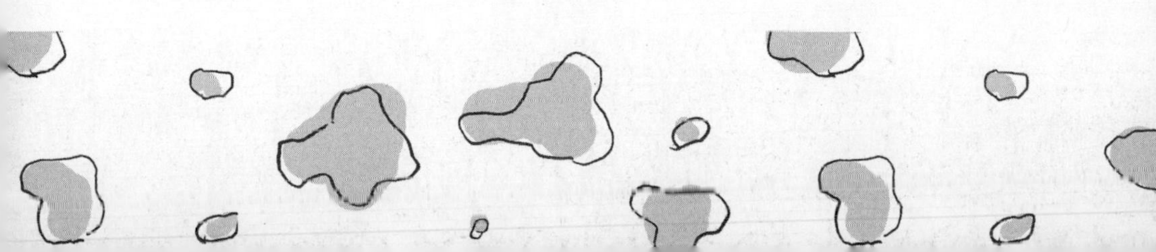

Nobody's sure where the expression "Curiosity killed the cat" started. But the rest of the expression goes: "but satisfaction brought it back." Don't forget the last half of the quote!

• • •

TODAY: Look around you and find at least five things to wonder about. Ask someone about them or look up the answers to find out more information.

CURIOSITY DID NOT KILL THE RAT

Ever wonder why scientists often choose rats to experiment on in the laboratory? One reason is because rats are curious—maybe even more curious than cats. Rats aren't afraid to tackle new challenges or scramble through mazes to see what lies around the next corner.

Today black rats inhabit forests in Israel, where they feed on seeds from pinecones. A long time ago, during a drought in Jerusalem, most animals from the pine forests were starving. But not the black rats. While starving animals stepped over fallen pinecones, the curious rats figured out a way to get at the seeds inside the cones. These creatures worked out a system of removing the rows of scales on the pinecone in a precise order that would free the seeds inside. The rats not only learned this skill but also taught it to their offspring. Curiosity (for better or worse) saved the rats!

Little kids tend to be so curious that they can drive a family crazy with *why* and *how come* questions. We all start out life curious, observing the world around us.

Unfortunately, most people lose that inborn curiosity once they hit the school years. You can get too caught up in yourself—how you look, how you feel, what other people think of you. You don't even notice your mom's new haircut, your sister's sadness, the bird singing outside your window, the frost on the trees, or the beauty of God's world around you. God could put a burning bush on the sidewalk and you'd dash around it without even asking what's going on.

Rats! Maybe we should take a lesson from the rats.

> *The angel of the* LORD *appeared to [Moses] in a blazing fire from the middle of a bush. Moses stared in amazement. Though the bush was engulfed in flames, it didn't burn up. "This is amazing," Moses said to himself. "Why isn't that bush burning up? I must go see it."*
>
> **EXODUS 3:2-3**

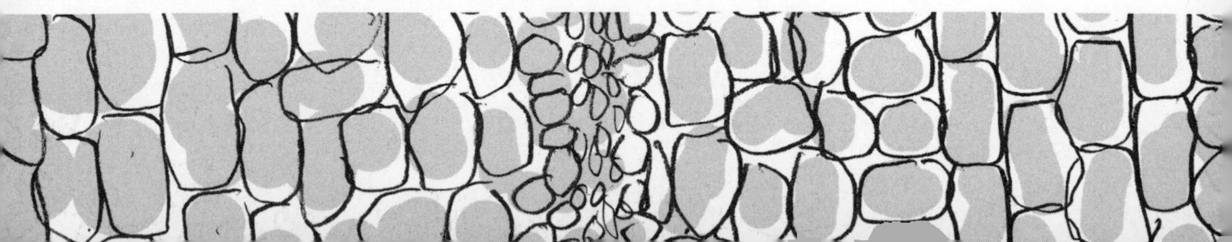

MADE TO ORDER

God thought of everything. Did you ever wonder how a giraffe can clean its ears? God built into this animal a 21-inch tongue. Made to order.

Sperm whales are mammals, so they don't have gills and can't breathe underwater. Yet that's where they live. They're able to breathe through specially made blowholes, which are basically big nostril flaps on top of their heads. Most have one blowhole, although some have two. The whales come up for air and snort out the old air, sending up a spray, then dive underwater, where they can hold their breath for more than an hour.

Buzzards have to eat, so God made their eyes so supersensitive to light that these birds can see a tiny mouse from 15,000 feet in the air.

Other animals are equipped with everything they need for life. Beetles and armadillos have hard protective shells, and butterflies and moths get delicate wings to fly away. The cheetah gets speed, while the praying mantis gets camouflage.

The hippopotamus spends its life sunning and never gets burned or dries out. Why? Because the hippo was created with the ability to produce a reddish lotion that oozes from its skin and moisturizes it.

God created each animal with the exact body it needs to live on earth. And God created your body too. Maybe you're not crazy about your nose. Or perhaps you want to be taller, or shorter, with different hair and eyes. Maybe you have a disability or you don't think you're as smart as other people.

Just remember that God created you with everything you need, and you are totally loved and valued exactly as you are. You were made to order.

Thank you for making me so wonderfully complex!
Your workmanship is marvelous—how well I know it.
PSALM 139:14

Polar bears have webbed paws that help them swim.
Slugs have four noses (sort of).
The octopus has three hearts.
The starfish has no brain.

• • •

TODAY: Talk to God about everything you don't like about your body. Don't leave out anything. Then thank God for creating you exactly as you are.

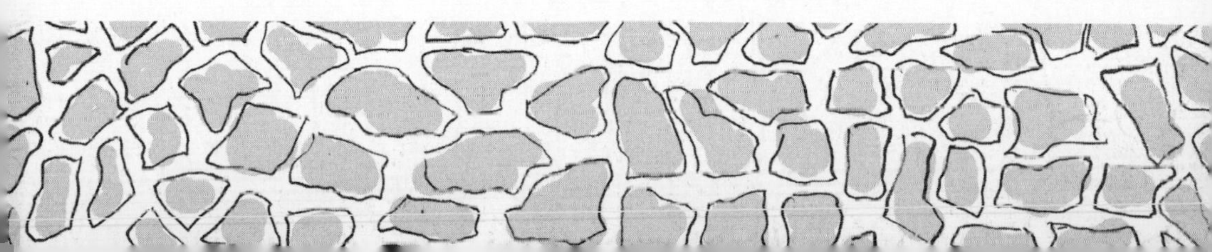

AWESOME!

Did you know that no two zebras and no two tigers have the same stripes? And that no two cows or leopards sport the same design of spots? Awesome!

Seeing birds migrate south for the winter and north for the summer, or hearing geese as they fly in their crooked V, should fill us with awe. How would they know where to go unless God wired them with fine-tuned instincts?

Some hummingbirds fly from Alaska to Mexico and back every year, a 6,000-mile round-trip. Every winter, the bristle-thighed curlew finds its way to islands in the Pacific, thousands of miles from home in Alaska. The arctic tern flies from the Arctic to the Antarctic and back again every year—you can't journey farther than that!

Birds aren't the only migrators. Green sea turtles journey 1,400 miles from Brazil to Ascension Island in the South Atlantic so they can lay their eggs on the exact shore where they were born. Salmon spend from six months to seven years in the ocean before swimming upstream in a river to lay their eggs thousands of miles away, back where they were born. Caribou walk 3,000 miles every year as they migrate to find food and to give birth. And some people consider the thundering wildebeest migration one of the wonders of the world.

Other creatures manage to be awesome underground. The *Japyx* insect uses its two-pronged tail like a fork to grab insects and chow down. One species of cicada spends 17 years underground and then comes up for only a few weeks to mate and lay eggs.

Don't become dulled to the awesome scenes going on all around you. Let yourself be awed and filled with wonder at what a great Creator we have.

If you're not continually amazed at the world around you, it's not God's fault!

> *How amazing are the deeds of the* Lord*! All who delight in him should ponder them.*
> **PSALM 111:2**

The basilisk lizard can walk on water by moving its legs fast and using special scaly flaps on its toes.

• • •

TODAY: Keep a little notebook with you all day and write down at least 20 awesome things you see in nature or discover by reading about animals.

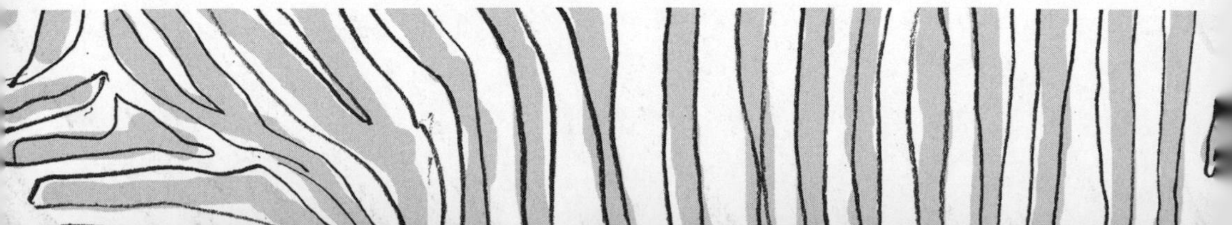

CALLING ALL SHEEP!

In Israel during Jesus' day, shepherds kept their sheep on hillsides, moving the flock to wherever there was grass. At night groups of shepherds camped together under the stars and took turns keeping an eye on the sheep. The common practice was to herd all their flocks into one central sheepfold at night. Whoever was gatekeeper for the night closed in the sheep and watched over them.

When morning came, it was time for the shepherds to reclaim their own flocks. You'd think it would have been impossible, since sheep are sheep, right? But all a shepherd had to do to get his own sheep back was to call out to them. The sheep in each flock knew their own shepherd and gladly followed him.

Jesus called himself the Good Shepherd, and he told the disciples that he would always know his sheep—his followers—and his sheep would know him.

Can you always identify your Good Shepherd and follow him? When you hear new ideas and philosophies, can you sort out which ideas fit into what Jesus taught and which ideas are out of line?

You don't have to be afraid of other people's ideas. We learn by listening to others. But you need to be able to sort out Jesus' teachings from all the other advice and claims that call out for your attention. How? By knowing the Shepherd so well that you can tell whether you're turning to follow him or starting to veer off track and follow somebody else.

I am the good shepherd; I know my own sheep, and they know me.
JOHN 10:14

Sheep were the first lawn mowers at the White House, thanks to President Woodrow Wilson's First Lady. She made sure that the grounds were inhabited by a flock of sheep that would keep the grass short.

• • •

TODAY: Talk to God about ways to get to know Jesus better. Make a plan to read through the Gospels and take notes on things you learn about Jesus. Sign up for a Bible study. Do whatever it takes to know the Shepherd well.

BLENDING IN

Certain animals have an uncanny ability to camouflage. They go beyond simply looking like their surroundings, the way a praying mantis resembles a stick, or a caterpillar looks like a leaf. These animals actually change their appearance to look like the objects or creatures around them.

The cuttlefish is a master of disguise. When it rests on a rock, it takes on the shape, form, and color of the rock. When it swims, the cuttlefish changes colors while in motion to match the ocean floor beneath it. It can change its shape to round, or stretch out flat to blend in with its surroundings.

A type of flounder in Europe, called the plaice, is so adaptable that if you place the fish on a checkerboard, it will change its color and shape to look exactly like the checkerboard.

We're a lot like the camouflage crew at times, ready to change so we fit in with everybody else. At first, it can be as innocent as changing your hairstyle or your shoes. But the need to be one of the group can lead to some bad decisions when everybody's smoking or wearing inappropriate clothes or experimenting with things that compromise what you stand for.

We become like the people we spend time with. That's why people in cliques look and act alike. You might not even realize you're changing. Cuttlefish change into all sorts of colors, but they're color blind.

Ask God to help you stay true to the person he's created you to be. Choose your friends, your group, carefully.

> *They may say, "Come and join us. Let's hide and kill someone! Just for fun, let's ambush the innocent! Let's swallow them alive, like the grave; let's swallow them whole, like those who go down to the pit of death. Think of the great things we'll get! We'll fill our houses with all the stuff we take. Come, throw in your lot with us; we'll all share the loot." My child, don't go along with them! Stay far away from their paths.*
>
> **PROVERBS 1:11-15**

The American weevil and the swallowtail butterfly caterpillar look like bird droppings.

• • •

TODAY: Take a hard look at the company you keep, and talk to God about the ways you've changed this year—in good and not-so-good ways.

HUNGRY?

Some animals' whole world seems to revolve around hunger. Caterpillars need to eat 24 hours a day, and if they don't get what they need, they'll die. You have to wonder if the little guy worries there won't be enough leaf to go around.

The polyphemus moth larva eats constantly. It needs to consume about 86,000 times its birth weight in its first two months of life. That seems like an impossible feat, but it works out. And the larva eventually becomes a moth.

It's hard to feel too sorry for a vampire bat, but they do have to deal with a huge appetite. A colony of vampire bats in Latin America might need to feed on the blood of around 15,000 chickens a night, or maybe 25 cows if they're up for a change of menu.

Giant pandas spend 14 hours a day eating. And grazing animals, like horses, eat nearly all day long, unless they're sleeping. Birds spend most of their time looking for food. A baby robin might eat as much as 14 feet in earthworms a day.

Yet somehow the animals get the food they need.

Most of us don't have to face that fear and worry about where our next meal is coming from. Although many families have tight budgets, most people in our country barely know what it feels like to be really hungry.

Yet we still worry. Maybe your family has had to tighten finances and you've had to give up your phone or shop at different stores. Or maybe you're worried you won't have enough money to do stuff with friends or eat out or get the right kind of shoes.

Or maybe your worries are more urgent. Your parents have lost their jobs, and you're worried you might have to move out of your home. Hard times can happen to any of us. But God's here. He provides for the animals, and he will take care of us, too.

> *God will generously provide all you need. Then you will always have everything you need and plenty left over to share with others.*
> **2 CORINTHIANS 9:8**

Most birds definitely don't "eat like a bird." Birds down at least half their weight every day just to live.

• • •

TODAY: Ask God to use you to help people in need. Check out relief organizations, such as Samaritan's Purse, World Vision, Compassion International, or the Salvation Army, or ask your local church how you can help.

Dogs and cats both need fresh, cool water every day. Cats can't live on milk alone without water. In fact, cats don't need milk, and they might even get a stomachache from drinking it.

• • •

TODAY: If you don't really feel that thirst for God, act as if you do. Don't let even an hour go by without talking to God. Keep it up, and pretty soon you'll realize that you really are thirsty for God.

THIRSTY FOR GOD

The most important part of taking care of a pet's physical needs is to provide fresh water. Humane societies warn pet owners to keep dogs and cats supplied with fresh water at all times. Animals can survive much longer without food than without water. It's possible for them to lose most of their fat and up to half of their protein and still live. But if a pet loses only one-tenth of its body's water, it could die.

A lack of water—even just a small shortage—can give your pet a stomachache. It can also lead to kidney problems, malnutrition, and heart disease. Every living creature needs water, which may be why animals, like humans, feel thirst as a strong, all-powerful yearning. Thirst is a craving that can't be ignored.

Psalm writers, like David, wrote that they thirsted for God. They meant that they longed for God with such a strong craving it couldn't be ignored. They felt that if they didn't have a closeness with God, they couldn't survive.

What are you thirsty for? What, or who, do you long for? What keeps you awake at night or captures your brain during class or gets you daydreaming on your walk home? Baseball? Soccer? Horses? A computer game or TV show? A movie star or singer? A certain guy or girl?

The only thirst that makes sense is a thirst for God. Every other longing will fail to live up to everything we're hoping for. God is the only one we can't live without. We need him to survive. We need him just to get through another day.

I lift my hands to you in prayer. I thirst for you as parched land thirsts for rain.

PSALM 143:6

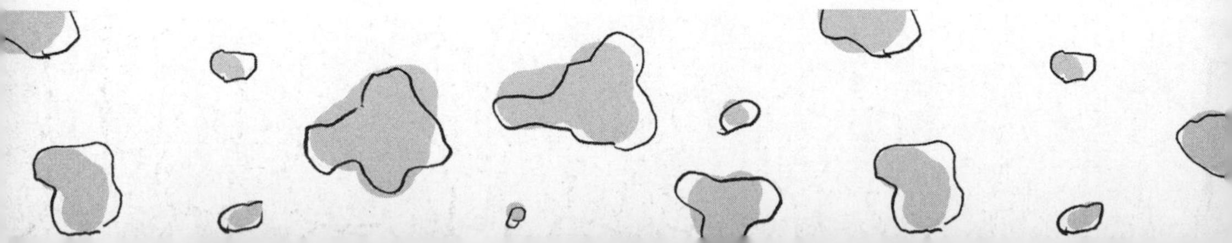

WHAT'S UNDER YOUR SKIN?

Pop quiz: Are animals' stripes or spots just part of their fur, or do they have striped and spotted skins, too?

Believe it or not, for most animals those stripes and spots aren't different designs found only on their fur. Each creature has a unique pattern as identifiable as fingerprints. You could shave a tiger and the same stripes would return, because the pattern is rooted in the skin.

Our Christianity needs to go deep, past the surface actions that most people see. It's not that hard to be a "Sunday Christian"—someone who goes to church and can talk the language, but doesn't live it out the rest of the week. People aren't drawn to "churchy Christians," whose actions are barely skin deep.

Real Christianity is a deep relationship with Christ, a friendship that marks the entire believer from the inside out.

You can't always tell a Christian by outside appearances, right? There's no handy checklist of dos and don'ts that will prove whether someone is a Christian or not. True, the way you act as a follower of Christ should make you stand out (in a good way). People should be able to see your "stripes" and "spots." And what they see should demonstrate how you're living for Christ. But those stripes need to be real and deep, with your actions coming from inside your heart—not from a shallow list of dos and don'ts.

Let Christ get under your skin. Being a Christian goes to your core being, who you are deep down inside. Christian = Christ-in-one. Christ in *you*.

> *When I think of all this, I fall to my knees and pray to the Father, the Creator of everything in heaven and on earth. I pray that from his glorious, unlimited resources he will empower you with inner strength through his Spirit.*
>
> **EPHESIANS 3:14-16**

The stripes on a zebra seem like they'd make the animal easy to spot. But it's actually the opposite. In sunlight and shadows, a zebra's stripes can look blurry. To a predator far away, a zebra creates an optical illusion when it runs, and the predator gets even more confused.

• • •

TODAY: Talk to God honestly about how deep your faith goes. All throughout the day, think about how deep God's love is for you. If you're feeling confused, talk to someone you trust who has a deep relationship with Christ.

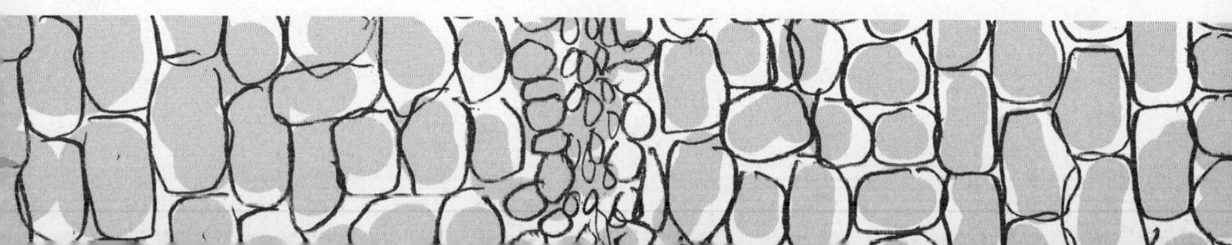

FADS COME AND GO (FOR WHICH SOME ANIMALS ARE EXTREMELY GRATEFUL):

goldfish swallowing
ant farms
Mexican jumping beans (actually seeds with caterpillar larvae trapped inside)
dyeing Easter chicks purple and pink
Chia Pets and pet rocks (okay—not so bad, if you're an animal)

• • •

TODAY: What fads are considered cool at school? Ask your parents and grandparents about the fads when they were in school. Talk about whether the things that were considered wrong in their day are still wrong today.

NEW THINGS

Sometimes the newest and latest things aren't the best.

The kea is a 19-inch mountain parrot from New Zealand. Funny and entertaining, the kea can also drive people crazy. Kea parrots are attracted to everything new that comes along. If they haven't seen it, they have to try it out. They've wrecked—and been wrecked by—electrical wires, ski lifts, RVs, and tires. They often search trash bins on the lookout for something new.

But this drive to be part of everything new can be dangerous. The kea is growing extinct because the parrots are so drawn to tourists . . . and to tourists' cars. Not a good mix.

As long as there have been humans, there have been fads. From poodle skirts to miniskirts, sock hops to discos, to karaoke, each generation believes it's the first group to be cool. Since you've been in school, you've probably gone through a few fads and trends yourself.

If you wait long enough, the coolest clothes—print leggings, hip-slung jeans, straight-legged pants—will go out of fashion . . . and come back in again. Curly hair might be out of fashion for a while, but eventually it will come roaring back into fashion, sending the long, straight-haired girls back to the hairstylist.

It's fun to be part of new crazes and fads. But just because something is new doesn't mean it's better. Clothes and hairstyles are one thing. Truth is another. Truth doesn't change. Just because some people today think it's okay to stretch the truth, try drugs or sex, or live with someone before getting married, the truth is still the truth. God's standards and expectations haven't changed.

History merely repeats itself. It has all been done before. Nothing under the sun is truly new.
ECCLESIASTES 1:9

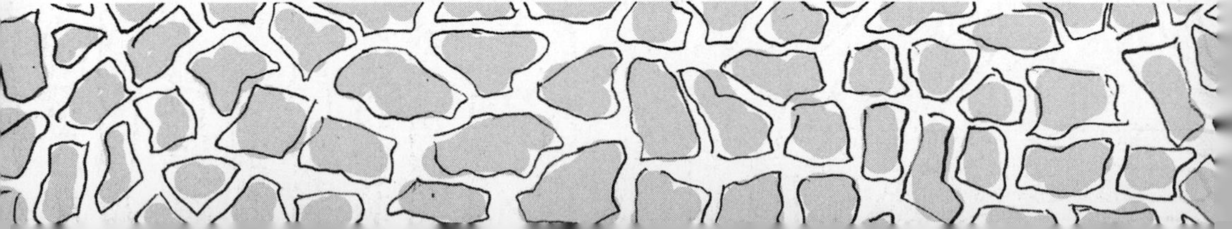

WHAT A LOVELY TONGUE YOU HAVE . . .

Isopods, distant cousins of bigger crustaceans like lobsters and shrimp, are pretty strange creatures. You've probably seen the isopods called sow bugs or pill bugs, which are often called "roly-polys" because some of them roll into a ball when they're frightened.

Another isopod, a parasite called the tongue-eating louse, latches onto the tongue of the spotted rose snapper fish. The isopod lives there, eating away at the snapper's tongue until the parasite actually becomes the fish's tongue, replacing its own tongue.

The book of Proverbs talks a lot about the tongue and flattery. Proverbs 26:28 warns, "A lying tongue hates its victims, and flattering words cause ruin." So what's up with that? How can somebody telling you how good you look or what cool shoes you're sporting be a bad thing?

Definition-wise, *flattery* means a compliment that isn't sincere. So you might find yourself doing your hair a certain way just to get those thumbs-ups, and the flatterer didn't really mean it in the first place.

The poor snapper fish loses its own tongue when the isopod takes control. It's kind of like the way other people's opinions about you hijack the way you think about yourself. If nobody tells you that you look great in your new jeans, do you stop wearing them? If people laugh when you talk about God, do you stop bringing him up?

Don't live for flattery. It's nice to get compliments, but God's praise is the only kind that matters.

> *I'm not trying to win the approval of people, but of God. If pleasing people were my goal, I would not be Christ's servant.*
>
> **GALATIANS 1:10**

Cows have long, rough tongues. Less than 10 percent of your classmates can touch their noses with their tongues, but all cows can touch—and lick—their noses with their tongues. So there.

• • •

TODAY: List five things you've done in the last few days to please other people (parents don't count). List five things you'll do today to please God.

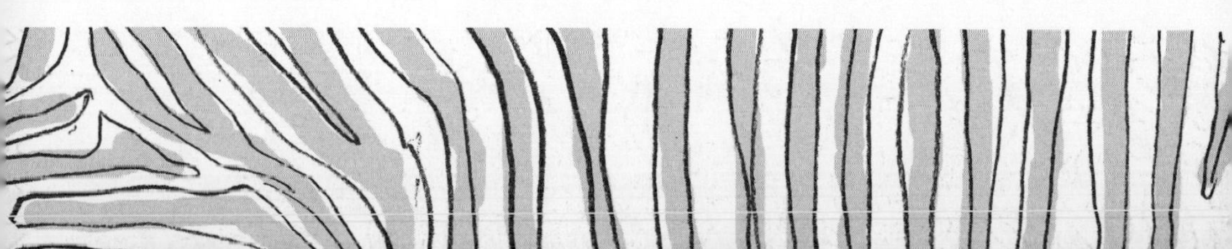

Whales sing with "accents," with whales from one area or generation sounding the same, but songs from their relatives across the sea having distinct differences.

• • •

TODAY: Make yourself listen to a style of music you normally wouldn't listen to, and see if you can find a way to praise God through it.

HEAVENLY MUSIC

Animals seem to love music as much as we do. A nightingale might have a few hundred songs in its repertoire. But birds aren't the only musicians in the animal kingdom.

Humpback whales are champion music makers. They've even cut their own CDs and recordings (with a little help from their friends). A humpback whale's song is complex and can last for 30 minutes. Only the male sings, belting out a series of repeated hums, chirps, and mysterious whale songs. Another male whale can then pick up and repeat the song exactly, not missing a note. Or the song can be improved—jazzed up a bit.

Humpbacks aren't the only animals that have had their music recorded by humans. Coyotes, sea lions, Mexican bats, frogs (like the boreal chorus frog), and chipmunks have too.

Animal sounds vary from soft, sweet, and slow to loud, fast, and teeth rattling. For horse lovers, there's no music more welcomed than the nicker of a horse, but the sound means nothing to the non–horse lover. Cricket music puts some people to sleep and keeps others awake at night.

Human music works the same way. You might hate classical or love jazz. You may groan at your parents' "goldie oldies," and they may constantly beg you to turn down your "noise."

Church music and song selection can split great churches right down the middle. Maybe your church service majors in the old hymns, when you get more out of contemporary Christian. Or maybe those country western solo numbers put you over the edge. So which music is best? The music that helps you praise God and connect with other believers. If you'll be open and at least listen to the words of the songs at church—no matter what style they are—you can turn that music into praise. And that's what music's all about.

Sing to him; yes, sing his praises. Tell everyone about his wonderful deeds.

1 CHRONICLES 16:9

March 4

WATER OFF A DUCK'S BACK

You've probably heard the expression "like water off a duck's back." It means that criticisms and mean words slide off certain people without affecting them in the slightest. Picture a perfectly dry and content duck—in the middle of a pond, in the midst of a downpour.

God has fashioned the feathers of ducks to keep them dry and warm. Ducks' outer feathers are waterproof because they have built-in oil glands near the tail. All a duck has to do is spread that oil over its outer coat, and water runs off it . . . like water off a duck's back.

Even in extremely cold water, ducks can swim around and be just fine. The duck has soft feathers closest to its skin, keeping it insulated and protecting it from the cold.

How do you handle it when people talk about you behind your back? Or to your face? Do their comments roll off you like water off a duck's back? Or do you think about their words, going over and over the insult or slam? Do you get angrier and angrier as you think about it? Or do you get more and more depressed?

There will always be people who get their kicks by making fun of others or by tearing down other people. You're bound to get a few cutting remarks from time to time if you talk about God or if you stand up for what's right.

God's love is your oil, insulating you. You don't have to absorb every mean thing people say about you. Let their words slide off you like water off a duck's back.

And let the things God says about you stick.

Your former friends are surprised when you no longer plunge into the flood of wild and destructive things they do. So they slander you.

1 PETER 4:4

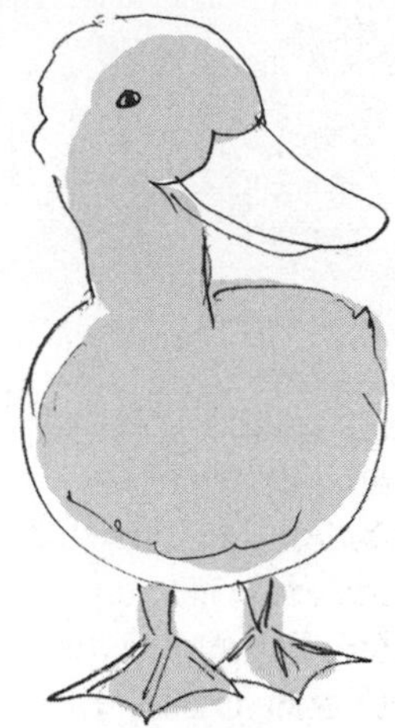

Even a duck's webbed feet stay warm in icy water. That's because duck feet don't have blood vessels or nerves.

• • •

TODAY: This week if anyone says something that hurts your feelings, toss those words up to God and tell God you'd rather hear what he has to say about you. Then start reading through the Psalms.

Peacocks aren't the only show-offs in the animal kingdom. The male moorish idol fish struts and shakes its tail feathers too. When the moorish idol fish meets another male, it tries to look better than its competition. The fish even manages to change colors and become brighter.

• • •

TODAY: What abilities or possessions or characteristics make you proud of yourself? Talk to God about each one today, and be sure to express your gratitude, rather than your pride.

PROUD AS A PEACOCK

When peacocks strut around, what are they so proud about?

It's most likely not because they're helping their fellow peafowl or making the garden a better place for all bird-kind. We assume they're proud of the way they look, with those gorgeous, iridescent fanned feathers spread out behind them—that blue or green train with the colorful "eyes" on the feathers.

Maybe they're proud because they're so popular. Peahens usually pick the biggest peacock with the most colorful train, after all.

Pride is a tricky emotion. People tell you that you should have some pride in yourself or that you should be proud of that A on your history test. Then later they come down on you for being too prideful. So is pride a good thing or a bad thing?

That depends. Pride in yourself is listed as a sin in the Bible. Are you proud because you're so good looking? such a great athlete? so smart?

On the other hand, there's a legitimate sense of pride that's based on knowing that an accomplishment is really God's, and you're just proud to be part of what he's doing. If you're part of a mission project that irrigates land so people can water their farmland and you see those crops come in, you might be overwhelmed with pride and gratitude. That's different from being proud of the fact that your family has the biggest house in town or drives the best car.

Be grateful for your talents and gifts, but nail yourself if you see that you're proud as a peacock. Pride makes you strut and stick your nose in the air. Gratitude drops you to your knees, with your head bowed.

Haughty eyes, a proud heart, and evil actions are all sin.
PROVERBS 21:4

PRIDE BEFORE A FALL

A group of lions is called a pride, with between two and eighteen females—sisters, aunts, nieces, moms—and a male or two, or even more. The male lion who leads the pride seems to have it made. He gets his pick of any females in the pride he wants. Not only that, but the women do most of the hunting. Then they bring back the carcass and let the male lion eat first.

But if the male leader of the pride has . . . well, pride, he'd better enjoy it while he can. Few male lions last longer than three years in this king role. Pride comes before a fall—and a very hard and violent fall, at that, as the younger male lions take over by force.

Just because people might be willing to treat you as if you're better than others doesn't mean you have to accept that treatment. Paul and Barnabas traveled around modern-day Turkey, telling people about Jesus. In one city after they healed a man, people were so impressed that they began showering Paul and Barnabas with gifts and flowers, calling them gods. But Paul and Barnabas wouldn't allow it. They made sure God got the credit and the glory.

People are fickle. Right after the crowd cheered for Paul and Barnabas, some people from another city showed up and changed the minds of the crowd so fast that Paul and Barnabas were in danger of being stoned to death. The crowd went from trying to sacrifice *to* the disciples to trying to sacrifice them (Acts 14:8-20).

The crowd that cheers for you when you hit a home run to win the game just might boo you next time when you strike out in the bottom of the ninth. That's a good reason to stay humble.

> *Human pride will be brought down, and human arrogance will be humbled.*
> **ISAIAH 2:11**

When a male lion takes over a pride of females, the first thing he does is kill all the cubs. He wants his own kids around, and nobody else's.

• • •

TODAY: What role do you play in your group of friends? Leader? Brain? Clown? How would your relationships change if you lost that role? Ask God to help you refuse any kudos that don't ultimately go to God.

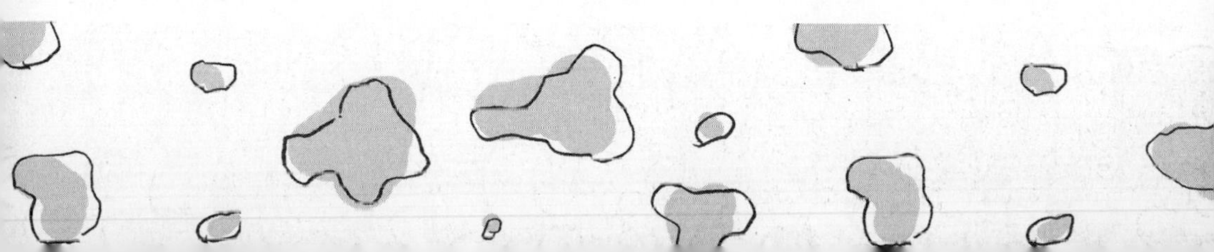

Bush babies, a kind of big-eyed, fuzzy monkey, let out a cry that sounds like a human baby. The bush babies' sense of hearing is so sensitive that they have to cover their ears to sleep.

• • •

TODAY: When's the last time you had a good cry? Talk to God about it . . . and about anything else that has you close to tears.

A GOOD CRY

Did you know that some animals shed tears? Scientists don't all agree that the tears come from sadness, like our tears do, but pet owners will vouch for their pets' emotions.

Dogs cry. So do chimpanzees. Seals shed thick, oily tears that make them look like they're crying. Even bears and elephants shed tears. Some elephants mourn the loss of a fellow elephant—a buddy that might have traveled with the herd for 70 years.

Even when baby animals don't shed tears, there's no doubt that they cry when they're left alone or separated from Mom. Baby bears cry out until the mother returns. And baby birds are incessant in their pitiful calls from the nest. Anyone who has been around the barn when a colt is weaned from its mother knows that they're both crying over the separation.

Everybody cries. Some shed tears more often than others, and some just cry on the inside, where others can't see.

But God sees. And when you feel those tears coming, remember that God sees every teardrop. You're not alone. The God of all compassion is right there with you.

We cry over different things, and sometimes we aren't sure why we feel so sad. But even when you can't put your finger on what's the matter, God can. God collects every one of your tears. And he promises that someday he will wipe away every single tear.

> *You keep track of all my sorrows. You have collected all my tears in your bottle. You have recorded each one in your book.*
>
> **PSALM 56:8**

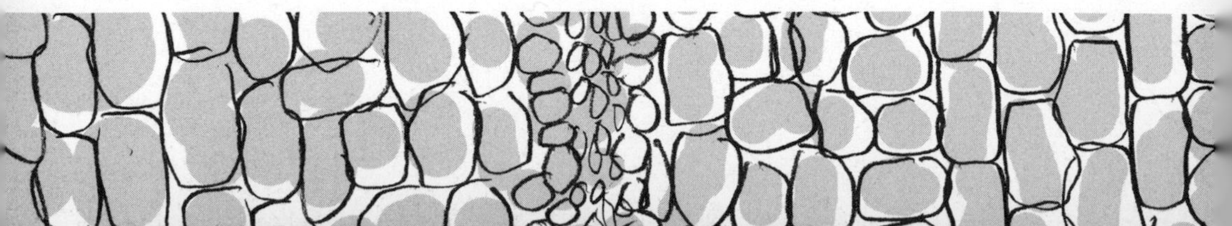

SORRY ABOUT THAT

One of the most soulful sounds in the universe has to be the call of the mourning dove. These birds live all over North America, in forests and farmlands, deserts and inner cities. There's no mistaking the deep-throated whistle that would make a great background for almost any scary movie: *oooo-OO-ooo oo oo oo oo oooo-OO-ooo oo oo oo.*

Some people love the moan of a mourning dove, but others hate it, complaining that it's just too sad.

Sometimes it's okay to be sad, as long as it leads to something better. The apostle Paul told the believers in Corinth that it was good that they'd gotten sad over his last letter because that sadness had led them to repent and change the way they'd been living.

Paul said there were two kinds of sorrow: (a) godly sorrow, which makes you stop sinning and turn to God—that's the good kind—and (b) worldly sorrow, which doesn't cause you to change your actions but just makes you sadder and further from God.

What are you sorry for? Are you sorry that you lied to your parents? Sorry that you're pretending to be someone you're not? Sorry that you keep getting deeper in unhealthy relationships? Then do something about it! Change. That's what it means to repent: turn around and go the other way.

Don't waste your sadness on the worldly kind of sorrow that just makes you feel worse. Use godly sorrow to make you turn to God for solutions.

> *The kind of sorrow God wants us to experience leads us away from sin and results in salvation. There's no regret for that kind of sorrow. But worldly sorrow, which lacks repentance, results in spiritual death.*
> **2 CORINTHIANS 7:10**

When a pair of mourning doves builds their nest, the male gathers sticks and then stands on the female's back and hands over the sticks. She takes it from there and weaves the nest. Hmm . . . that could be why she sounds so sad.

• • •

TODAY: List the things you're sorry for. Divide your list into two sections: "godly sorrow" and "worldly sorrow." Apologize to God and to anyone else you need to, and commit to changing your ways. Let God turn the sorrow into joy.

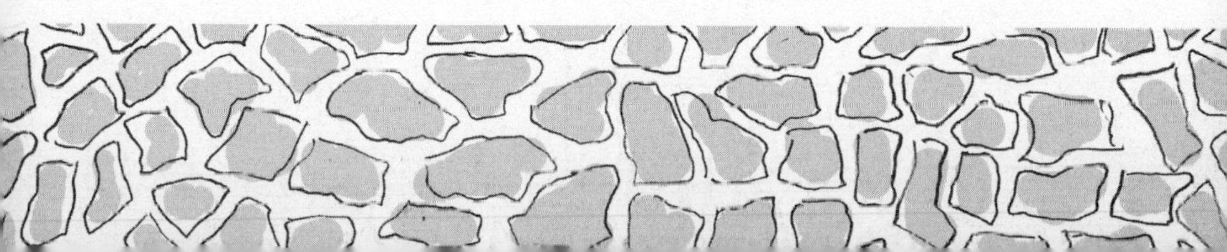

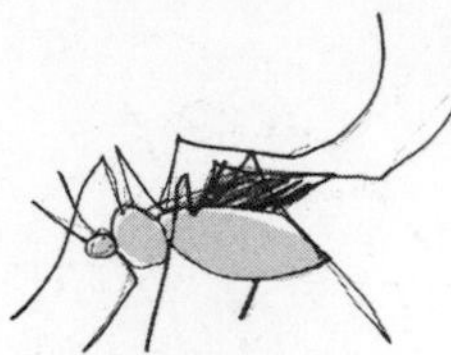

GETTING UNDER YOUR SKIN

Mosquito bites itch. That's because when a mosquito bites you, she sticks her needlelike nose, the proboscis, into you and injects her saliva under your skin. The saliva keeps your blood from clotting so that she can drink fast. But the saliva causes a reaction in your skin that ends in an itchy red bump.

On a bad day, botflies lay their eggs on a mosquito's proboscis and get a free ride under your skin. The result is a double dose of itchy!

Other insects inject venom, or poison, under your skin when they bite or sting. Fire ant stings (like bee and wasp stings) can kill a person who's allergic to the venom. About 20 to 30 kinds of spiders carry venom that can be dangerous to humans, with the brown recluse and the black widow topping the list.

Sometimes the things people do or say can feel like poison injected under your skin. A friend betrays you, a parent lets you down, a classmate won't stop bashing you. Like a mosquito bite, something gets under your skin and keeps pricking you. You can't let it go. You scratch at it, going over and over what that person did to you, and the hurt gets deeper and deeper, gnawing at you until you can't see any way out.

But there is a way out. And you need to take it, if you ever want real peace. God is the one in charge of justice. He sees and feels what has been done to you. So hand over your hurt—Jesus is the salve to stop the itching. Bitterness harms *you*, not the other guy, not the person who hurt you. *You.*

Somebody said that hanging on to bitterness is like drinking poison and expecting the other guy to get sick. Don't go there. In life, you're going to get bitten—you can count on it. But you don't have to let the bites get under your skin.

> *Watch out that no poisonous root of bitterness grows up to trouble you, corrupting many.*
> **HEBREWS 12:15**

Only the female mosquito bites. If you get a bite, she may be attracted to your sweat or body odor, or she might just be so hungry and thirsty that she'll bite anybody.

• • •

TODAY: Talk to God and be honest about the things that you've let get under your skin. Ask him to help you let go and forgive.

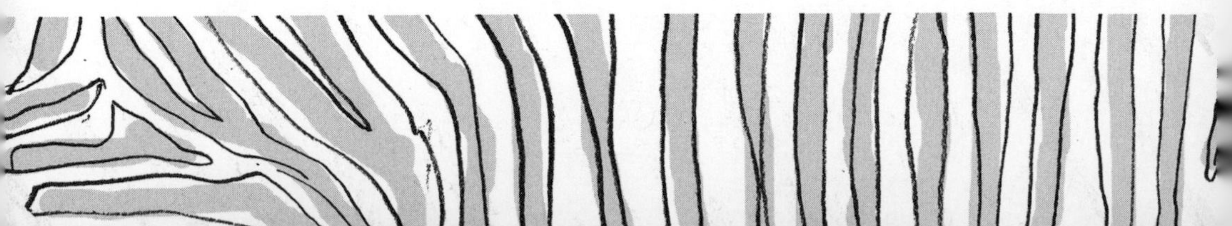

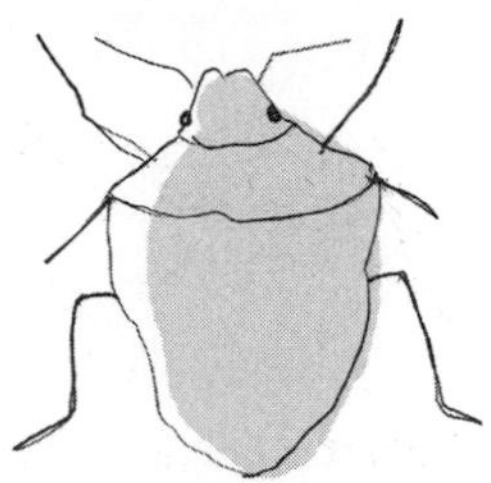

DON'T BUG ME!

There are roughly 10,000,000,000,000,000,000 bugs in the world, give or take—that's 10 quintillion. How do you feel about bugs? Seriously. Do they make you want to hug them, to cuddle up with them and make them your best buddies? How about cockroaches and june bugs, or rat fleas, earwigs, lice, and chiggers?

Chiggers grab on to your clothes and keep moving in until they find bare skin—at the waistband of your jeans, around your sock, or up your sleeve and straight to your armpit (they love armpits). Once chiggers get going, they don't stop. They bite and inject a fluid that isn't exactly poison, but it wears down the skin. Chiggers dissolve cells and then suck up the liquefied tissue. And the more you scratch, the worse it itches.

Has anybody ever pleaded with you, "Stop bugging me!"?

Most kids worth their title know how to wear down a frazzled parent. It goes something like this:

"Mom, can I go to Chris's house tonight?"

"Not tonight. You've got homework and a room to clean."

"*Ple-e-ease?* Everybody's going to be there."

"No. You put off cleaning that room all week. And I know you have a report due."

"*Mom!* That's not fair!"

"I have to get to work."

"Just say I can go. *Please?* I'll clean my room later. I won't stay long."

"But you know how—"

"Don't you trust me?"

"Of course I trust—"

"Then you gotta let me go. Please? *Please?* I'll never ask for another thing ever. Please, Mom? Can I? Just this once?"

"Oh, all right."

More or less, that's how it's done. Nagging and bugging parents might even work sometimes, but a bug-infested house will never be as comfortable as a home filled with respect and understanding. Give your parents a break. Sometimes the magic word isn't "*Please.*" It's "Okay."

Do everything without complaining and arguing.
PHILIPPIANS 2:14

Although all bugs are insects, not all insects are bugs. True bugs belong to the Heteroptera suborder, which includes the likes of stinkbugs, bedbugs, bloodsucking assassin bugs, and giant water bugs, known as "toe biters."

• • •

TODAY: What things have you been bugging your parents about lately? In what other ways have you been a pest? Make your apologies, and ask God to stop you before you bug, bug, bug people.

A mule is a cross between a female horse and a male donkey. A cross between a male horse (a stallion) and a female donkey (a jennet or jenny) is a hinny. Mules can't make babies. An ass is another name for a donkey, and a jackass is a male donkey. A burro is a small donkey.

• • •

TODAY: Catch yourself every time you resist advice or input today. Ask God to point out any stubbornness in you and give you the kick you need to get past it.

MULE-HEADED

A mule is a cross between a female horse (a mare) and a male donkey (a jack). As far as we know, George Washington was the first person in America to own mules. People in Spain were already using mules for farmwork then, and Washington liked the idea. He asked the U.S. ambassador to Spain to check it out. Word reached the king of Spain that Washington had an interest in mules, and in 1785 King Charles III presented Washington with a little gift: a jackass, or male donkey.

The expressions "mule-headed" and "stubborn as a mule" aren't generally considered compliments. Some mule owners claim these animals make great workers, but many people have found that they have a serious stubborn streak. If a mule decides it wants to go in one direction, or nowhere at all, even a bit and bridle won't help. Nobody says, "He's as teachable and flexible as a mule."

A person who's teachable will probably get further in life than someone who's stuck on doing things one certain way. Flexible people don't usually get the ulcers stubborn people get. Would you rather have friends who are agreeable—who might change their minds and do what you want to do on occasion—or friends who are so set in their ways that they won't even listen to your ideas?

When your dad tries to explain a better way to study, are you open to his ideas? Or if your mom has input on your wardrobe, do you give her a chance? If a friend warns you that you need to think about the way you've been acting lately, are you willing to hear that person out?

Or are you stubborn as a mule?

Do not be like a senseless horse or mule that needs a bit and bridle to keep it under control.
PSALM 32:9

PUT YOUR FOOT DOWN

You can lead a horse to water, but you can't make it drink . . . especially if it's not thirsty. Cats won't likely dive into the swimming pool just because you want them to join you and your buddies for a cool dip. Most animals have certain things they refuse to do.

Overly alert or nervous horses can drive a rider crazy, but there have been cases when a horse had good reason not to step onto a faulty bridge or gallop into danger. Horses have run away from earthquakes before humans sensed danger. They've refused to enter a forest when a developing forest fire was no more than a spark.

You might know the story of Balaam's donkey from the book of Numbers in the Old Testament. Balaam was a prophet who was summoned by Balak, the king of the Moabites, but God didn't want his prophet to go. After resisting the invitation of the officials from Moab, Balaam finally agreed to follow them. But along the way, an angel blocked the path. Balaam didn't see the angel, but his donkey sure did. And the donkey put his foot down and refused to go.

There's a time to give in and a time to put your foot down. Have you ever gone somewhere with friends, even when you knew it wasn't somewhere God—or your parents—would approve of? How many conversations have you joined when someone else was being trashed or when gossip was flying?

Have you ever witnessed bullying—in person or through e-mails or texts or social networks? You knew people were being mean and feelings were being hurt, but you didn't stand up or do a thing to stop it.

There's a time to put your foot down.

> *You have had enough in the past of the evil things that godless people enjoy—their immorality and lust, their feasting and drunkenness and wild parties, and their terrible worship of idols.*
>
> **1 PETER 4:3**

If a horse refuses to go when you want it to, a good technique is to make it circle. Tug on one rein and keep going in little circles until you can get past the problem. On the other hand, if you're heading for a cliff, your horse is right. Stop.

• • •

TODAY: Talk to God about things you've said and done to go along with the crowd (or things you've failed to say and do). Thank God for the forgiveness that covers you. Then make your apologies to anybody you know who was hurt. And the next time, put your foot down.

13 March

SAFE HAVEN

Jumping spiders look courageous when they leap more than 40 times the length of their bodies and land on their intended victims. But they're only brave because they know they can get back to safety in an instant. The spider produces a silky lifeline and secures itself to the line before it jumps. The spider's silk line is its ticket back to a safe haven.

Animals like safe havens. Prairie dogs venture out of their burrows, but they're ready to dive back underground at the first sight of danger. Bees hightail it back to the hive. Ants trail back to their ant nests. Ladybugs (you guessed it) fly away home.

You need a safe haven too. Hopefully your home is one. Your house should be the one place you can feel safe and say what you're really feeling and thinking. Maybe your parents don't always understand, but they love you anyway.

When the early Christians started spreading the Good News about Jesus farther and farther into surrounding cities and countries, they ran into intense opposition. But they kept going. At the end of their missionary journeys, they returned to Antioch, the city they'd been sent out into the world from. In Antioch the disciples could refuel their energies and faith in a safe haven.

Your local church and youth group can be that kind of safe haven for you too. You need a safe place where you can bring up questions about faith and the Bible, where you can get answers that will help you live for Christ.

> *When [Barnabas] found [Saul], he brought him back to Antioch. Both of them stayed there with the church for a full year, teaching large crowds of people. (It was at Antioch that the believers were first called Christians.)*
> **ACTS 11:26**

Although most adult tigers live alone, a male tiger insists on "marking his territory." He may only visit that territory once or twice a year, but he needs to have a place to come home to.

• • •

TODAY: Take a step of commitment to become involved in a local church or to get more involved in your youth group. Talk to your pastor or youth leader about what you can do to make your group a safe haven for members who are venturing out to help others.

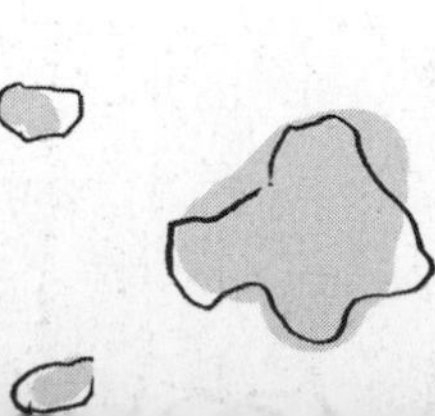

BARN SOUR

Have you ever gone on a short trail ride where the horses knew the route blindfolded and couldn't wait to get the ride over with? Sometimes horses don't want to leave the barn, and it may take the help of a trail boss to get some of them moving away from home.

The poor horses go through the motions of the ride, trudging along . . . until they turn to come back to the barn. Then they kick into gear and want to get back *now*. The same horses that seemed too tired to move are suddenly ready to trot or gallop back to the barn. But when the next trail group shows up, those riders will have the same trouble you did getting the horses to leave the barn.

It's called being "barn sour." The horses get so attached to their barns that they don't want to go anywhere else.

We can fall into the same trap. When Jesus went back to the Father, the disciples stayed pretty close to home in Jerusalem, meeting behind closed doors. When God's Spirit came to live inside of them, they were able to speak out for Christ. But it really wasn't until persecution drove the believers out of Jerusalem that they began to fulfill Jesus' command to be his witnesses to all parts of the world.

It's great to be part of a Christian community—a group of church friends or a youth group. But you need to be careful not to stay in the "barn." God has places for you to go, people only you can talk to about Christ. Christian fellowship is meant to give you the strength you need to get out into the world and make a difference.

Go and make disciples of all the nations, baptizing them in the name of the Father and the Son and the Holy Spirit. Teach these new disciples to obey all the commands I have given you.

MATTHEW 28:19-20

Horses in a stable or barn can come to rely on the security of the stalls so much that when they're frightened, they'll run back into the barn—even when it's on fire.

• • •

TODAY: Come up with two ways you can leave the "barn." Prayerfully step out in faith today.

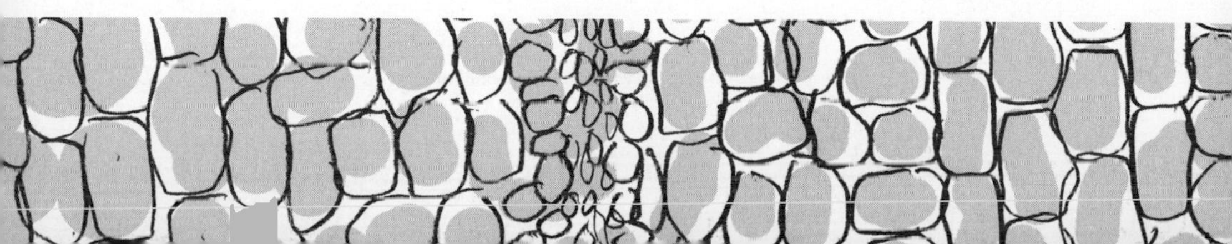

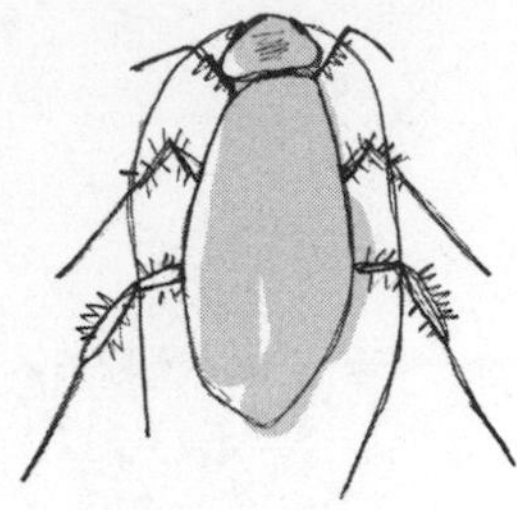

PRAYING MANTIS . . . OR PREYING MANTIS?

Take one look at the praying mantis poised on a leaf of grass or among the flowers, and you just know it's got to be one of the good guys. With its long front legs raised in a prayerful position, no wonder it got the name "praying" mantis.

But looks can be deceiving. If you happen to be a moth, grasshopper, fly, or cricket, the mantis is no good guy. It is, in fact, a deadly predator—better named a "preying" mantis than a "praying" one.

The mantis waits on a twig or leaf, blending in with the surroundings, rotating its neck 180 degrees until it spies its victim. Then it strikes out with those "praying" legs and impales the unsuspecting insect with sharp spines that hold the victim in place, helpless, while it's being eaten alive. Scientists do not believe the mantis is saying grace.

Mantis is Greek for "prophet" or "fortune-teller." The praying mantis may look like a good prophet, but it's not. The Bible warns people about false prophets who preach about God but really only want to get people off the track of faith.

You probably hear all kinds of things about God from many different sources. One TV speaker might tell you that unless you join his church and never miss a Sunday, you won't go to heaven. Turn the channel, and you'll hear another speaker claim that everybody goes to heaven, no matter what they believe. A friend from your own church might try to convince you that the Bible doesn't apply to us today, especially not when it comes to things like money and dating.

Test the "prophets" in your life. Rely on God's Spirit inside of you, plus the Bible, to tell who's praying and who's preying.

> *Dear friends, do not believe everyone who claims to speak by the Spirit. You must test them to see if the spirit they have comes from God. For there are many false prophets in the world.*
>
> **1 JOHN 4:1**

The closest relatives to the praying mantis are cockroaches and termites.

• • •

TODAY: Make a list of 10 things that you know are true and won't change, no matter what. Ask God to help you see through people who say and teach things that just aren't true.

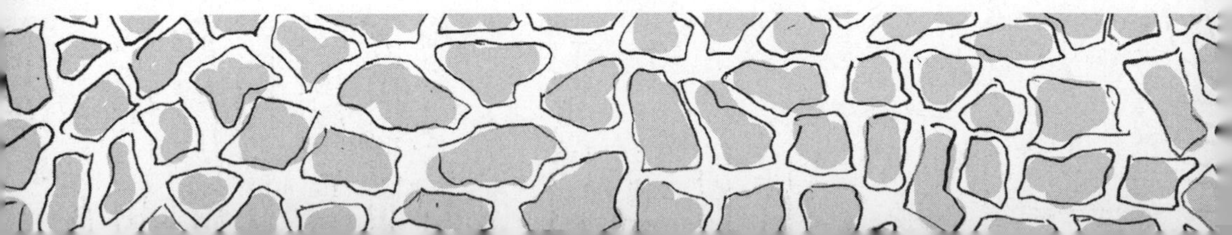

DON'T TOOT YOUR OWN HORN

Sea unicorns aren't unicorns at all. They're actually in the same family as whales and dolphins. They have twisted tusks, which hunters used to sell as magical unicorn horns.

But the hunters had no business "tooting their own horns" about their discoveries. The "unicorns" were just narwhals, an odd type of whale with only two teeth. A female narwhal's teeth usually stay embedded in the lip, but the male's left tooth shoots through the lip to form a tusk up to eight feet long. Sometimes both teeth break through the lip and twist together, forming a spiraled "unicorn" tusk.

When you do something you think is pretty awesome—win an award, clinch the game for your team, sing a great solo, ace a test—it may be tempting to tell everybody. It's not really bragging—you just want to share, right? Or do you want to make sure everybody knows so they'll think better of you? Tooting your own horn isn't a great idea, and here's why:

1. You may be wrong. Maybe you weren't as awesome as you think.
2. Even if you're not really bragging, you'll probably come off that way.
3. If you take your praise now, you just might not have any left when you get to heaven.
4. Only God can judge your motives for doing whatever great thing you did. You can do something that looks awesome, but it isn't worth a unicorn's horn if you have the wrong motive.
5. Finally, even if you do something wonderful for God, with the purest of motives, big deal. That's what we're supposed to do!

When a servant comes in from plowing or taking care of sheep, does his master say, "Come in and eat with me"? No, he says, "Prepare my meal, put on your apron, and serve me while I eat. Then you can eat later." And does the master thank the servant for doing what he was told to do? Of course not. In the same way, when you obey me you should say, "We are unworthy servants who have simply done our duty."

LUKE 17:7-10

Narwhals are unusual whales that are found only in the Arctic Sea. The name means "corpse whale," due to its pale color and because when these animals swim belly-up in pods of 10 to 100, they look like a mass of dead whales.

• • •

TODAY: Talk to God about what you think your three best accomplishments were in the past year. Did you make sure everybody knew about them? Did the praise from others really bring you lasting satisfaction?

WHO CARES?

Sparrows are the most common birds in the world. They show up in every state in the United States and nearly everywhere on the planet. Small and brownish-gray, with short tails, they're not much to look at. And they have more than their share of annoying habits. They like to take over the nests of other birds or build their own nests on top of existing nests. Some sparrows even build a nest right on top of a nest with another bird's babies in it!

About 50 years ago, Chairman Mao Tse-tung of Communist China tried to get rid of sparrows. He made peasants kill the birds in their fields until sparrow corpses were piled high in various regions of the country. The result was that the following year, since the sparrows weren't there, insects took over the fields, and a locust plague caused a countrywide famine.

Sparrows weren't considered valuable in Jesus' day either. That's why he used the sparrow as evidence that God cares about us. Since God knows every time a sparrow falls, he certainly won't miss a thing when it comes to you. God cares about every little part of your life.

When you do your best on a quiz and still fail, God feels for you. If you say the wrong thing or if you trip and somebody laughs at you, God notices. And he cares. When you're having a bad day or feeling lonely or you don't have anybody to sit with at lunch, God sees and cares.

The next time something happens to you and you're tempted to think, *Who cares?* the answer is *God.*

> *What is the price of two sparrows—one copper coin? But not a single sparrow can fall to the ground without your Father knowing it. . . . So don't be afraid; you are more valuable to God than a whole flock of sparrows.*
> **MATTHEW 10:29, 31**

The white-throated sparrow has two distinctive color patterns: tan striped or white striped. Instead of mating with a bird that looks like it, this sparrow always mates with a bird that has the opposite color pattern—a tan striped with a white striped.

• • •

TODAY: At least once every hour during the day, thank God for caring about your every move: when you choose your cereal, when you brush your teeth, when you pick out clothes, when you sit by someone on the bus, when you walk into the cafeteria, when you get a bad grade or a good one. And remember—God cares.

BITING OFF MORE THAN YOU CAN CHEW

Black swallower fish live in the deep sea and grow to be just seven to ten inches long. But the swallower preys on fish three times its size . . . and swallows them whole. The mouth and throat of the swallower can stretch like a balloon, and its stomach can expand to three times its normal size.

On occasion, the black swallower bites off more than it can chew. It swallows the too-big prey but can't digest it—and the swallower dies. One eight-inch swallower in the Cayman Islands was found dead with a 34-inch snake mackerel in its belly.

Have you ever bitten off more than you could chew? The result can be disaster. Humane shelters claim that the number one problem in crowded animal shelters is owners who don't know what they're getting into. When new pet owners discover how much work caring for an animal can be, some of them dump the poor pets at the nearest shelter.

Jesus warned the disciples that they needed to seriously consider what it would take to follow him. He wanted them to know the cost so they wouldn't quit when things got tough.

Same goes for you. Everything you say yes to—being on a team, leading a discussion group in Sunday school, aiming to get into a great college—means you have to say no to other things (that favorite TV show, reaching the next level of your computer game, texting friends).

Knowing more about your commitment up front will help you later on when you feel like quitting.

Don't begin until you count the cost. For who would begin construction of a building without first calculating the cost to see if there is enough money to finish it?
LUKE 14:28

About 5 to 7 million pets go into animal shelters in the United States every year. At least half come from homes where the owners changed their minds about owning a pet. Sixty percent of the dogs and 70 percent of the cats in animal shelters are euthanized, or killed.

• • •

TODAY: Talk to God about anything you've dropped out of this year, and figure out why it happened. Then pray about new commitments coming up. Ask God to help you count the cost.

More than 60 percent of all households in the United States have a pet. About 85 million are cats, and around 75 million are dogs.

• • •

TODAY: List five of your responsibilities, including pet care, if you have a pet. Talk to God about how you've been handling your responsibilities. Ask God to help you kick it up a notch.

UP TO YOU

Whether you get a spunky puppy, a slithering boa constrictor, a cuddly kitten, or a nearly immovable newt, there's nothing like getting a pet. You may have lobbied for a pet because you wanted the companionship and fun of owning your own cat, dog, guinea pig, or parrot. Maybe your parents felt the same way. But it's likely they had another reason to allow you to be a pet owner: to teach you responsibility.

If you own a dog, you have to feed, water, walk, brush, bathe, and watch out for it. If you get a cat, you have to be careful so it won't run away. You also need to keep the litter box clean and make sure your cat has fresh food and clean water. Other pets require cages or aquariums that have to be cleaned by somebody—you.

If you're paying attention, you can learn a lot about yourself through your pet. Are you trustworthy and responsible, never forgetting to feed and water your pet? Then you're probably your pet's favorite person.

Pets come to depend on the most faithful person in their lives. Think about it. If you don't feed that puppy (and your parents refuse to pick up the slack for your lack of responsibility), the dog won't survive. If your mom ends up feeding and walking your dog, then your dog probably likes Mom best.

Jesus taught that if we're faithful in little things, we'll be faithful in big things down the line. There's no better place to begin being responsible than by faithfully caring for the jobs you have right now, whether it's your pet, your schoolwork, or your chores.

If a man cannot manage his own household, how can he take care of God's church?
1 TIMOTHY 3:5

WHAT'S IN YOUR MOUTH?

The male jawfish of the Philippines incubates the female's eggs in his mouth. A father sea catfish keeps the eggs of his young in his mouth until they're ready to hatch and swim out. Dad catfish won't even eat until the babies are born, which means he goes without food for several weeks.

A species called Darwin's frogs live mostly in Chile. This small male frog with a pointed snout slurps up the female's eggs. Then he keeps the eggs in his vocal sac until they hatch and pop out of his mouth.

Some African cichlids are mouth brooders, which flirt by locking lips and fanning fins. After the eggs are laid, it's the female fish that scoops them into her mouth and holds them until hatching time. As her babies grow and get bigger, her throat gets bruised, but she keeps those babies inside until it's safe for them to come out.

The Bible is filled with advice and warnings about the things that come out of our mouths. What we say matters.

Here are some verses about our mouths (and the trouble they can cause):

> *Too much talk leads to sin. Be sensible and keep your mouth shut.*
> **PROVERBS 10:19**

> *Jesus called to the crowd to come and hear. "Listen," he said, "and try to understand. It's not what goes into your mouth that defiles you; you are defiled by the words that come out of your mouth."*
> **MATTHEW 15:10-11**

> *May the words of my mouth and the meditation of my heart be pleasing to you, O LORD, my rock and my redeemer.*
> **PSALM 19:14**

Darwin's frog, that hatches eggs inside the male's vocal sac, was a common sight in Chile until 1978, when the frogs seemed to disappear. Scientists believe the frog may now be extinct.

• • •

TODAY: Ask God to help you control every word that comes out of your mouth today. Check out your words with God first. Then let them out.

Arapaima fish, which live in swamps, can breathe through their gills, like normal fish, or gulp down air like we do.

• • •

TODAY: As you go about your normal routine, pay attention to moments when you feel inadequate, like you can't do or say what you wish you could. Then remember that God promises to use you, no matter what. And speak up, or step in, relying on his power.

PRETTY FISHY

Tilapia is the name of a fish that started out in the Nile River and the Mediterranean Sea. After World War II, Europe and the United States began to farm the delicious fish, and tilapia spread all over the world. Today you can order a tilapia dinner in many restaurants across the United States.

Some people call tilapia the Nile snapper, cherry snapper, or sunshine snapper. But one of the most interesting names for it is Saint Peter's fish.

You can read about this now-famous fish in Matthew 17. Jesus and the disciples were in Capernaum when some tax collectors got Peter off by himself and asked him if Jesus paid taxes. On the defense now, Peter said Jesus did.

Before Peter said a word to Jesus about the tax problem, Jesus pointed out that kings shouldn't have to pay taxes in their own kingdoms. Yet he went on to say that he and the disciples would pay the tax so they wouldn't offend anyone.

Jesus told Peter to go to the lake and throw in his line, then open the mouth of the first fish he caught, and there he'd find a silver coin to pay their taxes. Tradition says that this fish was the tilapia. People might have guessed this by the markings of the fish, with lines like golden fingerprints. "Peter's fish" coughed up the silver coin for the tax.

Did you ever feel as if God can't use you because you're too young, or too shy, too ordinary, or too weird? Everyone on earth feels like he or she is too something, or not enough of something else—not smart or quick enough, not cool or talented enough. But God can use anyone. In fact, God delights in using people others might think are "unusable."

God can use anyone and anything, even a fish.

Remember, dear brothers and sisters, that few of you were wise in the world's eyes or powerful or wealthy when God called you. Instead, God chose things the world considers foolish in order to shame those who think they are wise. And he chose things that are powerless to shame those who are powerful.

1 CORINTHIANS 1:26-27

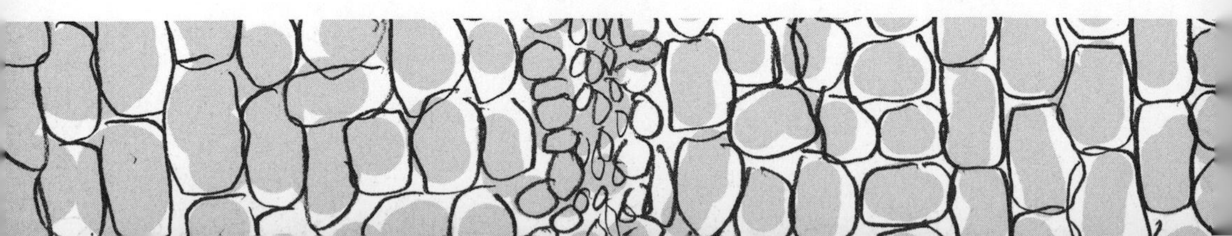

TONGUE POWER

The tongue of a woodpecker can be as long as the woodpecker itself. Unlike the tongues of most birds, the woodpecker's tongue isn't attached to its head. Instead, it curls around its skull. The long tongue can worm its way into the hole of a tree to draw out grubs (little unhatched insects).

Dogs' tongues are pretty amazing. The tongue of a dog has eight sets of muscles to control it. It can be a radiator, cooling off the whole animal, or it can lap up water, lick the dog's wounds, or check out a possible food source. A dog can also lick its master's face to show how glad it is to see its buddy.

Cat tongues are rough, making the tongue a comb for grooming or a tool to help get meat off the bone.

Our tongues have power too. The Bible uses the tongue as a metaphor for things we say. If God is going to speak through us, we'll need to use our tongues wisely to pass along the message to other people.

So how's your tongue? Are you putting it to good use? If you had a recording of the things you've said over the past week, would you enjoy hearing the playback? Do you let God speak through you? How many times have you brought up God or Christ in conversation?

It's not always easy to talk about God. But if you're listening to God and he's a big part of your life, you can't help but talk about him. You know how it is when you're excited about something—a certain sports team or music group, a new guy or girl in your class, a new member of your family. You can't stop talking about the things that excite you.

Let God's words overflow into yours.

The Spirit of the Lord speaks through me; his words are upon my tongue.
2 SAMUEL 23:2

Every known dog breed except the chow and the Chinese shar-pei has a pink tongue. These two breeds have blue-black tongues.

• • •

TODAY: Ask God to speak through you today. Then look for openings to bring up spiritual subjects in natural conversation.

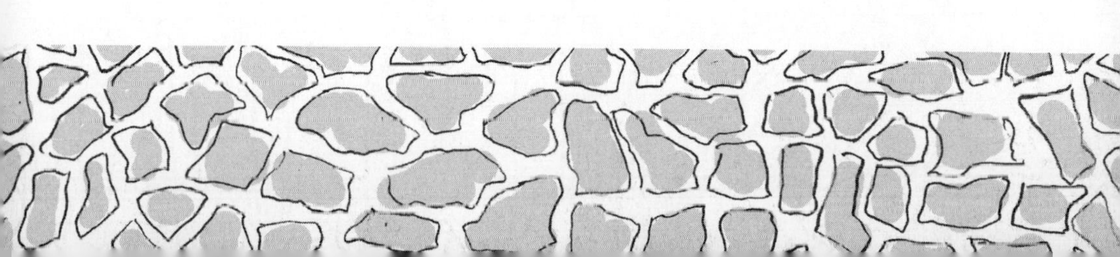

HYPOCRITES

What's with all the hypocrites in the animal world?

A jellyfish is not a fish. And it doesn't have the backbone (which *real* fish have) to admit it.

Who named guinea pigs anyway? They're not pigs, and they don't come from Guinea.

Inchworms may be about an inch long, but they're not worms—they're caterpillars.

The flying fox isn't a fox; it's a bat. And polecats aren't cats; they're European weasels.

Hypocrites are people who pretend to be moral and religious, or to hold beliefs that are popular with a certain group of people, while not actually believing those things in their hearts or demonstrating them in their lives.

If you feel great about yourself and your Christian life just because you go to church, then you might want to think again. Jesus called the Pharisees in his day "blind guides" and "whitewashed tombs," and they were constantly in the Temple.

All the things that you think you're doing for God—even great things, like going to church, reading the Bible, praying, or giving—don't give you points or gold stars. God cares about your heart—*why* you're doing those good things.

Christianity is not a bunch of rules that make you feel great about yourself because you're better at rule-keeping than someone else is. Christianity is a relationship.

Out of all the people Jesus talked to when he walked on the earth, the religious hypocrites received his harshest words. Make sure you never get counted in that group!

> *Jesus replied, "You hypocrites! Isaiah was right when he prophesied about you, for he wrote, 'These people honor me with their lips, but their hearts are far from me. Their worship is a farce, for they teach man-made ideas as commands from God.'"*
>
> **MARK 7:6-7**

Houseflies may pretend to be harmless pests you can shoo away at a picnic. But there's a good reason to shoo them away from your food. A fly lands on your hot dog to taste it . . . with its feet. The fly loves it and so pukes all over it. The fly's saliva turns that piece into hot dog soup so the little pest can mop it up with the spongy pad at the end of its mouth. *Then* you can shoo it away (and maybe toss the rest of that hot dog).

• • •

TODAY: Ask God to point out anything hypocritical in you. If you catch yourself being fake, back up and be honest—with yourself, with other people, and with God.

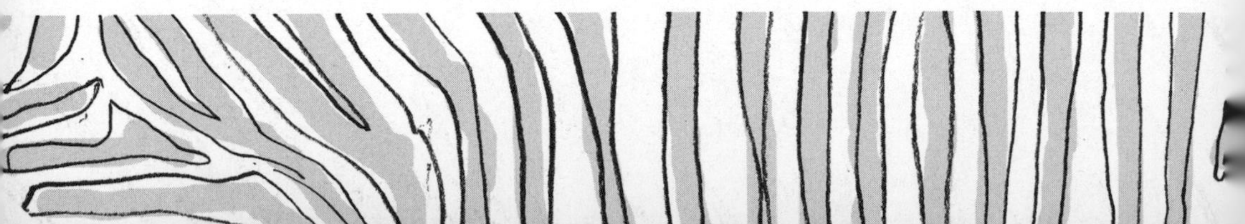

March 24

GOOD TASTE

Monarch butterflies may have good taste, but their sense of taste is in their feet. They land on brightly colored flowers and take a taste. Meanwhile, the pollen sticks to their heads and body parts so the butterflies can fly from flower to flower spreading pollen.

Although monarchs have good taste, they don't taste good. Not to birds and other animals, anyway. In fact, they taste so bitter that other butterflies, such as the viceroy, mimic the monarch's color pattern to make birds think they're yucky tasting too.

Dogs don't have as many taste buds as we do—about 2,000 to our 9,000—but they make up for the difference with more than 200 million scent receptors to our 5 million.

Nearly every day we get a chance to "taste" life, or to try out something new. It might be as simple as sampling tapioca in the cafeteria. Or finding a new way to solve a math problem. Maybe somebody invites you to play ball after school or to join the band. You might get an invitation to a party or a sleepover at a friend's house where you've never gone before.

But the best invitation you'll ever get is the one God offers in Psalm 34. God invites you to taste and see how good the Lord is. You can take God up on the offer by coming to him when you're in trouble. Or you can dip into the Bible or try talking to God on a real and deep level. And you can sample God's goodness by noticing the beauty of the world all around you.

The buffet of God's goodness is sitting in front of you. Taste and see how good it is.

Taste and see that the Lord is good. Oh, the joys of those who take refuge in him!
PSALM 34:8

A marine catfish can taste with any part of its body. It likes to swim upside down while it eats.

• • •

TODAY: "Taste" the goodness of God by spending 30 minutes reading through the Psalms. Be a detective and sense God's presence and grace as you go through your day.

Not all turtles can draw their heads and legs inside their shells. Hawksbill and loggerhead turtles can't, and neither can certain other marine turtles that live in the sea, like the leatherback, which weighs in at half a ton.

• • •

TODAY: Imagine that you're inside a bubble, where nobody can hurt you. Smile at everybody and try to connect with them. But relax. Nothing they say or do can hurt you because you're inside your bubble with God. Cool!

BUILT-IN PROTECTION

Turtles have it made. Whenever danger comes—a growling dog, a lizard, a gull—turtles can withdraw into the safety of their shells.

Turtles spend a lot of time in the water, but tortoises are land dwellers, usually showing up in dry, hot climates. Tortoise shells are so hard that they work great as built-in protection against predators. The tortoise can pull in its legs, arms, tail, and head.

Parrot fish can be gorgeous, in colors ranging from coral to electric blue, reds, yellows, and oranges. Their mortal enemy is the moray eel, which can kill them with no problem, except for one amazing built-in protection. The parrot fish makes a big bubble out of its own mucus and closes the bubble around itself so it can safely sleep away the night. The eel, which hunts by smell, swims right on by.

Wouldn't you love that kind of protection? Well, guess what? You've got it! God's got your back . . . and your front. Maybe you know the 23rd Psalm, which promises us that even in the valley of the shadow of death, we're protected by God's rod and staff.

In the book of Job, Satan complained to God that Job had a God-built hedge around him, protecting him on every side (Job 1:10).

Psalm 121:5 says that God stands over you like a protective shade—a perfect umbrella, guarding you against the scorching sun. And Psalm 125:2 promises that God surrounds you like the mountains surround Jerusalem.

Mountains, hedges, shade, rods, staff . . . you should feel safer already.

You bless the godly, O Lord; you surround them with your shield of love.
PSALM 5:12

DEFENSE! DEFENSE! DEFENSE!

The Texas horned lizard has more than one line of defense:

1. Camouflage: It can lighten or darken its coloring to better blend in with its surroundings.
2. Spines and thorns: Thorns—like bumps on its head and body—help the lizard blend in to the underbrush, while spiny bones can pierce the throat of an attacking snake.
3. Freezing: When scared, the lizard can flatten its body and *freeze*, so it looks dead.
4. Hissing: The sound will scare off some snakes and birds.
5. Squirting blood: The Texas horned lizard is the only lizard that can squirt foul-tasting blood from its eyes.
6. Puffing up: When all else fails, it can puff itself up so it's too big to swallow.

Ultimately, God is our protector, and we don't need to walk around scared of our shadows. But when sin entered the world, so did danger. Yet God hasn't left us defenseless. He has given us:

1. A brain: Use it to stay away from places you know are dangerous.
2. An inner warning system: Listen to that inner voice. It's a defense God's given you.
3. Parents: Pay attention to safety tips, and obey your parents.
4. Bodily defenses: You've got legs that kick, fingers that poke, fingernails that scratch, elbows that hit, teeth that bite, and a voice that can scream and yell. No matter how small you are, you do have defenses. God gave them to you.

Praise the Lord, who did not let their teeth tear us apart! We escaped like a bird from a hunter's trap. The trap is broken, and we are free! Our help is from the Lord, who made heaven and earth.
PSALM 124:6-8

The Texas horned lizard can squirt blood from its eyes (actually, from sinuses behind the eyes) at its attacker. When it squirts out blood, the lizard loses one-fourth to one-third of the total blood in its body. (Don't worry. The blood builds back up, and the lizard lives to fight another day.)

• • •

TODAY: Thank God that you have some natural defenses. Think about how you could be better prepared to use those defenses if you had to.

27 March

What do macaroni, gentoos, chinstraps, and emperors have in common? They're all types of penguins.

• • •

TODAY: Write down a list of qualities you think make a great dad. Then thank God that he is so far better than any "superdad" we might imagine.

HEAVENLY FATHER

Most of the time in the animal kingdom it's the moms who win the "best parent" award. They give birth to, feed, care for, and even give their lives for their babies when necessary.

But a number of animal daddies prove to be pretty heavenly. A father emperor penguin places eggs of his offspring on his feet. For 60 days or longer, Daddy Penguin stands in the cold and icy winds of the Antarctic and protects those eggs. He refuses to eat during the whole time of incubation and may lose as much as 25 pounds waiting for the eggs to hatch. When the eggs finally hatch, Dad feeds the penguin chicks a special liquid from his own throat.

A father phalarope, a long-legged bird from the Alaskan tundra or marshes in the western United States, makes the nest, incubates the eggs, and then cares for the young himself.

The male giant water bug takes charge of over 150 eggs and carries them on his back, washing them and protecting them until they hatch.

The lumpsucker fish uses suckers to hang on to the rocks with his eggs when the tide goes out. He leaves himself open to attack from enemy birds that might otherwise steal the eggs.

We all know that our heavenly Father is the best parent ever. God loves us completely, no matter how we mess up, no matter what we do or don't do. He wants the best for us and leads us in his footsteps. He listens, understands, and has all the right answers.

God the Father loves us so much that he calls us his children and sacrificed his Son, Jesus, so we could spend eternity together.

> *See how very much our Father loves us, for he calls us his children, and that is what we are!*
>
> **1 JOHN 3:1**

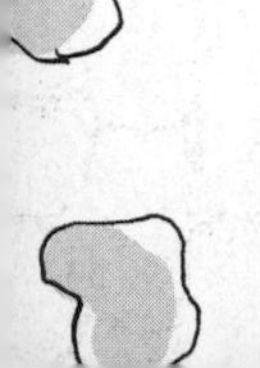
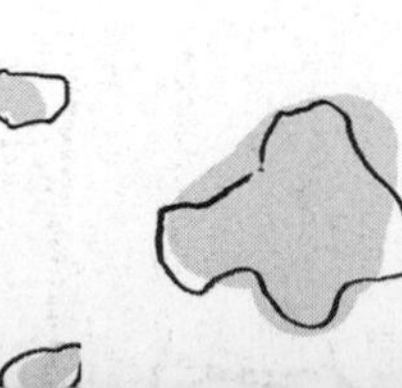
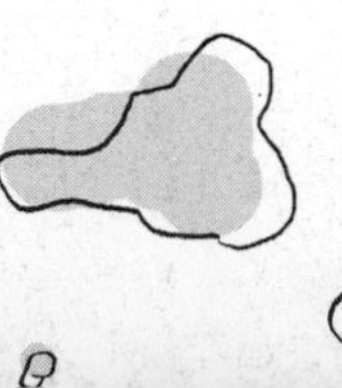

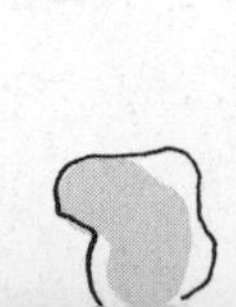

March **28**

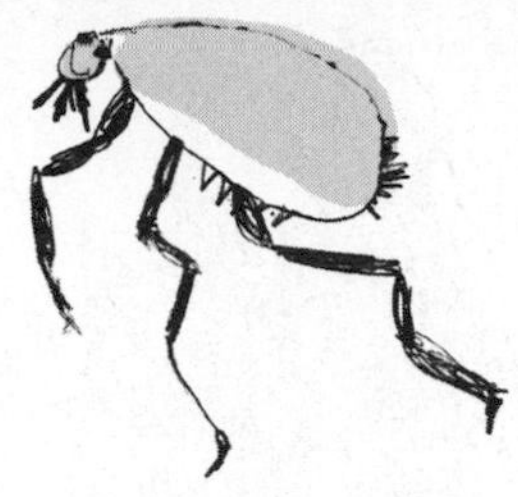

ONE OF A KIND

The hummingbird is unique. It's the only bird that can fly backward. The unique structure of its shoulder joints allows the bird to hover and fly in all directions, even upside down. Its wings move in a figure eight instead of flapping up and down, like all the other birds in town.

Individual gorillas, chimpanzees, and koala bears have unique fingerprints—no two animals are the same. A Holstein cow's spots are its own special trademark.

Other animals can do unique feats we might never give them credit for. A kangaroo rat can go longer without water than a camel can. A bat can eat 1,200 mosquitoes in about an hour. The list of one-of-a-kind traits goes on and on in the animal kingdom . . . and in the human world too.

You're unique. Nobody has your fingerprints or your DNA or your personality. No one will ever have your combination of thoughts and experiences and gifts. God creates us one at a time. Every morning when you get ready for school, what do you think about? Do you try to fix your hair and wear the clothes that will make you fit in and look like everybody else? Or are you free to be your own person? Don't waste your effort trying to be like everyone else.

Did you know that *holy* means "set apart"? If you believe in Christ, God sets you apart so that you can be the person God wants you to be. God fashioned you individually. Dare to be different. There has never been anyone like you.

> *You made all the delicate, inner parts of my body and knit me together in my mother's womb.*
> **PSALM 139:13**

A flea can jump 100 to 200 times its own length. That's like you jumping over a 100-story building. Plus, fleas always land backward.

• • •

TODAY: List 10 ways you're different from your worst enemy and 10 ways you're different from your best friend. Thank God for making you exactly the way you are.

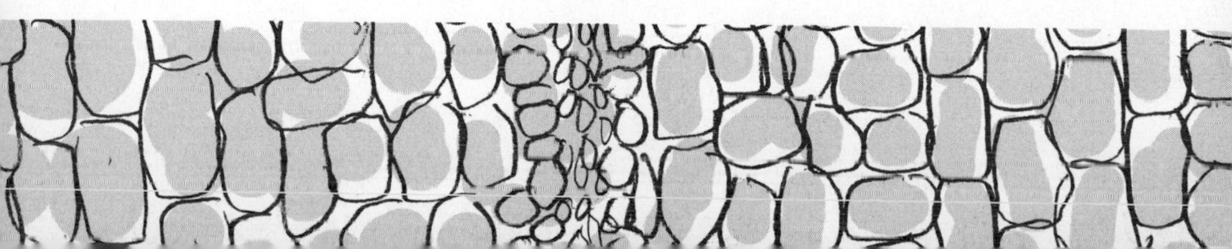

When a dog eats grass, it might be a sign that it has a tummy ache. On the other hand, grass-chewing may have turned into a favorite pastime.

• • •

TODAY: Think about a sin that you've done more than once. Don't forget that sins can be things you *don't* do, as well as things you do. Confess those sins to God, and ask for help so you never return.

NOT AGAIN!

Dogs make fantastic pets. They didn't get the title "man's best friend" for nothing. But you have to admit that dogs can do some pretty gross things. They vomit easily—sometimes from indigestion or stomach irritation, other times from eating too fast or scarfing up something they shouldn't have. But still, you can't blame them for that.

The gross-out comes from what many dogs do after they vomit. They return to their own vomit and chow it down again.

King Solomon, the guy who asked for wisdom and got it some 3,000 years ago, said we do the same thing as gross-out dogs sometimes: "As a dog returns to its vomit, so a fool repeats his foolishness" (Proverbs 26:11).

What do you think? Have you ever done the same dumb thing twice? You leave your books at school on purpose because you really don't want to study for that science test. You tell Mom you don't have homework (not quite a lie, right?). Then you bomb the test the next day and realize that wasn't such a smart trick after all. But a month later, you leave your history notes at school, knowing you'll have a quiz over them the next day. Or worse, do you keep repeating the same sins, even though you know they're wrong?

Because Christ died and paid for our sin, we don't have to return to the same sins over and over. That's part of being free from the power of sin.

So when you sin the first time, be sure to "clean it up" thoroughly by confessing it to Christ. Then ask God to keep you from returning to the same old mess.

> *When people escape from the wickedness of the world by knowing our Lord and Savior Jesus Christ and then get tangled up and enslaved by sin again, they are worse off than before. . . . They prove the truth of this proverb: "A dog returns to its vomit." And another says, "A washed pig returns to the mud."*
>
> **2 PETER 2:20, 22**

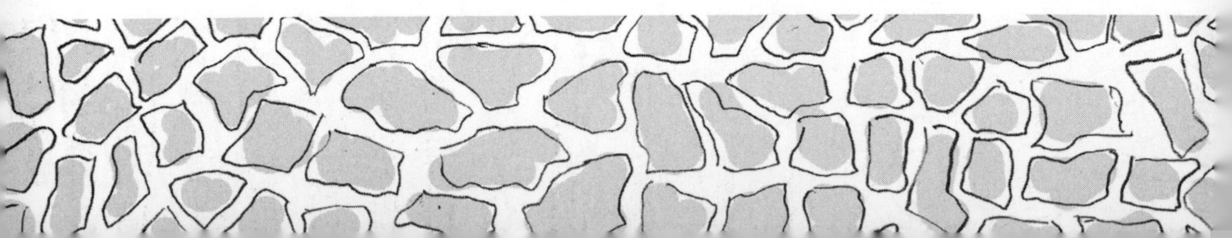

March 30

WHITE ELEPHANTS

White elephants have been a subject of mystery throughout the ages. Truly white elephants are albinos, which means they have a genetic defect and lack color in their skin.

In parts of Asia, white elephants were considered holy. If one appeared anywhere in Thailand, it became the property of the king. But the elephant needed expensive food and care and turned out to be a burden. In fact, if a Thai king wanted to get rid of a political enemy, all he had to do was smile and give him the white elephant. The expense would ruin the new owner.

In America in the late 1800s, P. T. Barnum thought a white elephant might be just what he needed to beef up his circus. He paid $200,000 for a white elephant from Southeast Asia, but his investment didn't pay off: circus-goers weren't flocking to see it. Barnum found himself stuck with an animal that threatened to eat him out of house and circus. The elephant cost much more to keep than it brought in as a circus draw.

Today "white elephant" means something that has value but the owner can't use it. It's more trouble than it's worth.

In a way, we're all white elephants—hard to get, harder to maintain. As much trouble as we give God, you'd think he might want to kick us out of the palace. But God doesn't work that way.

God proved how valuable we are to the Father when he sent his Son to die for us. That's the highest price possible, and God paid it for us! We're called children of God, and God claims us as his inheritance.

If you're ever feeling like you're not worth the skin you live in, think again. You're made by God, bought by God, and considered his treasure.

I pray that your hearts will be flooded with light so that you can understand the confident hope he has given to those he called—his holy people who are his rich and glorious inheritance.
EPHESIANS 1:18

In Thailand, elephants have always been loved and valued. A white elephant is on the flag of the Royal Thai Navy. And one of the highest honors a king can give to a faithful warrior is "the order of the white elephant."

• • •

TODAY: Have a nice long talk with God and thank him for believing you're valuable and worth the trouble. Start seeing yourself through God's eyes.

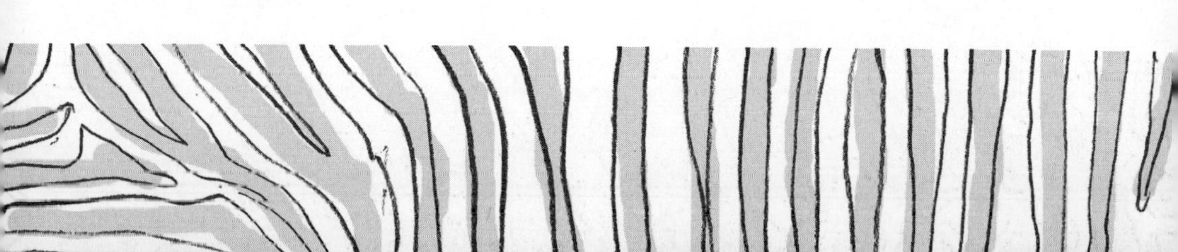

Red foxes aren't always red. About one-fourth of red foxes are called cross foxes because they sport a black stripe down the back, intersected by a black stripe across the shoulders, forming a cross.

• • •

TODAY: Ask your parents or your pastor what you can do to help the homeless in your community.

FOX HOLES

Foxes have holes, or dens.

Most of the year, the male red fox hangs out by himself, prowling and hunting at night and sleeping in the shade during the day. But when winter comes, the fox finds a wife and starts digging a den for his family. The fox den usually has a great location near water, but where drainage is good. Still, the den is nothing to write home to Mom Fox about. Some foxes simply take over groundhog holes and enlarge the opening.

When Jesus lived on earth, he didn't even have that much. Not a den, and not a nest. No place to lie down. He wandered through deserts and cities, sometimes staying with friends. He didn't have a place to call home. And that's something most of us on earth long for.

So Jesus was homeless for most of his stay on earth. That would be terrible, no matter who you are—but he was the Son of God. We can't even imagine the home Jesus left to come to earth. Heaven: A place with no sin. Continual fellowship with the Father. Perfect love and understanding.

Not having a home on earth was a big sacrifice for Christ, and it should give us an inkling of how much he loves us. But even that sacrifice doesn't begin to explain what coming to earth cost. The suffering. The rejection. The separation from the Father. And eventually death.

Yet thanks to Jesus' death and resurrection, we'll be able to share his home someday.

> *Jesus replied, "Foxes have dens to live in, and birds have nests, but the Son of Man has no place even to lay his head."*
>
> **MATTHEW 8:20**

FOOLED YOU!

Lightning bugs are famous for flashing white dots of light across the night skies. But the flashes aren't for our enjoyment. They're codes. Most guy fireflies are showing off for girl fireflies, each species with its own pattern of blinks. If a girl likes what she sees, she flashes back to him after his final flash. They flash back and forth a bit as the guy moves in closer. And if they like each other, they hook up.

Except some of the female fireflies don't play fair. A female of one species observes a male of a different species doing his flash dance. Then she imitates the female firefly of his species, lures the poor guy in, waits until he's close, and captures and devours the unsuspecting firefly.

What can you expect from insects with false names? Fireflies aren't flies. Lightning bugs aren't bugs. They're beetles.

Abe Lincoln said, "You can fool all of the people some of the time, and some of the people all of the time, but you cannot fool all of the people all of the time." True. But even more important, you can never fool God.

No matter how you smooth-talk a teacher, charm your classmates, or fool your parents . . . God is never fooled. He sees everything and knows the truth. God will keep you honest, because when it's just you and God, you can't pretend.

When you came to Christ, you were given his Spirit, the Spirit of truth, to live inside you. That's why you feel a gnawing inside when you're pretending to be someone you're not. When you talk to your heavenly Father, you can let it all out. Isn't it a relief to realize that Someone knows the whole story already?

God knows people's hearts.
ACTS 15:8

A decoy fish has a clever way of fishing for smaller fish in the ocean. It fans out a fin on its back to reveal what looks like the eye and open mouth of a big fish. The frightened little fish sees that open mouth and swims away . . . right into the fish's real mouth.

• • •

TODAY: Go to a place where you can be alone with God. Talk to God about everything fake in your life, and ask him to help you be real—with him and other people.

Bald eagles aren't really bald! They were given the name "bald" when English usage defined bald as white.

• • •

TODAY: Improve your eyesight today and be on the lookout for things you've never really noticed before. Make a list of 10 of these "wonders."

THE EYES HAVE IT

An ostrich's eye is bigger than its brain. When it comes to land animals, the ostrich has the biggest eyes, followed by the horse. Elephants and humans fall far behind.

But overall the squid wins. Colossal squids have the largest eyes of any living animal—one of their eyes is bigger than your head!

The crayfish's eyes are on movable stalks that can swivel around. Most spiders have eight eyes. Jumping spiders can see 360 degrees around them.

Hawks and bald eagles probably have the best vision in the world. A hawk can see a mouse from a mile up. The tufts of hair around their eyes serve as sunglasses to make hunting in the daytime easier.

Animals have different techniques for seeing. Birds have muscles in their eyes that can change the thickness of the lens and the shape of the cornea. Whales have a kind of built-in hydraulics system to move their lenses closer and farther away from the retina so they can see in and out of the water.

How's your vision? (And we're not talking about whether you need glasses.) Are you seeing clearly? Did you notice that first bud on the tree outside your bedroom window? Have you seen the way your sister is changing? Have you noticed the colors in the sky, the shape of the clouds, the way the moon changes night to night?

Ask God to open your eyes to everyday wonders of his wonder-full creation. There's a lot more to seeing than meets the eye.

Look and see, you blind!
ISAIAH 42:18

BIG-HEARTED

Animal hearts come in all sizes. The heart of a blue whale weighs around 2,000 pounds and is about the size of a car. Human hearts weigh 7 to 15 ounces, while a cow's heart weighs in at a good five pounds.

Python hearts aren't all that big. But a python's heart grows every mealtime.

A butterfly's heart is long and tubular, but no animal's heart, including our own, is truly, well, heart shaped.

To God, it's not the size of our hearts that counts but what fills the heart. One way people explain becoming a Christian is by saying that we "invited Jesus into our hearts." We turn our hearts—the control center for the mind, emotions, will, and spirit—over to Christ. And Christ fills us—our hearts—with his Holy Spirit.

Then what? What else fills the heart? Is there room in there to care about people who don't know Christ? How about room for a classmate who doesn't seem to have a single friend? Or room for a sibling who's going through a tough time? Are you willing to ask God to break your heart with the things that break his?

On the road to Emmaus, Jesus met up with two disciples who didn't recognize him until he'd gone. Then they said: "Didn't our hearts burn within us as he talked with us on the road and explained the Scriptures to us?" (Luke 24:32).

Maybe it's time to open your heart wider, to care deeply about the things God cares about, and to get a good case of "heartburn."

> *That is why the Lord says, "Turn to me now, while there is time. Give me your hearts. Come with fasting, weeping, and mourning."*
> **JOEL 2:12**

People always said that the famous racehorse Secretariat had a big heart. But it wasn't until the horse's autopsy that the owners had any idea how right they were. A normal Thoroughbred's heart weighs around nine pounds. The vet estimated that Secretariat's heart weighed about 22 pounds.

• • •

TODAY: Come up with three things in your life, or three people, you think might be on God's heart. Talk to God about them. Be open to spiritual heartburn.

Mallard mothers have special calls that they give while incubating their eggs. As soon as the eggs hatch, Mother just has to give out her special call, and her chicks rush to her for protection.

• • •

TODAY: Don't hold back from God. Stay in touch with him all day. Tell him about your deepest sadness. Give him the cries you scream out loud and the ones you swallow.

CRY, BABY

Very early on, baby birds discover the power of an offspring's cry over its mother. In fact, in some species, chicks learn to cry out while they're still inside the egg.

Quail chicks communicate with their mother long before they're hatched. From inside their eggs, they even cry to each other and coordinate hatching so they'll all come out about the same time.

A pelican chick cries to let its mother know it's too cold or too hot inside the egg.

Chicks inside their eggs know enough to listen to their parents' voices too. Then when they finally hatch and come out into the world, they can recognize Mom or Dad from the first minute, just by hearing that sound.

Alligators lay their eggs along the banks of rivers in mounds of decaying vegetation. Although Mom Alligator may swim around while her babies hatch, when she hears their cries, she comes running over and tears open the nest to set her babies free from the garbage heap.

We're God's children, and it's okay for us to cry out to him.

If you have hurts you don't talk about with anyone else, cry out to God. If somebody razzes you at school and you laugh it off but feel like crying, cry to God. And the cool thing is that God's waiting for your cry. He's always right there, ready to help you break out or to pull you out of the garbage heap.

> *In my distress I cried out to the* LORD*; yes, I cried to my God for help. He heard me from his sanctuary; my cry reached his ears.*
>
> **2 SAMUEL 22:7**

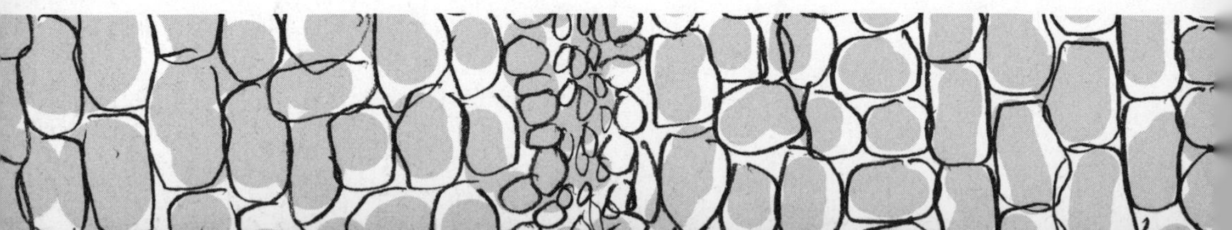

EARS TO HEAR

There are as many different kinds of ears as there are animals. Look at dogs—from the tiny, pointy ears of a terrier to the stand-up ears of a German shepherd to the short "rose" ears of a bulldog to the long, floppy ears of hound dogs. Dogs hear much better than we do, detecting high whistles humans can't pick up.

The fanlike ears of elephants help them communicate with each other in sounds that are too low for humans to hear. Bats can also hear sounds we'll never be able to hear, thanks to their big ears. The bat-eared fox has such great hearing that it finds insects by hearing them instead of seeing them.

Hedgehogs have rotten eyesight but terrific hearing, which lets them detect crawling insects underground.

Most human ears look more or less the same, but our hearing isn't necessarily the same. Over and over, Jesus told his disciples and the crowds, "Anyone with ears to hear should listen and understand" (Mark 4:9, 23).

What could Jesus have meant by "ears to hear"? Probably everyone around him had ears. God invented ears. Jesus knew better than anyone else that ears were made to hear. So what was he saying?

Have you ever sat through an entire sermon at church, then couldn't remember what it was about? Ever read a chapter in a devotional (not this one!) and then forgotten everything you'd read?

On the other hand, what if you've been waiting for months for the next book in a series to come out and you finally sit down to read it? Or your favorite TV show is finally back on? Or you know you have to listen closely to every word in math class because the big test is tomorrow? You'll have "ears to hear."

We listen to things we value. What God says can change our lives. We should always have ears to hear him.

A time is coming when people will no longer listen to sound and wholesome teaching. They will follow their own desires and will look for teachers who will tell them whatever their itching ears want to hear.
2 TIMOTHY 4:3

The long-eared jerboa, a nocturnal rodent that lives in dry parts of Africa and Asia, is sometimes called "the Mickey Mouse of the desert" because of its enormous ears.

• • •

TODAY: Name three things you paid close attention to yesterday. Now choose at least one thing you'll tune in to today. Determine to have "ears to hear" when you read your Bible, when you pray, or when a friend is asking for help.

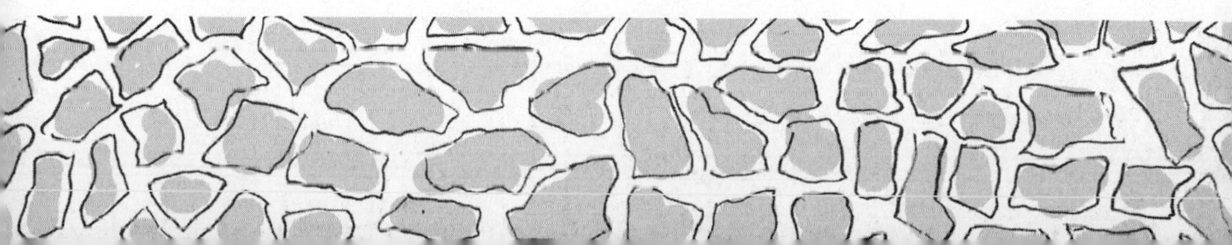

The most famous water-animal mystery is the Loch Ness Monster. It's usually described as having a horselike head, a long neck, and a serious humpback.

• • •

TODAY: Talk to God about things you just don't understand, like why you look the way you do, why you get treated the way you do, or why you suffer in ways you think are unfair. Thank him that even though you don't get it, he understands.

ASKED AND ANSWERED

As much as we keep learning about the animal world, there's still so much we don't know.

Like what's the deal with the Loch Ness Monster, or "Nessie," the large sea creature that supposedly lives in a lake in Scotland?

Or the dreaded chupacabras that are rumored to attack livestock in rural villages of Latin America?

Why have there been so many reports of that hairy ape-man, known as the yeti, in the Himalayan mountains? Or alleged sightings of other hairy ape-men—Bigfoot or Sasquatch—in wooded areas of North America?

Or how about the reported sightings of Mothman, serpent monsters, giant lizards, giant frogs, and dinosaurs?

Not all unanswered questions are about monsters. Why do puppies wag their tails when they're happy to see you instead of, say, sticking out their tongues? Why does a horse that was glad to be ridden last week want to buck you off this week? Why does your cat seem to favor the only friend you have who's allergic to cats?

There are a lot of questions we might never get answered (like where God got the stuff to make elephant skin and butterfly wings and peacock colors). But God knows. And it's good for us to realize we don't know everything.

God gave Job a good talking-to for blaming God just because Job didn't understand what was happening to him. God pointed out that there are a lot of things we don't know.

Nobody has all the answers except God. When you don't understand why you're going through something—a family breakup, a difficult loss, or an unfairness of some kind—remember that God knows. And nobody has all the answers except God.

> *The Lord said to Job, "Do you still want to argue with the Almighty? You are God's critic, but do you have the answers?"*
>
> JOB 40:1-2

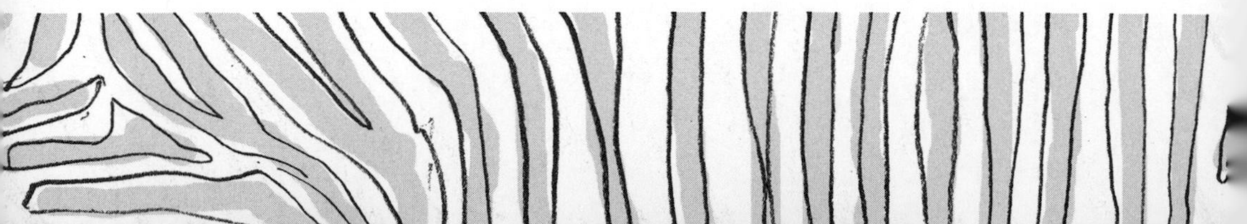

CUCKOO FAMILIES

Animal families vary as much—or more—than human families. Geese generally mate for life and stick around to act as a two-parent family. But that's not the case for all animals.

Take the cuckoo bird, for instance. A cuckoo mom might wait until another bird leaves her nest for food. Then she flies in and leaves her egg in that stranger's nest. The cuckoo egg will be the biggest in the nest and the first to hatch. But the mother bird will raise the cuckoo as her own. She'll work as hard as she can to get food for her adopted baby.

Cuckoo bees lay their eggs in the nests of other bees, and those moms treat the cuckoo bee eggs as their own in an adoptive family.

Tiny wasps called chalcids lay eggs in the eggs of other insects. Their young hatch first, and sometimes they feed on the host eggs. But a new family forms.

God intended for families to consist of a mom, a dad, and children. But things don't always work out that way on earth, and we often end up with a variety of family groupings. Maybe you resent the fact that you're part of a single-parent home or that your stepmother isn't your real mother or that you're adopted. But God is in charge. And God knows what family is the best place for you.

When we belong to Christ, we all join a wonderful family—the family of God. God says he's our Father and we're his kids. So no matter how tough things get in your earthly family, you can be grateful that you're part of the family of God.

God places the lonely in families.
PSALM 68:6

Newborn dolphins travel with their mothers in such tight formation that they look like one huge animal to predators. Close relatives sometimes relieve Mom from her child-care chores and let the kids play in "nurseries." Young dolphins are weaned at 18 months, but they hang around home for up to 6 years before setting out on their own.

• • •

TODAY: Thank God that he handpicked your family for you. Then talk to all the people in your family and tell them you're glad God gave them to you.

Animals give off signals that they want to play. The invitation comes through facial expressions or body positions. Monkeys sometimes bend over in football-hike formation and peek between their legs at a playmate.

• • •

TODAY: Ask God to join you while you have some fun on your own. Try to track a creeping insect or learn to identify the birds you hear. Splash in a puddle. Go on a bike ride.

PLAYTIME!

Most young mammals in the wild do three things: eat, sleep, and play. Playing is as important to the growth of a bear cub or a tiger cub as eating and sleeping. When cubs play together, they learn how to interact with each other and the world. Cubs invent games, like follow the leader, king of the castle, and races. Playing helps their muscles develop. Plus, playing is fun!

Other animals play in their own ways. Otters slide on muddy riverbanks or icy slopes for no apparent reason . . . except for fun. Penguins get a kick out of body sledding on the ice. Cheetahs play with their food. Dolphins balance things on their noses, blow bubbles, and play catch-and-release, often catching a fish, releasing it, then catching it again before finally eating it.

Domestic animals play too. Watch colts and lambs kick up their heels in the pasture. Dangle a string in front of your cat. Or play fetch with your dog until you can't take it anymore. Sometimes animals play for the sheer joy of playing.

Do you? Can you play with your friends just to have fun, or do you always have to win? Does every ball game and every race turn into a heated competition, with the winner being the only one who enjoys it in the end? Do you like seeing how fast your buddy is, or does it make you mad that you're not that fast? Play is supposed to be fun.

You should even be able to play by yourself. Go on a long walk or a fast run. Shoot hoops, play the guitar, or read a book. You don't always have to be entertained by TV, music, the Internet, or video games.

Take your cue from the animals. Learn to play.

God . . . richly provides us with everything for our enjoyment.

1 TIMOTHY 6:17, NIV

SETTLING INTO A PECKING ORDER

Have you ever watched horses grazing in a pasture or racing to the barn for feed?

It's not hard to pick out which horse is the natural leader of the herd. She (it's usually a mare) gets to eat first. And after the dominant mare has claimed her spot, the others go to their feed bins in an order set by the horses themselves, from first to last. That's called the "pecking order."

It's built into a horse to find its place in the herd. Instinctively, horses know they need to function well as a group and not constantly be fighting for superiority. Once the order is settled, life becomes peaceful. The dominant mare takes over and offers security and leadership to the other horses.

The rest of the herd respectfully submits to the leader. And in return they get to relax in the field and graze all day, knowing that the dominant mare is looking out for them. They don't have to be afraid of predators, because the leader has them covered.

There's a peace for us, too, when we settle into our own "pecking order." We can trust that Christ, our leader, is looking out for us.

Another "herd" we belong to is the local body of Christ—a church. There's a sense of peace in belonging to a good church, where you know you fit in as part of the herd and where Christ is the leader.

> *God has put all things under the authority of Christ and has made him head over all things for the benefit of the church.*
> **EPHESIANS 1:22**

The term *pecking order* came about in the early 1900s when scientists studied birds and chickens. They observed that chickens organize themselves from "top chicken" to "bottom chicken." Chicken bosses keep the others in line by pecking.

• • •

TODAY: Talk to God about your "herd." If you're not part of a good church, make plans to find one and become involved. Take a good look at the groups you hang out with and decide whether Christ is the dominant influence in the company you keep.

Some ribbon worms will eat themselves if they can't find any food. Yum . . .

• • •

TODAY: Catch yourself before you're drawn into sniping, bickering, griping, cutting people down, or backbiting. Don't do it. And if you slip up, tell God—and the other person—that you're sorry. One person can change a whole group.

WHAT'S EATING YOU?

Sometimes two-headed snakes are born and survive. But they seldom live happily ever after. The two heads fight over food, even though everything either head eats goes to the same stomach. Even worse, if one head smells prey on the other, it may actually try to swallow its Siamese twin.

Most animals won't eat members of their own species, but count on the rat to be an exception. Rats will eat just about anything, including dead rats or fellow rats that aren't dead yet.

If you were an invisible visitor at your house, what impression would you get about your household? Is everybody nice to everybody else? Or is there constant bickering, with kids yelling familiar phrases like, "He started it!" "She's hogging the bathroom!" "You always go first!"

Are mealtimes peaceful, or is everybody complaining and squabbling, eager to get out of there? Even if nobody shouts, do you fight on the inside, letting family feuds grow and fester?

Is it a dog-eat-dog world at school, too? Do you have to be quick-tongued in your group just to keep up with the sniping? Are there cliques and factions, even among your friends, with gossip and name-calling?

Be careful. God hears every word and knows every thought. Talking down to people or ripping them apart behind their backs doesn't just hurt them. It hurts you, too. Then you're not much better off than . . . a two-headed snake.

> *Some people make cutting remarks, but the words of the wise bring healing.*
> **PROVERBS 12:18**

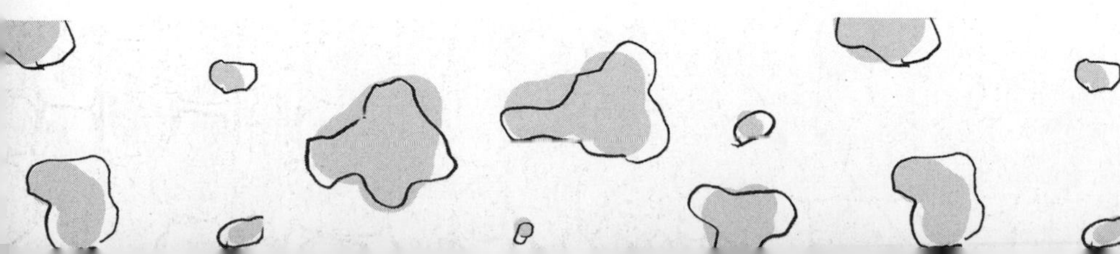

GUY-GIRL STUFF

If you could hang out in the hills with a group of feral (semi-wild) mustang mares, you might be surprised how much you have in common with them. The herd operates peacefully, with mares looking out for one another. A couple of females guard the rest from predators. Other mares without colts might step in as nannies.

Until a stallion comes along.

When a male presents himself, the mares just might turn on each other. They bite, kick, and threaten the other mares just to be with the stallion.

Horses aren't the only boy-crazy animals. Spotted hyenas take guy-girl stuff to a whole new level. When those females fight over a male, it's not a pretty sight.

Humans can pull the same nastiness once boy-girl stuff enters the picture. You sit at your table in the cafeteria and conversation flows easily. But when a cute guy joins you, there may be some competition for attention. And if a girl gets a chance to hang with that guy, sometimes it's bye-bye to her other friends.

Guys go through the same thing. Even if you don't let on, you might resent the guy who gets the girl you've had a thing for. Or you may end up doing something crazy just to impress her.

Life doesn't have to get off track when guy-girl stuff happens. If you keep being yourself in every situation, whether a person of the opposite sex is around or not, you'll have a better chance of overcoming awkwardness—and keeping your friends.

And don't forget that God created us male and female on purpose. We can learn a lot from the opposite sex when we're not trying so hard to be something we're not. They may even become great friends.

Among the Lord's people, women are not independent of men, and men are not independent of women.
1 CORINTHIANS 11:11

Even though most male birds have brighter colors than female birds, male and female lovebirds look alike.

• • •

TODAY: Pray about your feelings toward the opposite sex. Be honest with God if you feel strongly about one particular person at school. Ask God to give you solid friendships with guys and girls.

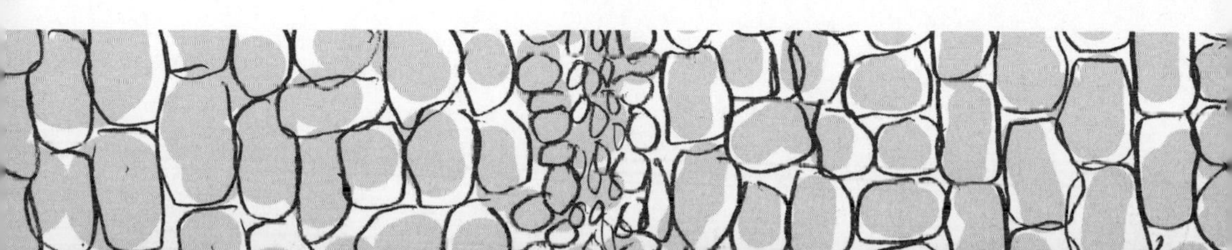

BAD HABITS

Dogs never mean anything by it, but even the sweetest puppy can develop bad habits that will plague the household unless something is done.

Puppies love to chew anything—socks, shoes, furniture, hands, ankles, couch cushions. It may seem harmless at first, but eventually nobody will find the habit cute.

Barking is natural. A dog will bark for a warning, out of fear, or for the sheer fun of hearing its own bark. But barking will become a problem when your parents are trying to sleep through the hound dog serenade.

Your dog won't know what's off limits unless you teach it. Puppy will think this is still playtime if you don't make it clear where the line is. And if you let your dog get away with the bad behavior, you'll have a bad habit on your hands.

You have bad habits too. We all do. Maybe you use bad language. You started letting yourself swear with your buddies, but now you can't stop, even at home. Or maybe you overeat. You know it's not healthy and you don't like the way you look, but you can't seem to stop.

True, bad habits are hard to break. But the good news is, you're not in it alone. You can break the habit with God's help. God's power raised Jesus from the dead and created the universe. Think that much power ought to do it? So be encouraged—you really do have a way out. It may take you 100 times of failing, confessing, then asking God for help again. But you can do it because he can do it.

And when you do, God will use you in other people's lives. They'll see for themselves that God's power is working in you.

> *God is working in you, giving you the desire and the power to do what pleases him.*
> **PHILIPPIANS 2:13**

Think you've got a bad habit of overeating? Check out the polyphemus moth, a member of the giant silkworm moth family, which some claim is the biggest overeater in the animal kingdom. In the first 56 days of its life while still a caterpillar, this moth eats about 86,000 times its own body weight.

• • •

TODAY: Talk to God about one or two bad habits you want to ditch. Ask for God's power (all the power in the universe!) to help you break the cycle and get rid of those habits.

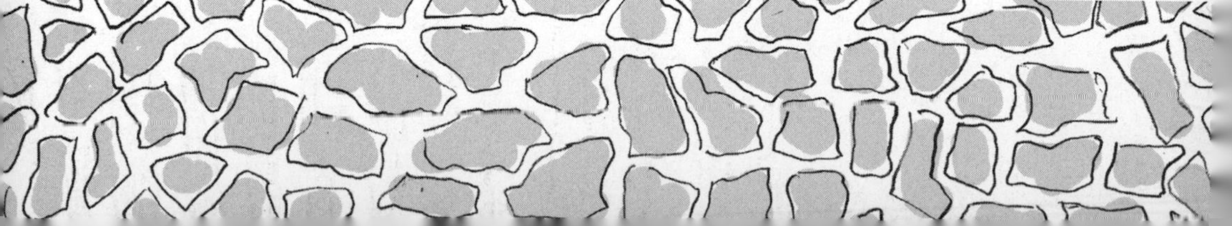

CARRY ME

You've probably seen pictures of a baby kangaroo, called a joey, riding comfortably inside its mother's pouch, under her chin. Other marsupials, like wombats and bandicoots, have pouches that face backward. That way, when they dig into a burrow, the pouch and baby won't get filled with dirt.

Baby kangaroos start out tiny and not fully developed, weighing less than an ounce. But they can climb. A baby can climb all the way inside the pouch to nurse and stay warm and safe. For about seven to ten months, the joey is carried in that pouch by Mom.

Even after the joey jumps out to freedom, it may jump back in when it's sleepy or frightened. The joey dives in headfirst, with its back legs and tail sticking out. Then it twists until it flips over and can safely peek out from the pouch.

Koala babies are carried by their mothers too. When the koala is about six to eight months old and is too big for the pouch, it just climbs aboard Mom's back and gets carried until its about a year old.

Joeys in the pouch seem to have it made. They can experience life without being seriously threatened by danger as long as they take refuge in that pouch.

We have the same kind of protection. The Psalms celebrate the fact that the God of the universe cares deeply about us as individuals. We're called God's children. He carries us through our tough times on earth.

So whenever you're frightened or just looking for a good night's sleep, pop back into the pouch. Trust that God has you surrounded. He'll look out for you. Let him.

> *Praise the Lord; praise God our savior! For each day he carries us in his arms.*
> **PSALM 68:19**

Koala bears aren't bears. They're relatives of kangaroos, wallaroos, wombats, wallabies, bandicoots, and opossums—but not bears.

• • •

TODAY: Every time something upsets you today, imagine that you're climbing back into God's "pouch" for safety.

Female elephants teach the ways of survival and community to the younger females in the herd. One day one of the younger females will take over the herd and start teaching and passing on what she has learned.

• • •

TODAY: By asking good questions, and by being sincerely interested in the answers, get some stories out of two members of your family. For example, call your grandparents and ask about school when they were your age. Or ask how they met.

PASS IT ON

Animals pass certain physical and personality traits to their offspring. That's why people started breeding lines for racehorses. If a horse's lineage goes back to Man o' War, a famous racehorse, that newborn foal will be sold for a big price—more than, say, the great-great-great-great-grandson of the Old Gray Mare who ain't what she used to be.

When you buy a puppy, it's a good idea to spend time with the puppy's parents, if possible. If the adult dogs don't like children, the puppy may have inherited that dislike of kids. On the other hand, if the parents are friendly and good natured, their pups may be friendly pets for you.

Bald eagles have an interesting inheritance that they pass along to their eaglets, which pass it on to the next generation, which . . . (you get the picture). Eagles that mate for life usually pass along their nests to their offspring. And we're talking *big* nests. An eagle's nest might measure 10 feet across and 12 feet deep, and weigh more than a ton.

What are you hoping your grandparents will leave you as an inheritance? A big house? An awesome car? An heirloom that's been in the family for generations? The best inheritance is a strong faith. And one of the best ways for you to get that inheritance is through stories. Get your great-grandparents talking about life when they were your age. Ask your mom what the hardest thing was for her when she was growing up. Ask your granddad to explain how he came to know Christ.

Then pass it on!

I will speak to you in a parable. I will teach you hidden lessons from our past—stories we have heard and known, stories our ancestors handed down to us. We will not hide these truths from our children; we will tell the next generation about the glorious deeds of the Lord, about his power and his mighty wonders.

PSALM 78:2-4

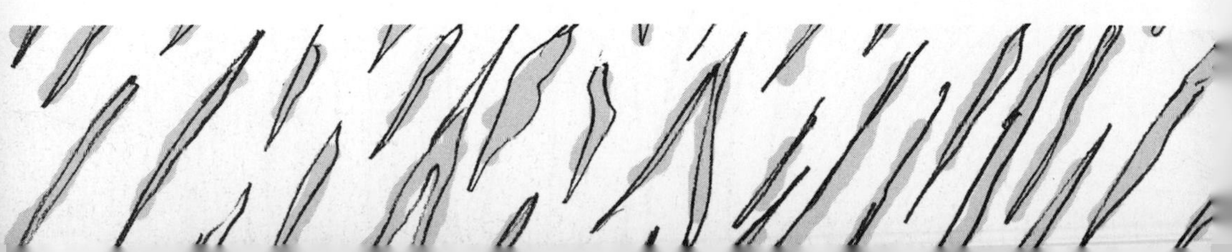

ON GUARD!

There are some great reasons lions are called kings of the jungle. A lion's roar is so loud it can be heard up to five miles away.

Lions prowl. They skulk. They hunt (the females more than the males). They come equipped with long, sharp canine teeth that make them look like something to beware of. Lions have powerful claws, like the house cat, only deadlier—the better to claw you with, my dear . . . and to rip their prey to shreds.

When the prey least expects it, a lion dashes up from behind and grabs the animal or knocks it over. The poor prey never sees it coming.

In his first letter to churches, Peter warned new believers that they should be on guard. Everywhere they went, evil would be waiting, just as a lion prowls around waiting to pounce. But the warning followed Peter's promise that God would be with them and that they should give him all their worries.

It's not easy to be on guard but to stay free of worry. Yet both commands are important and true. We shouldn't walk around peeking behind every bush and being scared of our shadows. God is on our side—bigger than a lion, stronger than Satan.

But in an instant, evil could pounce. Prisons are filled with people who lost everything in one minute of stupidity. Someone who would never smoke a joint or shoplift gives it a try, on the spur of the moment. And *pounce*!

Trouble is waiting, lurking. It only takes one second to ruin a life. Be on guard.

> *Stay alert! Watch out for your great enemy, the devil. He prowls around like a roaring lion, looking for someone to devour.*
>
> **1 PETER 5:8**

Lions sleep or rest most of their lives away—up to 20 hours per day. But watch out for the other four hours. . . .

• • •

TODAY: Talk to God about past mistakes you've made on an instant's notice, when sin took you by surprise. Ask God to help you be on the lookout from now on.

Fairy terns don't build nests. They lay a single egg on the forked branch of a tree, and the female fairy tern can never leave her egg.

• • •

TODAY: After you've finished your homework or your chores, take another look. Can you put in a little more effort to make your work more excellent?

GREAT WORK!

God has filled the world with animals that are master builders, especially among birds. The masked weaver bird of East Africa knots grasses together so it can hang its nest from a tree limb. With the strips of grass, the male bird makes a sling at an exact 90-degree angle. No more, no less. If he goofs up, he'll pull the whole thing apart and start over again. Meanwhile, the female masked weaver bird waits for her perfect nest.

The meadowlark lines its nest with hair and grass, builds a canopy, and makes little pathways leading through the grass to the nest.

The bowerbird has a flair for home decorating. The male bowerbird gathers twigs for the nest and adds feathers, berries, string, and anything else he can find—all to attract chicks (or at least one lovely female bowerbird).

Other birds, like swifts and swallows, build with spit and mud, showing the skill of a potter. Others sew nests out of leaves.

Wouldn't you think it would be all right to simply make a nest? To just throw together some sticks and get on with it? But God has built a sense of style and excellence into his creation. Why? Because God's creation reflects the Creator.

The work you do reflects on you. But much more important, your work reflects on God. It might seem pretty cliché to hear a teacher tell you to "do your best," but it's still good advice. Getting a C on an English report doesn't cut it if you're capable of getting an A with a little more work. Don't just get by. God wants us to challenge ourselves to excellence, to reflect his creativity.

We request and exhort you in the Lord Jesus, that as you received from us instruction as to how you ought to walk and please God (just as you actually do walk), that you excel still more.

1 THESSALONIANS 4:1, NASB

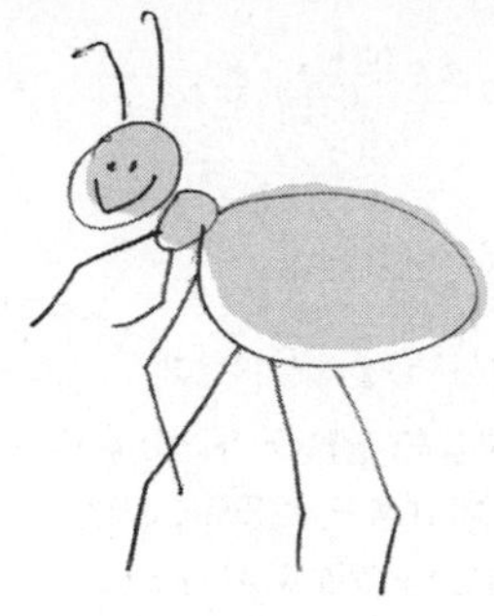

TEAMWORK

Ants and bees understand teamwork. Each member works hard at a certain job for the good of the whole group. Army ants of South America have over 700,000 members in their colony, yet they manage to move as if they're one giant ant.

Here are some other jobs in the division of labor among ants:

Leaf-cutter ants harvest leaves to take back to the ant colony. They grow a special fungus in the nest by chewing leaves into a pulp.

Farmer ants care for aphids that give them "ant milk."

Horticulture ants cultivate underground gardens for ant food.

Army and security ants patrol and keep others safe.

Engineering ants can dig a tunnel from opposite ends and meet up exactly in the middle.

Baker ants form chewed-up grain into patties and bake them in the sun.

Nannies, teachers, and babysitters all have roles to play in the ant colony. They virtually raise the young ants.

How do you function on a team? Are you content with the role assigned to you, even if it's not the starring role? If you're not first-string quarterback, can you be happy as second-string defense? If you don't get the best part in a school program, will you still be rooting for your class to succeed?

Do other kids always want you involved in their group projects because you're known as a team player? Or do you fight for the best, or easiest, part of the assignment? In youth group, are you eager to help the cause, no matter what job you get?

"Teamwork! Teamwork! Teamwork!" We shout it at games and demand it from our sports teams.

Maybe we should demand it of ourselves, too.

I appeal to you, dear brothers and sisters, by the authority of our Lord Jesus Christ, to live in harmony with each other. Let there be no divisions in the church. Rather, be of one mind, united in thought and purpose.

1 CORINTHIANS 1:10

Ants divide their jobs into farming, gardening, tending the young, and on and on. But it's not unusual for an ant to make a career move and change jobs.

• • •

TODAY: Talk to God about the group projects you've worked on in the past, or about any teams you're on now. Ask God to make you a great team player.

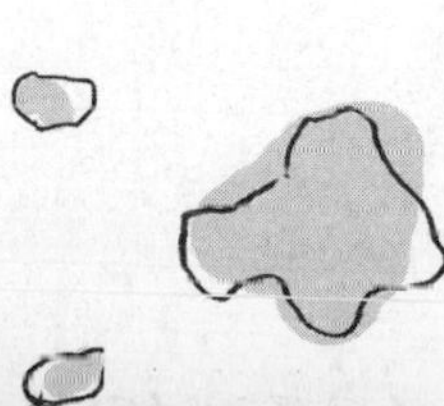
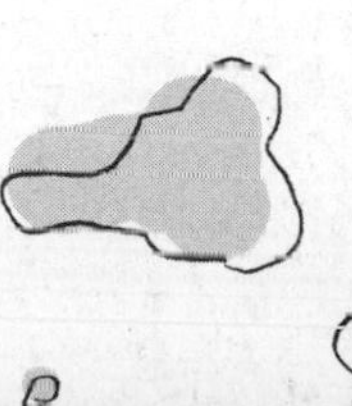
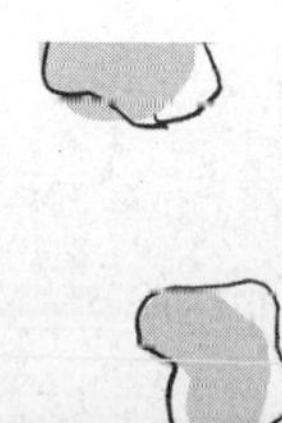

Aardvarks average 6 feet long and 100 pounds, and they still get scared. When they do, they burrow into the ground at warp speed. *Aardvark* is Afrikaans for "earth pig" (but don't go calling people aardvarks).

• • •

TODAY: Think about the last time you were afraid. What did you do? Did you share the fear with anyone? Talk to God about that fear, and about any others looming over you. Thank God that he's on your side.

NEVER FEAR

Animals get frightened just like you do, and they can do the craziest things when they're scared (also like you). You've probably "played possum" when you wanted people to think you were sleeping. But possum aren't playing. They're actually so scared that they pass out.

The weevil of East Africa drops to the ground when it's frightened and curls up its legs to look good and dead.

Ladybugs know how to "bleed," but not when they're hurt—when they're scared. Blister beetles shoot off a chemical that makes skin blister.

A number of creatures opt for a stinky solution to their fears:

The desert skunk beetle shoots a stinky spray from its abdomen.

Squash bugs spray when they get scared. And they're not nicknamed stinkbugs without good cause.

The devil's coach horse beetle lifts its tail to look like a stinging scorpion. It can't sting, but phew! The stink will send predators running.

What do you do when you're scared? Do you go to God? Do you talk to someone you trust? Or do you hide out or act tough?

Sometimes we create our own fears, imagining and expecting the worst. Or we don't study, then wonder why we get so worked up over a test. David trusted God to help him defeat the giant Goliath. But he'd practiced with his slingshot, and he'd had practice trusting God, who had already helped David defend his father's sheep from wild animals (1 Samuel 17:32-37).

Do all you can to reduce your fears (study, do your homework, stay out of dangerous situations, follow the rules and guidelines you've been given). And when you're afraid, remember that you have the God of all creation on your side.

You came when I called; you told me, "Do not fear."
LAMENTATIONS 3:57

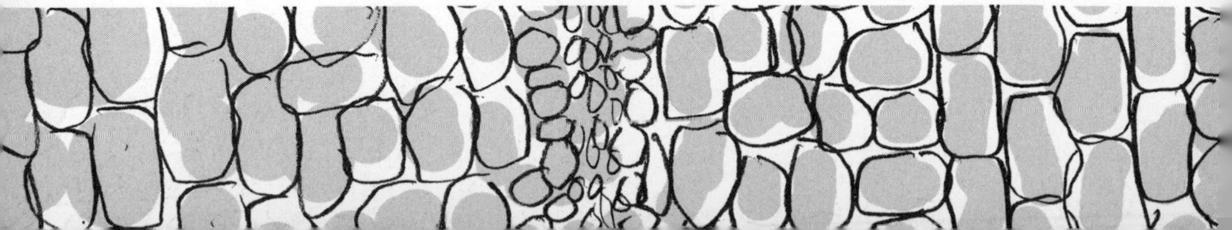

BE STRONG

Some people think the lion must be the strongest animal. Others believe it's the draft horse or an ox or maybe an elephant. But in proportion to its size, the ant beats them. It can carry 50 times its own weight. That's like you lifting five horses.

Mites, the cousins of ticks, are strong when they cling onto a rough surface. They can hold their own against a force pulling at them at 1,200 times their own weight. But they don't really lift, so they're out of the "strong man" contest.

So the winner is . . . the rhinoceros beetle. It has two forked horns that act like pincers in a fight. This little guy can lift up another beetle 850 times its weight and then slam it to the ground.

How strong are you—not physically, but emotionally and spiritually? Can the slightest injustice (real or imagined) make you feel like you can't go on? When your friends use language you'd never use in front of your mom, do you join them, or are you strong enough not to? When it would be so easy to cheat and copy your buddy's quiz answers, are you strong enough to look the other way?

Paul wrote to the Ephesians, who were facing persecution from all sides. He told them to put on the armor of God—to read the Bible and pray, to carry the Good News with them wherever they went, to live righteous lives. And finally, when he encouraged them to be strong, he told them how. They were to be tough in the strength of God's might, not in their own.

God is a bottomless ocean of strength, a never-ending source of the power that's always available to us through his Spirit.

Be strong in the Lord and in his mighty power.
EPHESIANS 6:10

Not counting bugs and beetles, the strongest land mammals are probably the elephant, the hippo, and the rhinoceros. A black rhino is much more likely to charge and attack than the peaceful white rhino.

• • •

TODAY: Talk to God about something in your life that's going to require extra strength—a change, a move, righting some wrong, admitting a lie, resisting temptation, talking to someone about Christ. Ask God for his strength to do it.

Animals don't just grow at different rates—they move at different speeds. Peregrine falcons dive at speeds up to 200 miles per hour. The cheetah can run at 70 miles per hour, the sailfish can swim at 68 miles per hour, and the ostrich can get up to 40 miles per hour.

• • •

TODAY: Talk to God about what's holding you back from living the kind of spiritual life he wants you to live. Ask God to help you mature in your prayers, Bible study, and interactions with people.

SLOW GROWING

Some animals develop faster than others. Elephant babies grow slowly, nursing for up to five years and not reaching maturity until they're in their teens.

The Hercules beetle spends three whole years as a tiny grub before it matures. Saturniid moths, like the emperor moth, are extremely slow-growing creatures. They spend three months as caterpillars. Monarch butterflies, on the other hand, only crawl around as caterpillars for about 10 days.

Some insects might develop faster if they had better conditions. Lack of humidity, a low temperature, not enough food—these factors can slow down the speed of development.

People grow at different rates too. That girl who was the tallest kid in second grade might end up the shortest in high school. Sometimes it feels like you outgrow your clothes overnight. Other times your last year's sneakers seem to fit forever.

We grow at different rates spiritually, too, and that's okay. But if you find yourself making the same mistakes over and over or giving in to the same temptations, then it's time to size yourself up and see where you stand. Are you praying more and connecting with God on deeper and deeper levels? Have you followed through with your decision to read the Bible every day? Do you talk about God with your friends? Are you growing?

You can't make yourself grow spiritually. God causes you to grow. But it's possible to go into "coasting" mode spiritually, to get stuck on a plateau where you do the bare minimum to try to ease your conscience. The writer of Hebrews basically called believers like that babies.

Instead, you can trust God to grow you up as you step out and let him use you more and more.

You have been believers so long now that you ought to be teaching others. Instead, you need someone to teach you again the basic things about God's word. You are like babies who need milk and cannot eat solid food.

HEBREWS 5:12

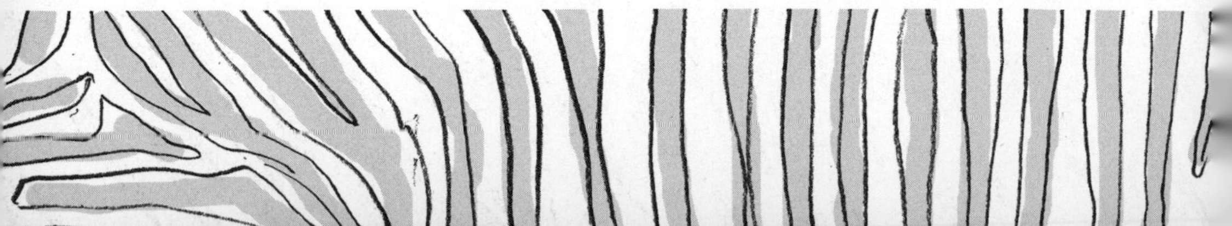

EAGLE WINGS

Everything about a bird is made for flight. The majority of birds breathe faster, have higher heart rates, and keep a higher body temperature than other animals. Everything about a bird is fast, fast, fast because birds need high-energy motion to keep moving through high elevations.

Plus, birds have wings.

The bald eagle is a miracle in lightweight design. The female's wingspan can reach up to eight feet as she sails through the sky. Eagles' wings are covered with feathers and down, and each feather is tough but flexible, light but strong. The eagle has over 7,000 feathers, but those feathers all put together weigh less than a pound and a half. Pound for pound, an eagle's wing is stronger than the wing of an airplane.

Isaiah 40:31 is an amazing promise: "Those who trust in the Lord will find new strength. They will soar high on wings like eagles. They will run and not grow weary. They will walk and not faint."

Imagine running and never getting tired, walking but never winding down or running out of gas. When we're in heaven, that's what it will be like. We're created with the promise of eagles' wings, and we can't even imagine how fantastic we'll feel in the presence of God.

But we don't have to wait for heaven. True, you probably won't fly under your own power yet. But with God's power, you can do so much more than you can on your own.

Are there people in your family who don't know Christ? Instead of keeping quiet and hoping somebody else will talk to them, trust God. Eagles don't soar through the skies when they stay perched on the mountaintop. When the time is right, they jump, knowing that God has given them wings to catch the wind.

Get outside of yourself and soar.

There are three things that amaze me—no, four things that I don't understand: how an eagle glides through the sky, how a snake slithers on a rock, how a ship navigates the ocean, how a man loves a woman.
PROVERBS 30:18-19

When the bald eagle was chosen as the symbol of the United States in 1782, Ben Franklin suggested that our nation's symbol should be the wild turkey instead.

•••

TODAY: Ask God to show you where he wants you to soar like an eagle today. Trust that he'll help you find the right words and do the right thing.

OUCH—TAKE IT BACK!

Porcupine comes from the Latin word for "pig" and the French word for "thorn." Some people call porcupines quill pigs, and others call them prickle pigs.

A porcupine has over 30,000 quills on its body and tail. And each quill is so sharp that it can easily pierce the toughest animal skin.

When the porcupine is attacked, it swings its tail and zaps the attacker (such as a dog) with needle-sharp quills that will send the poor animal squealing. But that's not the worst. The numerous barbs on each quill point backward so they lodge into the attacker. That makes the barbs really hard to pull out. And if even a slight piece of a barb breaks off under the skin, it can cause infection.

Like sharp quills, sharp words hurt. Sticks and stones may break your bones, but words hurt too. The same words you might think are funny could cause someone pain.

There are so many good uses for words. Don't waste yours on name-calling or slams. Think of ways to build people up with your comments.

It's not easy to undo the hurt your words cause, either. You let an insult fly in less than a second, but that insult might stick for years.

Kids sometimes shout at each other, "Take it back!" when somebody says something they don't like, something that hurts. But it's not that easy. Once the words are out there, it's tough to take them back, as tough as pulling porcupine quills from an injured dog's face.

Don't use foul or abusive language. Let everything you say be good and helpful, so that your words will be an encouragement to those who hear them.
EPHESIANS 4:29

Contrary to popular belief, porcupines don't throw their quills. They usually wave their tails or jump and let the predator stick itself.

• • •

TODAY: Stop the barbs! Ask God to help you think before you shoot out words that will hurt. Instead, say some encouraging words to at least two people today.

STINKERS

Some animals deserve to be called "stinkers." The skunk that lets go of its chemical mix can stink up everyone in breathing distance. Clothes that catch the stink may have to be pitched. Skunks don't stink all the time. But if you ever see a skunk stamping its feet, it's time to run away.

Skunks aren't the only stinkers. Weasels, ferrets, mink, and badgers can all make themselves stink when they're threatened. Stink badgers are well named because they squirt their foul liquids at their attackers. The Indonesian stink badger squirts out a greenish liquid that is said to cause blindness in dogs and make people sick to their stomachs.

Caterpillars and squash bugs stink enough to keep most birds from eating them. Every cockroach has its own individual smell . . . and they all stink.

This isn't a devotional on BO but on other ways you can end up being a "stinker." Paul wrote to the Romans about people whose talk was foul, like the stench of an open grave.

Is your talk ever foul? It's easy to fall into swearing and rotten language when you're with people who drop a bomb every other word. Add to that the language you hear on TV shows, movies, and music, and pretty soon those words that once sounded so awful don't sound that bad anymore. You're used to bad language.

It's not just the "bad words" that send off a stench either. Blasphemy is taking God's name in vain—calling on him when you don't mean it. If you use "Oh my God!" as an exclamation, you may not even realize you're doing it. But it's definitely using God's name in a vain, or empty, way.

And that stinks.

Their talk is foul, like the stench from an open grave. Their tongues are filled with lies. Snake venom drips from their lips. Their mouths are full of cursing and bitterness.

ROMANS 3:13-14

Most snakes are said to smell like strong fried chicken. But the poisonous copperhead snake smells like freshly cut cucumbers.

• • •

TODAY: Ask God to make you super aware of your language. Don't let yourself get away with stinking up conversations.

24 April

WORTH THE WAIT

When your mother was pregnant with you, nine months probably felt like a long time to wait to see your little, scrunched-up face.

Here's a list of how many days some animals have to wait for their babies:

mice: 20 days
rabbits: 33 days
ferrets: 52 days
foxes: 62 days
dogs: 60 days
cats: 63 days
pigs: 114 days
rhesus monkeys: 164 days
baboons: 187 days
chimps: 237 days
dolphins: 276 days
cattle: 284 days
camels: 406 days
giraffes: 410 days

And the winner . . . or loser . . . is the elephant, which has to wait as long as two years to have that baby.

Have you ever prayed for something and had to wait *forever* for an answer? That's what the prophet Daniel felt like when he heard that the city of Jerusalem lay in ruins. He started praying and waited for weeks. Then an angel came and told him: "Don't be afraid, Daniel. Since the first day you began to pray for understanding and to humble yourself before your God, your request has been heard in heaven. I have come in answer to your prayer" (Daniel 10:12).

Daniel's prayer was answered by God long before Daniel saw that answer.

If you're praying with the same heart as God and you know it's something God wants, then that prayer is already answered—even if you have to wait for months to see it in action. When you were in your mother's womb, her prayer was answered, even though she had to wait all those months to see you.

Keep on praying. It's not like you're trying to wear down God. But by continuing to pray, you become part of the answer, and your faith grows. Don't give up.

We are confident that he hears us whenever we ask for anything that pleases him. And since we know he hears us when we make our requests, we also know that he will give us what we ask for.

1 JOHN 5:14-15

When kindergartners and first graders were asked how long it takes to get a prayer answered, one seven-year-old boy answered, "It takes three years. I know because I asked God for a puppy when I was four, and I just got me one."

• • •

TODAY: Start a prayer journal and write down your prayer requests and God's answers. Thank God for all those answered prayers you forgot about!

April 25

HORSE SENSE

If you've ridden a horse that shies at every waving flag, bolts at the unexpected appearance of a rabbit, or refuses to come in out of the rain, you may wonder where the expression *horse sense* comes from.

In horses' defense, though, most of them have good reasons for reacting like they do. They can't fight an enemy, so they run. (Is it the horse's fault that you happen to be on its back at the time?)

Nobody's really sure how the expression *horse sense* came to mean "common sense," but it probably dates back to the mid-1800s, when the American West valued a rugged, dependable horse over an elegant, high-strung one.

You should crave good horse sense because it can keep you safe. Good sense boils down to making good choices—not acting on impulse, but taking the time to do the right thing.

When Solomon got to ask God for one thing, he asked for wisdom. God made him the wisest man on earth. But not even Solomon was born wise.

Nobody is born wise, and you don't come by horse sense genetically, either. The more you think through decisions—even little decisions—the better your horse sense gets. You develop good judgment.

So where do you get wisdom? Psalm 111:10 says, "Fear of the LORD is the foundation of true wisdom. All who obey his commandments will grow in wisdom. Praise him forever!" If you respect God and follow his commandments, you'll grow in wisdom . . . and horse sense.

A person with good sense is respected; a treacherous person is headed for destruction.
PROVERBS 13:15

Hippotherapy is the practice of treating human problems and disabilities with the help of horses. The horse's walk is therapeutic and rhythmic, and riding can help a person's balance and coordination, and even speech.

• • •

TODAY: Make a list of 10 recent decisions you've made, and analyze them to see if you used good horse sense. Talk to God about each decision and how you'll decide next time.

Some of the sporting breeds of dogs are actually a little farsighted. Golden retrievers, Labrador retrievers, Chesapeake Bay retrievers, cocker spaniels, and springer spaniels are more likely to see objects better when the objects are far off.

• • •

TODAY: Pray throughout the day for two concerns that are bigger than you, beyond your own little world.

NEARSIGHTED

Moose are nearsighted, meaning they can see well close-up, but not so well far away . . . which explains why they sometimes run into cars.

Rhinoceroses tend to be nearsighted too. They can see that big horn on the end of their snouts, but may not see a predator creeping up.

Dogs can be nearsighted. Some breeds have more problems with eyesight than other breeds. Nearsightedness has been found in rottweilers, miniature schnauzers, and German shepherds. (So if they bite you close-up, they know it's you.)

We can live our lives as if we're spiritually nearsighted—as if there were no heaven, no hell, and no future except what shows up tomorrow. School, friends, and activities take over all our strength. Our thoughts are consumed with what other people think about us. Every little thing that goes wrong can take on life-and-death dimensions.

You don't get invited to a party, and you think you'll never live it down. You get picked last on a sports team, and you don't want to show your face. Or things are so tough at home that you're too depressed to talk to anybody about it.

You're nearsighted. Put on your spiritual glasses and take a good look beyond yourself. God says that when the game's over, no matter how tough the game is, you'll be a winner. You're not going to fail, because the victory is already won.

Keep looking. When you're not so nearsighted, you can notice people who are hurting more than you are, people you could help if you'd just see them. There's a world out there that needs Christ.

Get the big picture.

You belong to God, my dear children. You have already won a victory over those people, because the Spirit who lives in you is greater than the spirit who lives in the world.

1 JOHN 4:4

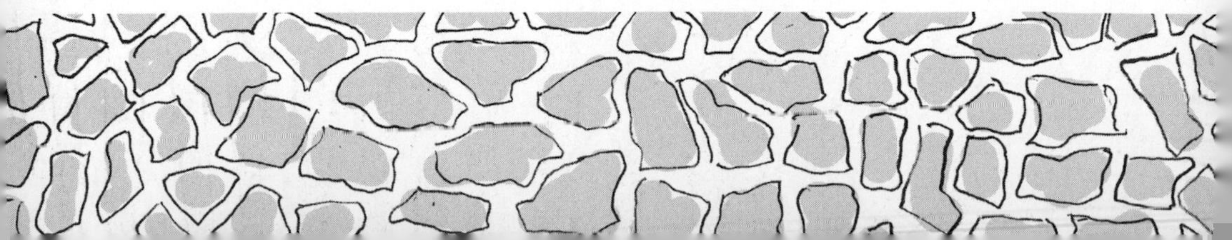

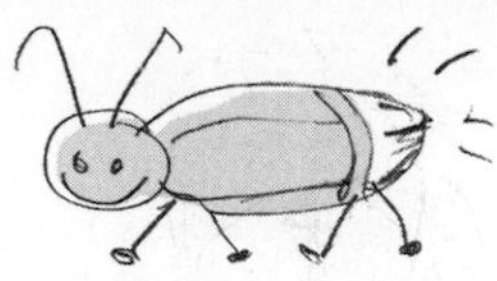

LIGHTEN UP

You may have seen fireflies flashing in the summer night's sky. But fireflies aren't the only bright ones in the insect world.

Springtails love to live inside your house and inhabit dark rooms, where they flicker light. Click beetles and gnats can light up too. Although mammals, reptiles, amphibians, and birds can't light up, certain invertebrates and bacteria can—just a little.

Sometimes it takes only a little light to transform an entire environment. Once your eyes grow accustomed to the dark, your tiny night-light can seem so bright you can't go back to sleep. And the lighted numbers on your clock make you pull the covers over your head.

If you have Christ, the Light of the World, living inside you, then you're filled with light. And that light needs to shine everywhere. Let people see Christ in you.

Are you a different kind of person when you're in church or youth group than you are in the lunchroom or on the soccer field or at the mall?

Is your light as bright in cyberspace as it is when you're with your parents? You don't always have to be a blinding searchlight. If your friends are cyber-bullying or sending hurtful texts to someone, you might be able to stop it by simply saying, "Let's not go there." "Not cool." "Not funny."

Little things count. Make someone's day with a compliment. Pick up somebody's dropped candy wrapper as you're walking along. Stop someone from kicking a cat, from gossiping, from planning something you know is wrong.

Let your light shine.

In the same way, let your good deeds shine out for all to see, so that everyone will praise your heavenly Father.

MATTHEW 5:16

A lightning bug makes light using a chemical process when three chemicals in its cells combine with oxygen. An electric eel can give off a shock so powerful it could light up a house.

• • •

TODAY: Thank God that you have the Light of the World living inside you. Do two things today that let your light shine.

COOL IT!

God built cooling systems into animals that need them. The ears of the African elephant can grow as big as 30 square feet. Each ear contains blood vessels that act like a coolant, or air-conditioning. All the elephant has to do is flap those ears, and the breeze is better than a fan.

Dogs have cooling systems too: their noses. A dog's nose is a maze of moisture. So when your dog pants, it breathes in cool air through its nose. The air flows over the wet surface of the nose and evaporates, cooling off your dog.

How effective is your cooling-off system? When something makes you angry, what do you do? Do you react before giving yourself time to think? If a teacher tells you that you have to do your report over, it's a good idea to keep your mouth shut until you've cooled off. When your parents say you can't go to someone's party, it doesn't do any good to get angry with them. Cool off. Then you can at least talk about it.

People have devised different ways to keep their anger in check. You've probably heard the one about counting to 10. Not a bad idea really. Those 10 seconds give you a little time to fire up an immediate plea to God for help.

Other people find it helpful to just walk away. Probably a good idea if the other guy is as angry as you are or if you don't trust yourself to rein it in.

But don't store up your anger inside either. Some situations need to be resolved. Just give yourself time to let off steam before dealing with it. (Punch a punching bag. Scream into a pillow. Take deep breaths.)

Cool it . . . and talk to God.

Don't sin by letting anger control you.
EPHESIANS 4:26

A dog has very few sweat glands, so his cooling system comes through his nose. But the main way a dog gets rid of heat is by panting. Bulldogs and pugs, who can't pant well, can overheat easily and are subject to heat strokes.

• • •

TODAY: Whenever you feel yourself getting angry, immediately turn to God and give your anger to him. Then count to 10 before reacting. Give yourself time to cool off.

TELL TAILS

Some animals have pretty strange tails. The tail of a kangaroo weighs almost 200 pounds. It's not much to look at (sort of like the tail of a giant rat), but it comes in handy for balancing every step a kangaroo makes and for support when it sits.

A monkey's tail is so long that it can wrap around a tree branch and hold the monkey up as it dangles. Or monkeys can use their tails as extra hands for grasping things.

Tails of horses and cows are great flyswatters. Cats can puff out their tails to make them look fierce or wave them to warn an intruder to back off.

Pigs have curly tails. Cats and most dogs have straight tails, although the Manx cat has no tail at all. Gorillas, apes, chimps, and the tailless tenrec don't have much of a tail to speak of.

Ever wonder if a straight-tailed dog wishes he had a curly pig tail? That tailless tenrec might long for a giant kangaroo tail. Sounds ridiculous, but most people have wishes that are just as silly.

Is there some feature you wish you didn't have? Your dad's nose? Your mom's hair? Do you think you're too short? Too tall? If you only had a build like your buddy, life would be better. Or if you had a face like that popular girl in your class, you'd be popular too.

God made every part of you with great care. You can't believe that he didn't do his best work on you. You're handcrafted, made by God. You are priceless!

> *How foolish can you be? He is the Potter, and he is certainly greater than you, the clay! Should the created thing say of the one who made it, "He didn't make me"? Does a jar ever say, "The potter who made me is stupid"?*
>
> **ISAIAH 29:16**

The prize for the longest tail goes to the animal that also has the longest neck. A giraffe's tail is about eight feet long.

• • •

TODAY: Talk to God about one part of your body that you just don't like. Be honest. Then thank God that he made you the way you are and that he doesn't make mistakes.

With the face of an owl, framed by whiskerlike feathers, the kakapo bird of New Zealand is the world's biggest, and weirdest, parrot. Weighing in at about eight pounds, the kakapo can't fly. Sadly, the bird is nearly extinct.

• • •

TODAY: Make a list of your strengths and weaknesses—five of each. Then thank God for all 10.

INADEQUATE—WHO ME?

Killer whales, also called orcas, are the scariest predators in the sea, feared by seals, sea lions, and other whales. At 20-some feet long and weighing 10,000 pounds, they have no natural enemies. But when a whale is beached—stuck in too-shallow water or on the shore—it's virtually helpless and will eventually die.

Penguins are magnificent swimmers, but they can't fly. They're the only bird that swims but doesn't fly.

Cheetahs may be the fastest animals on land, but even they have weaknesses. Since they're so tall and lean, cheetahs can't catch big prey, like zebras and buffalo. And they're no match for lions and hyenas.

The tarsier is a tiny primate with long anklebones. The tarsier can turn its head almost 360 degrees, but its big eyes can't move.

All animals have weaknesses. And the same goes for people. No one on earth is, or ever has been, perfect . . . except Jesus. The rest of us have strengths and weaknesses. It's when we focus on our weaknesses that we're struck with feelings of inadequacy.

If God calls you to do something, he'll help you do it in spite of your shortcomings. In fact, God can work best through our weaknesses. Then we'll know he did it. We'll give him the credit.

A star athlete may not sense God's help as strongly as an average player does when he has a super game. A classmate who loves getting in front of people might forget to count on God when she gives her oral report. But you won't forget—not if you're nervous in front of people.

You may not have the skill or talent or personality for every situation, but God has more than enough for everything you'll ever be asked to do. Give God a chance to work through your weakness.

> *Each time [the Lord] said, "My grace is all you need. My power works best in weakness." So now I am glad to boast about my weaknesses, so that the power of Christ can work through me.*
> **2 CORINTHIANS 12:9**

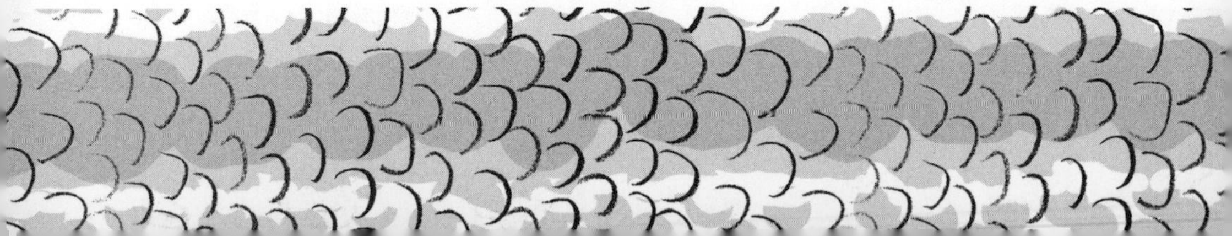

PAY ATTENTION

Most animals pay closer attention to the weather than we do. The European weatherfish is extremely sensitive to changes in barometric pressure. When the pressure decreases, the fish gets jumpy and restless, and researchers know that a storm is on the way.

Many animals can sense earthquakes, hurricanes, and natural disasters long before humans do. Some people believe animals have special powers, but they really just pick up faint warning signals we miss.

Before earthquakes hit, there are changes in electrical activity, creating static electricity—that force that makes your hair stand up, your clothes cling, and your finger become a weapon of shock when you touch someone. Animals' fur makes them more sensitive to static electricity. Fish and birds sense the changes in the earth's magnetic field. They're paying attention.

Have you ever had a friend blow up in your face and leave you wondering, *Where did that come from?* Have you ever had a parent break down in tears or a teacher burst out in anger, and you think, *Man, I didn't see that coming*?

You probably didn't see it coming because you weren't paying attention. Your friend might have been dropping hints. Your parent probably wore a sad expression all week. And you should have seen the anger building in your teacher.

A study came out a few years ago that concluded many kids are losing the ability to read physical expressions and gestures. The more time someone spends on Internet friendships, the worse they are at interpreting facial expressions.

Take time to read people. Pay attention.

> *Jesus turned to the crowd and said, "When you see clouds beginning to form in the west, you say, 'Here comes a shower.' And you are right. When the south wind blows, you say, 'Today will be a scorcher.' And it is. You fools! You know how to interpret the weather signs of the earth and sky, but you don't know how to interpret the present times."*
>
> **LUKE 12:54-56**

Racehorses traveling from the East Coast to California can get nervous and flighty because they sense earth tremors we don't. And California horses get nervous out East because they don't feel those tremors.

• • •

TODAY: Pay attention to the facial expressions of your family and friends, and see if you can figure out what's going on beneath their surface talk. Ask God to make you sensitive.

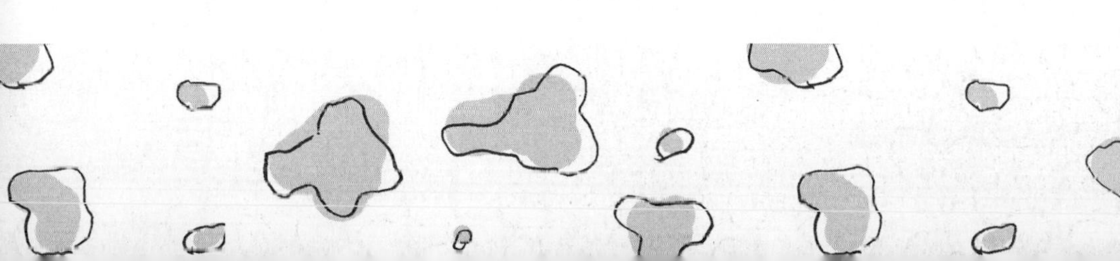

2 May

SHOCKING!

The electric eel can deliver a shock powerful enough to stun you and make you wish you hadn't messed with it. The electric eel isn't a true eel though. It's an electric fish, like the knifefish, the ghost fish, and the aba aba. Most electric fish create weak electric fields around themselves so they can sense an attacker and swim away. But the electric eel of South America and the electric catfish of Africa deliver shocking jolts.

The torpedo ray, or the Pacific electric ray, is the most shocking of all. It's not afraid to go after divers. And if it wraps itself around you, the charge can knock you down flat.

You can count on the fact that over the next year shocking things will happen—maybe a job loss in your family, a natural disaster, a terrorist attack, a national crisis, or something at your own school.

So what are you going to do? You could pretend that bad things only happen to other people. Or you could give in to fear, playing the what-if game. What if something happens to me at school? What if my dad gets in a wreck? What if my mom loses her job? What if a tornado hits my house? What if there's a terrorist attack?

It's okay to be alert. We shouldn't ignore potential dangers. On the other hand, worrying about what's coming won't keep shocking things from happening. So the only solution is a calm trust in God. He has you covered, no matter what's down the line.

What an amazing gift to know that no matter what comes, God will get you through it.

> *In God, whose word I praise, In God I have put my trust; I shall not be afraid. What can mere man do to me?*
>
> **PSALM 56:4, NASB**

The ancient Greeks and Romans called rays, such as the torpedo electric ray, "numbfish" because their shocks caused numbness. Hoping that the numbness might cure gout and headaches, people applied the rays to their bodies and were shocked numb. Our English word *narcotic* comes from the Greek *narke*, for "numbness."

• • •

TODAY: On a sheet of paper, list every shocking thing you think could happen in the next year. Talk to God about each item. Tear up the sheet and toss it into the garbage. Trust that God is bigger than any of those things.

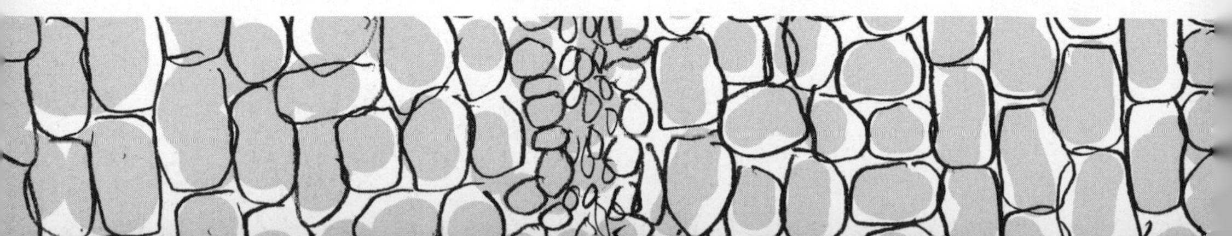

ARE YOU POISONOUS?

The golden poison dart frog lives in only one region in the rain forest of Colombia. The little froggy doesn't look that threatening. But it's probably the most poisonous animal in the world. All it has to do to poison you is touch you, because its poison is in its skin. One frog has enough poison in it to kill 100 people. The Chocó natives used the poison from the frog on the tips of their blowgun darts.

Rattlesnakes warn you with their rattles. Scorpions look like they'd happily poison you. But the cute frog, which seems harmless, turns out to be the most deadly.

As sins go, gossip doesn't feel like one of the most deadly. After all, you're not killing, cheating, or stealing. Although some gossipers spread lies, others just pass along juicy secrets that are true. Besides, there's something so satisfying in being the one who knows the juicy tidbit. . . .

But gossip is poison. If you've ever had a friend betray a confidence and spill your secret, you know that gossip hurts. If you've ever been verbally attacked in person, by phone, or over the Internet, you know there's poison in gossip.

And gossip spreads—fast. You can't take it back, and you can't slow it down. The time to stop it is when someone first passes information to you. Instead of being amazed and delighted, don't reward the gossiper. Just remember that gossip is poison, and then politely change the subject.

Proverbs on gossip:

> *A gossip goes around telling secrets, so don't hang around with chatterers.*
> **PROVERBS 20:19**

> *Telling lies about others is as harmful as hitting them with an ax, wounding them with a sword, or shooting them with a sharp arrow.*
> **PROVERBS 25:18**

> *Fire goes out without wood, and quarrels disappear when gossip stops.*
> **PROVERBS 26:20**

These animals have a bite, sting, or touch that can kill you: the poison dart frog, the death stalker scorpion, the blue-ringed octopus, the box jellyfish, the stonefish, the marbled cone snail, the Sydney funnel-web spider, the inland taipan snake, the king cobra, the Brazilian wandering spider, the puffer fish, and more.

• • •

TODAY: Be hyper-aware of gossip at school, over the Internet, and even at home. Ask God to give you the strength to say, "No thanks. Not interested." Stop the poison.

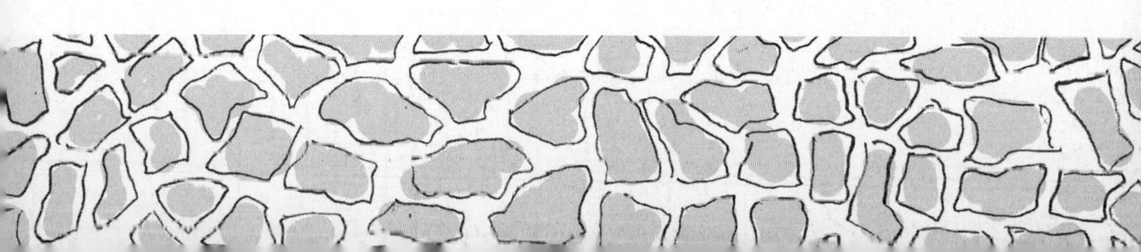

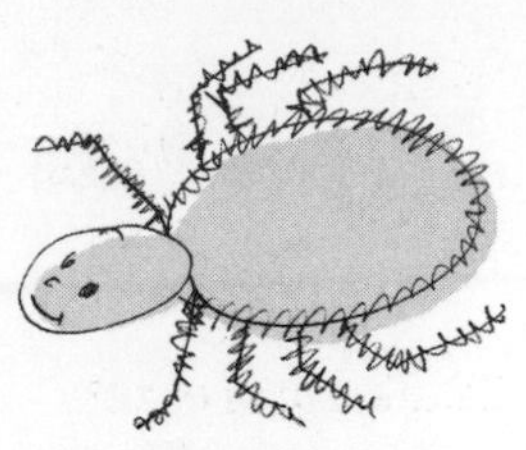

GIVE 'EM A CHANCE

Butterflies are masters of imitation and disguise. Hungry birds that love the taste of a yummy viceroy butterfly will leave it alone because the viceroy looks like a monarch. And monarchs are too bitter tasting from eating all that milkweed. So the bird misjudges the viceroy and goes away hungry.

The Indonesian moth doesn't look much like a praying mantis until it goes into mimicry mode. Then it changes its stance and holds its abdomen above its wings so that predators will think it's a mantis and stay away.

Some moths even manage to mimic sounds to fool predators. Good-tasting moths imitate the sounds of their foul-tasting relatives, and bats leave them alone.

In the animal world, mimicry and misjudgments work well for the would-be victim of a bigger predator. But with people, misjudging someone fills the world with inequality and unfairness. Prejudging is prejudice.

Are there people in your school you've never taken the time to know just because they don't look like you? Maybe you've prejudged someone because of his skin color, her ethnic background, where he lives, what she wears. On the other hand, maybe you've misjudged someone you thought would be cool to know just because she's a great dresser or he's a good athlete.

It's not your job to judge—especially based on appearances. Don't be too critical of anyone. You don't know the whole story. Only God knows. So leave the judging to God.

> *Don't speak evil against each other, dear brothers and sisters. If you criticize and judge each other, then you are criticizing and judging God's law. But your job is to obey the law, not to judge whether it applies to you.*
> JAMES 4:11

Ant spiders, jumping spiders, and sun spiders mimic flies, wasps, and ants. Most animals think ants taste gross. Some spiders manage to smell so much like an ant that ants let them stroll into the anthill, where they steal the babies!

• • •

TODAY: Admit to God that you've prejudged someone—at school, at church, in the neighborhood. Then give that person a chance.

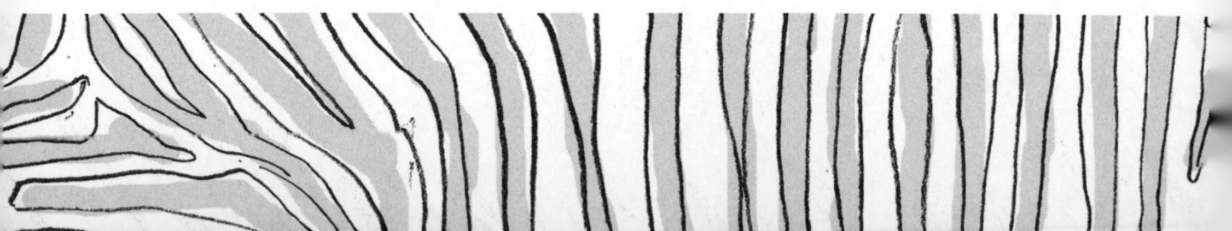

May 5

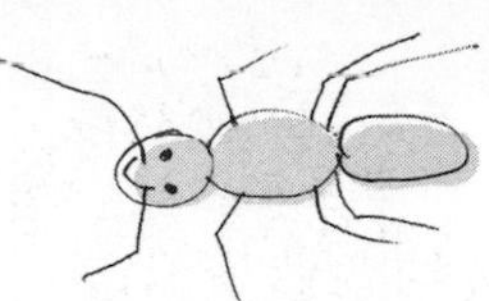

EXPLODING

The bombardier beetle lives on every continent except Antarctica. Inside its abdomen, the beetle houses a powerful mixture of chemicals, along with a special chemical to keep the others from exploding.

When the bombardier beetle is disturbed, look out! It mixes hydrogen peroxide and hydroquinone. Then it fires the mix into the attacker's face, where it explodes. The chemical mix would explode inside of the beetle if the bombardier didn't have that special chemical (called an inhibitor) that prevents the explosion.

When the beetle wants to set off the bomb, it has yet another chemical to override the inhibitor. And bang! The spider or frog that thought this beetle might make a good snack gets shot in the face with a chemical mix that's as hot as boiling water. The attacker gets attacked.

What do you do when you're attacked? If somebody yells in your face, does that person get yelled back at even louder? If someone pushes you, do you shove back? When you find out somebody has been gossiping about you behind your back, do you explode with gossip in return?

Explosions only make your problems worse. Jesus could have fought back when he was arrested. He could have called thousands of angels to his rescue. But he taught his followers to live peacefully with all people, to turn the other cheek. He said that we should be kind to our enemies and overcome evil with good, not with more evil. And he gave us his Spirit inside us, the "inhibitor" we need when we feel like we're going to explode.

> *Never pay back evil with more evil. Do things in such a way that everyone can see you are honorable.*
> **ROMANS 12:17**

Certain types of soldier ants can shoot out chemicals from a horn on their heads . . . or from a hole in the head.

• • •

TODAY: Talk to God about any anger you're carrying around inside you. Be specific. What made you so angry? What have you thought about doing to even the score? Then give the anger to God and ask for the help of God's Spirit to keep your anger from exploding.

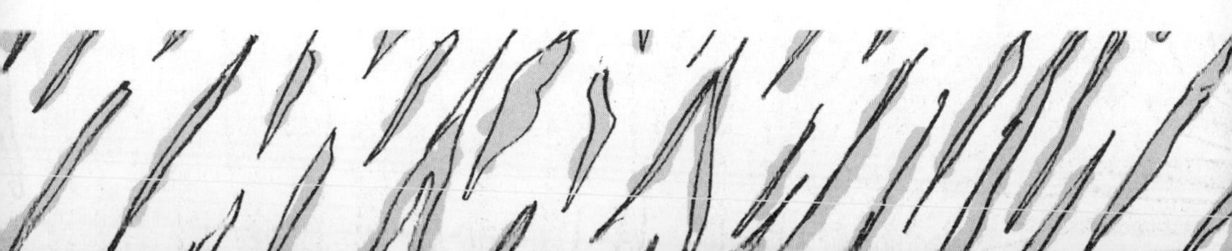

For a cat, licking itself constantly is so built in that if a cat stops licking, it's time to take the animal to the vet. It means something must be wrong.

• • •

TODAY: Practice spiritual breathing throughout your entire day. The second you realize you've broken your fellowship with God by something you thought or did or said, tell God you're sorry. Tell him that you know it was wrong. Then thank God for filling you with his Spirit, so you're as good as new.

CLEAN UP YOUR ACT

Cats compulsively clean themselves. If you have a cat, you've probably noticed how many of your cat's waking hours are spent on grooming.

Cats lick themselves for several reasons. They like clean, smooth fur, and using that rough tongue does the job. Cleaning also gets rid of the cat's smell, just in case a predator may be on the hunt. Fluffing up the fur helps keep a cat warm in the winter. And licking helps cool the cat in the summer.

In a way, we need continual cleaning too. If you've accepted Christ, then Jesus' payment for your sin happened on the cross, once for all time. But that doesn't mean you automatically stay close to God every day. Sin blocks our friendship with God, our fellowship with him through Christ.

How do you stay clean? By spiritual breathing—exhaling the sin and inhaling God's spirit of forgiveness. Exhaling is confessing—admitting to God that what you did, said, or thought wasn't right. You agree with God. Then you inhale, breathing in God's Spirit of forgiveness, power, purity, and love.

You may have to breathe spiritually dozens of times a day, and that's okay. In Leviticus 5:5, Moses instructed the people: "When you become aware of your guilt in any of these ways, you must confess your sin."

Keep short accounts with God. Don't let sin keep you from enjoying the fellowship of God.

> *If we confess our sins to him, he is faithful and just to forgive us our sins and to cleanse us from all wickedness.*
>
> **1 JOHN 1:9**

DANCING BEES AND ARMY ANTS

Insects that pitch in and work together are considered "social" insects. They may not be animals you'd choose to hang with—ants, bees, termites, wasps—but you have to admire the way each insect has found its niche, its place in the community.

Bees have a few choices about how they'll serve the group. True, if you're not a queen (poor you), you're a drone or a worker. Not much choice there. But you still get to dance when you discover fresh pollen. Ants have scores of possible jobs, from gardener and farmer to warrior and slave driver.

If you've chosen to follow Christ, you belong to a community, too—the community of believers. But it's up to you how well you fit into that community. Ants and bees pull together through instinct. Unfortunately, Christians have been known to fight over little things, to struggle for position, or to forget the community and simply live their own lives.

God has given everyone at least one gift so that we'll find our place, our niche. You have something to offer the body of believers that no one else has. God has jobs for you to do that nobody else on earth could do. Nobody will ever have your exact set of experiences, talents, or opportunities.

Don't lose sight of the community of believers. Connecting with your local church is a good place to start. As you get more involved and serve in different ways, God will show you exactly how you fit in.

> *He makes the whole body fit together perfectly. As each part does its own special work, it helps the other parts grow, so that the whole body is healthy and growing and full of love.*
>
> **EPHESIANS 4:16**

The killer bee is a strange combination of a fierce African bee and a European honeybee. During a scientific experiment in Brazil in 1957, the bees got loose and started flying north. By 1980, killer bees had hit Mexico, and they kept on going. Now, in the southwestern part of the United States, you can find swarms of killer bees.

• • •

TODAY: How are you fitting into the body of Christ? Talk to God about what you think your niche might be. Try out different ways of serving in your church. Volunteer for at least one job.

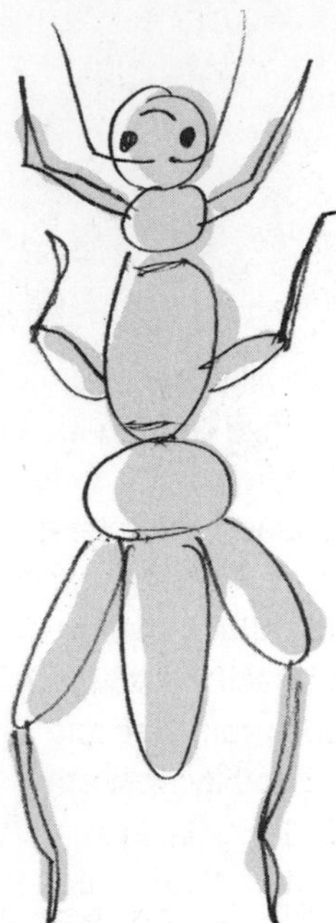

DIFFERENT STROKES

God must love variety. Pick any tree in the United States, and there will be about 100 to 200 different species of insects in it. If you checked out a tree in a rain forest, you'd find about 600 species of insects.

Moths range from the pygmy moth, with a wingspan of two-tenths of an inch, to the giant agrippa moth, whose wingspan reaches 12 inches. There are insects too small to see under a microscope. And there are giants, like the foot-long giant stick in Indonesia or the Hercules beetle in Central and South America.

God could have made people look alike—with the same skin color, hair color, shape, and height. Instead, not only do we look different, but we each get unique fingerprints and DNA. No matter how many people will be born down the line, they'll never get your DNA.

But what do we do with the variety? In most schools, if you watch students before classes start or at lunchtime or after school, you can see little groups of people who basically look similar. One ethnic group here. Another over there. Another one there. There's a table of cheerleaders. A table of people going grunge. A table of people with expensive clothes, their labels showing.

And a table of you and your friends. How's the mix there? Does it reflect the variety of creation and the Creator? Does your church reach people who come from different backgrounds and races, different levels of income? Do you, personally, make the effort to get to know people who come from a different culture and aren't like you?

Reach out farther than your neighborhood. If the apostles had kept in their own clique instead of spreading out from Jerusalem, you might not have heard the Good News.

They worshiped together at the Temple each day, met in homes for the Lord's Supper, and shared their meals with great joy and generosity—all the while praising God and enjoying the goodwill of all the people. And each day the Lord added to their fellowship those who were being saved.

ACTS 2:46-47

About 80 percent of the world's animals are insects. And approximately 8,000 new species of insects are added to the list each year as new ones are discovered.

• • •

TODAY: Make an effort to talk to at least three people you rarely talk to at school or in an extracurricular activity. Ask God to point out kids who could use your friendship.

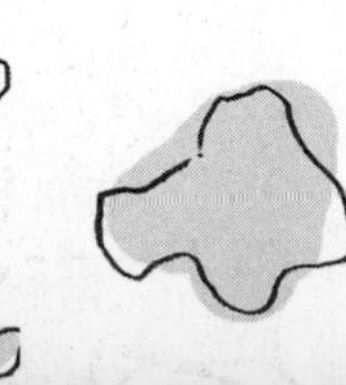
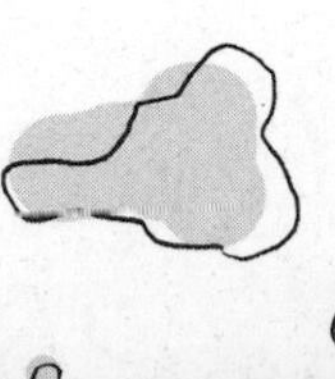

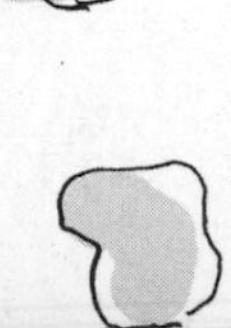

VOICE RECOGNITION

Some animals have amazing voice recognition. Your dog probably knows your voice, and your horse recognizes your call or whistle. Sound is often more important than sight when babies need to find their parents. A tern chick can pick out its parent's voice from thousands of squawking and peeping birds in the colony. In a crowd of hundreds of sea lions, a sea lion pup can find its mom easily by hearing her voice.

Turkeys need to hear their own chicks in order to recognize them. Deaf female turkeys can't pick out their little gobblers.

Not all parent birds can recognize their babies' voices right away. Herring gulls take about five days to pick out the sounds of their chicks, and the chicks take about that long to recognize Mom's voice. Kittiwakes, a kind of seabird, may need up to five weeks to recognize their babies' voices.

How good are you at identifying the voices of people in your life? Can you pick out your friend's voice at a crowded football game, or your mom's voice at the grocery store? Humans are fairly limited in the number of voices they can recognize compared to the number of people they can recognize by sight. You should be able to recognize your family's voices, a couple of buddies', and a few more, but usually that's about it.

Sheep recognize their shepherd because of the sound of the shepherd's voice. Jesus explained this to his disciples: "He calls his own sheep by name and leads them out. After he has gathered his own flock, he walks ahead of them, and they follow him because they know his voice. They won't follow a stranger; they will run from him because they don't know his voice" (John 10:3-5).

Voice recognition works both ways. You recognize Jesus' voice, and Jesus recognizes yours. He knows you and hears you.

I love the Lord because he hears my voice.
PSALM 116:1

A one-year-old sheep is called a hogget. If you see a hogget on its back, lend a hand! Sheep can't get up from that position.

• • •

TODAY: At least three times throughout the day, confide in God. Isn't it amazing that the God of the universe recognizes your voice? Listen closely for his.

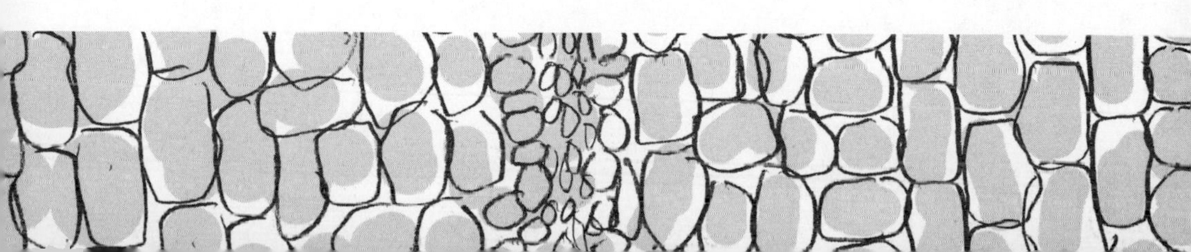

When a cat catches a mouse, Kitty can move her whiskers to touch the mouse and make sure it's dead before letting go of the poor creature.

• • •

TODAY: Brush up your whiskers. Tell God you want to sense every leading of his Spirit, all day long.

PUT ON YOUR WHISKERS

Cats have whiskers on the inside of their front legs, right above the paw. They depend on the feeling they get from those whiskers to help them snatch mice. God also gave cats whiskers on their faces—on the upper lip, cheeks, and forehead. Whenever a whisker touches anything, messages are sent through the nerve endings. That's why cats can prowl at night. Whiskers help guide the cat through the darkness.

God has given you spiritual whiskers. He knew you'd have to find your way through some tricky situations. So he has given you his Spirit, a sense of right and wrong, and a conscience.

Say you're at school and the cool guys tell you to eat at their table in the cafeteria, but you're sitting by your best buddy, who isn't invited. You get up to change tables, but something nags at you inside. You turn to your buddy. He tells you to go ahead. But you feel a twinge in your stomach. Maybe that's a whisker. You sit back down.

Sensing that little whisker deep inside can keep you out of danger too. A cat walking down a dark alley feels the trash can on one side and the brick wall on the other because of those sensitive whiskers. God can give you a sense of uneasiness when you're headed in the wrong direction. But if you barge ahead and ignore the warning, those warnings gradually get harder to hear. And you can end up on the wrong path.

Since we are living by the Spirit, let us follow the Spirit's leading in every part of our lives.
GALATIANS 5:25

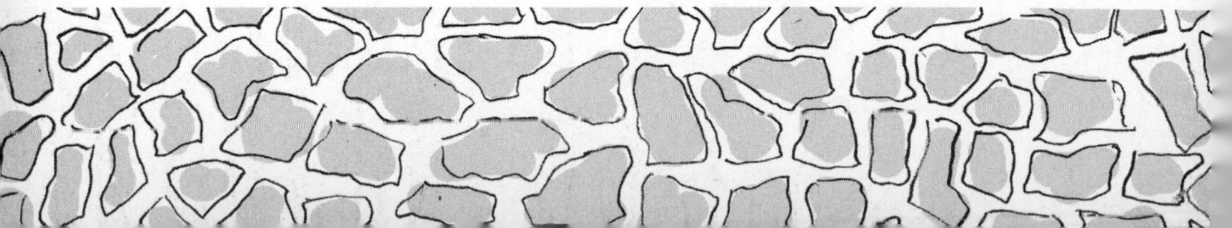

May 11

GIVE IT UP

You've probably heard about "horse whisperers," people who gentle horses instead of breaking them. In the past, most trainers believed they had to break a horse's spirit and teach it who was boss, even if that meant using a whip and force. But the best horse trainers today reject force and use gentle ways to train horses.

Horse whisperers train horses with love and respect. One of the goals of training is for the trainer, or owner, to be accepted by the horse as the leader. The horse might be allowed to run in circles in a round pen, with the trainer in the center. The trainer asks the horse to do something—stand still, be haltered, or be saddled, for example. If the horse refuses, the trainer encourages him to run in circles again. When the horse stops, the trainer tries again. And they keep it up until the horse gives. When the horse does what it's asked, the trainer praises the horse.

And a relationship of trust begins.

Round-pen training is a good illustration of how God handles us sometimes. God asks us to do something—talk to that new kid at school, study hard for that test, apologize to someone—but God won't force us to do it. So we fight it. We run in circles. And when we've worn ourselves out with our little rebellions, we finally take a cue from the trainer and quit trying to run the show ourselves.

God doesn't even say, "Told you so." He just whispers, "Good job. Well done." And we see how crazy we were not to give in sooner.

> *Since we respected our earthly fathers who disciplined us, shouldn't we submit even more to the discipline of the Father of our spirits, and live forever?*
> **HEBREWS 12:9**

Horses have great memories that put elephants to shame. If a horse has one second of extreme fright, that second will be committed to memory, possibly for years. And the next time the horse is in the same location or meets the same person or hears the same sound, terror will strike again.

• • •

TODAY: Talk to God about everything you've been fighting against—your curfew, what you can't wear to school, house rules, school rules, chores, standing up for Christ. If you find yourself bucking against God, it's time to give in. Whatever it is, it's not worth the fight. You can trust God as your leader.

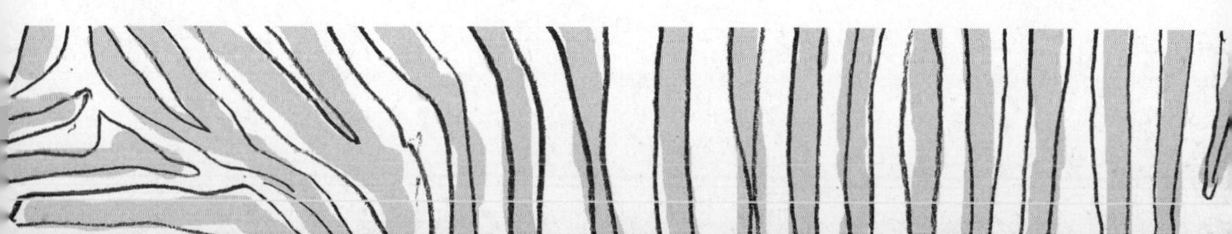

When a male Clydesdale horse finally stops growing, he may weigh as much as 2,400 pounds. His hoof is twice the size of a racehorse's hoof . . . about the size of a dinner plate.

• • •

TODAY: List five ways you've grown physically in the past three years. Then list five ways you've grown spiritually. Thank God that he's in charge of growth.

GROW UP

Lobsters take a year to be full grown. Cats as young as five months can have kittens, but they're not really mature until they're 12 to 24 months. Dogs can keep growing up to two years. Some people call a horse mature at two years, when it has reached its maximum height, but it will keep developing up to five more years.

The white sturgeon (the largest freshwater fish in North America) spends 20 years maturing in the ocean, where it grows to 12.5 feet long and 1,200 pounds.

TTT! **T**hings **T**ake **T**ime.

Maybe you can't wait for the day you get your driver's license. Or until your parents let you go out with someone. You've been in a hurry to move to the next grade level each year.

Slow down—growth takes time. Don't miss what's going on now. You'll never be this age again. So enjoy it.

You should be growing spiritually, too. Are you as eager for the day when you're more spiritually mature?

You can help your spiritual growth by reading the Bible and staying in tune with God. But when it comes down to it, it's God's job to grow you up in your relationship with him.

Keep getting to know Jesus better, and he'll take care of growing you up—physically and spiritually. TTT.

Dear brothers and sisters, I close my letter with these last words: Be joyful. Grow to maturity. Encourage each other. Live in harmony and peace. Then the God of love and peace will be with you.

2 CORINTHIANS 13:11

May 13

LOVING YOUR ENEMIES

It's a mystery why dogs that have been horribly abused by their owners remain faithful to them. Workers for the humane society and other organizations have shown up to rescue dogs from thoroughly rotten humans. Dogs that have been beaten, starved, and totally neglected whine when taken from their abusive owners.

Dogs seem to have the ability to love their "enemies," even when it makes no sense.

Jesus said that we should love our enemies and pray for them. But why should we? They don't deserve it, right? What about that kid at school who has it in for you and can't wait to make you look bad in front of your friends? Or the bully who makes your life miserable? Or the person who spread lies about you all over the Internet? They don't deserve love or forgiveness, surely! They're your enemies.

But the truth is that we were all God's enemies before forgiveness came our way through Jesus Christ. Romans 5:10 says, "Since our friendship with God was restored by the death of his Son while we were still his enemies, we will certainly be saved through the life of his Son."

We became God's friends when Christ died for us. We didn't deserve forgiveness. We were God's enemies, after all. But God forgave us. And we're supposed to forgive our enemies just as God has forgiven us.

> *Love your enemies! Pray for those who persecute you! In that way, you will be acting as true children of your Father in heaven.*
>
> **MATTHEW 5:44-45**

Most animals have natural enemies, but the only real enemy of the great horned owl is another great horned owl.

• • •

TODAY: List all the things God could hold against you, and thank God for the forgiveness you don't deserve. Then make a list of people you consider your enemies. Pray for the people on your list. Then wad up that list—with God's help, you have no more enemies.

Caribou, cousins of the reindeer, live in forests on the edge of the cold Arctic. Caribou calves are born with warm fur and open eyes. They can walk and run soon after birth.

• • •

TODAY: For a whole week, catch yourself whenever you say—or think—"I can't . . ." Talk to God about it, and thank him for giving you all you need in Christ.

EVERYTHING YOU NEED

God thought of everything. When a fish hatches, it has all the scales it will ever have or need. As it grows, the scales grow. And the fish will keep growing its whole life.

When puppies are born, they have lungs, kidneys, hearts, and every other organ they'll need for life. The same is true for horses, cats, tigers, lions—every animal.

And you. When you were still in your mother's womb, waiting around to be born, you had everything you needed to become a fully formed little human. She could look at the ultrasound and see your heart beating. God had already knit you together in there. You had it all.

And you still do. Maybe you wish you had more spending money. Or you don't see how you can survive school this year. Or you can't stand it that you don't have a single friend you can count on.

Ever feel like you were in the wrong line when God was handing out brains? (You weren't.) Or like you missed out when talents got divvied up? You can't play ball, and you're a lousy singer. Your art projects are the worst, and you freeze up if you're in front of a bunch of people.

Maybe you can't draw like your best friend or sing or throw a football like your buddy. But you have everything you need to do everything God has called you to do.

Seriously, you have it all. God has built you so that whatever happens, or doesn't happen, for the rest of your life, you can handle it. But even better, you have Christ. It's in Christ that you have everything you need.

By his divine power, God has given us everything we need for living a godly life. We have received all of this by coming to know him, the one who called us to himself by means of his marvelous glory and excellence.

2 PETER 1:3

May **15**

POWER

The old English mastiff may be the most powerful dog around. The name *mastiff* probably comes from the Anglo-Saxon word for "powerful." Weighing in at 200 pounds, this dog will fight off anyone who threatens its territory.

Mastiff dogs are so strong that the Romans once used them in battles. They even signed up mastiffs as gladiators to fight tigers, bears, and lions in exhibitions, where crowds cheered them on.

Today people own mastiffs as guard dogs. These gentle giants love kids but will attack strangers to protect the family. And you wouldn't want to be that stranger!

Think of the most powerful animal you can imagine. A bear? An elephant? Now picture the most powerful vehicle . . . the most powerful natural disaster . . . and the most powerful evil imaginable.

Even if you added all those things together, God is way more powerful than that.

You knew that already, right?

But did you know that *you're* more powerful too? Christ plus you equals *power*. The same power that raised Jesus from the dead is at your fingertips.

If you think you don't have the power to talk to your friend about Christ, you're wrong. Ask God to give you the words and the guts to start talking.

If you think you don't have the power to quit that bad habit, you actually have more than enough power. Are you afraid you can't give that talk or admit you did something wrong? Afraid you can't say no . . . or yes?

Yes, you can—you've got the power!

I also pray that you will understand the incredible greatness of God's power for us who believe him. This is the same mighty power that raised Christ from the dead and seated him in the place of honor at God's right hand in the heavenly realms. Now he is far above any ruler or authority or power or leader or anything else—not only in this world but also in the world to come.

EPHESIANS 1:19-21

The English mastiff has held a couple of world records for the heaviest dog in the world. Dogs in the breed range from 100 to 342 pounds.

• • •

TODAY: Remind yourself that you're powerful because you can draw on God's power. Talk to God about one situation where you need his power today.

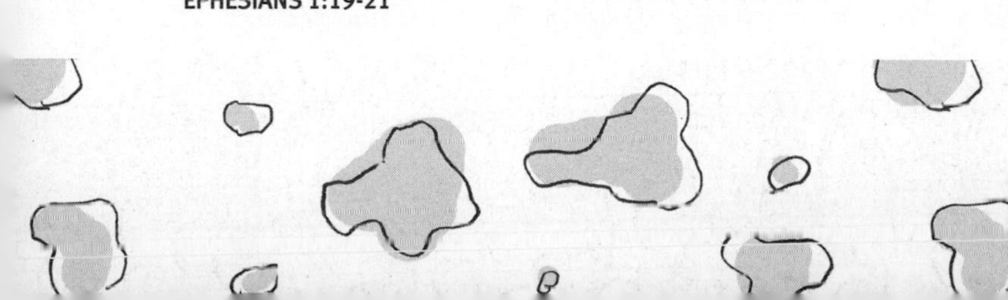

LITTLE GIANTS

The smallest breed of dog in the world is the Chihuahua, named after the state of Chihuahua in Mexico. Chihuahuas max out at 6 to 10 inches and just 2 to 6 pounds.

Chihuahuas are little, but don't tell them that. It's not unusual to see Chihuahuas take on a dog several times their size. Their bark is loud, and they seldom back off, as if they don't realize they're smaller than a Great Dane.

On the other hand, take the Clydesdale. Clydesdale horses stand about six feet tall at the shoulder and weigh over 2,000 pounds. But if you pick up a Clydesdale foal and hold it, for the rest of its life that horse will believe you could still lift it anytime you want.

The way you think about yourself sets you up for success . . . or failure. After Moses led the Israelites out of slavery in Egypt, they cheered their amazing success. All they had to do now was enter the land God promised them. So Moses picked 12 spies to check out the land. Two spies returned with terrific reports about a rich and fertile land.

The other 10 spies had a different perspective. They saw men so big that they felt like grasshoppers next to those giants.

All 12 saw the same things in the new land. But their perspectives were completely different.

How's your perspective? Do you defeat yourself before you even start something? *I'm not going out for the team because they're all better than I am. I might as well give up trying to make a friend in this school.*

Don't give in to the grasshopper perspective. You can do anything through Christ.

> *The other men who had explored the land with him disagreed. "We can't go up against them! They are stronger than we are!" So they spread this bad report about the land among the Israelites: "The land we traveled through and explored will devour anyone who goes to live there. All the people we saw were huge. We even saw giants there, the descendants of Anak. Next to them we felt like grasshoppers, and that's what they thought, too!"*
>
> **NUMBERS 13:31-33**

Chihuahuas are the only dogs born with a soft spot in the skull, where the skull hasn't come together yet—like human infants.

• • •

TODAY: Where do you feel the most like a grasshopper, like you don't belong and can't compete? Ask God to change your perspective, starting today.

May 17

FISH OUT OF WATER

Fish were made for water. On land, a fish is . . . well, a "fish out of water."

The old "fish out of water" cliché refers to people who have gotten themselves into a situation they're not made for or one they aren't equipped to handle.

But now and then, even fish break the mold. Goosefish, frogfish, and a few other bottom-dwelling fish don't just swim. They walk underwater on short, stout fins.

Mudskippers are truly fish out of water. They live in shallow water and get swept to shore when the tide comes in. When it's low tide, they can hop and skip around on the mud.

When do you feel like a fish out of water? During those minutes before school starts, when everyone is talking in the hall, by the lockers, or in your classroom? Do you wait and hope nobody notices you? Or maybe you get sick to your stomach every time the coach assigns starting positions for the big game. You just know you'll be warming the bench again. So you stare at the floor and pray you become invisible.

Believe it or not, even the coolest kids at school feel out of place in certain situations. Some people hide those feelings better than others, but everybody feels like a fish out of water now and then. Even your parents.

Jesus is the only one who fits in everywhere. He was at home with tax collectors and doctors and children. He could talk to the rich about how to enter heaven and the poor about how to be happy on earth.

And the great thing is that when Christ lives inside of you, you belong. You belong to God, and that gives you a sense of caring that takes you outside of yourself and lets you connect with other people, no matter who they are.

I can do everything through Christ, who gives me strength.
PHILIPPIANS 4:13

Walking fish and climbing perch are able to hoist themselves out of the water and onto mangrove roots by the shore, where they'll take a little stroll on land.

• • •

TODAY: Whenever you feel like you don't belong today, talk to God. Ride his coattails and know that you're able to do anything with Christ giving you strength.

Most racehorses run faster when they're out of their comfort zones. When they compete against faster horses, they run faster themselves.

• • •

TODAY: Tackle at least one thing outside your comfort zone today. Start a conversation with someone you don't know. Bring up Christ over lunch in the cafeteria or with someone from your neighborhood. Volunteer to help on a community project. Start a Bible study. Fly!

LEARNING TO FLY

Baby birds must love their nests. Everything is taken care of. They're protected. Mom keeps them warm. Food is delivered straight to them—all they have to do is open their beaks. That nest is a baby bird's entire world, and life is good.

Before long, a baby bird's feathers grow, and its wing muscles develop. The bird's parents know the chick needs to learn to fly. And flying lessons might be a little rough.

Some bird parents start by dangling a worm away from the nest so the hungry baby will reach for it . . . and fall. Other parents nudge Baby out of the nest. It sounds cruel, but the parents are there to supervise and urge their baby to hop back to the nest.

Next time, Baby will stretch its wings to break the fall. And after a few more falls, it will discover flight . . . and a whole new world outside the nest.

Christians need to learn to fly too. There's a great sense of safety in sticking with people and activities you're comfortable with. You could go though elementary, middle, and high school attending church and youth group every week. You feel safe. Those guys are in your comfort zone, your nest.

But if you never venture out of your comfort zone, it's hard to learn to fly. Maybe you'll have to leave the safety of your two best Christian friends to go talk to that new kid. You'll need to spread your wings and trust Christ to help you.

Isaiah was content to give God's message to Israel. But God told him he had bigger plans for the prophet. God wanted Isaiah to take that message to the whole world. What "flight plan" could God be calling you to?

> *[The Lord] says: "It is too small a thing for you to be my servant to restore the tribes of Jacob and bring back those of Israel I have kept. I will also make you a light for the Gentiles, that you may bring my salvation to the ends of the earth."*
>
> **ISAIAH 49:6, NIV**

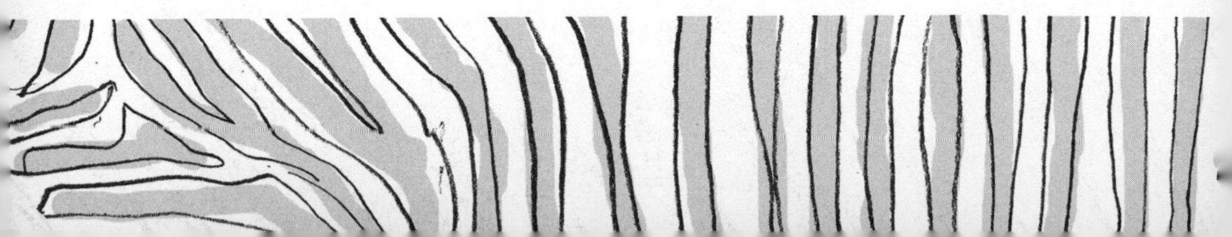

May 19

BETTER THAN THOSE GUYS?

If you've gone on a trail ride from a rental stable, your experience might have ranged from fun to frustrating. Some stables buy worn-out horses and make them trudge over the same trail a dozen times a day with riders who may not know what they're doing. So the horses run the show. They go where they want, at a pace they want, and they stop to eat when they want.

Most horse people don't allow their horses to eat with the bridle on. Yet the trail horses stop and pull leaves from trees. Or they manage to jerk the reins so they can actually graze, holding up the line of riders.

Imagine a trail ride where eight horses stop and eat constantly. But the horse you're on only stops now and then. You might think you had a well-behaved horse, right?

Wrong. That horse may be acting better than the others, but it's not behaving well. The standard of a good horse doesn't depend on what the others are doing.

Have you ever claimed that something you did wrong wasn't really so bad because other kids were doing things that were much worse? You told a white lie, but they actually stole something from a store. They made fun of someone, and you just laughed along. Your parents don't like what you're wearing, but they should see what your best friend gets away with wearing.

You're a good kid, compared to them.

The problem is, you're not compared to them. You're compared to Christ. That's our standard. Don't look to any other for comparison.

> *They are only comparing themselves with each other, using themselves as the standard of measurement. How ignorant!*
> **2 CORINTHIANS 10:12**

If your horse fights putting the bit in its mouth, or keeping its head down to be bridled, spread a drop of molasses on the bit.

• • •

TODAY: Ask God to show you one thing you've been letting yourself get away with because everybody else is doing worse things than that. Compare what you're doing with what you think Christ would be doing in the same situation. Ask for grace to be like him.

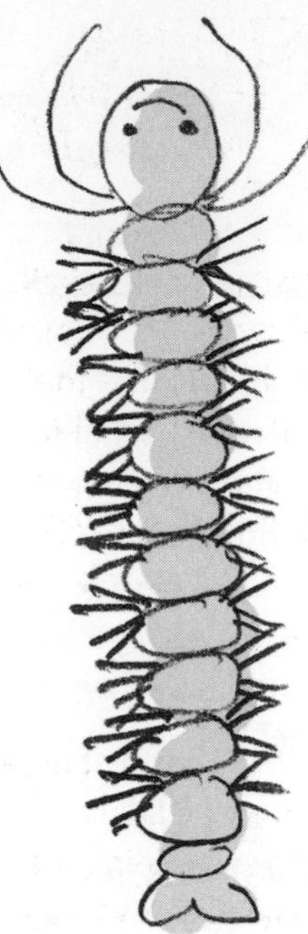

The caddisworm, or larva, builds a house around itself out of bits of stones, wood, or other material, making it look like a tiny stone chimney or a tube-shaped log cabin. The house is exactly the right size because the larva uses sensory tips on its tail to measure.

• • •

TODAY: Talk to God about your "house." Ask God to help you rebuild your sense of security on the Rock.

ROCK ON

There are about 3,000 species of the caddis fly (Trichoptera), and most of them look like small moths with see-through wings. A caddis lives only one month as an adult, but it has to survive a full year in the larva stage first. And it's the larvae that "rock on."

The tiny caddis larva builds a house around itself. The ones that live in streams take in bits of stone and glue them together into underwater "homes." For a year, the caddis carries around its own stone shelter. Whenever a fish comes along, the caddis tucks inside its stone house, and all is well.

Jesus told a parable about people who build houses on stone and others who build on sand. Both houses work fine . . . until a storm comes. The house built on rock is left standing, but the sand house crumbles. If you've ever built a sand castle by the ocean, you know what happens to your beautiful castle when high tide comes.

What does it really mean to build your house on the rock or the sand? Ask yourself what makes you feel secure. Is it when you're in the right group at school? Do you get your self-confidence from knowing you're good looking or smart or talented or well liked?

So what happens when you're eased out of your group? Or when you go through an awkward phase or you hate your hair? Or when somebody appears who's cuter or smarter or more talented?

Crash! goes the house of sand.

On the other hand, if you base your security on the fact that God loves you and Christ has made you part of the family of God, that will never change. Everything else could be stripped away, and you'd still have your relationship with God, the Rock.

Anyone who listens to my teaching and follows it is wise, like a person who builds a house on solid rock. Though the rain comes in torrents and the floodwaters rise and the winds beat against that house, it won't collapse because it is built on bedrock.

MATTHEW 7:24-25

May 21

STANDING YOUR GROUND

Turtles are no wimps. They survive on every continent except Antarctica and swim in every ocean of the world. Turtles range in size from the four-inch bog turtle to the 1,500-pound leatherback turtle. The loggerhead sea turtle weighs in at 500 pounds. Its favorite dish is the poisonous man-of-war. Several species of turtle, like the American box turtle, live to be over 100 years old. There's nothing wimpy about a turtle.

The turtle has a unique plan of attack in battle. It can't exactly run away from its predator. The snapping turtle can deliver a good blow, but even it isn't exactly up for a fistfight. So what's a turtle to do? It draws in its legs and head, stands its ground, and waits for the attacks to end.

Quietly standing your ground could be the best thing you can do in certain fight situations. If somebody calls you a name, what good does it do to call one back to that person? If a bunch of kids accuse you of thinking you're too good for them, does it help to hurl words back in their faces?

Sometimes the best solution is to stand your ground, quietly and peacefully, knowing that God has placed a protective shell around you. Instead of tuning in to what other kids are saying to you or about you, you can tune in to God and remember what he says about you. If you stand your ground, sooner or later they'll run out of accusations and names to call you.

Standing your ground isn't retreating. It's the path to a quiet victory. Give it a try.

A gentle answer deflects anger, but harsh words make tempers flare.
PROVERBS 15:1

A true turtle can't crawl out of its shell. Its bones are fused to its shell. And is that shell ever tough! A turtle shell is made up of about 60 different bones, all connected.

• • •

TODAY: The next time someone says or does something that makes you want to strike back or yell in return, stop. Consider your options. Try the turtle approach of standing your ground, knowing you're protected.

TREASURE-HUNTING

Have you ever eaten a chestnut roasted on an open fire? How about an acorn?

Acorns may not be your favorite snack, but they're pure gold to squirrels, chipmunks, certain birds, and a few insects. Some of these creatures spend most of their waking hours treasure-hunting for acorns and burying their treasures.

Take the acorn woodpecker. He pecks away, drilling holes in dead trees or in fence posts. In certain parts of the country, you can see posts covered with nice round holes. Then the acorn woodpecker hunts for acorns and pops one into each hole, trying to hide them for later.

The problem is that rival squirrels would just as soon pirate the treasures of others as "squirrel away" their own treasures. They'll happily steal every last acorn hidden by the poor acorn woodpecker.

But those squirrels rarely get to hang on to their treasure. Bears happily steal the treasured acorns too.

Red squirrels don't even bother hiding their acorns. They just drop the nuts in piles all over the ground—easy pickings for hungry bears.

What's your treasure? Money? Clothes? Music? The latest computer game?

Jesus warned against storing up treasures on earth. Nothing lasts here. You could buy the perfect baseball bat and hide it for years, only to find that it rotted while you weren't looking. You could save up gobs of money, only to have someone steal it or to have it go up in flames.

Instead, Jesus invites you to store treasures in heaven, where nothing rusts or wears out or gets stolen. If you're kind, loving, and helpful, those treasures will be waiting for you in heaven.

Wherever your treasure is, there the desires of your heart will also be.
MATTHEW 6:21

Some insects bore holes into acorns and deposit their eggs inside so the larvae will have a great meal as soon as they hatch.

• • •

TODAY: Do one thing to store your treasure in heaven. Stand up for someone at school. Help your parents or a younger sibling. Give your allowance to someone in need.

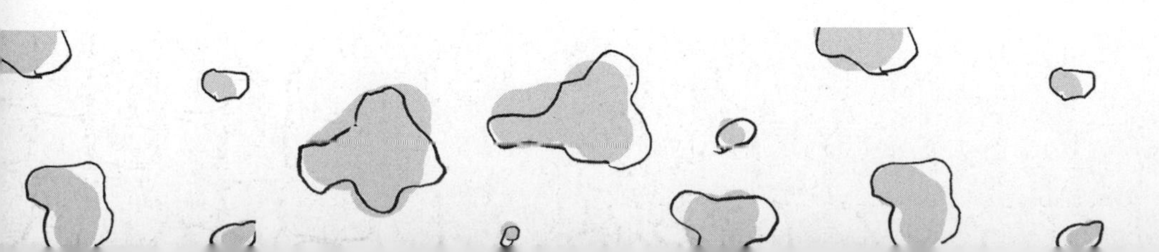

May 23

IF IT LOOKS LIKE A PIG . . .

There's a weird-looking animal that lives in the deserts of Texas, Arizona, and New Mexico and in the wilds of Central America and northern Argentina. This creature has rough, slightly hairy skin, like a pig or a hog, weighs up to 60 pounds, and has a flat pig snout. And it stinks—all the time.

Many people call this creature a skunk pig. Figures—it looks like a pig; it smells like a skunk. Others call it a musk hog, another fitting name.

But it's not a pig (it has three toes on each hind foot, unlike pigs). And it's not a skunk (it smells all the time, not just when it's frightened). It's really a collared peccary or javelina, and it belongs to its own family, tayaussa.

Hey—if it walks like a duck and quacks like a duck, it's a duck, right?

Wrong. At least, technically. But people form their own opinions based on appearances, and everybody gets confused.

Paul wrote the Christians in Thessalonica that they needed to avoid the appearance of evil. People would be watching the new believers to see what they were like. Paul didn't want the observers to be turned off to Christ because of something they *thought* they knew about Christians.

If you're a believer, people may be watching you to see what Christians are like. Obviously we're real, flawed, and forgiven, and we shouldn't pretend to be perfect or "holier than thou." But we don't want to give out false impressions of what Christians are about either.

Say you go to a party where there's drinking or smoking, or where there's an unchaperoned house to party in. Even if you don't do a thing wrong, you could get branded with the partyers just by being there. Hey—if it walks like a partyer, and quacks like a partyer . . .

Abstain from all appearance of evil.
1 THESSALONIANS 5:22, KJV

What's the favorite food of the javelina or skunk pig? Prickly pear cacti.

• • •

TODAY: Talk to God about the reputation you're giving off as a Christian. Let him point out any areas where you need to watch out for the appearance of evil.

24 May

The misunderstood pig is one of the cleanest animals around. If pigs are given clean stalls, they'll arrange separate areas for eating, sleeping, and going to the bathroom.

• • •

TODAY: Get alone with God and talk about any feelings of guilt you have. Write your sins on a piece of paper, and tell God you agree that what you did was wrong and that you want to be clean. Then tear up the paper and thank God for his total forgiveness.

DIRT-FREE

Nearly every animal likes to be clean. Even the ones that roll around in the dirt and mud get dirty for practical reasons, like to scratch themselves or to prevent sunburn.

Elephants long to be clean, but it's tough when you weigh 6 tons and stand 10 feet high, especially if you're standing in a shallow pool of water. That's why one of the first skills baby elephants develop is the art of a good shower from their own trunks. And until a baby elephant can pull that off, its mother will provide the shower for it.

Domestic animals usually prefer to be clean too. Birds preen, dogs and cats lick. Even mice lick their paws to clean themselves. And some geckos use their long tongues to clean their eyes. Animals like to be clean.

So do people. Not just clean on the outside but clean on the inside. God created you with a built-in longing to be right with him. In every corner of the world you can find people who know they need to be "clean" before God. They just may not know how.

Christ is our way to be right with God. Through his sacrifice, we are clean. At the Last Supper, Peter begged Jesus to wash him completely. But Jesus assured Peter he was already clean because he believed in Jesus. Still, the disciples needed their feet washed. And we still need regular cleaning by confessing our sins and experiencing forgiveness in Christ.

Feeling guilty is like feeling dirty. Nobody likes that feeling. If you can't get rid of your guilt, take it to Christ. He's the one who can help you feel clean again.

Purify me from my sins, and I will be clean; wash me, and I will be whiter than snow.
PSALM 51:7

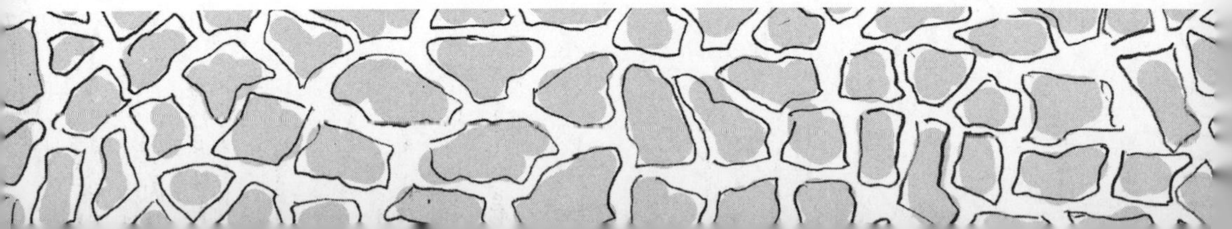

LIKE MOTHER, LIKE . . .

The praying mantis mother is a lousy parent for a number of reasons:

1. She eats her children's father.
2. She can lay lots of eggs with no problem at all, but as soon as the eggs hatch, Mommy takes off, leaving the tiny insects to fend for themselves.
3. Thanks to Mom's great example, when the praying mantis young are by themselves, they eat each other.

Other animals are blessed with great parents. Male sea horses incubate their eggs in stomach pouches. Frogs lay eggs to feed their tadpoles. Pigeons puke up their own food to feed their chicks. And snakes sometimes shiver to boost their body temperature and incubate their eggs.

Certain mammal mommies can be great parents—or horrible ones. Some polar bear moms carry their cubs in wicked weather to keep them safe. Others leave poor baby bear on an ice floe in the ocean and swim to safety alone.

Human parents come in all varieties, and we don't get much say about which ones are ours.

If you've been blessed with loving, disciplining parents, be grateful and follow their example. Nobody's perfect, so don't expect perfect parents. But thank God—and your parents—for your family.

If your parents aren't setting good examples, then look beyond them to your heavenly Father. God calls you his child, and he is the best example of a parent ever. Love your parents and pray for them. Know that God can parent your parents.

> *Even if my father and mother abandon me, the Lord will hold me close.*
> **PSALM 27:10**

The praying mantis prefers its dinner to be alive and squiggly. The mantis will eat almost any bug, including bees and wasps. And the worst thing is . . . it chews with its mouth open.

• • •

TODAY: Thank God for five great things about your parents. Now go and share that list with your parents.

26 May

GOOD OUT OF BAD

The Kirtland's warbler is an endangered North American bird. It builds its nest in a few counties in Michigan, in Wisconsin, in the Canadian provinces of Ontario and Quebec . . . and nowhere else.

The funny thing is that the survival of this warbler depends on a disaster happening every now and then: forest fires. Kirtland's warblers need young jack pines so they can live and thrive. When the pines grow too tall, the warblers have to leave and search for somewhere else to live.

But in a forest fire, not only are the old trees wiped out but their seeds are released so that new trees can grow. It takes the intense heat of a fire to force open the tight cones of the jack pine, releasing the seeds that will spawn a new forest, where the warblers can live happily ever after.

When something bad happens in your life—a friend drops you for somebody else, people start ganging up on you, you don't get a part in the play or a spot on the team—it's hard to see anything good in it. And it may be a long while before you do.

But God promises that if you trust him, he'll work things together and bring some good out of that disaster. Maybe you'll end up making friends with someone who's more loyal than your old friend. Or after getting turned down from acting or basketball, maybe you'll discover a different talent that God has built into you. Or maybe you'll just determine to work harder at the activity the next time around.

Only God knows how he'll work things out and weave events together for your best, but that's his style. So hang in there.

> *We know that God causes everything to work together for the good of those who love God and are called according to his purpose for them.*
> **ROMANS 8:28**

Cowbirds are one of the biggest threats to the Kirtland's warbler. Mama cowbird lays her egg in a warbler nest. Her baby hatches first and destroys some of the warbler eggs or chicks. If Mama cowbird lays two cowbird eggs in the warbler's nest, none of the warbler chicks will survive.

• • •

TODAY: Talk to God about one thing in your life that has gone way wrong this year through no fault of your own. Thank God that he can, and will, bring something wonderful out of the mess.

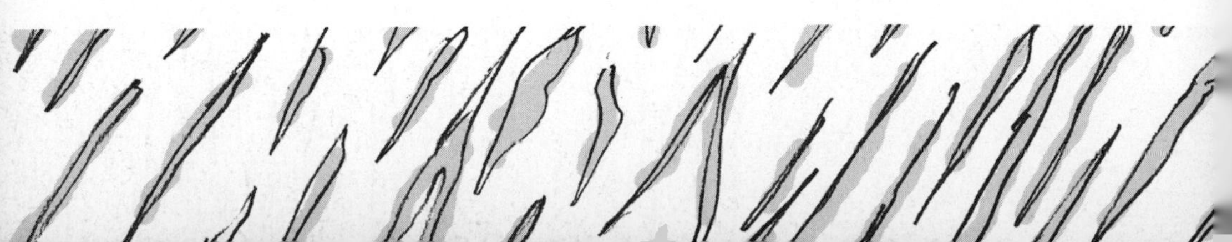

BRAGGING RIGHTS

Peacocks are beautiful, all right. But the beauty isn't exactly something they can take credit for. Peacock feathers are really brown. Each feather is made up of layers of keratin, the material we have in our hair, fingernails, and toenails. The layers of the feather are grooved so they catch and bend light. It's the light's refraction that makes the beautiful colors.

The same thing happens to a bubble or an oil slick. When light strikes a puddle of oil on your driveway, the ugly puddle looks green, blue, bronze, yellow, and orange. But you don't see the oil puddle bragging.

Doesn't it drive you crazy when people brag? They can't wait to tell you where *they* spent their summer vacation, what they got for Christmas, how much money their parents make, how much that purse cost. They're the first to let you know they got invited to the party when you didn't.

Why do people brag? If things are so great, why the need to wave it in other people's faces? Because they're insecure. They don't think people will like them if there's not something brag-worthy about them.

And how about you? Do you slip your successes into conversation, making sure people know how good you are? Do you name-drop if you've been hanging out with the most popular kid in school? Do you keep talking about that great hit you got in the ninth inning or how well you did on that test?

Even your best accomplishments come from God, who gave you your brain, your athletic potential, your talent. If you have to brag, brag about God.

Only God has legitimate bragging rights.

What gives you the right to make such a judgment? What do you have that God hasn't given you? And if everything you have is from God, why boast as though it were not a gift?

1 CORINTHIANS 4:7

Only gorillas (and some people) beat their chests as a way of showing off. And gorillas are an endangered species.

• • •

TODAY: Thank God for everything you like about yourself, everything you're proud of. Remember that all those things are gifts from him.

Prairie dogs earned their name from settlers traveling across the plains. These settlers thought that the warning calls they were hearing sounded like dogs barking.

• • •

TODAY: Talk to a parent, a pastor, or a Christian friend and make sure that you've made an honest commitment to Christ. Thank God for the warning.

FALSE WARNING

Animals have come up with some pretty cool ways to look out for one another. Prairie dogs, for example, bark—but not just any old bark. One high-pitched warning bark could signal the exact predator spotted—say, a fox or a wolf. A different bark might send all the prairie dogs underground.

The white-winged shrike-tanager of South America has a more clever warning system. One tanager acts as a scout to guard the flock and warn the others of danger. The shrike-tanager is so good at giving the warning cry that other birds rely on its call for their warning too.

Only sometimes, the tanager gives a false alarm—on purpose. When it gives the alarm, all the other birds flee the area, and the shrike-tanagers have clear sailing to get the food the tanager spotted. Tricky, tricky, tricky.

God's prophets throughout history sounded a warning that people should stop sinning and turn to God for salvation. Before Christ lived on earth, died, and was resurrected, people looked forward to a Messiah who would be God's gift to save them. Now we look back at that Messiah, Jesus, and at what he did for us.

The warning still exists for those who don't know Christ, and there's nothing false in the alarm. We need to accept the gift offered by God. A gift isn't yours until you take it. Nobody is born a Christian. Going to church doesn't make you a Christian any more than going to a hospital makes you a doctor. It's not enough that your parents are Christians and you try to be good. You need to thank God for dying for your sins, and then accept his offer of forgiveness, based on Christ's death and resurrection. The flip side of the warning is the promise that if you heed the warning, you belong to God.

Be on your guard, not asleep like the others.
1 THESSALONIANS 5:6

LOOK OUT!

In the early 1900s, dalmatians could be seen in nearly every firehouse in the United States. The breed made great firehouse dogs because they weren't afraid of horses, and the fire engines back then were pulled by speeding horses. When dalmatians first became part of the team, they were vital to successfully fighting fires. They learned to run ahead of the fire engine and bark to warn people to get out of the way.

Later, the dalmatians' role changed. Fire departments switched to gas-powered fire engines, and the dogs were afraid of the loud motors. Plus, it was dangerous for them to run along with the big trucks. So firefighters let the dogs ride up top on the trucks to the scene of the fire. Eventually dalmatians became mascots, just to keep the tradition alive.

Dalmatians were entrusted, or commissioned, with the important job of warning people to safety. Have you ever heard the term *the great commission*? Before Jesus left earth to return to his Father, he gave his followers an important assignment, a job that's come to be called the great commission. Jesus commanded his disciples to go and tell everybody the Good News about salvation through Christ.

Imagine that you knew you were leaving everybody on earth and you had a chance to make one final statement. It would probably be the most important thing on your mind, right? In Jesus' final moments before returning to his Father, he gave the disciples his great commission and charged them to tell everyone about him. If we're his followers, then the great commission applies to us, too.

Now fire trucks use a siren instead of a dalmatian to warn people to get out of the way—but people still need to get out of the way. And people still need to hear the Good News. Are you ready to share what Christ has done for you? Could you explain to a friend how to become a Christian? Can you ask just the right question at the right time and show Christ's sincere concern? You're part of the great commission.

> *Go into all the world and preach the Good News to everyone.*
> **MARK 16:15**

Dalmatian puppies are born pure white—they don't develop spots until a few weeks after birth. About 12 percent of dalmatians are born deaf.

• • •

TODAY: Talk to God about one person in your life who may not know Christ. Ask God to show you an opening to talk about Jesus—and for the guts to do it.

30 May

PEOPLE RESCUE

Those of us who love animals can't help but be concerned about the rate of wildlife extinction. *Science Daily* quoted a botany professor at the University of Texas who believes that half of all living bird and mammal species will be gone in 200 to 300 years.

Among the wild animals listed as endangered are African and Asian elephants; several species of whale, including blue whales; hybrid spider monkeys; gorillas; red wolves; leopards; cheetahs; cougars; tigers; and pandas.

Not only are wild animals endangered, but domestic breeds of animals need rescuing too. Hundreds of different kinds of yaks, buffalo, cattle, sheep, goats, ducks, and ostriches are also in danger of disappearing. According to www.Infoplease.com., an online resource of Pearson Education, one-third of the recorded 259 types of domestic farm animals in the United States and Canada could disappear soon. Animals need to be rescued.

And so do we.

What do you need rescued from? Feelings of depression? Maybe you're not sharing the way you feel with anyone. You keep acting like everything is okay, but you feel yourself sinking . . . hopeless.

A friend decides on a "better" best friend than you. Life is tough at home. Your parents fight.

Or you dread going to school every morning. Your stomach aches when you think about that bully waiting to push you around. Or those lies and rumors someone started about you. You need rescuing.

God is in the rescue business. There's nothing that God doesn't understand, because Christ experienced everything we experience. He gets it. So go to God. Talk to him. Let him rescue you.

There is no one like the God of Israel. He rides across the heavens to help you, across the skies in majestic splendor.

DEUTERONOMY 33:26

Over 1,000 animal species worldwide are on the endangered list. In the United States, about 500 animal species and one-third of fish are threatened or endangered.

• • •

TODAY: Start by being totally honest with God and telling him everything you need to be rescued from. Then pray about telling someone else how you feel—a parent, a sibling, a pastor, or a friend from church.

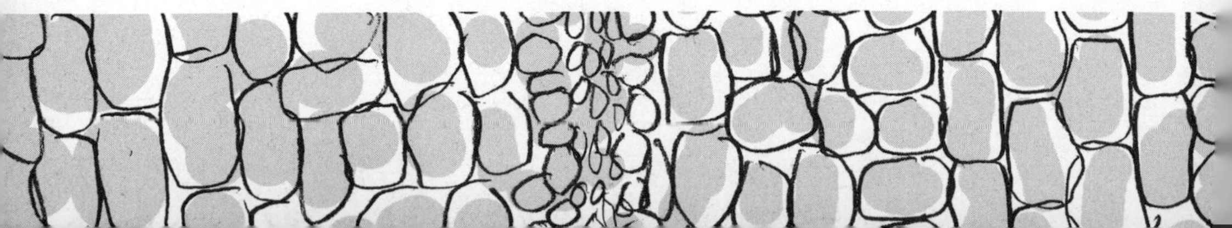

May 31

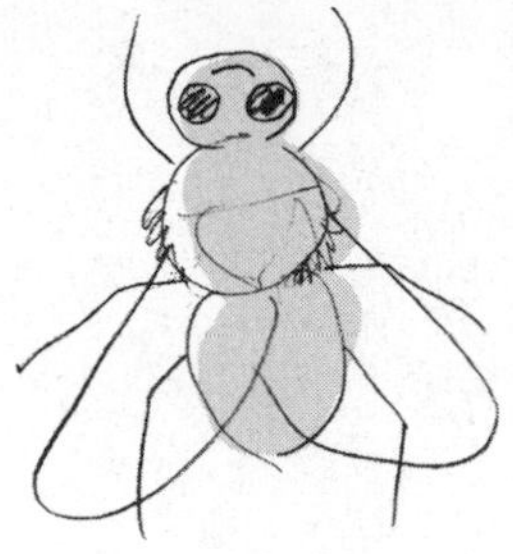

MUSCLE UP

Never enter a muscleman contest with a grasshopper. Grasshoppers may not look muscle bound to you, but a grasshopper has 900 different muscles, compared to your measly 700 or so. That explains why a grasshopper can jump 20 times its length, which would be like you jumping about 40 yards straight up—the height of a 10-story building!

Don't enter a jumping contest with a flea either. A flea speeds up 50 times faster than a space shuttle and can jump 100 times its own height. That's like you leaping over a 45-story skyscraper.

Speaking of muscles:

A caterpillar has 4,000 muscles, beating out humans and grasshoppers.

Cats have 32 muscles in each ear.

An elephant's trunk has 40,000–100,000 muscles. It can uproot a tree or pick up a tiny blade of grass.

You were born with muscles. But for muscles to develop, you have to exercise them. It takes disciplined workouts to get strong and develop big muscles. You can't buy them or just wish you had them. You need to exercise.

In a way, faith is a muscle. God gives us our faith, but we need to use it, to exercise it. If you're nervous before a test at school (and you've studied), exercise your faith. Pray that God will calm you down so you can recall the answers you know. When you see the way God comes through for you, your faith grows. Then the next time you're nervous about a test or a speech, you ask for help again. Your faith will get stronger when you see God answer your prayers and as you understand more about his character.

No training is more important than spiritual training. Start exercising that faith muscle!

Train yourself to be godly.
1 TIMOTHY 4:7

A fly can react to a swat 10 times faster than you can swat. (Hint: Flies take off backward, so aim from behind.)

• • •

TODAY: Ask God to show you a small thing you can trust him for today. Overcome your shyness and talk to a new person. Raise your hand in class. Stand up for something you know is right.

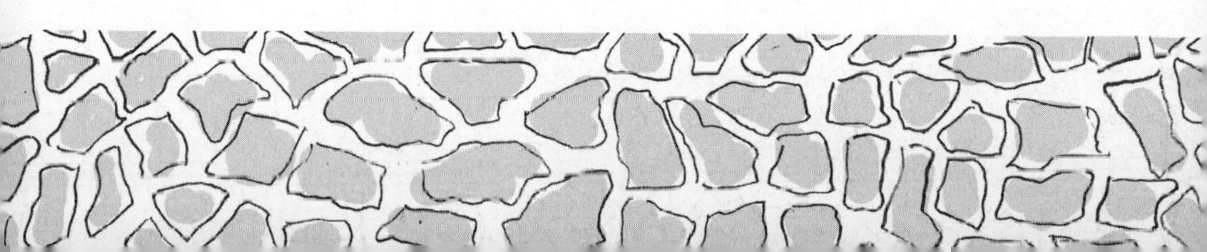

The following animals are true hibernators: bats, squirrels, hamsters, hedgehogs, chipmunks, swifts, and nighthawks.

• • •

TODAY: Write down three major goals for your summer. Then prayerfully make detailed plans about how to reach each goal.

LAZY, HAZY, CRAZY DAYS

Some animals get through the winter by hibernating—going into a deep sleep, usually retreating to a den or burrow or some other kind of shelter. There are different degrees of hibernation. True hibernators, like woodchucks, appear to be dead because their heart rate slows and their body temperature drops, and they're almost impossible to wake up.

Brown bears sleep in caves during the winter, but they're not true hibernators since they can be awakened. Reptiles, lizards, and snakes go into an inactive state called a torpor, and they can be awakened too.

Diapause is a period of suspended animation—temporary dormancy—that insects and butterflies enter when it's cold, and they come out of when they're warmed up. Spring peepers, small tree frogs, also go into a partially frozen hibernation.

All three states of sleep are pretty tempting when the lazy, hazy, crazy days of summer roll around. Without school, why get up early, right? All you have to do is roll over and go back to sleep. Sure, eventually you'll want to get up because you're hungry. But there's nothing going on after that. And there's always room for one more nap.

Maybe you don't want to sleep your summer away. You prefer the "torpor" state of dozing. Or you could find exactly the right television show to let you drift into a state of suspended animation as your mind numbs to everything else around you.

And then summer's over, and it's time for another year of school.

Make this summer different! Declare this the summer you accomplish a big goal you haven't had time for during the year. Read through the New Testament on your own. Get in great shape by walking or jogging every day. Learn to play tennis or chess. Make regular visits to a nursing home and develop friendships there. Volunteer to help at a community soup kitchen. Don't waste your summer. Give it to God.

As a door swings back and forth on its hinges, so the lazy person turns over in bed. Lazy people take food in their hand but don't even lift it to their mouth.
PROVERBS 26:14-15

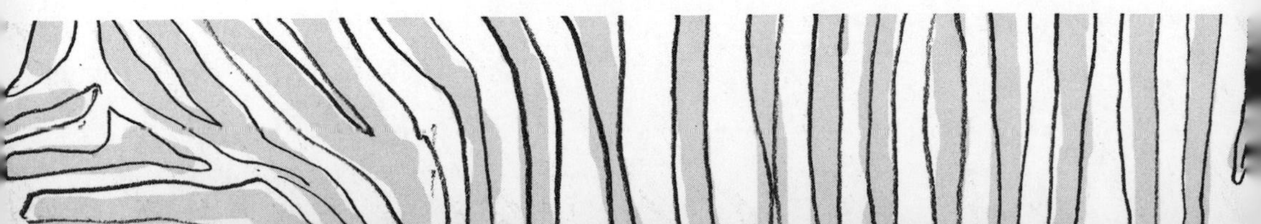

LITTLE STEPS

Otters are the best swimmers in the weasel family, but they're born afraid of the water. At birth, Mom and Dad Otter have to dig a special land exit out of their dens for their babies because they'd be too scared to take a water exit.

Yet if they're going to make it in the world, young otters need to learn to swim. That's why their parents have developed a clever long-term strategy for getting their babies to be swimmers.

First, the baby otters are encouraged to play on the shore. Otters love to play. They wrestle with each other and ride on their parents' backs. The young otters watch while their parents dip into the scary water and come back with food for them.

Next, on one of their piggyback rides, the parents wade into the water. Their young cling to their backs for dear life, and the parents go back on land and play some more. Pretty soon, those dips into the water go so deep that the parents are swimming with their babies clinging to their backs.

Before long, Mom and Dad Otter swim underwater, dumping off their riders, which thrash and fight against the water until their parents swim back and rescue them. Eventually, the young otters realize that when they stop fighting, they simply float. And from there, swimming comes easily.

Sometimes big fears can be conquered through little steps. If you're terrified of giving a speech in front of your class, start small. Make it a point to answer questions in class. If you're afraid to learn a new skill, like babysitting or yard work, start by shadowing someone else and then becoming an assistant.

God may have given you a talent—swimming, running, singing, writing—but you probably won't start out winning the Olympics, starring in an opera, or writing a best-selling novel. Take little steps. As you use your talent, God will give you more.

To those who use well what they are given, even more will be given, and they will have an abundance. But from those who do nothing, even what little they have will be taken away.
MATTHEW 25:29

Otters would rather play than eat much of the time. An otter will sneak up behind a fish, arch its back, dart forward, and grab the unsuspecting fish with its bare paws. Often the otter will let the fish go, ending its game of catch and release.

• • •

TODAY: Talk to God and figure out one talent you think you might have but you've been afraid to try out. Prayerfully develop "little steps" to reach that goal.

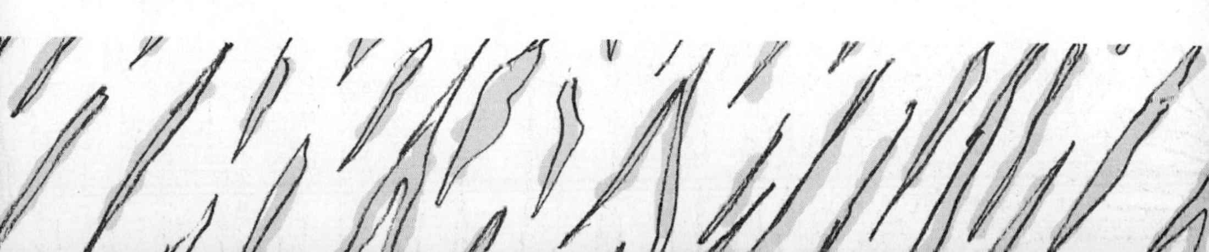

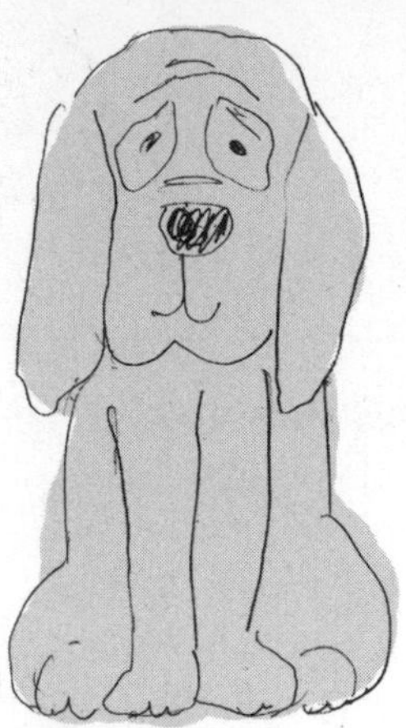

DETECTIVE DOGS

Bloodhounds have found fame in the movies as ace crime-fighting dogs. Before that, Sir Arthur Conan Doyle wrote about bloodhounds in Sherlock Holmes novels.

With their great sense of smell, bloodhounds really do make good detectives. If they're well trained, they can sniff out the bad guy or find the innocent victim.

You have about 5 million olfactory sensory cells that pick up smells. Not bad. But before you pat yourself on the back, you should know that dogs have you beat. A bloodhound has 220 million olfactory cells in his nose. That's 44 times as many as you have.

How's your spiritual sense of smell?

When you hear somebody talking about a new way to "commune with the universe" or "become one with nature," are you automatically drawn in? Or can you sniff it out, test it, and see if it's true to what you know about Christ and the Bible?

New religions and new takes on old ones spring up every year. Some of them sound pretty good. God loves everybody, so doesn't it make sense that everybody would go to heaven? Or what about the idea that there's nothing after death, so we should enjoy life and do whatever we want?

When you hear things like that, your spiritual detector should go off. Just because something sounds good doesn't mean it's true. Paul praised the people of Berea when he visited them with the Good News about Christ because they checked out everything he said against the Scriptures (Acts 17:11).

Scripture and God's Spirit inside you can make you an ace spiritual bloodhound.

You will know the truth, and the truth will set you free.
JOHN 8:32

The bloodhound is the only animal whose testimony can be used as evidence in a U.S. court of law.

• • •

TODAY: Write down any of the things you've heard people say about God (on TV, in the classroom, or at a friend's or relative's house) that don't ring true to you. Check out those thoughts by comparing them with what the Bible says. Ask someone you trust to help you search through Scripture if you need to.

June 4

SACRIFICE

The killdeer is a type of plover (wading bird) that gets its name from the alarm call it makes: "Kill-deeah." It's about as big as a robin and looks like a small sandpiper, with long legs. But the most impressive thing about the bird is that it's a sacrificial parent.

Killdeers mate for life after the male woos the female by singing to her and making several nests for her to choose from. Each nest is scraped from a graveled area on the ground, with rocks and pebbles that look like their future speckled eggs. When the eggs are laid, Mom and Dad Killdeer take turns incubating them.

When anyone approaches the nest, the killdeers swing into action. If both parents are there, one stands by the nest to block the sun while the other begins its sacrifice. The bird moves away from the nest, dragging one wing along the ground, pretending to be hurt with a broken wing. It's a convincing act, and animal predators are usually fooled into going for the adult and leaving the eggs (or babies) alone.

When the act works, just as the predator lunges for the grounded killdeer, the bird flies away. When the killdeer isn't quick enough, it sacrifices its life for its babies.

We know that the ultimate sacrifice was what Christ did by dying on the cross for us while we were still sinners.

Since Christ has sacrificed so much for us, it makes sense that we would want to sacrifice for him. Yet making sacrifices has always been tricky. In Old Testament times, people made animal and grain sacrifices to show their need for God's forgiveness. But God made it clear that he wanted their love and their hearts, not empty sacrifices.

In the Bible's original language, the word *sacrifice* is the same word as *gift*. God has given us everything, so it's hard to give him a gift. The best we can do is to love him and do what he tells us—walk with him, love others, help the poor, and tell others about Christ.

> *Let us offer through Jesus a continual sacrifice of praise to God, proclaiming our allegiance to his name.*
> **HEBREWS 13:15**

People like the killdeer because the bird's favorite foods are insect pests, like flies, ticks, mosquitoes, beetles, and grasshoppers.

• • •

TODAY: Throughout the day, thank God for everything in your life. As part of your "continual sacrifice of praise to God," thank him for the hard parts of your life.

Loons only lay two eggs, and one is laid a few weeks before the other. The first hatchling will be the dominant loon in the nest and will always get to eat first. If the parents can't find enough food, they will only feed their older offspring, even when it means the younger loon will die of starvation.

• • •

TODAY: If something is bugging you, have a heart-to-heart with God. Be free to let it all out, knowing that God loves you, no matter how crazy you sound.

CRAZY AS A LOON

Loons are migratory birds that hang out on lakes and large ponds in Canada, the northern United States, Iceland, and Greenland. With bright red eyes, a black head, and a body that reaches three feet long, the bird looks awkward and clumsy when it comes on land.

But the feature that earns loons the cliché "crazy as a loon" is their cry. Loons make four basic, crazy cries:

Hoot: The hoot is the least crazy call, made to the loon's mate and chicks on the lake.

Yodel: When a male defends his territory, he lets out a loud, weird yodel.

Tremolo: This "insane laughter" is sounded in times of fear.

Wail: The haunting wail of a loon comes only at night and can be heard for miles around, never to be forgotten.

Be honest. Have you ever felt as crazy as a loon? You want to scream out loud, punch a pillow, hit a person, kick the nearest puppy, ram your fist (or head) through the wall?

You're human, loaded with complex emotions that can build up like volcano lava and threaten to erupt. Feelings can make you wonder if you really are crazy.

But you don't have to give in to those feelings. You have a much better option than screaming, hitting, kicking, and going crazy. You don't have to take your anger and frustrations out on other people. You have God.

God understands completely. He loves you no matter what you're feeling. He accepts you, craziness and all. Let him help.

> *Delirious, I chattered like a swallow or a crane, and then I moaned like a mourning dove. My eyes grew tired of looking to heaven for help. I am in trouble, Lord. Help me!*
>
> **ISAIAH 38:14**

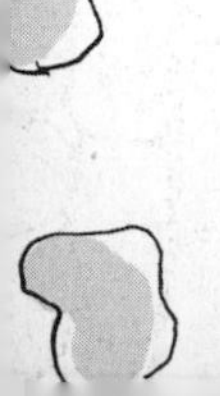

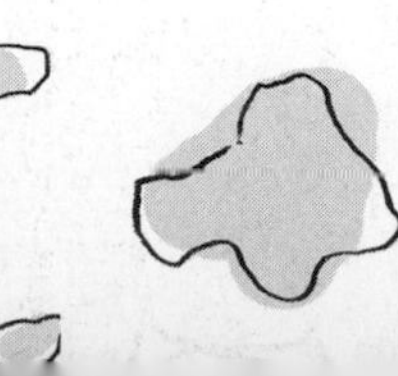

SOMETHING TO CROW ABOUT

Crows understand the art of helping each other out of tough situations. They've worked out intricate ways to come to the aid of a fellow crow in need.

First, they communicate. More than 50 warnings have been observed by scientists, and each communication is based on one syllable: "caw." Depending on the volume and tone, "caw" can signal where to get food or when it's time to fly away. It can be an all-clear signal or a sympathetic mourning call over a dead crow.

Communication travels so fast to the other crows that if one crow is shot in the air, its friends gather to help the wounded bird before it even hits the ground.

Owls are the crow's biggest enemy, and a crow by itself is no match. But sometimes a number of crows gang up and close in on the owl, cawing so loudly that the owl can't stand it. Soon, the owl gives up and leaves.

If necessary, crows may join in a counterattack. Several crows draw the owl's attention in front of it, with hecklers staying ahead to confuse the owl. Meanwhile, other crows sneak up and attack from behind.

Crows have discovered that there is strength in numbers.

When you're in trouble, you don't have to go it alone either. One of the best ways to build solid friendships is to open up to a friend. Share your honest feelings, even if you think they make you look weak or strange. When you open up, chances are your friend will too. And your trust will grow as the friendship deepens.

Helping a friend works both ways. If you think your friend is going through something hard, ask if you can help. No one should have to go it alone.

A person standing alone can be attacked and defeated, but two can stand back-to-back and conquer. Three are even better, for a triple-braided cord is not easily broken.
ECCLESIASTES 4:12

Scarecrows don't work on crows. The birds are too smart. They watch the scarecrow for movement. When they don't see any motion, they go back to calmly devouring the corn.

• • •

TODAY: Ask God to show you someone who needs your help—a kind word, a listening ear, a friend to sit by in class or at lunch.

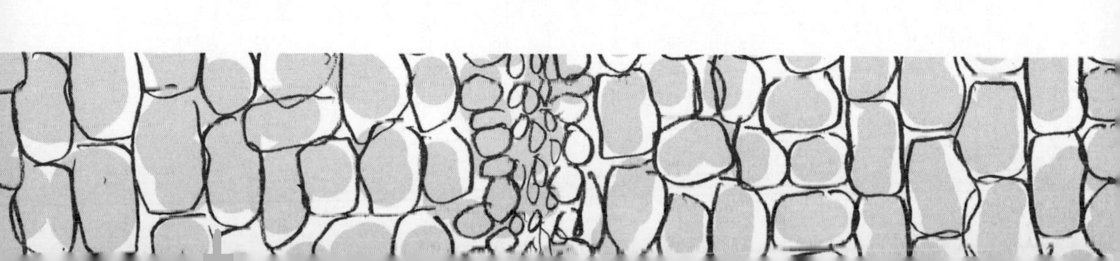

The owl's mouth isn't just an opening between its beak like other birds', but an opening that stretches from ear to ear. All the better for Mr. Owl to swallow a mouse or bird whole. Since owls have no teeth, Mr. Owl simply pukes out the hair, bone, and feathers.

• • •

TODAY: This week, be early on at least one assignment at school and one chore at home. Start developing the habit of not procrastinating.

WISE UP

When other animals of the frozen forests of North America see the great horned owl making a nest in February—the dead of winter—those creatures might not call the owl wise. It's too early to be nesting. The other birds won't surface for a good two months.

But the female owl goes about her business in the snow, finding an abandoned nest and making it her own. Soon she lays her eggs with the howling wind ruffling her feathers. For weeks she sits on her eggs, trapped on top of the nest. If she leaves, her eggs will freeze. Somehow she weathers storms and fends off hunger for four weeks until her owlets hatch.

Then the real work begins, and the reason for early nesting becomes clear. Owlets have giant appetites. It takes both parents to get enough food to fill their babies' bellies. For the next three months, owlets grow so fast that they need food constantly. The owls can supply food because they started so early. With leaves still off the trees, they can easily see prey. And snow still on the ground makes spotting rodents easy.

The early owl gets the mouse. Maybe that's why owls are considered so wise.

Are you the early bird or the last-minute type? When you get an assignment on Monday that's due Friday, when do you start on it? Monday after school? Or Thursday night in a panic?

Don't be a procrastinator, a person who puts things off. Nobody enjoys that last-minute cramming for a history test or the all-nighter to get that book report finished. But life is sweet when you can turn in an assignment a day or two early.

Procrastination is a habit—a bad habit. But it's not genetic, and it doesn't have to be permanent. You don't have to stay the last-minute type. Give yourself a break. Just do it . . . now. You won't be sorry.

Those too lazy to plow in the right season will have no food at the harvest.
PROVERBS 20:4

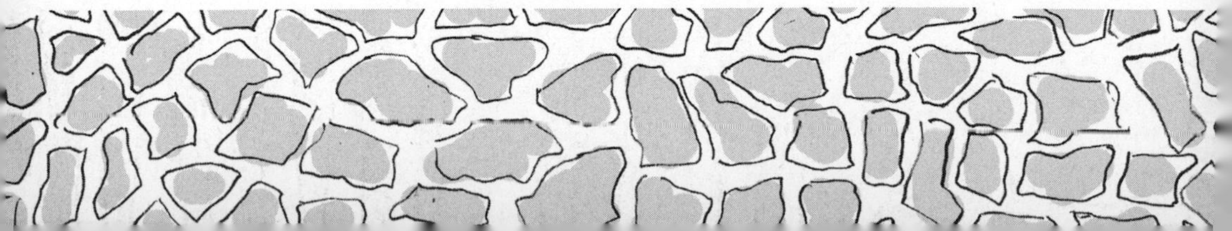

TO BEE OR NOT TO BEE

We know that bees are amazing team players. They all work toward building the hive, making honey, and serving the queen. But what's even more amazing than the bees' ability to work together is their ability to pull together when disaster strikes.

If a hive is destroyed or the queen is injured, honeybees kick into high gear and take on new responsibilities. Bees that were hive cleaners might instantly turn into repair-bees. Nurse bees take on double duty as guards. Normally each bee contributes its own kind of "bee juice" to the honey. In a crisis, bees may change their fluids to balance out the hive.

Honeybees see the need and immediately jump in to help. They're willing to change their normal way of life—at least temporarily—to do more than their assigned duties.

How do you function in a crisis? If your mom is in the hospital, do you see the needs at home and jump in to help without being asked? You could make lunches for your little siblings. Or you could do the dishes or empty the dishwasher or run the vacuum cleaner.

Outside of your own family, if you see a friend in crisis, do you do what you can to help? If your friend has to miss classes, you could take him the assignments. Or if she needs a place to retreat when things are crazy at home, you could invite her to hang out at your house.

When the Old Testament Israelites were led away in captivity, the people who were left with the ruins of Jerusalem had to kick into gear and rebuild. Sometimes we have to do the same thing.

> *The Lord says . . . Be strong, all you people still left in the land. And now get to work, for I am with you, says the Lord of Heaven's Armies.*
>
> **HAGGAI 2:4**

A young honeybee's first job is to clean its room. Shortly after the bee is born, it cleans its cell in the hive, then leaves it so another bee can be raised there.

• • •

TODAY: Ask God to show you specific places where you can jump in and help—with your family, with your friends, or at church.

Some small monkeys, such as marmosets, don't make great mothers. The female hands over her babies to the father immediately after birth. Except for the nursing, Father Marmoset does it all from there on out.

• • •

TODAY: Be honest with God and talk about other families you've believed are better than yours. Admit that you have no idea what goes on in other families. Then thank God for the family he has given you, and pray for them.

GOLDILOCKS, SCHMOLDILOCKS

Once upon a time, Papa Bear, Mama Bear, and Baby Bear lived happily ever after in the woods . . . until Goldilocks came to visit.

Wrong.

Unfortunately, bear families don't work that way. Male and female bears are great during courtship, spending time together and acting lovey-dovey. But afterward Mama Bear goes off all by herself to have her babies—away from Papa Bear.

Once the babies are born, Mama Bear raises her cubs by herself and refuses to let Papa Bear come near them. He doesn't even try. But if he did, he'd be very sorry.

So the truth is, that happy little bear family doesn't exist. And any chairs in the cave belong to Mama Bear and Baby Bear.

Sometimes other people's families look ideal. But you never know what goes on inside someone else's house. You might think you got shortchanged in the parent department, but your buddy may believe your parents are the best.

Don't waste time envying anyone else's parents or family. Thank God for where he has placed you, and pray for your own parents.

The psalmist in Psalm 73 declared that all he desired was God. He didn't need anything or anyone else. That's a pretty good attitude. If you are going to wish for more of anything or long for somebody, let it be for God himself.

Whom have I in heaven but you? I desire you more than anything on earth.

PSALM 73:25

PERFECT LOVE

When baby animals get frightened, they run straight to their parents. Whether it's a tiger cub or a kitten, a baby looks to the one it loves and trusts whenever there's trouble.

Pets are the same way. A dog frightened by a vacuum cleaner will probably hightail it to its owner and best friend.

People who know how to gentle horses understand that big horses can be scared by little things. Out on a ride, if there's a flag waving in someone's yard, the horse might stop cold and freeze with fear. The wise rider won't answer that fear with anger or punishment. Shouting and abuse aren't the way to help anybody through fear. Instead, a practiced rider will talk soothingly to the horse, stroke its neck, and assure the animal that everything is okay.

Love conquers fear.

Everybody is afraid of something from time to time. You might be afraid to start classes at a new school or begin a new year in an old school. Maybe you have to perform—in a big game, at a concert, or in a school play—and you get the jitters. Or you might be afraid that your parents are going to get a divorce or that a grandparent is dying.

Where do you go when you're afraid?

In Daniel 10, Daniel has a vision in which a man or an angel appears to him, frightening him. The man calms Daniel and tells him not to be afraid because he is very precious to God.

There's no better reason to stop being afraid than this: God loves you.

> *Such love has no fear, because perfect love expels all fear. If we are afraid, it is for fear of punishment, and this shows that we have not fully experienced his perfect love.*
> **1 JOHN 4:18**

FANCY NAMES FOR SOME OF OUR FEARS OF ANIMALS:

agrizoophobia: fear of wild animals
arachnophobia: fear of spiders
herpetophobia: fear of creepy, crawly things
hippophobia: fear of horses
ichthyophobia: fear of fish
melissophobia: fear of bees
musophobia: fear of mice
selachophobia: fear of sharks
ephebiphobia: fear of teenagers

• • •

TODAY: Talk to God honestly about anything you're afraid of. Think about how much God loves you, and let his love put out the fear.

THE PET JURY

Poor cats. They get blamed for so many of our allergies. People tend to give dogs a free pass when it comes to allergies, especially short-haired dogs. After all, it has to be those fuzzy, furry, long-haired cats that make us allergic. Guilty, guilty, guilty!

But the truth is we're not allergic to cat hair. We're allergic to a cat's saliva. If cats didn't like being clean, there would be no problem.

Cats bathe by licking themselves. Licking leaves saliva on their coats. The saliva dries and flakes off. Then sensitive people breathe in tiny airborne particles of saliva and have an allergic reaction.

Knowing what causes your cat allergies isn't going to stop you from sneezing. But it might help you understand where your cat's coming from. The cat isn't out to get you—it's only trying to keep clean. And that's a good thing, right?

It's easy to judge animals harshly, but it's even easier—and more destructive—to judge other people harshly. Do you write off a classmate because he looks weird? Do you take one look at the new girl and decide she's not cool enough to hang with your group?

Even worse are the judgments that come out of prejudice—prejudging someone because of race, culture, or even religion.

God alone is Judge. You're not. And Jesus, who had every right to judge, loved and accepted people. He didn't even judge the people who were considered the biggest sinners of his time—financial scammers and the sexually immoral. Instead, he won them over with love and acceptance, in spite of what they'd done. How can we think we have the right to judge anyone?

God alone, who gave the law, is the Judge. He alone has the power to save or to destroy. So what right do you have to judge your neighbor?

JAMES 4:12

About 10 percent of people have some kind of cat or dog allergy. About 20 to 30 percent of people with asthma have pet allergies too.

• • •

TODAY: Look around at the people you see and admit to yourself and God that you've judged some of them. Tell God you're sorry. Then make an effort to get to know at least one of the people you've judged.

FREAK OUT OR FLEX?

If cats have a fall, they nearly always land on their feet. They need to fall from a height great enough to let them flip over, but not so high that their legs can't absorb the shock.

Why can cats land on their feet when most other animals can't? Because they're so agile. Cats have an extremely flexible spine. When a cat feels itself falling, it can twist its back so its head and forelegs are pointing toward the ground. Then all it has to do is whip its tail over to help it hoist its rear end up. And the cat lands on its feet.

Flexibility is a plus for most animals. Equestrians work with their horses to develop flexible backs and get rid of stiffness. When a horse is flexible, life is easier for the horse and the rider.

How flexible are you? Can you do a back bend? touch your toes? do the splits?

More important, how flexible are you on the inside? When your parents change their minds and decide you can't go to the party on Saturday after all, do you freak out or flex? When you thought you'd be going on a great summer vacation but you end up at your grandparents' farm again instead, can you flex?

Every day you get opportunities to react to disappointments and letdowns. You can choose to be stubborn and angry, but it doesn't help. Or you can accept the change and make the best of it. You might even try to see what surprises God has in store for you with the new plan.

Change your hearts and stop being stubborn.
DEUTERONOMY 10:16

Cats don't always land on their feet. If they fall more than one or two stories, they'll probably be severely or fatally injured. More and more cats have been injured from falls in recent years because there are more high-rise apartment buildings. Cats that get hurt during falls from these apartments are said to have high-rise syndrome.

• • •

TODAY: List five things you're regularly stubborn about (bedtime, homework, school clothes, phone time, Internet use). Ask God to soften you and make you flexible.

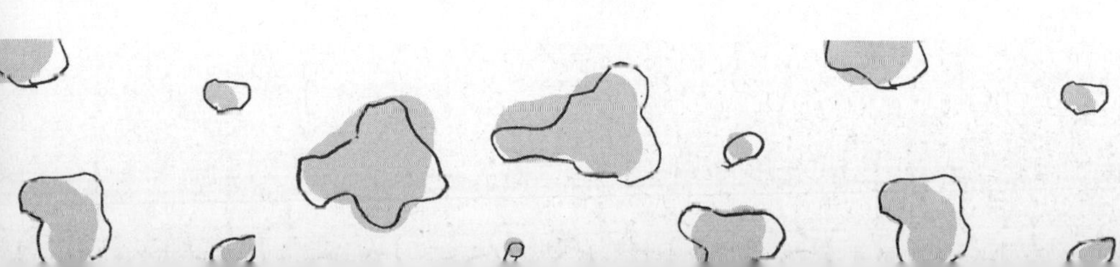

A reverse sneeze isn't really a sneeze at all. In times of excitement or stress, a dog's trachea can narrow so that not enough air enters the lungs and your dog appears to be choking. Most episodes go away on their own. But you might help by talking softly and stroking the dog's upper throat to help it relax.

• • •

TODAY: The next time something upsets you, see if you can excuse yourself and find a quiet place to be with God. Be still and realize that the God of the universe is on your side.

REVERSE SNEEZING

If you have a short-nosed breed of dog, like a pug or boxer, you might have seen it gag or appear to be choking. With legs spread wide apart, the dog gasps and snorts, trying to take in air. People call this a "reverse sneeze."

In a regular sneeze, a dog pushes air out through its nose. But in a reverse sneeze, it pulls in air through its nose, usually when it gets excited. Dog owners can get pretty scared because it looks like the dog can't breathe.

Yet as horrible as the whole thing looks and sounds, reverse sneezing isn't harmful to the dog. As soon as the pup calms down, it will be as good as new. Although you might be able to help the dog calm down faster, the episodes usually take care of themselves as your pet settles down.

You might not have had full-blown panic attacks, but most of us get panicky now and then. Maybe it's the big test coming up or the speech you're supposed to make. Maybe you feel the twist in the pit of your stomach every time you carry your lunch tray around the cafeteria, looking for a table that will have you.

Whatever sends you into a panic, you can handle it with God. Stop. Take a deep breath. And remember that God is in control. You have infinite resources to deal with every situation because the Spirit of Christ lives in you.

Be still, and know that I am God! I will be honored by every nation. I will be honored throughout the world.
PSALM 46:10

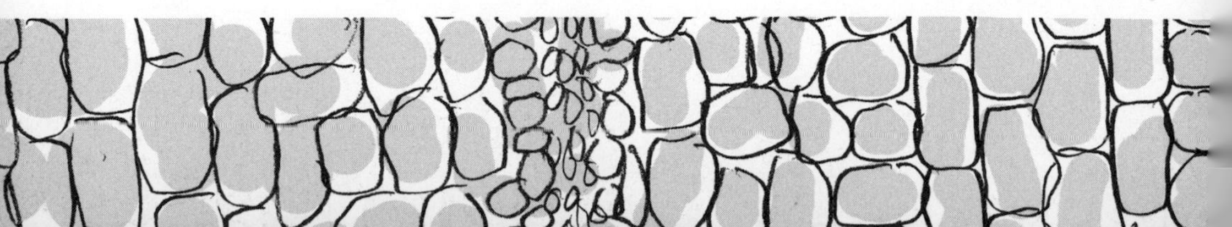

June 14

THE PERSISTENT BIRD GETS THE WORM

A woodcock doesn't look all that special. It's a brownish game bird with short legs and a long bill. But in tough situations, the woodcock proves to be resourceful and persevering. Normally the bird has little trouble getting worms, even though it has to eat its weight in food every 24 hours. With eyes set far back on its head, the woodcock can probe the ground for food with its long bill and still see 360 degrees around to keep watch.

But if the ground is hard and dry, the woodcock's normal techniques for getting worms don't work. Worms dig deeper into the ground to find moisture, and the bird's bill can't reach them. So the persistent woodcock flattens itself on the ground, spreads out its wings, and beats the ground, flapping its wings furiously. After a while the bird stops, listens, then does the whole operation all over again.

Underground, the worms think they are hearing rain instead of woodcock wings, so they burrow up toward the surface, where they're easy pickings for the waiting woodcock.

It's always a good idea to have a plan B.

How persistent are you? If you try out for the baseball team and don't make it, is that the end? Or do you practice every day so you'll do better at the next tryout?

If you need information and can't find it on the Internet, do you dig deeper and come up with other ways to get what you need—like a phone call, an interview, or a trip to the library?

If you don't understand a homework assignment, do you let it go and tell the teacher the next day that you couldn't do it? Or do you try harder, ask for help, reread the chapter?

Don't give up. God will always help you find a way.

Patient endurance is what you need now, so that you will continue to do God's will. Then you will receive all that he has promised.

HEBREWS 10:36

Woodcocks are pretty ordinary-looking birds, but they go by some extraordinary names: timberdoodle, owl snipe, big mud snipe.

• • •

TODAY: Talk to God about anything you've given up on lately. Prayerfully reconsider trying again and taking a different angle on it.

Some say woodchucks got their name from the Cree Indian word *wuchak*, a name used for several small animals that looked alike. Others claim English settlers coming to the United States saw the odd animal and called it chuck, which meant "little pig."

• • •

TODAY: Think of the messiest area you're responsible for (your room? your locker? your desk?), and come up with three things you can do to organize that space. Then do it—today.

AS ORGANIZED AS A WOODCHUCK

Woodchucks also go by the name of groundhogs. They're cousins to squirrels and marmots and spend most of their lives digging. A woodchuck can dig itself out of sight in minutes by loosening dirt with its front paws and kicking the dirt out with its back paws.

You might think that an animal digging in the dirt would be dirty, but not the woodchuck. Woodchucks are very disciplined about keeping themselves clean. They practice a routine of picking off burrs and licking themselves.

Woodchucks are organized in building homes too. A woodchuck digs a burrow with separate bedrooms, a bathroom, and a couple of exits, including a supersecret exit that's hidden until needed. Bedrooms are kept neat and clean, with Mom Woodchuck changing sheets of clean, dry grass regularly. Woodchucks just may be the animal world's best housekeepers.

Speaking of cleanliness and organization, how's your room? Neat and clean? And that locker and your desk at school? Would you call them organized?

Nobody's born organized. We learn organization skills and have to continually overcome our natural desire to be lazy and undisciplined. But keeping your room clean is bound to be easier than doing massive cleaning when your mom finally loses patience with your mess. Besides, being organized saves time and aggravation. It's no fun to lose homework assignments or forget when things are due.

If you're not sure how to start organizing your life, ask your parents or an organized friend for help. Charts and day planners can help you keep records all in one place.

Proverbs says that discipline brings happiness. Why not give it a shot?

> *If you reject discipline, you only harm yourself; but if you listen to correction, you grow in understanding.*
> **PROVERBS 15:32**

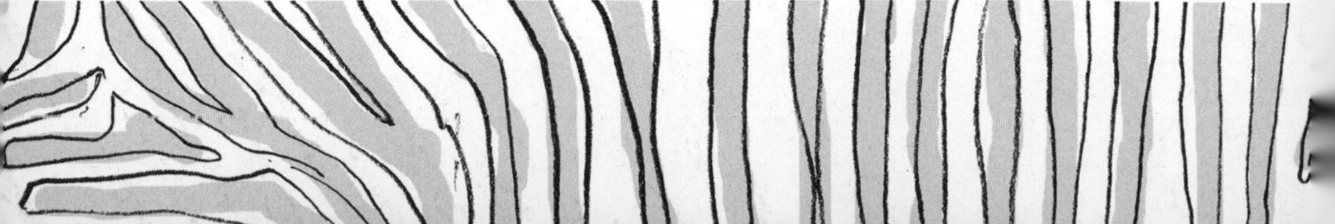

June 16

DID CURIOSITY KILL THE RACCOON?

When it comes to curiosity, cats have nothing on raccoons. Raccoons are born inquisitive, a characteristic that can help them survive . . . or get them killed.

Raccoons love to explore and can find food in all sorts of places, from trash cans to hollow trees. Their cleverness leads them to unique ways of getting dinner. To catch a crayfish, the raccoon runs its finger underwater until a crayfish snaps its claw around the finger. Then the coon sweeps the crayfish out of the water and into its mouth.

Raccoons have fewer saliva glands than dogs, so swallowing some food is difficult. But the coon dips the food into water first, earning it the name "wash bear" in German.

The same curiosity that helps the raccoon find food can also get the coon into trouble. Farmers make traps with shiny objects because raccoons can't resist investigating something shiny. Raccoons break into houses, undoing locks and hinges, and making themselves pests.

God-given curiosity is a wonderful gift. Little kids have it. They can drive you crazy with questions, from why the sky is blue to where puppies come from. You should hang on to your own childlike sense of excitement. Explore the world God has given us.

But don't forget that curiosity can sometimes lead us into traps. Don't be in a rush to try everything new. If a friend claims to have a pill that will keep you awake to study for a test or help you forget your problems, put on your brakes.

Give God your curiosity, and let him help you use it in the right ways.

> *Don't act thoughtlessly, but understand what the Lord wants you to do.*
> **EPHESIANS 5:17**

Raccoon prints are easy to pick out by the water's edge or in mud or snow. The prints are about three to three and a half inches long and look like a child's handprint, with long fingernails.

• • •

TODAY: Find out one thing about God's world today—the name of a tree in your yard, the type of cloud in the sky, the dynamics of a rainbow.

A group of swans is a flight or a wedge, although some call the group a bevy or a herd.

• • •

TODAY: Prayerfully look for opportunities to step up and take leadership in at least one area of your life.

STEP UP, SWANS

The tundra swan, often called the whistling swan because of the sound of its wings in flight, is smaller than the trumpeter swan. Most people agree it is the most graceful bird on the water or in the air. These swans migrate from winters in North Carolina to northern Alaska and Canada, traveling up to 3,700 miles to get there.

Their flight north is hurried because the nesting season is so short. A swan has to build a nest, lay eggs, and raise the babies before the water freezes again and all the swans have to fly south.

Although there might be as many as 500 swans in a flock, they take off with a strong flurry of wings at the same time and rise 6,000 feet into the air, where they can soar above storms and mountains.

To reach the nesting area in time, they fly up to 100 miles per hour, a feat they can only accomplish by flying in a V. One swan has to step up and take the lead, blazing the trail for the others and reducing air resistance for the ones behind it. When the lead swan tires, it drops back, and a new leader steps up. In this way, the whole flock can fly 70 percent farther than one swan could fly alone.

When you live for Christ and for others, there will be countless times when God's Spirit urges you to step up. It might mean that you should take the leap and tell your youth leader that you want to lead a small group Bible study. Or it might mean that when everyone else at your lunch table is gossiping about the girl who isn't there, you step up and stop the meanness.

The world needs leadership, and God could call you to lead at any minute. Even if you don't take on a grand position of leadership, you need to be ready to step up.

> *Speak up for those who cannot speak for themselves; ensure justice for those being crushed. Yes, speak up for the poor and helpless, and see that they get justice.*
>
> **PROVERBS 31:8-9**

June **18**

TAMING THE SHREW

At a distance, shrews are pretty cute looking creatures. One of the world's smallest mammals, some shrews are only three inches long and weigh less than a dime. If you saw a family of shrews out for a night's walk, you couldn't help but say, "Awwwww." Mom would be in the lead. Behind her, each baby shrew would be locked onto the tail of the little shrew in front of it, each hanging on with its teeth. The family definitely sticks together.

But there ends the compassion of the shrew.

Nervous and short-tempered, the shrew lives to eat. A shrew downs almost its entire body weight every day and spends day and night hunting food. Shrews hunt alone because they can't trust each other and are unsociable. In fact, they have no qualms about eating their fellow shrews if the opportunity arises.

The bite of a venomous shrew can be deadly. Its saliva is packed with poison, which paralyzes prey or even kills it. A shrew has no problem attacking and eating mice two to three times its size. It may leap onto the back of an even bigger animal and bite its neck, then eat it, bones and all.

Ounce for ounce, the shrew is one of the most vicious animals in a shrew-eat-shrew world.

It's easy to be nice to your buddies. But how are you doing with people outside your group? Jesus showed sincere concern and compassion for all kinds of people—the Samaritan woman with a bad reputation, despised tax collectors, social outcasts like lepers, people from other races and backgrounds (Gentiles), the rich, the poor. And he's our example.

Ask God to help you look past your own needs and your own friends, and to make room for people who need to see the compassion of Christ in you. Make sure your interactions with others are life giving, not poisonous.

> *Don't look out only for your own interests, but take an interest in others, too.*
> **PHILIPPIANS 2:4**

The saliva of a venomous shrew contains enough poison to kill 200 mice. But if the shrew goes without food for seven hours, it will die.

• • •

TODAY: Make it a point to look out for someone you wouldn't normally consider to be in your circle of friends. Start a conversation, invite this person to eat lunch with you, save a spot beside you in class.

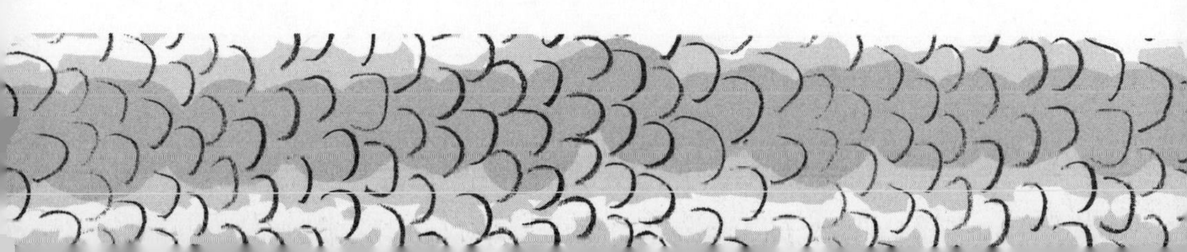

Blue-eyed white cats are more likely to be deaf than white cats with brown eyes. If a white kitten has gold or green eyes, or if it has a patch of dark fur on its forehead, it probably won't be deaf.

• • •

TODAY: Have an honest talk with God and figure out if you've plugged your ears to certain things he wants you to do. Ask for God's help to do them.

DEAF CATS DON'T MEOW

Only 1 in 100 cats is deaf, but pure white, blue-eyed cats are often deaf. Half of all white cats have genetic deafness. The same gene that gives a cat a white coat causes a defect in the inner ear. When the defect comes into play, the sound vibrations can't be changed into nerve impulses, and the cat can't hear. Unfortunately, there's no cure for this kind of deafness.

Sometimes people own deaf cats and don't realize they're deaf. The owner might just think the pet is stubborn, refusing to come when called.

It's important to recognize the signs of deafness in your pet. A deaf cat may sleep too much. It may seem lost in the world, disoriented and forgetful. A deaf cat won't come running at the sound of its favorite cat food hitting the food dish. The cat might not meow because it has never heard the sound before.

You can find out if a cat is deaf by doing a simple hearing test. Clap your hands or shout behind your cat. If the cat doesn't turn around, it probably can't hear you.

Do you need a hearing test—a spiritual hearing test? The Bible warns us about spiritual deafness, which means tuning out God and what God says in the Bible. In Zechariah 7:11, the Lord tells the prophet Zechariah, "Your ancestors refused to listen to this message. They stubbornly turned away and put their fingers in their ears to keep from hearing."

When you know God wants you to be kinder to your little brother but you keep being mean, you're plugging your ears. When you know God wants you to hang out with different friends who won't get you in trouble but you don't change, you're becoming spiritually deaf.

The good news is that there's a cure for spiritual deafness: obedience. Do what God tells you to do. And your spiritual hearing will get better and better.

Faith comes from hearing, that is, hearing the Good News about Christ.

ROMANS 10:17

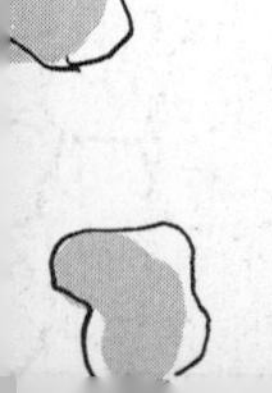
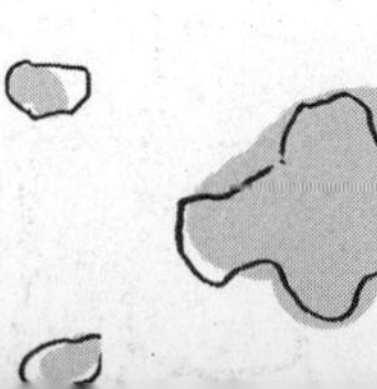
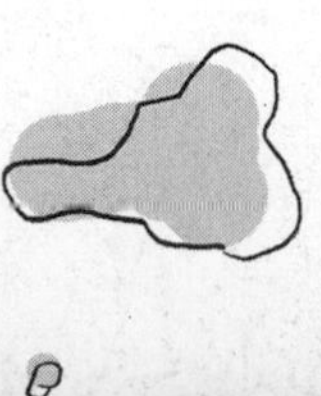

FLAKY ANIMALS

Most animals lose their hair. Even though you may not see a dramatic change in some creatures, they gain and lose fur according to their growth spurts or depending on the season.

Horses in the north grow a thick coat to keep themselves warm in the winter. The colder the winter, the fuzzier the horse. When spring comes, horses shed.

Other animals lose cells and body coverings so slowly you might not notice. Water turtles gradually lose their leg coverings as they swim. Other animals lose dry skin to make room for new cells and moist skin.

When Christ comes into our lives, we're born again and changed forever. But we're still on earth, stuck in these bodies—still capable of sinning, even though we don't want to.

We need to keep changing, losing some things and taking on others. It won't happen fast, but it will happen. You kick a bad habit, such as eating too many sweets or spending too much time in front of the television or computer. Then you start a good habit—healthy eating, going on long walks or runs, taking up a new hobby.

God changes you on the inside, too, making you more caring toward others. You grow kinder, and the kindness shows in little ways, like helping your mom or dad with dinner or sticking up for someone at school. As we follow Christ, we should become more like him.

God isn't finished with you yet. Change is coming. Are you ready for it?

> *Throw off your old sinful nature and your former way of life, which is corrupted by lust and deception. Instead, let the Spirit renew your thoughts and attitudes.*
> **EPHESIANS 4:22-23**

SOME DOGS THAT DON'T SHED (VERY MUCH):

Shih tzu
Yorkshire terrier
Maltese
Bichon frise
Poodle
Italian greyhound
Border terrier
Cairn terrier
Havanese
Miniature schnauzer
Boston terrier
Scottish terrier
Chinese crested
Australian terrier
Airedale terrier
Greyhound
Irish water spaniel
Basenji
Kerry blue terrier

• • •

TODAY: List five ways you've changed (for the better) in the last two years. List five ways you still need to change. Ask God to change you on the inside.

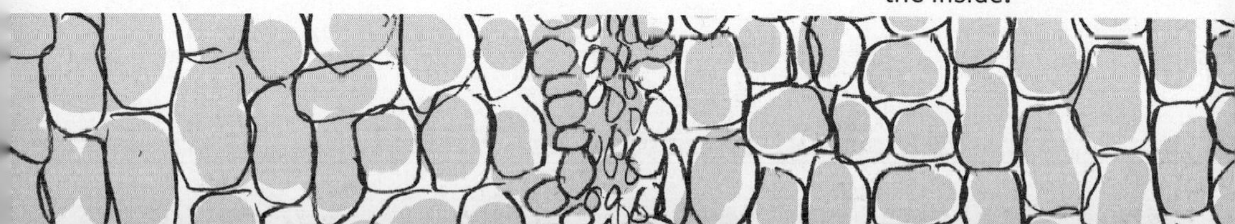

Horses age about 2.2 years to our one, although the formula changes when the horse gets older.

• • •

TODAY: Pay special attention to the clock and notice the difference in how the hours feel. Which hours seem to fly by, and which drag? Ask God to help you use all those hours wisely.

DOG YEARS

People used to try to figure the age of a dog in human years by using the formula of one human year equaling seven dog years. So your three-year-old dog would be 21 in human terms.

More recently, a new formula has been devised to take into account a dog's fast growth in the early years: 10.5 dog years per human year for the first two years, and four dog years per human year after that. So your three-year-old dog would be 10.5 + 10.5 + 4, or 25 years.

Cats are on a similar time line as dogs. A cat is considered to be middle-aged at age seven and old at age 10.

Time is a funny thing. That last hour you sit in school watching the clock may feel like several hours, but recess or lunchtime flies by in minutes. Christmas seems like it will never get here, but your book report deadline arrives before you know it.

Maybe you can't wait to get out of the school you're in. You can't wait until you're in high school or college or out on your own.

Hang on. God created time, and he controls it. Don't be in such a hurry to rush through your days.

On the other hand, you don't have to regret the passing of time either. Time is a gift. God gave it to us because he knew we'd need it to accomplish everything he's planned for us to do. All we have to do is live within it.

> *You must not forget this one thing, dear friends: A day is like a thousand years to the Lord, and a thousand years is like a day.*
>
> **2 PETER 3:8**

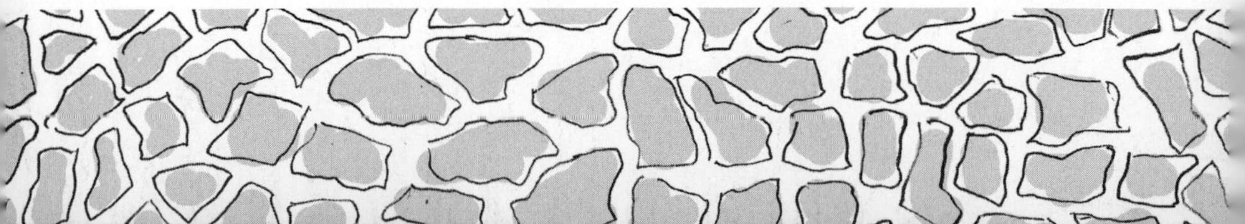

MICE IN MOTION

Most people aren't that crazy about mice, but you have to feel sorry for the creatures. Mice are constantly in motion. They have a very high metabolism, and their bodies never stop to rest. A mouse's life is tough, and it takes all the little guy's energy just to live through the day. All it can think about is getting enough food.

As a result of so much hurrying and scurrying, mice don't live long. The average life span of an indoor mouse is four or five years at best.

Do you feel like you're hurrying and scurrying through your own life? Sometimes you can get so caught up in school, activities, and friends that there's no time for you to stop and think. You run from sports practice to band, from class to the mall with friends. And in between, you have to text your friends, make a few phone calls, and go online.

Do you ever want to yell, "Stop!"?

Even Jesus tried to take a few time-outs to refuel and get out of the rat race of life. He went off to the wilderness to be alone with the Father (Luke 5:16). He prayed all night on a mountain (Luke 6:12). He tried to have a retreat on the other side of the lake with his disciples, but the crowds got there ahead of him (Matthew 14:13).

Don't be afraid to say no to friends so that you can steal some one-on-one time with God. Even 15 minutes alone in your room can help you refuel. A no-computer/no-phone Saturday could give you the break you need to get refreshed.

If the Son of God needed time alone, so do you.

Better to have one handful with quietness than two handfuls with hard work and chasing the wind.
ECCLESIASTES 4:6

You could keep a pet mouse on a table without a cage because the mouse would be afraid to jump from such a height. (Your mom might not like it if you use your dining table though.)

• • •

TODAY: Make a "date" with God—a time when you can get alone with God, read through the Psalms, pray, or go on a long walk and appreciate the beauty of his creation.

23 June

WALKING THE DOG

You can learn a lot by walking a dog. Not only can you pick up some pointers by observing what your dog does right, but you can even learn from the things your dog does that drive you crazy.

Maybe your dog is one of the well-trained ones, and your walks are orderly. Your clever dog responds to voice signals and the slightest nudge or tug on the leash, so you are always in control. Walks are fun and relaxing for both you and your dog.

Walking with God goes more easily when we follow his commands too. It's up to us whether we'll do what we know God wants us to do or fight and struggle every step of the way.

If God nudges you to tell someone about Christ, either you can do it or you can try to stall or run the other way. If you tell yourself that this year you're going to read the Bible every night before you go to bed, you can do it or you can go back on your promise. If you do what you've told yourself you would do, though, you'll fall asleep content, knowing you did something that will help you in life and deepen your relationship with God.

Or you can keep forgetting to read the Bible, and the struggle is on.

Some dogs drive their masters crazy by stopping every minute to smell the roses . . . and the fire hydrant . . . and the invisible rabbit path . . . and the footprints of the neighbor's dog . . . and. . . . If you're in a hurry, you probably don't appreciate your dog's laid-back attitude.

But there's something to be said for doing exactly what your dog does on those frustrating walks—you can stop and notice what's around you. Sometimes you have to take time to sniff.

We are merely moving shadows, and all our busy rushing ends in nothing.
PSALM 39:6

No matter what the economy is like, two jobs that are needed more than ever are babysitting and dog walking. By the way, male dogs don't actually have to lift their legs to do their business. The action is more about marking territory and letting other dogs know how tall and fit this male dog really is.

• • •

TODAY: Take a walk and don't come back until you've noticed 10 things you never really noticed before. Talk to God on your stroll.

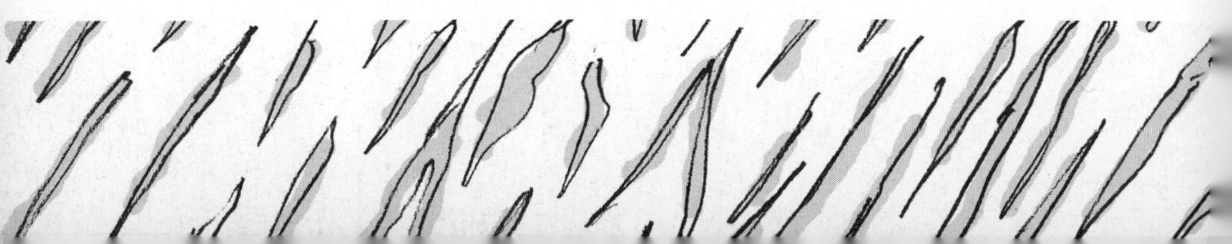

June 24

TO BARK OR NOT TO BARK

Dogs bark. The number one complaint of neighbors about other people's pets is barking dogs. Most dogs bark so much that they end up useless as watchdogs. They continually bark at the vacuum cleaner or a woodpecker, and eventually the "bite" goes out of the bark.

Domestic dogs bark more than wild dogs. Puppies of wild dogs bark, but when they grow to adulthood, wild dogs stay silent unless it's an emergency. Otherwise any sound might give away their location. If a wild dog barks, it means it. The bark is usually a warning to its puppies, telling them to hide, or an alert for the pack.

The exception to the barking domestic dog is a truly fearless watchdog intent on attacking. If that dog is silent, look out.

Do the members of your family bark at each other? Shouting can be catching. If your parents shout at each other or at you, you might have developed the habit of shouting back. Or you might have come up with shouting all on your own. You shout at your older sister for hogging the bathroom or at your little brother for coming into your room without knocking. You shout at your dad when he tells you to go do your homework or at your mom when she tries to wake you for school.

Shouting isn't just a bad habit that's rude and abusive. It's also fruitless. It doesn't work. You don't get your way by shouting. You just get anger and hostility in return.

It takes less effort to talk in a nice, calm voice of reason than it does to shout something snotty. Plus, it's more effective to be nice.

Besides, if you bark too much, somebody could hang a Beware of Dog sign around your neck.

Get rid of all bitterness, rage, anger, harsh words, and slander.
EPHESIANS 4:31

There's one breed of domestic dog that's the exception to the barking dog: the basenji. Some basenji never bark. Others will bark only if they learn to do it from another dog.

• • •

TODAY: Catch yourself if you so much as raise your voice at anyone today. Then stop it. Shoot off a prayer to God and ask him to help you control what comes out of your mouth.

Puffer fish have extremely poisonous internal organs. Any animal that eats it will have trouble breathing and may even die. Yet many humans find puffer fish delicious and risk eating the fish . . . but only when it's prepared by an experienced chef who knows how to get rid of the poison.

• • •

TODAY: Talk to God about any bullying you've done yourself or watched being done to another person. Next time you see a bully in action, defend the victim, not the bully. Ask God for the courage to stand with the weak against the strong.

BULLY TRAP

The animal world is filled with bullies. Mothers of the slow loris know this and set a trap of sorts for those bullies who would try to hurt her babies. The loris is a small, wooly primate with huge eyes and the cuddliness of a teddy bear. A newborn loris clamps onto the belly of its mother or father for safety.

When the young loris gets a little older, it's placed on a branch while its parent goes off in search of food. That's when Mom sets her trap. The loris produces a toxin that can poison most any enemy when mixed with saliva. Mother Loris licks this toxin onto her babies before leaving them. When a bully attacks, it ends up a victim of its own meanness.

The South American false-eyed frog has bright blue eyespots on its rump that look like real eyes. When a bully predator comes close for an attack, the frog faces the attacker rump first and the false eyes give off a stinky, gooey liquid that repels the bully.

Bullying is wrong. But it goes on in every school and everywhere in cyberspace. Bullying can take the form of physical pushing and shoving or threatening to use force. Or it can be verbal and emotional abuse—picking on someone and saying hurtful things to them and about them.

Hopefully you're not a bully, physically or emotionally. But it's just as bad to watch bullying take place or to go along with it. It can happen at a sleepover, when the girls e-mail hurtful things to someone who isn't there. It can happen on the ball field, when teammates gang up on the weakest player.

Bullies eventually get caught in their own traps. Nobody really admires a bully or wants to be friends with one. Bullying another person shows your flaws, not the other person's. God expects us to help the weak, not hurt them.

If you set a trap for others, you will get caught in it yourself. If you roll a boulder down on others, it will crush you instead.

PROVERBS 26:27

SWIMMING UPSTREAM

The king salmon weighs in at 20–100 pounds, lives in fresh and salt water, and has one of the most amazing life cycles in the animal kingdom:

Salmon begin life as eggs laid in the gravel of a riverbed. Only 5 percent survive and hatch.

The fry, or baby salmon, are swept out to a lake. But their amazing sense of smell locks in the smell of the exact location where they were hatched.

In the parr stage, the parr, or growing salmon, get bigger in the freshwater lake.

In the smolt stage, the parr leave the lake and travel to the mouth of a river, where they grow and wait.

The salmon swim into the ocean and live there for one to four years.

Finally, the salmon return to freshwater and prepare for a six-month journey upstream. The fish will not eat during the whole journey.

The salmon's journeys upstream might be hundreds of miles, filled with danger from birds and predators, as they jump 15 feet in the air over the top of waterfalls.

The salmon arrive at the exact spot where they were hatched. The females lay their eggs, and the males fertilize them. Then they swim away to die. Mission accomplished.

Salmon set quite an example! How's your stick-to-itiveness? Could *you* accomplish a goal if you knew it would take you four years? Big goals take big staying power.

Do you want to work out and build muscles, or maybe lose weight? It won't happen overnight. You have to commit to a plan to reach your goal. Same goes for mastering a new language, learning to play the guitar, or becoming a writer, musician, or artist. The secret is to set small goals that will take you to your big goal.

With Christ's power at work inside you, there's nothing you can't accomplish.

Dear brothers and sisters, never get tired of doing good.
2 THESSALONIANS 3:13

Many of the salmon species are officially endangered. Salmon runs are now only one to three percent of the numbers of migrating salmon Lewis and Clark met up with on their journeys in the early 1800s.

• • •

TODAY: Prayerfully tackle one big goal you want to accomplish. Split that goal into five to ten little goals—things you can see yourself doing. Ask God to help you commit to the long-term goal.

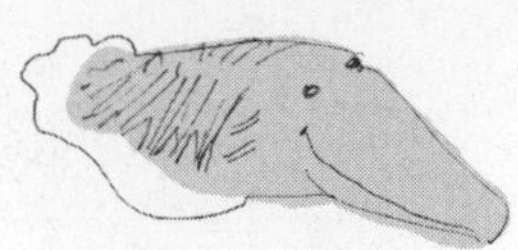

WHAT'S YOUR SMOKE SCREEN?

The brown inky squirt from the body of the cuttlefish was once used by artists as the main ingredient for the dye sepia.

• • •

TODAY: Have a long talk with God and be totally honest and sincere. Talk to God like you'd talk to your closest friend, with no special, fancy language—just love and truth.

Cephalopods are a group of animals that includes octopuses, squid, and cuttlefish. They carry around built-in defenses to hide themselves from their enemies. When an attacker comes close, they squirt a dark, inky fluid in the water that surrounds the enemy so the cephalopods can make a clean getaway.

The octopus has an added trick to throw the enemy off track. The moray eel loves to attack in the dead of night, when the octopus's inky smoke screen does no good. So instead, the octopus shoots out a chemical that confuses the eel's sense of smell.

You may not have an inky or chemical smoke screen, but you may have your own brand of defense to keep people from getting too close. Maybe it's sarcasm—the ability to say something snide to keep the other person off guard. Maybe it's humor. Just when things get serious and people begin to open up, you pull out your invisible joke book and turn everything into a big laugh.

Letting the right people in isn't always easy. But if you want your friendships to grow, you'll need to go deeper and be more open. You might have to work at being honest and sincere with people. And that's all right. You've got time. As trust develops with a friend, ask God to help you open up and to help your friend open up to you too.

But if you're putting up a smoke screen before God, that's a bigger problem. No one can pull the wool over God's eyes. God already knows whatever you think you're hiding from him. He knows you better than you know yourself. Trust him. God is the one person you can always be totally honest with.

> *Let us go right into the presence of God with sincere hearts fully trusting him. For our guilty consciences have been sprinkled with Christ's blood to make us clean, and our bodies have been washed with pure water.*
>
> **HEBREWS 10:22**

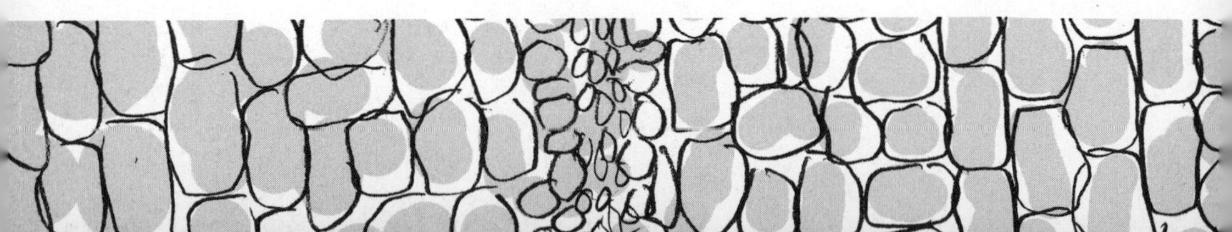

June 28

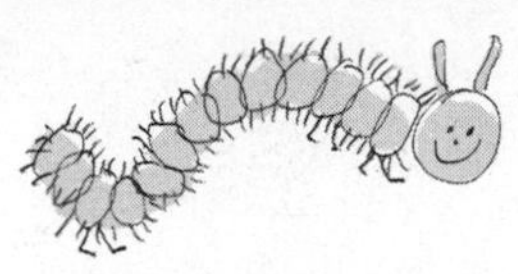

GUT INSTINCT

Instinct is the built-in way an animal acts in certain situations. Birds know when to migrate north and south. Newborn kelp gulls automatically peck at the red spot on their mother's beak to make her hurl out food for them. Sea turtles move toward the ocean the instant they hatch on the beach.

Spiders of the same species spin webs in exactly the same way. A spider that spins a silk cocoon fashions a base, then walls, and finally a lid after she lays her eggs inside. The building pattern is so set in the spider that if it is moved after finishing the base, it will continue where it left off, making walls that have no base, then laying eggs that fall through to the ground. Then the spider will make the lid as if all were well.

God gives us a kind of instinct too—a built-in sense of his existence. In every part of the world, people have known that there was more to life than what they could see, a god they either worshiped or feared. Pascal, a French philosopher, wrote, "There is a God shaped vacuum in the heart of every man which cannot be filled by any created thing, but only by God, the Creator, made known through Jesus."

God has given us other internal messages too. For the most part, we know right from wrong, good from bad. James wrote that God's Word has been planted in our hearts: "Get rid of all the filth and evil in your lives, and humbly accept the word God has planted in your hearts, for it has the power to save your souls" (James 1:21). Sometimes we may have to get rid of the junk that clouds our best, built-in instincts.

> *They know the truth about God because he has made it obvious to them. For ever since the world was created, people have seen the earth and sky. Through everything God made, they can clearly see his invisible qualities—his eternal power and divine nature. So they have no excuse for not knowing God.*
> **ROMANS 1:19-20**

Female wasps instinctively know how to count. A mother wasp lays her eggs in individual cells and supplies each egg with live caterpillars for her babies to snack on. The number of caterpillars is always the same for each wasp. Girl babies get more food than boys. In one species, Mom Wasp gives each baby boy wasp 5 caterpillars and each baby girl 10.

• • •

TODAY: Think about your earliest thoughts about God. Were there times you believed because you could see God through his creation? Can you recall moments when you instinctively knew right from wrong?

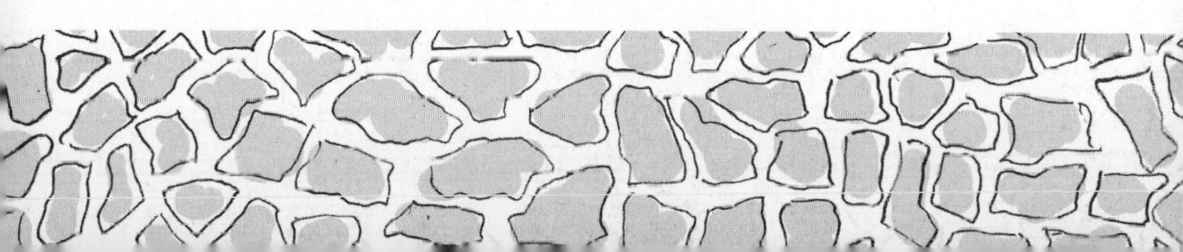

The *howler* in howler monkey is actually misleading. Male howls sound like a powerful roar, and female howls sound more like a pig's grunt.

• • •

TODAY: Ask God to whisper to you during the day. Be sensitive for that still, small voice. Whisper back.

GOD'S WHISPER

Some animals are loud! The blue whale, the largest animal on earth, is also the loudest animal on earth. When the blue whale lets out a cry, it reaches up to 188 decibels, a whistle that can be heard for more than 500 miles underwater. Jet planes only get up to 140 decibels, and anything over 85 hurts our ears. As loud as you shout, you'll probably never get over 70 decibels.

The next loudest animal is the howler monkey from Central and South America. The noise it makes can be heard from three miles away.

Several birds are in the running for the loudest bird award. The winner is the kakapo of New Zealand, a big parrot that makes a sound like a foghorn. Next is probably the nightingale. The song of a nightingale at 90 decibels can damage your eardrums if you're too close for too long.

Since God is the almighty Creator of the universe, you'd expect him to speak with a deafening roar. No doubt God has a loud voice. He called the world into being. He said, "'Let there be light,' and there was light" (Genesis 1:3).

When the prophet Elijah was running away from evil King Ahab, God met the prophet on a mountaintop. A windstorm hit the mountain, then an earthquake with fire. Elijah expected God's voice to come through those loud, catastrophic events. Instead, he heard God's gentle whisper.

Don't wait until you hear God shout. Listen for his whisper—that still, small voice inside of you that tells you to stop what you're doing or shows you something you should do. The more you listen to the whisper, the more naturally God's will and your will become one.

> *After the earthquake there was a fire, but the Lord was not in the fire. And after the fire there was the sound of a gentle whisper.*
>
> **1 KINGS 19:12**

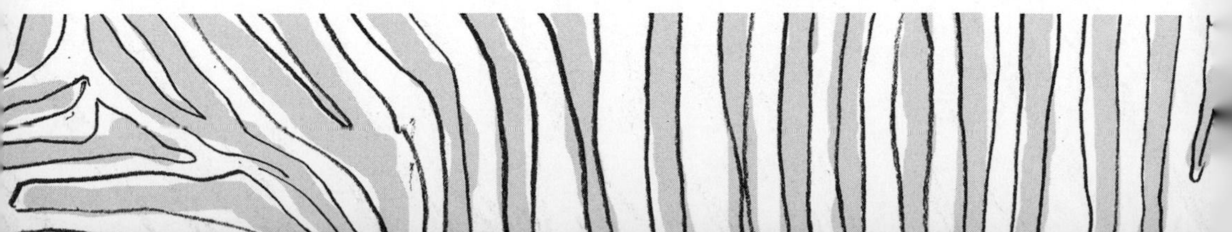

June 30

STRAYING FROM THE NEST

Bird nests come in all sizes and shapes. The most common nests in North America are songbird nests, like the robin's. Nests are cup shaped and rough on the outside but smooth inside, with layers of grass and other soft material.

Most tropical birds build hanging nests that are out of the reach of predators. Some of these nests contain a dead end, a fake entrance to fool predatory snakes.

Woodpeckers peck holes in tree trunks. Tailorbirds of Southeast Asia sew leaves together for nests. And the Polynesian megapode found on the islands of Niuafo'ou and Fonualei in the South Pacific buries its eggs in volcanic ash at the rim of a crater so the heat from the volcano will incubate the eggs.

Birds aren't the only ones who build nests:

A hare's nest is a form.

A possum's nest is a drey.

A wasp's nest is a vespiary.

In a way, you have a nest too: your home. And your home and your family are the most important things in your life (next to God). You might think it's cooler to hang out with friends than to even talk to your parents or siblings. Friends will come in and out of your life, but you will always have your family.

Are you as polite to your family as you are to your friends? Do you try to be as helpful? as kind? Sometimes we shortchange our family members because we're secure in their love, but we should never take them for granted.

Someday it will be time to "leave the nest"—to go off to college or a job and do whatever you're meant to do with your life. But even then, remember your nest. Family is important, no matter how old you are.

A person who strays from home is like a bird that strays from its nest.
PROVERBS 27:8

The edible-nest swiftlet of Southeast Asia makes its nest out of hardened saliva. The see-through nest is the main ingredient of bird's nest soup, a Chinese delicacy.

• • •

TODAY: Make an extra effort to be nice to every member of your family. Treat them as if they're your best friends. Ask them about their lives and listen to their answers.

Which is smarter: the dog or the cat? On the one hand, the brain structure of cats and humans is so similar that more cats are used for neurological studies than any other animal. On the other hand, did you ever hear of a Seeing Eye *cat*? Or a rescue *cat*? Or a police car with *Feeline* on the license plate, instead of *K-9*?

• • •

TODAY: Talk over with God any tough thing you're going through now. Look for ways this experience can help make you a better and stronger person.

PEA BRAIN

Which animal has the biggest brain, and which has the smallest? For sheer size, sperm whales win the biggest brain prize, even though they are not the biggest whale. Behind sperm whales come elephants, other whales, dolphins, walrus, giraffes, hippos, seals, horses, polar bears, gorillas, and cows.

But if you take into account the size of the animal compared with brain size, humans and ants lead the way, and the mouse looks pretty good too.

As for the smallest brain, it's a toss-up between anemones, sponges, jellyfish, and green lizards. (Actually, some scientists argue that anemones and sponges don't even have brains.)

An interesting phenomenon of brains in similar species is the difference between the brain of a wild animal and the brain of a domestic one. Wild dogs, for example, have bigger brains than domestic dogs. The life of your average family pet is a lot less challenging than the life of a dog in the wild. At home, Fido skips the hunt and finds dog food in his personalized bowl. The only predator your pet is likely to face is the neighbor's cat. So as pets' lives became easier, apparently their brains got smaller. In fact, the brain of a wolf may be up to one-fifth larger than the brain of a wolf-sized dog.

Challenges and trials make us grow! If everything in life were perfect and easy, we wouldn't need to mature as human beings. It was probably the hard times in your life that pushed you into becoming a better person or learning a new skill. Nobody played with you, so you learned to entertain yourself. The difficulty you had learning to read taught you perseverance. The loss of a loved one gave you empathy for other people who are hurting.

And you probably grew closer to God during times when you needed him the most. Trials and problems are what develop character, endurance, and hope.

> *We can rejoice, too, when we run into problems and trials, for we know that they help us develop endurance. And endurance develops strength of character, and character strengthens our confident hope of salvation.*
> **ROMANS 5:3-4**

IMITATION

Everybody hates lice. Entire school populations have been infected with the nasty little creatures. An adult louse is no bigger than a sesame seed. Nymphs, or young lice, are even smaller than that and mature to adulthood a week or two after hatching.

These wingless insects are parasites and choose to live among human hairs, feeding on blood from the scalp. Lice prefer to make their homes on the heads of children ages 3 to 12.

The color of an adult head louse depends on the color of the person's hair the louse lives in. For example, a louse living in blond hair will end up a light color. And a louse living in black hair will grow to be dark. Lice color imitates hair color.

Chances are you're imitating someone too. You may or may not realize it. Maybe you try to joke around like your dad or walk like your mom or look cool like your older sibling. Or you might try to act like the most popular kid in your class and hope some of the magic rubs off. We really do become like the people we spend time with and admire.

In Acts 4:13, people recognized the disciples as having been with Jesus. Something about them reminded people of Christ.

Paul was so confident that he was imitating Christ, he urged the people of Philippi to do as he was doing, to imitate him as he imitated Jesus (Philippians 3:17).

You can choose the person you want to imitate. Is there anyone better than Jesus?

> *Keep putting into practice all you learned and received from me—everything you heard from me and saw me doing. Then the God of peace will be with you.*
> **PHILIPPIANS 4:9**

Because lice imitate hair color, the little stinkers are hard to see. So if you suspect lice infestation, look for the nits, or tiny lice eggs. Nits hide on hair shafts, close to the surface of the skin. They look kind of like dandruff, but you can't brush them out.

• • •

TODAY: Talk to God and ask him to help you imitate Christ. Pray that you will do such a good job being Christlike that other kids will want to imitate you.

Arctic lemmings are one of the only rodents that change colors. In the winter they're pure white, but in summer they turn brown, gray, or red. Plus, in the winter, arctic lemmings grow long, two-pronged claws on the third and fourth fingers of their forefeet—perfect for shoveling snow.

• • •

TODAY: Make it a point all week not to be pulled along by the crowd. Talk to God about anything you've done in a group that you never would have done on your own, and ask him for forgiveness.

LEMMING MOBS

Maybe you've heard the myth about lemmings committing suicide or seen pictures of scores of lemmings leaping off a cliff to certain death. Lemmings do jump off cliffs and pile onto railroad tracks in front of speeding trains, but they aren't committing suicide.

A lemming is a small Arctic European rodent—about four inches long. At various times, the lemming population explodes. So many lemmings belong to a herd that they turn on each other, and fights break out. Stress increases.

Finally a few lemmings on the edge of the crowd see their chance to escape and take it. The runaways take off, and the entire lemming herd follows at breakneck speed. Nobody knows where they're going, but they stick together in a frenzied mob. Hundreds of thousands of lemmings race out of control.

Mobs of lemmings get run over by oncoming trains and crushed on highways. If the lemmings reach a cliff, the ones in back can't tell where they are. They keep running, shoving the lemmings in front off the cliff. Then the mob rushes after them. If the lemming mob ends up at the ocean, they dive in and swim frantically until they run out of energy . . . and drown.

Nobody can fully explain the lemming mob mentality as they follow the leader to sudden death. And the same is true of human mob mentality. How do we explain spectators at a soccer match pouring onto the field and declaring all-out war on one another? How do we explain riots, when ordinary people get caught up and do things they would never do alone?

You may not actually become part of a mob, but the mob principles apply to some groups. Don't give in to the pressure of a crowd. Remember that your leader is Christ. Follow him.

You must not follow the crowd in doing wrong.
EXODUS 23:2

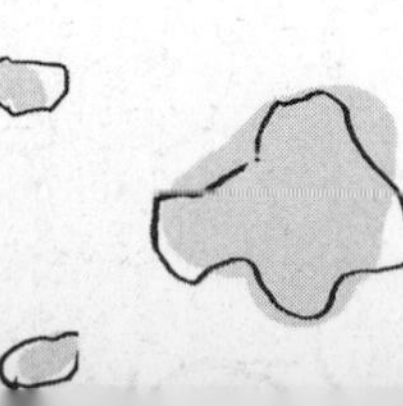

INDEPENDENCE DAY

For the most part, cats are fine on their own. If your family has to be gone overnight, your cat will probably be okay with its litter box, food, and fresh water. The cat may miss you, or it may not. This quality of independence is a big reason cat people love their cats.

Ferrets are so independent that until a pet ferret is one or two years old, you might not think it wants you around. But if you give it enough attention, your ferret will eventually bond with you, especially if you give it plenty of love and food.

How independent are you? Are you okay if you're in the cafeteria alone or by yourself at home for a few hours? Can you stand by your own decisions, even when your friends are trying to talk you into something you don't want to do? Independence can be a valuable trait, especially when the alternative is to be dependent on the opinion of a group. Do your own thinking.

What are some things you think you just can't live without? TV? Music? Sports? Your hobby? All good things have their place when taken in the right perspective, but any one of them can be unhealthy if you're really dependent on it.

On the other hand, there's such a thing as being too independent. If you've already made up your mind that your ideas are the best and nobody else can teach you anything, you're failing to realize that we're all dependent on one another. You can learn something from just about everybody.

Cultivate your own independence, but remember—only a total dependence on God is healthy.

> *The Lord is good to those who depend on him, to those who search for him.*
> **LAMENTATIONS 3:25**

INDEPENDENT PETS:

Snakes: They only have to be fed every week or so.

Rats and mice: They're easy to care for, but hard to cuddle.

Birds: You never have to walk them, but they're not so easy to hug.

Hamsters and gerbils: They don't need vaccinations and rarely get sick.

Fish: They never need baths or combing, but they refuse to play fetch.

• • •

TODAY: Write your own declaration of independence, noting things you don't want to be dependent on. Then write a declaration of dependence on God, thanking him for always being dependable.

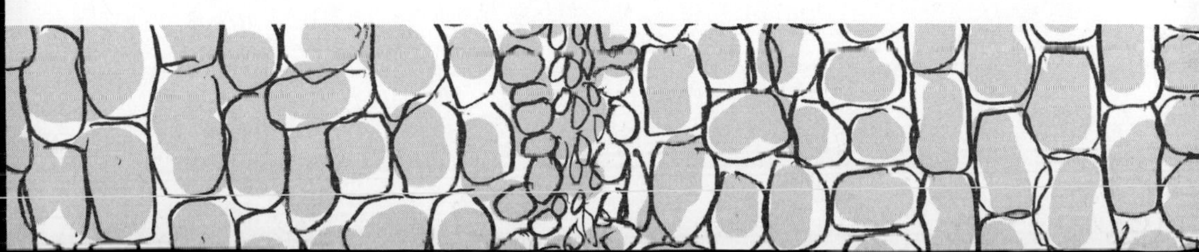

Because monarch butterflies feed on milkweed, they taste bitter to birds, and birds leave them alone. The viceroy butterfly imitates the coloring and markings of the monarch so birds will leave it alone too. You can tell a viceroy from a monarch by the extra black stripe on the viceroy's back wings (but birds don't seem to notice).

• • •

TODAY: Think about the metamorphosis you'll undergo when Christ returns. Try to imagine it, and thank God that you'll be more like Christ.

METAMORPHOSIS

Imagine if you had to hold on to life by clinging to a milkweed leaf. Day and night, you'd have to keep eating or you'd die. You could see enough of yourself to know you weren't much to look at—plain, creepy, dull.

You're not athletic. You can scrunch up your long body and unscrunch it to slither forward a little, but that's about it. So when a bird flies at you, all you can do is hope it will choose somebody else. Or maybe the bird has heard how foul tasting you are, and it won't bother you.

Two weeks go by, and you're still only two inches long. Sometimes you think you're not growing at all. What's the use?

But your skin itches, and something tells you to hang upside down on the twig, so you do. You begin to form a chrysalis, a waxy covering around yourself. Something is happening to you. You're changing, growing, transforming. A miraculous metamorphosis is taking place.

Soon you emerge as a glorious butterfly. You can fly, soar, and join thousands of others who have transformed too. It's a miracle!

Okay. Maybe caterpillars don't think like we do. But if they did, surely they'd never dream they'd end up as butterflies.

If you're a Christian, one day you'll undergo an even more miraculous transformation. First Corinthians 15:52 promises: "It will happen in a moment, in the blink of an eye, when the last trumpet is blown. For when the trumpet sounds, those who have died will be raised to live forever. And we who are living will also be transformed."

We don't understand what we'll look or feel like when we join Christ, but the transformation is bound to be much more dramatic than the metamorphosis of a caterpillar to a butterfly.

Dear friends, we are already God's children, but he has not yet shown us what we will be like when Christ appears. But we do know that we will be like him, for we will see him as he really is.

1 JOHN 3:2

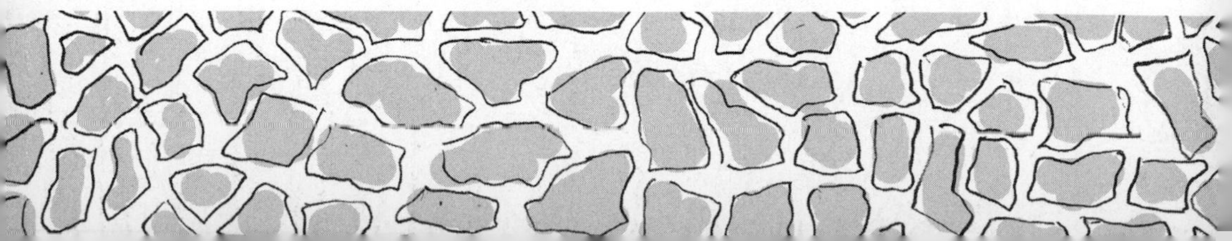

SEEING EYE DOGS

The first Seeing Eye Dog in the United States was a female German shepherd named Buddy, born in the 1920s. American Dorothy Eustis, who raised and trained German shepherds, learned about dogs being trained in Switzerland specifically to help blind soldiers from World War I resume normal lives. She began working with her own dogs.

Back in Tennessee, a young blind man named Morris Frank heard about Eustis's work and wrote to ask for her help. Morris and his dog, Buddy, trained together with Ms. Eustis.

With the success of her first student, Dorothy Eustis founded the first guide dog training school in the United States in 1929: The Seeing Eye.

The biblical prophets had a lot to say about blindness—spiritual blindness. Jeremiah 5:21 says, "Listen, you foolish and senseless people, with eyes that do not see." The people had seen so many miracles with their own eyes, and yet they still couldn't believe in God's power.

Jesus called the religious leaders of his day "blind guides."

Have you ever bought into the idea that "seeing is believing"? A friend assures you that you're getting a great teacher, but you won't believe it until you see it. And even then, you might be waiting for the teacher to show her true colors.

God turns the saying upside down and tells us that faith is the conviction of things *not* seen. We have so much evidence to go on for our faith—the facts of Jesus' birth, life, and resurrection, and his love. But if everything sat in front of us in plain sight, we wouldn't need faith. And we'd no doubt question our own eyes.

Seeing isn't believing. Believing is seeing.

Faith is the confidence that what we hope for will actually happen; it gives us assurance about things we cannot see.
HEBREWS 11:1

When a Seeing Eye Dog is matched with a visually impaired person, the two spend a minimum of four weeks in training together, during which the dog learns, among other things, to walk in the center of the pavement in a straight line, to stop at a curb and wait for instructions, not to turn unless told to, and to judge heights and widths so its new owner won't bump his or her head or fail to get through an opening.

• • •

TODAY: List all the things you believe without seeing (electricity, the existence of Mars, gravity, etc.). Ask God to help strengthen your faith.

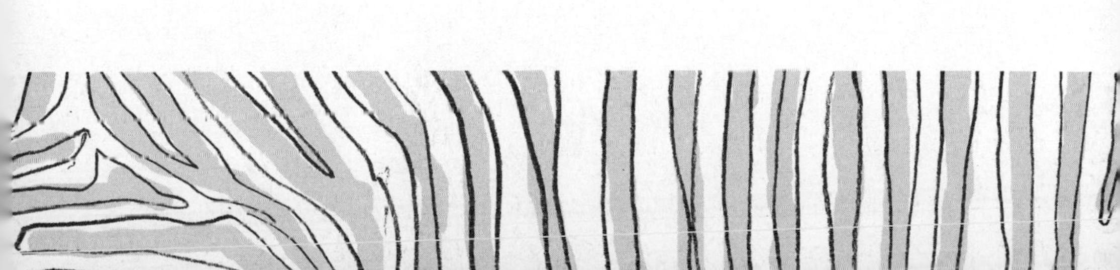

All golden hamsters come from a single pair of hamsters found in Jerusalem in 1930. You can influence the sex of the babies from your dwarf hamster. Keep the mother in a warmer room, and she'll have more boys. Turn up the AC, and she'll have more girls.

• • •

TODAY: Talk to God about your stuff. What are you hoarding? What can you give?

HOARDING HAMSTERS

Hamster comes from the German word *hamstern*, meaning "to hoard." And the hamster certainly earns the name.

A hamster's cheek pouches are designed to hold as much food as possible. Although mainly vegetarian, hamsters will eat just about anything, including insects, frogs, rodents, birds, and lizards. They'll even eat their own babies during the first week of the pups' lives.

In the wild, hamsters search for food all night long, traveling as much as eight miles a night.

Since they can't eat all the food they find and gather, hamsters hoard. They dig burrows with chambers to store more and more food. Stashes of hamster food have been found with hundreds of pounds of seeds hoarded for winter, even though hamsters hibernate, waking only for short food breaks.

It's easy to hoard. Because of our inborn selfishness, we like to keep everything for ourselves. So what if we have three pairs of tennis shoes? One might wear out, right? Can't give those two extra ones away.

Yeah—we know children all over the world are starving and we probably should send money to help. But it's hard to part with that birthday or Christmas money. And the babysitting or lawn mowing money? You're saving that for something really good.

Jesus had a different attitude about stuff. He said that if somebody wanted your coat, you should give him your shirt, too. He told a story about man who kept storing and hoarding his crops, building bigger barns to hold his wealth. But what the man didn't know was that he would die that night and lose everything he'd worked so hard for (Luke 12:13-21).

Hoarding may feel safer in the short run. But it's not. Giving is the real path to security.

A person is a fool to store up earthly wealth but not have a rich relationship with God.
LUKE 12:21

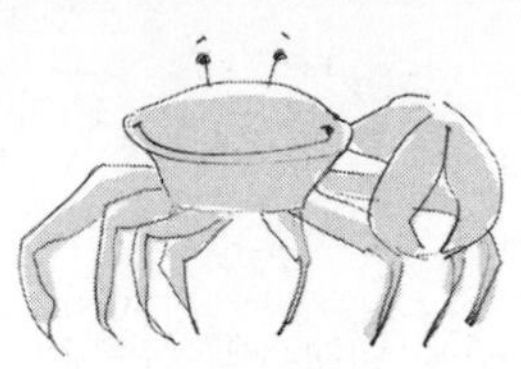

FIGHTING OVER CHICKS

Many animals in the wild fight, but they usually have good reasons for combat. A male "king" of a lion pride has to earn his royal title by defeating other males. Tigers, deer, elks, and many other animals fight to win the female, or females, of choice.

Male birds of many species have to compete for a female. The lucky ones simply build a better nest or flash a better set of feathers. Others have to fight for the lady's hand . . . or claw.

The male gladiator frog of Latin America has to conduct an elaborate courtship ritual to win Ms. Frog. Males fight, often to the death, using spikes on their forearms to mortally wound their competitors.

In the wild, most fights take place for one of three reasons: territory, food, or a mate.

What are fights over in your world? When you get into a fight or an argument, could it be because you're jealous of the other person? Maybe you want something he or she has. You're jealous of all the attention he receives, or you're envious because she gets whatever she wants. And it makes you mad.

Next time you feel like fighting, stop and talk to God first. Let God's Spirit convict you if your motives are selfish or if you're jealous. If you are, thank God for all he has given you. And walk away.

> *You want what you don't have, so you scheme and kill to get it. You are jealous of what others have, but you can't get it, so you fight and wage war to take it away from them.*
>
> **JAMES 4:2**

The hot-tempered male fiddler crab goes looking for a fight. He waves his big claw as a threat when he gets mad, and his body turns bright red, purple, or black.

• • •

TODAY: Prayerfully analyze the last fight you were in or the last argument you had. Looking back now with a cooler head, can you see any jealousy or envy at work?

Eagles don't have to sink to the level of attacking crows. Instead of fighting crows, eagles sometimes simply rise above them to an altitude where crows can't fly. We can do the same with people who want to fight us.

• • •

TODAY: The next time you feel like snapping back at somebody, ask God to help you be meek. Thank him for sending Jesus, the perfect example of power under control.

MEEK—NOT WEAK

What do you think of when you hear the word *meek*? If somebody at school said you were one meek guy, would you take it as a compliment? Or would you want to fight to prove how "not meek" you are?

It's easy to confuse meekness with weakness, but the two characteristics are nothing alike. Meekness is a kind of strength. It's power under control.

When a horse trainer first tries to gentle a wild horse, that horse might kick and buck, rear, bare its teeth, and refuse to let anybody near it. There's no doubt that this is a powerful animal, and the horse makes sure you understand that fact.

But take that same horse after it has been properly handled and won over with love and respect. Now the horse may obey voice commands. It lets its owner ride it with a loose bit, passing through a trot, canter, or gallop without resistance. The horse might even nuzzle its owner and nicker when he or she enters the barn.

This gentle horse is every bit as powerful as when it was wild. Only now, that power is under control.

That's what meekness is—power under control. When you're meek and don't yell back at someone who's yelling at you, you're not being weak. You're the strong one, reining in your power. If somebody at school calls you out for a fight, you don't have to give away your power. Keep it. But keep it under control.

Jesus said that the meek would inherit the earth. Let Jesus help you grow in meekness.

Blessed are the meek, for they will inherit the earth.
MATTHEW 5:5, NIV

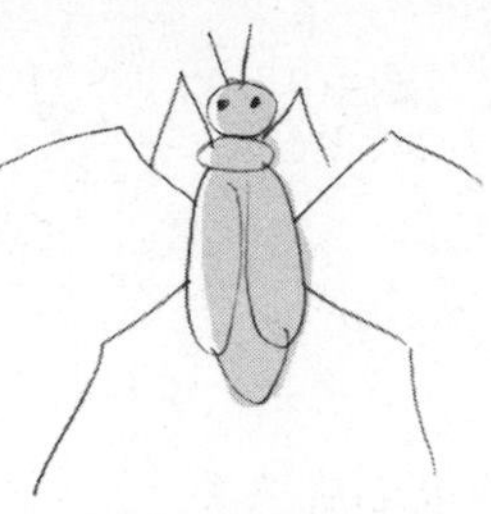

SENDING OUT VIBES

Animals depend on good vibrations, and some animals can't live without them. Here are some of the animals with built-in motion detectors:

The cockroach feels motion we could never detect.

Cat fleas lie dormant in the pupa stage in a carpet for years until a cat (or human) walks through. Then they jump on the warm flesh to eat.

A leaf-cutting ant buried during a cave-in taps a signal on the underground walls, and worker ants come running to the rescue.

When termite scouts hear an enemy coming, they beat a warning on the tunnel walls so worker termites can escape.

The African mole rat bangs its head on its burrow to signal a mate.

A female planthopper beats her abdomen against a leaf 20 times a second to announce she's ready to mate. The guy feels the vibes and beats back 20 times faster.

A whirligig beetle can skate on top of a still pond by sensing the vibrations in the pond ripples.

Have you thought much about the "vibes" you send out? When you wake up in the morning, are you met with smiles and greetings of "Good morning" from your family because they can tell you got up on the right side of the bed? Or do they take one look at you and know to leave you alone?

Some people aren't approachable. You smile, and they sneer in return. Other people are so friendly that you want to talk to them first if something goes wrong.

How do people react to your vibes?

It's important to send out Christlike vibes—signals that let everyone know you care, you're interested, and you'd willingly listen to their story or plea for help. Send out vibes that show you've been with Jesus.

Let everyone see that you are considerate in all you do.
PHILIPPIANS 4:5

Water striders beat the surface of the water looking for a mate. A male will beat 90 times a minute. If a female is interested, she'll beat back, but with a less enthusiastic 10 beats per minute.

• • •

TODAY: If you've been sending out the wrong vibes, change that, starting today. Ask God to fill you with his Spirit. Smile, and be friendly and interested in others.

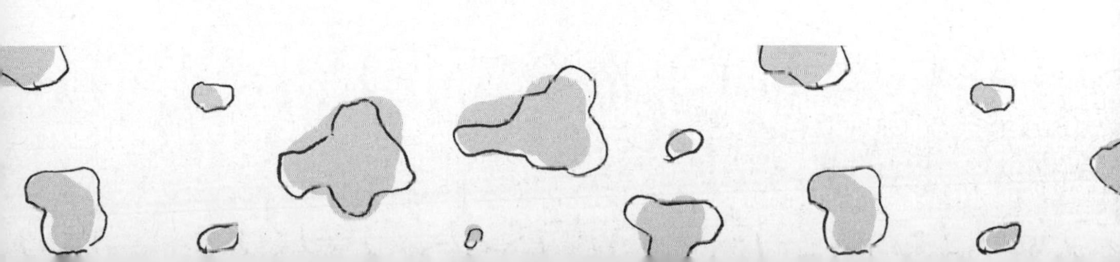

Spiders listen for sounds put out by mates, but sometimes they get mixed up. Certain spiders have been known to creep out of hiding when particular piano tunes are played because the sound of a piano wire matches the spider mate's cry.

• • •

TODAY: Ask God to point out parts of the Christian life you've been skipping—giving to the poor, telling others about Christ, turning the other cheek, etc. Make a specific plan to start listening fully and putting the whole plan into action.

NOW HEAR THIS!

Frogs don't hear much of what goes on in the world around them. Why? Because the frog's hearing is geared to only three things: food, mating, and predators. Everything else is filtered out.

Cricket frogs in the Northeast croak at 3,500 hertz, and female cricket frogs can only hear mating calls at that frequency. In the Midwest, cricket frogs croak at 2,900 hertz. So a Northeastern female transported to the Midwest would never hear the mating calls of Midwestern boys.

The male coqui frog of Puerto Rico lets out the first half of his call in a frequency heard only by other male coqui frogs. It's a warning to stay off his territory. The second half of his mating call is in a frequency not heard by other males but only by females.

Frogs have selective hearing, and so do we. You never miss the no-school-tomorrow announcement, but that announcement about a test on Thursday can fail to register.

There's a danger in selectively hearing the Bible, too. Who doesn't love the verses about the love of God and our freedom in Christ? But we might not be so alert to the ones about honoring parents, obeying, and turning the other cheek. We remember the verses about God forgiving us, but the part about us forgiving others? Not so much.

Don't settle for cafeteria-style Christianity, taking what you like and ignoring the rest. Every word of the Bible is true—it's a package deal.

> *If anyone removes any of the words from this book of prophecy, God will remove that person's share in the tree of life and in the holy city that are described in this book.*
>
> **REVELATION 22:19**

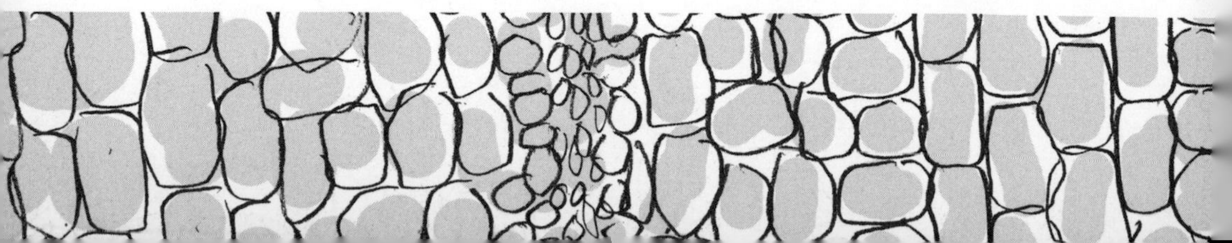

MAGNETIC APPEAL

What do pigeons, snails, honeybees, and migratory birds all have in common? They're sensitive to the earth's magnetic fields. Even robins are tuned in to the pull of the North Pole and the South Pole, but they can't always determine which is north and which is south.

The African knifefish has lousy vision, but it's clued in to the earth's magnetic fields. The knifefish is five feet long and a virtual magnet itself, with its head a positive force and its tail a negative force. The fish swims in its own force field of electrical impulses. The impulses it puts out aren't strong enough to hurt other fish or sea creatures, but the electrical charge can bounce back and alert the fish to food or enemies.

Are there people you know with "magnetic" personalities? They always attract attention. They're the stars of your class, maybe because they're great at sports or attractive physically. If you're honest, you're drawn to them too. You're flattered if they talk to you or single you out for friendship. You can't help being pulled in by them.

But the one person you should be most drawn to is Christ. When you're upset about something, he should be the one you turn to first. When you're happy, your thoughts should shoot prayers of thanksgiving to heaven.

We become like the people we admire. So the more you focus on Jesus, the more like him you'll become.

Let Christ be the magnet in your life.

When I am lifted up from the earth, I will draw everyone to myself.

JOHN 12:32

A knifefish is so sensitive to magnetic fields that you can hold a magnet above the water and attract a knifefish. The fish will approach the magnet and wait for the action to begin.

• • •

TODAY: Think about the people in your world who attract others. What is it that draws others to them? Talk to God about qualities in Jesus that should attract you to him above all others.

YOUR NORMAL BODY TEMPERATURE IS 98.6 DEGREES FAHRENHEIT, BUT THE BODY TEMPERATURES OF ANIMALS VARY:

Iguana: 108
Goat: 103.8
Canada jay: 109.4
Western pewee bird: 112.6
Anteater: 73.9

• • •

TODAY: Have a heart-to-heart with God and test your soul's "temperature." If you feel you've grown cold, make a warm-up plan of Bible reading and prayer.

COLD-BLOODED CATFISH

In general, fish, amphibians, reptiles, and insects are cold-blooded, and mammals and birds are warm-blooded.

Warm-blooded animals work to keep the inside of their bodies at a constant temperature. They make their own heat with their winter coats. They cool off because they have the ability to sweat and pant. Or they can simply move to the shade to get cool.

Cold-blooded creatures take on the temperature of their surroundings. In the summer their body temperature rises. In the winter it drops.

Fish are especially sensitive to a change in temperature. Catfish may be the most sensitive, fussing at a change of two-tenths of a degree Fahrenheit.

Animals have to seek warmth when it's cold. Warm-blooded animals spend much of their time keeping warm. Polar bears eat to gain layers of fat to insulate themselves. Birds ruffle their feathers to trap air at the body's surface. Even cold-blooded creatures like reptiles and lizards bask in the sun to warm up.

In the same way, we need to seek the warmth of God. When we keep our distance from him—accidentally or on purpose—we can grow cold. Nothing touches us. We don't feel compassion when we see someone getting picked on at school. We're not grateful for God's grace when we mess up in a relationship.

If your heart and faith have grown cold, warmth is a second away. That's the great thing about God—he's always there waiting for you to turn around and confide in him again. Get alone with God and pour out your heart to him. Read through some of the psalms. Then read about the way Jesus cares for people in the Gospels.

Being close to God again is all the warmth you'll need.

They said to each other, "Didn't our hearts burn within us as [Jesus] talked with us on the road and explained the Scriptures to us?"

LUKE 24:32

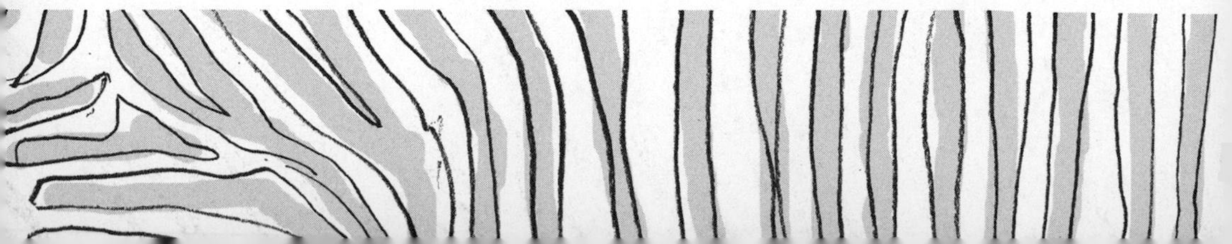

RATS!

Whatever else you may think about rats, you have to give them credit for persistence. Rats are virtually unstoppable. A rat can fall 50 feet and land on its paws in perfect condition. It can jump two feet straight up and four feet horizontally.

A fat rat can squeeze inside a pipe that's only one-and-one-half inches in diameter, and it can shimmy through a hole the size of a quarter. If rats are aboard a sinking ship, they simply plunge into the ocean and swim . . . and swim. Rats can swim nonstop for days.

As for food, just serve up whatever's on hand—wood, concrete, brick, mortar, sheet metal. Rats always have plenty to eat because they'll eat anything. They're unstoppable.

How unstoppable are you? If you have a goal—get your homework done on time, for example—what does it take to get you off track? The distraction of the computer or your phone? A bad grade that makes you just want to give up?

If you determine you're going to try to make peace with an "enemy" from school, how strong is your determination? If your enemy makes a mean crack or laughs at your attempt to talk to her, is that the end of it? They had their chance, and you're done trying to get along?

When we know we're in the center of God's will for us, we need to be unstoppable. Don't let the reactions of other people throw you off course. You're doing these good things for Christ, not to impress other people.

When things get hard, draw on the resource of endless strength and power available through Christ.

Don't give up.

Let's not get tired of doing what is good. At just the right time we will reap a harvest of blessing if we don't give up.

GALATIANS 6:9

Rats' teeth are unstoppable. They keep growing and growing—about four to five inches a year. If a rat doesn't gnaw enough to keep its teeth filed down, the teeth will curve over and grow into the rat's brain, killing it.

• • •

TODAY: Talk to God about anything you've given up on for the wrong reasons. Armed with the strength of Christ inside you, tackle that project again—and don't give up.

15 July

Moths, honeybees, ants, and some butterflies have no noses but have a terrific sense of smell. Sensory organs are located on their feelers.

• • •

TODAY: Ask God to help you stop yourself when you start getting too nosy. Instead of pressing for more information, pray for the person.

NOSY!

The proboscis monkey may have the most unfortunate-looking nose in the entire animal kingdom. The monkeys are born with small noses, but the noses grow fast. By the time the baby proboscis reaches adulthood, its nose takes up its whole face. Since the nose hangs down over its mouth, the poor monkey has to push its nose aside in order to eat.

The one positive thing about the giant nose of the proboscis is that the monkey can use its nose as a horn and blow it to warn off enemies.

How nosy are you? Whether your nose is big or little, it can be tempting to stick your nose into other people's business and into places it doesn't belong.

Curiosity can be a good thing. But there's a difference between being curious and being nosy. Curiosity wants to see what's going on; nosiness *has* to find out all the details, and it won't quit until it has enough to pass along.

Some family matters are strictly between parents. If your mom tells you something is none of your business, you need to respect that. Why press her for information and make things even more difficult for her? Instead, pray.

At school, if you hear a rumor, do you jump in the middle of it and try to find out all you can? That's being nosy. And it doesn't help matters. Being nosy fans the flames of gossip and keeps it alive. Instead, pray for the people involved, and do what you can to stop the rumors.

People deserve privacy. Even your little sister should be allowed to have thoughts that belong only to her and are known only by God. Don't sneak into other people's rooms, read journals, raid e-mails, or peek at anyone else's text messages. Keep your nose to yourself.

> *A troublemaker plants seeds of strife; gossip separates the best of friends.*
> **PROVERBS 16:28**

TOAD LICKING

In California a crazy and harmful game developed around the Colorado River toad, also known as the *Bufo alvarius*. Like other toads, the *Bufo alvarius* is warty and not much to look at. But it has a pair of poisonous glands on the back of its head. When the toad gets upset, it secretes several toxins.

One of those toxins is bufotoxin, a powerful poison that can cause mind-altering effects and hallucinations. Since this toxin comes out through the skin, certain people started a practice of "toad licking." Others discovered they could eat boiled toads and still get a kick from the bufotoxin drug. The results were often serious—harmful physically and emotionally. The poison in the toad, which is strong enough to kill a dog, is strong enough to make humans so sick they wish they'd never seen a toad.

Most of us know it's dangerous to play around with drugs and drinking. A good percentage of the regrets people have connect back to things they did under the influence of drugs or alcohol.

Like toad licking, sampling or just trying a drug can look so easy and harmless in the beginning. You're invited to a party where you know kids are sneaking in alcohol. You want to go, so you do, knowing you won't drink. Still, you don't tell your parents about the alcohol there.

That's the beginning. The next time you let someone pour you a drink so you're not the only one without a glass. You fake it, or you just take one sip.

Then the next time you decide to try what everybody else is having. Why not? It won't hurt anybody. You don't want to come off as judgmental, right?

Wrong. You are hurting somebody. Yourself. And others, too, who may be watching you to see what Christians are like.

Don't go there. It's not worth it.

Because we belong to the day, we must live decent lives for all to see. Don't participate in the darkness of wild parties and drunkenness, or in sexual promiscuity and immoral living, or in quarreling and jealousy.
ROMANS 13:13

Because of the practice of toad licking, it's now illegal in California to possess Colorado River toads.

• • •

TODAY: Get alone with God and write out a promise that with God's help, you'll stay away from any place where there's alcohol or drugs.

PICKING UP ON EMOTIONS

Certain animals are so good at picking up on emotions that they've proven useful in therapy situations with humans. A German shepherd, for example, can be trained to bark when it picks up on its owner's anger. This can help the owner tune in to his or her own emotions and control the anger before it takes over.

Horses are good at picking up on their riders' mood swings. A nervous rider will probably end up with a nervous horse. And a fearful rider can transfer that fear directly to his or her mount.

Other pets, like cats, seem to know when it's a good time to curl up on someone's lap or when it's wise to stay as far away as possible.

How good are you at reading your own emotions? Do you keep getting angrier and angrier without realizing it, then suddenly surprise yourself and those around you by losing it over a little thing?

Can you tell when you're not yourself? Do you know the early signs of depression so you can ask for help? Do you have mood swings, a sadness you can't shake, loss of appetite, no interest in activities you've always enjoyed, no energy, feelings of worthlessness and guilt? Pay attention!

Maybe you won't even admit to yourself that you're sad or down. Don't ignore the signs. Get help fast.

God wants you to talk to him about everything. Jesus invites you to toss your worries and cares to him. And the earlier you take him up on the offer, the better.

> *God is greater than our feelings, and he knows everything.*
>
> **1 JOHN 3:20**

Lions show a wide range of empathy and emotion. They like the closeness of other lions and often sleep with one paw on the head of another lion.

• • •

TODAY: Ask God to help you understand yourself the way he does. If you need to, tell a parent or counselor or pastor how you've been feeling lately.

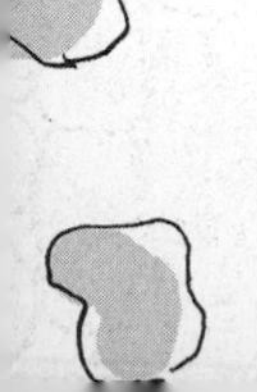
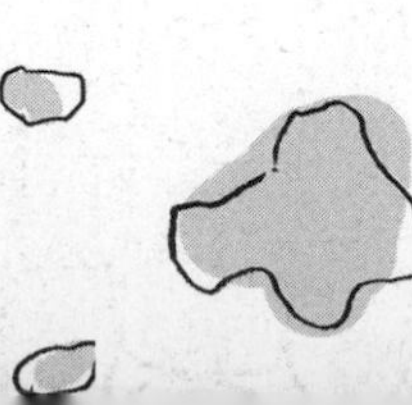
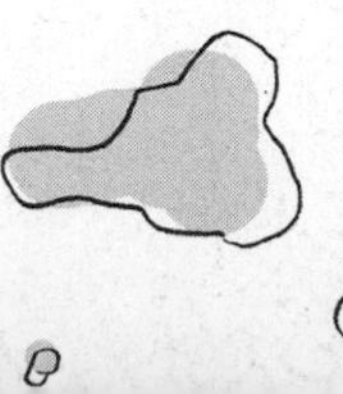

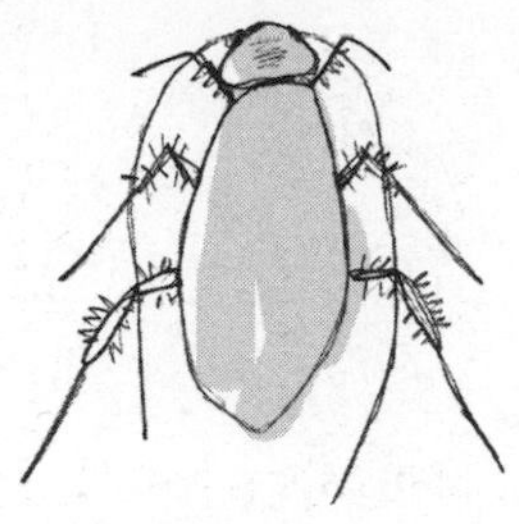

FLIRTING WITH DARKNESS

Roaches belong to the order of insects called Blattaria, a group that loves darkness and hates the light. There are about 4,000 species of these creatures, although we only get around 50 or 60 in North America. They love to creep into the darkest cracks of your house and feed on anything rotten they can find.

These darkness-loving creatures have managed to creep into every corner of the world, surviving in damp, dark burrows and sewers, inside rotten wood, in hot and steamy rain forests, and at the North Pole. They're everywhere!

Spiritual darkness is everywhere too. Paul wrote to the people living in Ephesus and explained that once they were full of darkness, but now that they'd come to know Christ, they had the light of the Lord and should live as people of the light (Ephesians 5:8).

Christ's light shines everywhere, more powerful than any darkness. Nothing is hidden from God, who promises that every little thing will come to light and be exposed sooner or later.

If you're doing things you won't talk about with your parents or with your Christian friends, you're flirting with darkness. Don't make excuses, saying that they just wouldn't understand or that they don't know what it's like to be you or that things have changed. Nothing you do is secret from God. One day everything you do will be out in the open.

You can't keep God in the dark, and you shouldn't want to.

> *Once you were full of darkness, but now you have light from the Lord. So live as people of light! For this light within you produces only what is good and right and true. Carefully determine what pleases the Lord. Take no part in the worthless deeds of evil and darkness; instead, expose them. It is shameful even to talk about the things that ungodly people do in secret. But their evil intentions will be exposed when the light shines on them, for the light makes everything visible.*
> **EPHESIANS 5:8-14**

Some people think cockroaches, especially the Madagascar hissing cockroach and the death's head cockroach, make great pets. Other people grind up a little bit of cockroach to add spice to a specialty sauce or seasoning. Still others believe cockroaches make the best medicine—a sure cure for indigestion, they say.

• • •

TODAY: Shine a spotlight on your heart and your actions. Would your life look much different if you weren't a believer in Christ? Are there things you keep secret because you're not proud of them? Ask God to help you walk in the light.

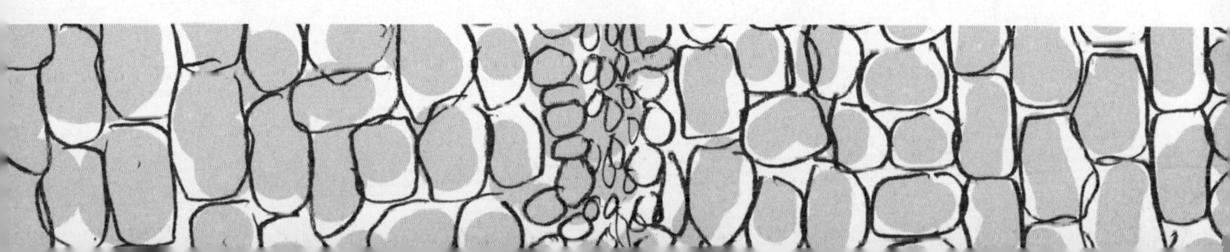

When a horse gets angry, its ears go flat back. Then it's time to look out. A cat's ears flat back could mean anger or fear, and the same goes for dogs.

• • •

TODAY: Whenever you do or say something that could make God angry, immediately thank him for his mercy and compassion, his understanding and forgiveness.

SLOW TO ANGER

Cats are so independent that they seldom stick around to show anger. If they want something and can get it themselves, they'll get it.

But cats do get angry. Their sense of well-being centers on four necessities they demand daily: food, water, a litter box, and the presence of their owner. So if your cat parades to its food dish in the morning but the dish is empty, your pet loses its sense of security. If you don't fill that dish, your cat will become angry and may meow at your heels until you do your job.

When you think about it, none of us has much reason to get angry, especially about the things we usually get angry over. Our anger is rarely on behalf of others, as Jesus' righteous anger was when he cleared the Temple of thieves and cheaters.

We get angry because we don't get our own way or because somebody doesn't appreciate us or maybe because someone said something we didn't like. But God provides for us in so many ways—food, shelter, family—that our anger is out of order.

If anyone has a right to get angry, it's God. Every day we sin against him. We forget about him and go through a whole day without talking to him, much less thanking him. We ignore the gifts he puts in front of us—a sunset, the smiling face of a grandparent, a buddy's laugh, a mom's hug. God sent his Son to die for us, but we act as if it never happened. And we keep the information to ourselves.

But God tells us he's "slow to anger." Instead, he's filled with unfailing love and faithfulness. Thank goodness!

> *Yahweh! The Lord! The God of compassion and mercy! I am slow to anger and filled with unfailing love and faithfulness.*
> **EXODUS 34:6**

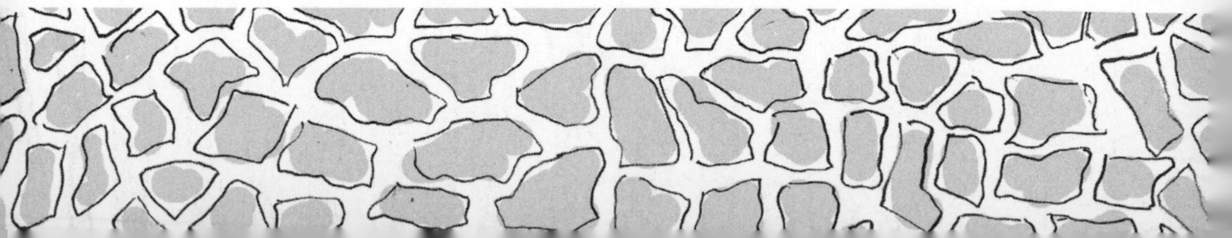

CONTENTED COWS

Have you ever seen a grouchy-looking cow? There are about 920 different breeds of cows, and out in a pasture, they all look peaceful and serene, with the possible exception of humped cattle, like the Brahman. The Pilgrims brought cows with them when they came to America, and cattle have been doing well here ever since. Cows can live for 25 years on a farm.

Most cows spend about six hours a day eating and another eight hours chewing their cud (food that's already been digested once, then brought back up from the stomach for round two). One cow drinks about 30 gallons of water and goes through around 95 pounds of feed per day. And for activity, a cow stands up and sits down an average of 14 times a day. Cows can see almost 360 degrees around them, and they see all colors except red. They can pick up smells from five miles away and can hear better than humans can. No wonder cows are so content.

Are you content? Or are you restless and bored, always wishing things were different?

Two giant contentment killers are jealousy and envy. If you want what your buddy has or if you wish you looked more like your friend or had someone else's parents, you're not going to be content with the life God has given you.

Being content doesn't mean you can't strive for the things you want in life. Healthy striving comes from a foundation of contentment and gratitude. You're thankful for what you have, and you're thankful that God will help you reach even higher.

A lack of contentment usually boils down to a lack of thankfulness. Change your outlook. Start noticing all you have to thank God for, and then do it.

Not that I was ever in need, for I have learned how to be content with whatever I have.

PHILIPPIANS 4:11

A mature female cow is called a cow, but an adult male is a bull. A female cow that hasn't had a calf yet is a heifer. Until the 1850s, almost every family had its own cow.

• • •

TODAY: For one day, thank God more than you've ever thanked him before. All day, thank God for the little things and the big things. Write down as many thanksgivings as you can.

NEVER MIND

Scientists, animal trainers, and pet owners will probably never agree on which animals are the most intelligent. Dog owners insist dogs are the most intelligent because they can learn so many commands, while cat owners insist cats are smarter because they're more independent. Dolphin trainers will tell you there's no smarter animal than the dolphin, which can even communicate with its trainer through whistles and hand signals.

Scientists look for objective evidence. Many agree that ants have the largest brains in the world—in proportion to their bodies. And the way they work in a colony, with advanced and specific division of labor, proves they're smart. An ostrich's eye is bigger than its brain. But others say birds have the biggest brains in comparison to their size.

Some people go so far as to list animals in order of intelligence. According to Edward O. Wilson, a behavioral biologist, the 10 most intelligent animals are chimpanzee, gorilla, orangutan, baboon, gibbon, monkey, smaller-toothed whale, dolphin, elephant, and pig.

A TV program on the Travel Channel came up with a different list of smartest creatures: ape, dolphin, monkey, elephant, parrot, pig, dog, raven, squid, squirrel.

How important is it to you to be smart? Do you compete for the best grades in your class, or are you embarrassed if you *do* get the highest grade? Some people, believing they're really smart, develop a bad attitude of looking down on other people. It's great to be smart, but it's even better to be wise, humble, and grateful.

The truth is, there will always be somebody more intelligent than you and somebody less intelligent. But what counts is what you do with the brain you've been given. A big brain with no persistence or understanding isn't really worth much. Most of the book of Proverbs teaches the reader how to get wisdom. Wisdom comes from letting God teach you through your experiences. So wise up!

Come and listen to my counsel. I'll share my heart with you and make you wise.
PROVERBS 1:23

Crows on the island of New Caledonia in the Pacific have surprised researchers by learning a skill it was thought only primates could master: the use of tools. Crows have learned to choose long twigs to spear grub worms deep beneath the bark of rotting logs.

• • •

TODAY: Ask God to teach you wisdom and make you wise. Start reading the book of Proverbs, a chapter a day, or even 10 verses a day.

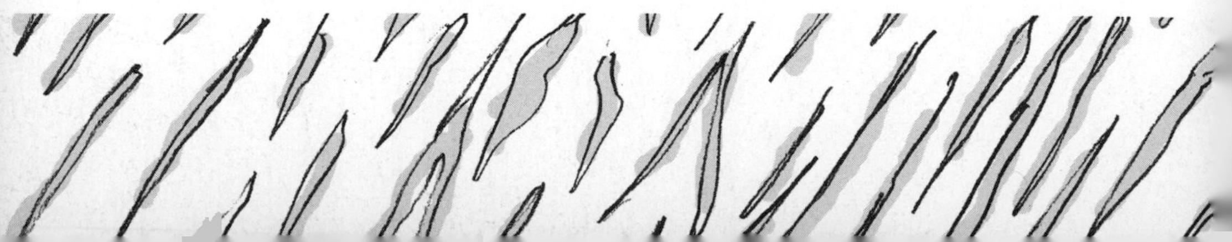

STICKY PROBLEMS

A spider's whole world depends on sticky problems. It weaves its web with one main purpose in mind: it wants insects to get stuck in the spiderweb.

Some spiders spin sticky silk from spinnerets on their abdomens. Sticky spiderwebs are perfect for capturing mosquitoes and other insects. But the spider's web is so sticky that even the spider itself could get caught in it if it didn't plan ahead.

Spiders know the secret of sticky. They know how to stay unstuck. The spider spins at least one long, nonsticky silk thread that crosses the entire web. And it usually leaves an unsticky center, where it can sit and wait for its dinner to drop in.

Do you ever feel like things you're worried about are stuck in your brain? You lie in bed and go over and over how stupid you acted around that person you really like who you wanted to like you. You replay every word of the failed conversation. Then you imagine what's being said about you behind your back.

Or maybe you're worried about something that *might* happen. Your parents are arguing so much. What if they got a divorce? What would happen to you? Or you know your parents' jobs are kind of shaky. Your buddy's mom lost her job. What if it happened at your house? What if your parents can't keep up their house payments? What if you have to move to a different city? a different state?

God invites you to give your worries to him. Some versions of the Bible use the word *cast* or *throw* your worries.

Trouble will come and so will problems and worries, but you don't have to build a home for them or glue them to you. Let go. Toss them up.

> *Give all your worries and cares to God, for he cares about you.*
> **1 PETER 5:7**

Some of the different kinds of spiderwebs are orb web, tangle web, funnel web, tubular web, sheet web, and dome or tent web. Ounce per ounce, a spider's silk thread is stronger than steel.

• • •

TODAY: Talk to God about the sticky problems that are following you around. Then toss them up to him!

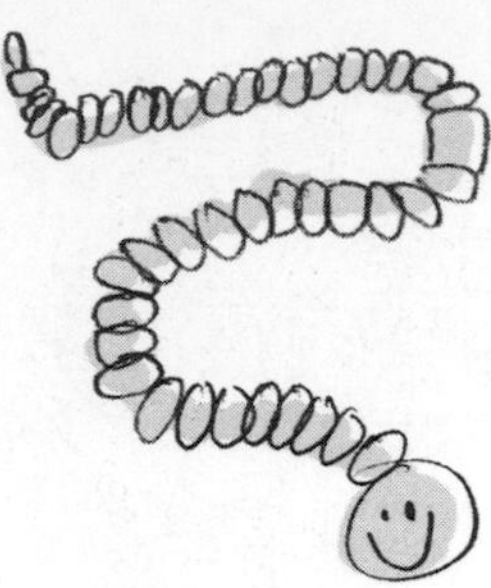

23 July

LOWLY WORM

Worms don't have much going for them. You could dig up any acre of land, and there would be more than a million earthworms in it. There are about 2,700 different kinds of worms, and they're all pretty creepy. No arms. No legs. No eyes.

Worms live anywhere they can get food, moisture, oxygen, and a decent temperature. They like to eat their weight in food every day, and they try to stay underground. If their skin dries out, the worms will die. If they're exposed to light for over an hour, they become paralyzed.

Still, worms can be used for good and end up giving a great benefit to people. When worms dig down into the soil, they bring up subsoil and mix it with the topsoil. Earthworms leave behind a slime that, although gross, contains nitrogen, an important nutrient for plants.

So you have to admit, worms aren't all bad.

In the Old Testament, Job declared that he, like all humans, was a worm compared to the Almighty. And you really can't argue with that. We're nothing without God. None of our great accomplishments count for anything—only the fact that we're God's kids and belong to Christ.

But since we do belong to Christ, and since the Father created us in his image, we're extremely valuable. It's confusing, but that's what humility is—seeing yourself as you really are. Not too low, and not too high. Even worms do some good now and again.

God is more glorious than the moon; he shines brighter than the stars. In comparison, people are maggots; we mortals are mere worms.
JOB 25:5-6

The Australian earthworm can grow up to eight feet long. It's considered a yummy delicacy by the locals. But the largest earthworm ever discovered was in South Africa and measured 22 feet long. Now that's a meal!

• • •

TODAY: Make a list that compares God and you. Then thank God that he considered you so valuable that he sent Jesus to die for you.

July 24

THE NOT-BOSSY BOSS

When you think about someone who's a leader, what image comes to mind? Someone who's bossy and shouts orders? Someone who makes sure he gets respect and demands obedience from his lowly followers?

We've all known bossy leaders, but whenever Jesus talked about leading, the ideas of gentleness and sacrifice weren't far behind.

In the animal world, leaders are often gentle. When lambs reach the age of 60 days or so, it's time to wean them from their mothers. If several lambs are being weaned, a breeder will usually leave a couple of ewes, adult females, to lead the lambs and help them find water and food. These leaders will do the job with the tenderness of a mother.

If you're the leader on a group project at school, do you lead by example and with a spirit of cooperation? Or do you love it that, finally, you get to be the one to boss everybody around?

There's a difference between being a leader and being a boss. Nowhere in Scripture do we see Jesus bossing his disciples around. He drew his followers in because of who he was. They wanted to be with him, to be near him, to be like him.

If you're ever given the opportunity to lead, that's the kind of leader you should strive to be. And that's the kind of leader you can pray that the leaders of our country and of other countries will be too.

> *Care for the flock that God has entrusted to you. Watch over it willingly, not grudgingly—not for what you will get out of it, but because you are eager to serve God. Don't lord it over the people assigned to your care, but lead them by your own good example.*
>
> **1 PETER 5:2-3**

A male sheep is a ram, a female sheep is a ewe, and a baby sheep is a lamb. In Chinese and several other languages, the word for sheep, goat, and ram is the same.

• • •

TODAY: Pray for the leaders of our country and the leaders of other countries around the world. Pray for your pastors and the leaders of your church. And pray that God will help you be the right kind of leader when you get the opportunity.

The most venomous snake is probably the inland taipan of Australia. But the box jellyfish is even more poisonous than the snake.

• • •

TODAY: Be honest with God and yourself, and admit any grudges you're hanging on to. Ask God to help you forgive the person. Then let it go.

DON'T TAKE IT OUT ON ME

Stonefish are the most poisonous fish in the world. They have 13 or 14 sharp spines on their backs, and the spines are fed from small sacs of venom under the skin. The slightest pressure against the skin or spine makes the poison flow from the sacs. If a spine pokes you, it will shoot the most deadly nerve poison into you. The result will be terrible pain, followed by a gruesome death in about two to four hours.

Revenge is like that. We can keep a past hurt stored in invisible sacs, wrapped in unforgiveness just under our skin. There, the anger grows more poisonous and hateful. It builds up, waiting, going deeper and deeper, until it explodes.

But the explosion rarely hurts the person you've got a grudge against. It hurts you. And you don't get rid of the poison by exploding.

Even if you never seriously try to get revenge on the person, just thinking revenge can poison your mind and heart. Those thoughts can eat away at you and take over your life.

The only way to get rid of the poison is by forgiving the person who wronged you. Forgive right away, before the poison has a chance to build up and sink into your skin. Don't store your poison. Get rid of it.

Let God handle your hurts. You may have to give your feelings of bitterness to God over and over again, but that's okay. He's ready to take care of the problem. Revenge, after all, belongs to him.

> *Dear friends, never take revenge. Leave that to the righteous anger of God. For the Scriptures say, "I will take revenge; I will pay them back," says the* LORD.
> **ROMANS 12:19**

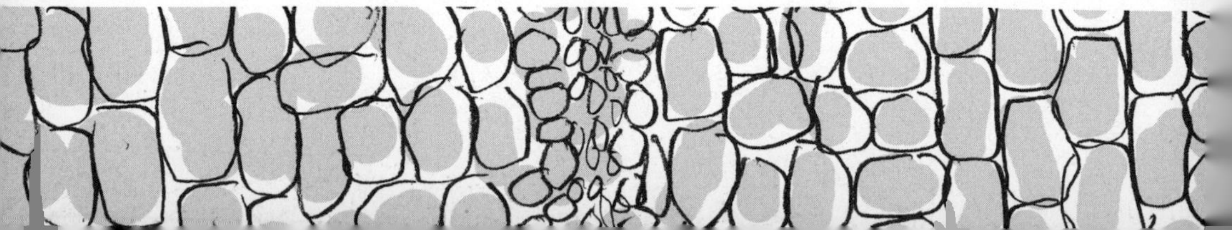

July **26**

EVEN A LITTLE LIGHT

Cats see about six times better at night than you do. They have the best night vision of all domestic animals. One reason cats see so well is because they have such big eyes to see you with. But even cats can't see in total darkness. They need a little light.

Butterflies need a little light too. They can't fly unless their wings and muscles are warm, so they soak up the light by basking in the sunshine. When they've gotten enough heat from the sunlight, they can fly again.

Deep at the bottom of the ocean, many fish count on the light given off by viperfish, or the siphonophores. The rows of lights on their bodies make them look like an underwater jet. Colonies of siphonophores string themselves together in lines 12 feet long and glow like fairy lights in the deep, dark ocean.

People need light too, and sometimes all they need is a little light from someone else. Don't hide yours. The Bible is filled with metaphors about light and darkness. Jesus is the Light, and he tells us that we shouldn't hide our little light from the world.

When you listen to people making fun of someone and you don't step up and try to stop it, you're hiding your light. When you laugh along as a buddy takes God's name in vain or trashes Jesus, you're hiding your light. When you don't go out of your way to be kind to someone, you're hiding your light.

Don't hide the Christ in you. Act as if the only light people around you may see is the bit of light you have. Sometimes all darkness needs is a tiny light, and you could be it!

> *You are the light of the world—like a city on a hilltop that cannot be hidden. No one lights a lamp and then puts it under a basket. Instead, a lamp is placed on a stand, where it gives light to everyone in the house.*
> **MATTHEW 5:14-15**

In the Arab-Israeli war of 1967, a shoal, or group, of flashlight fish was mistaken for enemy frogmen (military divers) and blown out of the water.

• • •

TODAY: Ask God to show you one specific way you can bring your light out of hiding today. (Maybe you could smile, say just the right word at the right time, or have a good talk with someone.)

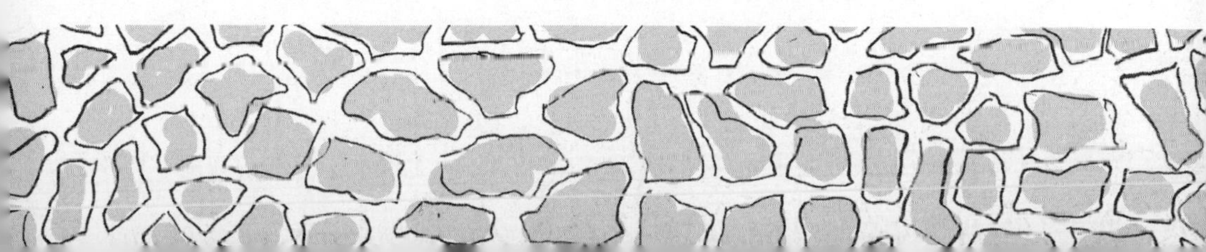

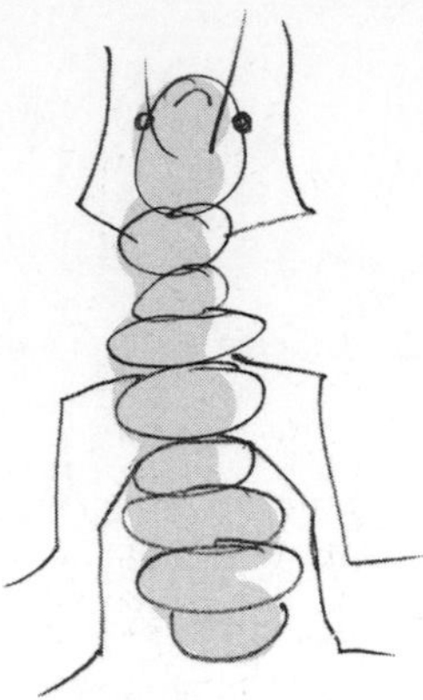

A queen termite may live between 15 and 50 years, laying as many as 6,000 to 7,000 eggs per day.

• • •

TODAY: If you're sure you have eternal life, thank God for his amazing gift. If you're unsure, talk to God, then ask a parent or pastor to help you understand God's grace.

ETERNAL LIFE

Different types of animals have wildly different life expectancies. Here are some of their average life spans:

aphid: 3 weeks
mouse: 1 to 3 years
hamster: 2 years
guinea pig: 3 years
rat: 3 years
rabbit: 6 to 8 years
chicken: 7 to 8 years
parakeet: 8 years
squirrel: 8 to 9 years
cow: 9 to 12 years
lion, pig, and duck: 10 years
dog, cat, pigeon, and wolf: 10 to 12 years
deer: 10 to 15 years
sheep and goat: 12 years
monkey: 12 to 15 years
periodical cicada: 17 years
bear: 15 to 30 years
donkey: 18 to 20 years
horse: 20 to 30 years
hippopotamus: 30 years

You can't know how long you'll live. But the great thing is that when we believe in Christ, we'll live forever with him. Death is a beginning, not an end.

If someone asked you straight-out where you were going when you died, would you hem and haw and end up saying you weren't sure? Would you say that you sure hope you're going to heaven? If those would be your answers, then you need to think about what it means to accept forgiveness because of Christ's death for you.

Christ's payment, death, and resurrection: either it's your ticket to heaven or it isn't. There's no "hope so" about it. And there's nothing boastful about claiming that you're going to heaven either. *You* didn't do anything to earn your way there.

You get to be with the Father in heaven for one reason: Jesus bought your way there with his death—for eternity.

> *This is what God has testified: He has given us eternal life, and this life is in his Son. Whoever has the Son has life; whoever does not have God's Son does not have life.*
>
> **1 JOHN 5:11-12**

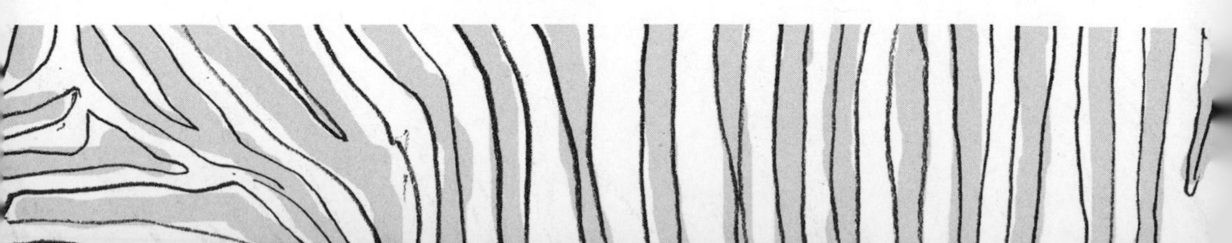

July 28

THE MIRROR EFFECT

Some pets (and some babies) love mirrors. A mirror in a parakeet's cage can cause some birds to fall in love with the mysterious mirror image. Other parakeets will aggressively peck at that phantom in the mirror.

Cats have their own built-in mirrors. At the back of a cat's eye is a layer of cells that make the eye more sensitive to light. Light strikes the eye, and the cells act like a mirror, reflecting light back through the retina. That way, the cat gets twice as much light. And the cat's eyes shine in the dark.

What do you see when you look in the mirror? Do you like gazing at your reflection, or do you look the other way when you pass a mirror? You might be surprised at the number of outwardly beautiful people who hate the way they look. They only see their flaws when they look in the mirror.

But look deeper. Do you like the person inside, the person you're becoming?

It's important that you love yourself, but how can you?

See yourself as God sees you. When God looks at you, he sees his creation and his child, whom he loves wholeheartedly. He sees a valuable, one-of-a-kind gift who is forgiven, ransomed at the highest possible price, and capable of doing great things.

You will never see yourself while you're on earth. You can only see your reflection. That's how we see everything now—as if we're looking into a cloudy mirror.

But one day everything will be clear. Then we'll see ourselves accurately, and we'll see our God face-to-face.

> *Now we see things imperfectly, like puzzling reflections in a mirror, but then we will see everything with perfect clarity. All that I know now is partial and incomplete, but then I will know everything completely, just as God now knows me completely.*
> **1 CORINTHIANS 13:12**

A parakeet's favorite toys are a rope, a swing, a bell, and a mirror. But if you have two birds, skip the mirror because one bird may fall for the reflected mirror bird and ignore the live bird in the cage.

• • •

TODAY: Stare at yourself in the mirror for one full minute. Try to see yourself as God sees you, and thank God for looking at you through eyes of love.

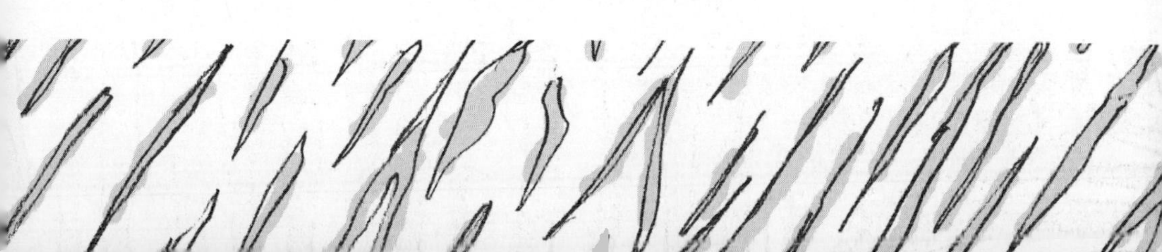

Dust mites are in the arachnid family, making them cousins of ticks, spiders, and scorpions.

• • •

TODAY: List 10 things in the "seen" category that you think about a lot during the day. List 10 things in the "unseen" category that you'd like to focus on more. Ask God for guidance and help.

THE UNSEEN

Maybe you've heard this sweet nighttime blessing: "Sleep tight. Don't let the bedbugs bite."

Bedbugs are real, even though you rarely see them. They're small, wingless insects that feed on the blood of warm-blooded animals, like us. At night they creep out of their hiding places—stuffed animals, piles of junk under your bed, clothes on the floor, clutter (they love clutter)—and sip your blood, after injecting your skin with their saliva to keep the blood flowing. And they're patient. You could be gone a whole year, and your bedbugs would be there waiting for you.

You can't see them, but dust mites live in those cute little dust bunnies under your bed. Mites are too small to be seen without a microscope, but a typical bed houses over 6 billion dust mites. They feed on dead skin that we shed from our bodies, plus potato chip crumbs and other goodies you've sneaked into your bedroom. Yet you can't see these little guys.

Think about all the things you believe in but can't see, like wind and magnetic fields. You can't see love or hate or jealousy, but you know they exist.

Most of the spiritual world and spiritual truths are unseen. You haven't seen God or the Holy Spirit. You may see the effects of kindness and goodness and faithfulness, but not the things themselves.

If you can see it, it won't last forever. Clothes, houses, money, cars, bikes, TVs, computers—none of them will last. So where do you want to spend most of your thoughts? Thinking about things that won't last? Or thinking about the unseen things that will last forever?

> *We don't look at the troubles we can see now; rather, we fix our gaze on things that cannot be seen. For the things we see now will soon be gone, but the things we cannot see will last forever.*
>
> **2 CORINTHIANS 4:18**

YOUR SERVE

In biblical times, donkeys were counted on to serve. Donkeys are mentioned almost 150 times in the Bible. Mary and Joseph probably counted on a willing donkey to get them from Nazareth to Bethlehem, where Mary eventually gave birth to the baby Jesus.

Later, Jesus rode into Jerusalem on a donkey, fulfilling a prophecy from Zechariah 9:9: "Rejoice, O people of Zion! Shout in triumph, O people of Jerusalem! Look, your king is coming to you. He is righteous and victorious, yet he is humble, riding on a donkey—riding on a donkey's colt."

Other animals served kings. Horses led charges into battle and pulled chariots. Oxen plowed fields. God's creatures fulfilled the roles he created them for—they served.

Serving isn't a very popular goal. How many of your friends have announced that when they grow up they want to be servants? Most of us want to be onstage, not behind it. Movie stars, athletes, and musicians are our idols. We don't even know the names of missionaries and other people who give their lives in service to others.

But God loves the servant's heart. Nobody else may notice if you carry in groceries for your mom without being asked, but God will. You might not get applause for walking your sister's dog when she's sick or for opening the door for a teacher whose hands are full, but God notices. If you carry a tray for a classmate who's having trouble in the cafeteria, a couple of kids might make fun of you. But God sees, and he is pleased.

Follow Jesus' lead. He said that he came to serve, not to be served. People might not consider being a servant something to work toward. But God does.

Never be lazy, but work hard and serve the Lord enthusiastically.

ROMANS 12:11

Donkeys are considered heroes of the Ethiopian highlands, where they carry food and water to millions—over rocky, barren highlands where no roads exist.

• • •

TODAY: Ask God to show you ways you can serve him by serving other people.

ONE LOST LAMB

Have you ever lost a pet? It's a horrible feeling. You're so desperate to find your dog or cat that you'll do anything to get that pet back.

Here are some tips to do *before* you lose your pet: take pictures of your pet and update your photos regularly; make sure your pet's name and your phone number are on its collar tags; consider getting a tracking chip put on your pet.

Here are some tips to help you find a lost pet:

1. Check all the hiding places in your house and yard.
2. Walk around your neighborhood, calling your pet and asking neighbors if they've seen it.
3. Make signs with your pet's picture, a description, your pet's name, and a number to call to reach you. Put "LOST DOG" at the top of the signs in letters large enough for drivers to read. Pass out flyers door-to-door. Hand them to dog walkers.
4. It helps to offer a small reward.
5. Read every sign and ad for "found pet."
6. Call your local newspaper and ask if you can post a lost pet ad. Read their lost-and-found ads.
7. Check the pound or animal control. Call local animal shelters. (Call every day.)
8. Post signs in vet offices, animal grooming shops, etc.
9. Check out some of the organizations listed in the sidebar on this page.

Think about the pain in your heart when you thought you'd lost your pet (even if you found it hiding in the yard). That's just a hint of what God feels for "the lost," for people who are still separated from him because they haven't accepted Christ's payment for their sins. God created every person and wants each one to come back to him.

If you've wandered or drifted away from God, it's always the right time to come back. Be found.

There is more joy in heaven over one lost sinner who repents and returns to God than over ninety-nine others who are righteous and haven't strayed away!
LUKE 15:7

HERE ARE SOME ORGANIZATIONS THAT MIGHT HELP YOU FIND YOUR LOST PET:

The local pound

Animal Control

Animal Care Services

Animal shelters

Petfinder (http://www.petfinder.com)

Pets 911 (http://www.pets911.com/services/lostandfound)

USDA's Missing Pet Network (http://www.missingpet.net/anlost.html)

• • •

TODAY: Ask God to show you people who are lost. Pray for them, and be ready to help them find their way back.

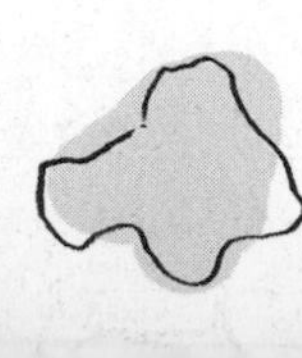
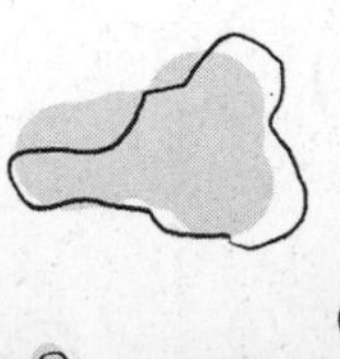

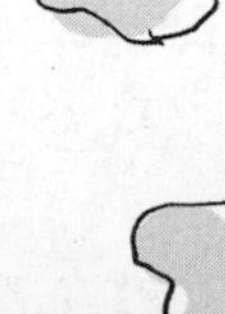

ON YOUR MARK!

Thoroughbred racehorses can gallop over 40 miles per hour. But they're not the fastest horses on earth. Quarter horses can outrun Thoroughbreds . . . as long as the race isn't over a quarter mile. A quarter horse can run 50 miles per hour for a quarter mile, which explains where it got its name.

The cheetah is the fastest animal on land, running up to 70 miles per hour. But after racing at breakneck speed, the poor cheetah has to stop for 30 minutes to catch its breath, a fact the nasty hyenas count on when they're tracking a cheetah for dinner.

Here are some speeds of other animals:

antelope: 61 mph	rabbit: 35 mph
gazelle: 50 mph	chicken: 9 mph
hunting dog: 50 mph	spider: 1.17 mph
coyote: 43 mph	tortoise: 0.17 mph
gray fox: 42 mph	sloth: 0.14 mph
hyena: 40 mph	snail: 0.03 mph

Did you know that your life on earth is a race to the finish? You only have a limited amount of time to accomplish God's will for you on earth. As in most races, obstacles pop up along the way. So here's some coaching advice:

Philippians 2:16: "Hold firmly to the word of life; then . . . I will be proud that I did not run the race in vain and that my work was not useless." Hold on to Scripture to make sure your whole race isn't useless.

Galatians 5:7: "You were running the race so well. Who has held you back from following the truth?" You were going great! Be careful not to let other people get in the way.

Hebrews 12:1: "Let us strip off every weight that slows us down, especially the sin that so easily trips us up. And let us run with endurance the race God has set before us." Don't let sin keep you from running your best.

Nothing is more important than the race you're running for God. On your mark, get set, go!

Don't you realize that in a race everyone runs, but only one person gets the prize? So run to win!
1 CORINTHIANS 9:24

Modern endurance rides are 100-mile races run by one horse and one rider in under 24 hours. To help make sure horses don't overdo it, each horse has to have eight checkups from a vet during the race, and the horse is required to rest for 30 minutes at each vet check. Plus, on occasion, riders may get off their horses and jog along with them.

• • •

TODAY: List five things, people, or habits that are slowing you down and getting in the way of you running the best race possible.

2 August

BROKENHEARTED

Hearts can hurt and be hurt.

An ant's heart is in its gaster, which is the prominent part of its abdomen. In with the heart are the ant's digestive system and its chemical weaponry. The ant can spray acid from its gaster and stun a predator or prey.

You're strong hearted, whether you realize it or not. Your heart has two pumps. One sends 2,000 gallons of blood a day through your system, and the other moves about the same amount. Over the span of your life, your heart will beat almost 3 billion times.

But as strong as your heart is, it's bound to get broken a few times.

You can feel brokenhearted for many reasons. When someone close to you dies, your heart may feel heavy and fractured, as if it will never work right again. Your heart takes a long time to heal, and a piece of you will always miss that person.

Or someone else may break your heart. A friend decides he doesn't want to be your friend anymore. Or that guy you thought was so crazy about you is talking to your best friend.

No matter how it happens, being brokenhearted hurts. Your heart aches. You need God's comfort more than ever. And you may even discover that you can feel his presence most when you're sad, lonely, or depressed.

Jesus knows what it feels like to be brokenhearted. He went through everything while he was on earth so that he'd understand. Take your broken heart to him and hand it over. He made your heart, and he can fix it up good as new.

> *The Lord is close to the brokenhearted; he rescues those whose spirits are crushed.*
>
> **PSALM 34:18**

In proportion to weight and body ratio, dogs have the largest hearts. Some dogs have been said to have died "of a broken heart" when their owners died.

• • •

TODAY: If you feel brokenhearted today, thank God that he cares how you feel. Ask him to help you spot people around you who may be brokenhearted. Pray about how you can help.

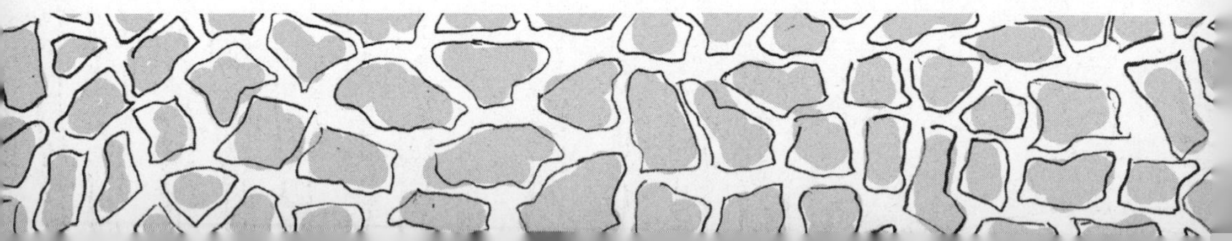

TRUE OR FALSE?

Toads cause warts. True or false?

A lot of people will tell you it's true. They might even swear that they themselves got warts from handling a toad. But they're wrong. The old myth is false. Although toads often have poison glands behind their eyes and many amphibians give off a poison that can irritate human skin, toads still don't give you warts. Warts are caused by a human virus.

The ostrich hides its head in the sand and thinks the enemy can't see it. True or false?

False. If ostriches buried their heads in the sand, they wouldn't be able to breathe. There are a couple of possible explanations for this rumor. Ostriches' heads are so tiny, compared to those big bodies, that when they're pecking the ground, it might look like the heads are buried in the sand. Ostriches do dig holes in the ground for nests, and an ostrich sticks its head into the nest several times a day to turn the eggs.

Today, in our technological information age, it's easier than ever to start rumors. People can post false information online, and within minutes, the so-called facts have been spread all over the Internet. It won't take long for the report to spread through the school.

Proverbs refers to rumors as "dainty morsels," like pieces of chocolate you can't wait to scarf down. But those morsels, those rumors, can do more harm than leading people to believe they can get warts from a toad. Rumors can cause people to misjudge another person or to distrust and fear other cultures and nationalities.

Don't fall for rumors, and don't spread them.

Rumors are dainty morsels that sink deep into one's heart.

PROVERBS 26:22

During the first year of life, a lobster sheds its shell 10 times. Sometimes a claw gets stuck in the old shell, and the lobster has to cut off its own leg to free itself.

• • •

TODAY: Prayerfully think back over rumors you've heard about people this year. Which rumors are you 100 percent positive are true? Ask God to keep you from repeating rumors.

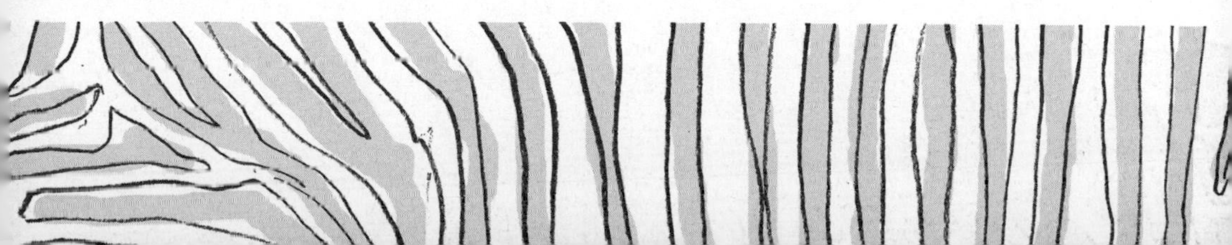

WEIRD BIRTHS

The European midwife toad has a unique system for hatching eggs. After the male and female mate and the eggs are laid, the male winds strands of eggs around his hind legs. Then he carries the eggs with him wherever he goes until the eggs hatch. Finally, he plops back into the water just in time for the tadpoles to swim out.

Male and female Surinam toads from South America do a kind of water dance together when the eggs are laid. The male manages to scoot the newly hatched eggs onto the female's back. Mom Toad grows a pocket when her skin swells, and the eggs get shoved inside the pocket. For two months her young develop inside this pocket, skipping the tadpole stage, until at last tiny toadlets pop out.

A duck-billed platypus lays eggs like a bird and incubates them for two weeks. When the babies hatch, the platypus feeds her young milk in an unusual way. The milk oozes from her fur, and the babies lick the fur to get their milk.

Animal births are wildly different. So we shouldn't be surprised that our spiritual births aren't all the same either. You may have been raised by Christian parents who helped you come to faith in Christ when you were young. Your buddy may have walked forward in a revival meeting. Your aunt may have finally found Christ in the hospital when she was only minutes from dying.

The essence of our faith, our salvation, is the same: Christ by faith. We don't make up our own brand of feel-good faith. All the how-tos are in the Bible and were taught by Jesus. But God will use any means to bring his children to faith. Just because your experience was different from someone else's doesn't mean one is right and the other is wrong. God is big enough to meet every person one-on-one.

> *All praise to God, the Father of our Lord Jesus Christ. It is by his great mercy that we have been born again, because God raised Jesus Christ from the dead. Now we live with great expectation.*
>
> **1 PETER 1:3**

The sand goby fish father starts out like an awesome dad. All by himself, he takes care of the eggs. He does have one hang-up, though, that denies him the "Fish Father of the Year" award. He eats about one-third of his offspring, even if he has plenty of food.

• • •

TODAY: Ask a couple of your Christian friends how they came to know Christ. Share the details of your own spiritual birth.

SPIRITUAL AMPHIBIANS

Amphibians lead a double life. The name comes from the Greek words *amphi*, meaning "both," and *bios*, meaning "life." Amphibians usually start life in the water, such as tadpoles emerging from jellylike eggs. Then they undergo a transformation so they can live on the land.

If you have Christ living in you, you've transformed too. Now you have a new, spiritual nature that can communicate with God and tune in to the Spirit of Christ.

There's only one problem. Even though you've been given this fantastic new nature, your old nature doesn't just disappear. It's still there. You have two natures, and they don't get along. That's why there's a struggle going on inside of you. Every day (maybe dozens of times a day), you have to say no to the old nature and yes to the new, listening to God's Spirit instead of going back to your old habits.

Your spiritual nature gets stronger as you trust Christ. But that old nature gets worse and worse, decaying with time. Which one wins the struggle? The one you feed the most.

Feed your spiritual nature by talking to God, reading his Word, and hanging out with people who want to grow spiritually too.

> *Put on your new nature, created to be like God—truly righteous and holy.*
> **EPHESIANS 4:24**

About one-third of the world's amphibians are endangered—on their way to extinction. The Palestinian painted frog used to live around the Sea of Galilee. When the swamps were drained in the 1940s so homes could be built, the frogs disappeared. No one has seen a painted frog since 1955.

• • •

TODAY: Ask God to make you extra-sensitive to the struggle inside you between your old nature and your new nature. Choose your new nature.

Not all animals flee or fight. Some play dead, standing still in a crisis or toppling over and lying stiffly on the ground. Still others, like certain species of fish, change colors in a crisis, choosing the camouflage option.

• • •

TODAY: Talk with God about the times in the past when you should have walked away—or run away—and you didn't. Ask God to remind you to flee the next time.

FLEE!

Some people don't understand why even a well-trained horse may try to run away. But horses have an instinct for self-preservation. When a horse feels threatened by a predator, it's left with two choices: fight or flight.

A horse's first instinct when there's any sign of trouble is to flee. Most horses don't really like to fight, but they will if cornered and left without the possibility of flight. With no claws or fangs, horses know they stand a better chance of survival by running away from a lion, bear, or wolf pack. The smart choice is to flee.

Sometimes that's the smartest choice for humans, too. Trouble might come in the form of a bully calling you out to fight, and you know the fight will get you kicked out of school. Is the smart move to be sucked into fighting? Or can you rely on wit, humor, words . . . and speed, if necessary?

Trouble can also come in the form of temptation. You're invited to a party, but when you get there, you realize it's not the kind of party you should be at. There are no adults around, and people are doing things you know are wrong.

Leave. Sometimes the bravest response is to walk away.

Or you're at the mall with friends, and some guys start following you around. At first, it's funny, maybe even flattering. They're older and pretty hot. Before you know it, you're walking with them. One of the guys puts his arm around your shoulder. They ask you to take a drive with them.

Don't dabble in trouble. Don't hang around until it's too late to get out. Flee.

> *Flee immorality. Every other sin that a man commits is outside the body, but the immoral man sins against his own body.*
>
> **1 CORINTHIANS 6:18,** NASB

LOYAL FRIENDS

Pets can be your most loyal friends. Dogs have been called "man's best friend" for centuries. Cats can stick by you, purring and promising everything will be all right. Most horse owners claim that their horses fill a friendship gap in their lives.

Sometimes people give pets to the elderly as loyal companions. Studies have shown that the right pet can help lower a person's blood pressure and heart rate.

Humans, on the other hand, aren't always so loyal.

When David was still a shepherd boy and a musician for King Saul, he and Saul's son Jonathan formed a friendship that stood the test of time. Jonathan remained loyal to David, even when King Saul tried to have David killed. And David remained loyal to Jonathan, even after Jonathan's death. King David took care of Jonathan's son.

What kind of a friend are you? If your friend isn't around and people are joking about her, do you stick up for your friend, or do you laugh along?

If you've had a best friend for a long time and a "better offer" comes along—someone from a more popular group—are you quick to leave your friend in the dust?

Sometimes people change. You may not always have the same best friend. Interests change, and you might find fewer things to talk about. But just because you end up with different best friends, you don't have to stop being friends altogether. You can have more than one friend, right?

Being loyal is continuing to care about your friend, no matter what.

> *Never let loyalty and kindness leave you! Tie them around your neck as a reminder. Write them deep within your heart.*
> **PROVERBS 3:3**

In a survey of small-animal vets, animal behaviorists Benjamin and Lynette Hart ranked chows, rottweilers, and Akitas as the most disloyal breeds of dog, based on reported rates of high aggression toward their owners.

• • •

TODAY: Talk to God about friends you used to have but no longer consider friends. Pray for them, and ask God to help you restore old friendships.

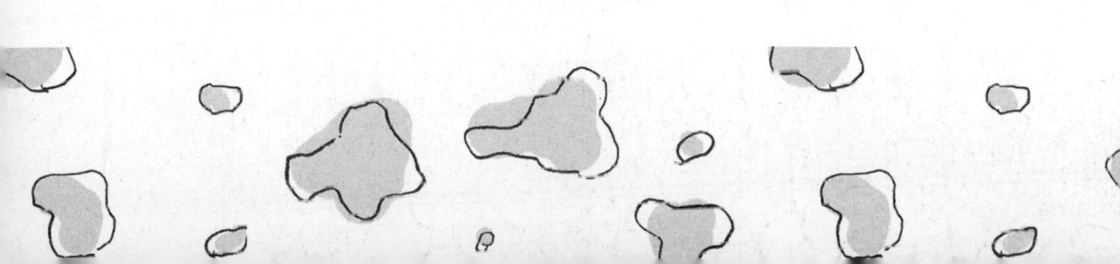

An emu father devotes two years of his life to training his chicks how to find food and how to dodge enemies.

• • •

TODAY: Write down five pieces of good advice you've gotten from your parents. Include those sayings that drive you crazy. Today, keep all the advice in mind and follow it.

TEACHABILITY

Animals in the wild have to learn fast how to protect themselves. But even wild animal babies aren't born with the survival skills they need to make it in the world. They have to learn from their parents and siblings, and sometimes from extended family members. If they're stubborn and rebellious, they may not make it. But if they're teachable, they can learn what they need to know.

Tiger cubs play and learn how far they can go when roughhousing with one another. But when their mother calls them back, they learn quickly to come running.

Baby birds have to learn how to fly. Sometimes the flying lessons can be pretty tough—getting nudged out of the nest, landing hard on the ground, scurrying back to the tree, reaching the safety of the nest . . . only to be nudged out again.

Humans have to learn too. And the learning goes on for the rest of our lives. Most schoolteachers would rather have a student who's eager to learn than a brilliant student who thinks he or she knows everything already.

Maybe you're ahead of your class academically. The math problem your teacher writes on the board is something you knew how to do last year. But being teachable means that you can always learn more.

Your parents know a thing or two. Being teachable means that you listen to your parents and take advantage of the wisdom they might have earned the hard way, through some tough experiences.

Learn from your own mistakes too. Don't let yourself off the hook when you keep repeating the same mistakes. Don't laugh it off with, "That's just me" or "How was I supposed to know?" Good judgment comes from learning from our mistakes.

> *My children, listen when your father corrects you. Pay attention and learn good judgment.*
> **PROVERBS 4:1**

GRIEVING GECKOS

The Madagascar day gecko is unusual in the animal world because it mates for life. If the female gecko dies, the male will spend the rest of his life alone. Since his eyes bug out naturally, the poor gecko looks like he's wandering the earth searching for his lost mate and in a continual state of shock when he doesn't find her.

When two horses have pastured together for a long time and one dies, the remaining horse can go through a period of grieving, involving listlessness and poor appetite. Dogs may go through the same thing.

If you've lost someone close to you, you know how much it hurts. You can know the "right answers"—that your loved one is in heaven and happier than he or she ever was in this life, that you'll see the person again in heaven, that it's for the best, that you'll always hold that person in your heart. But it still hurts. And you're still so sad, you don't think you can stand it.

When it feels like you can't stand it or like nobody understands, remember that God does. God the Father knows what it's like to see his Son killed, to suffer separation and death. He gets it.

God grieves with you. When Jesus' friend Lazarus died and his sisters and friends wept at the funeral, Jesus wept too. He knew he was going to bring his friend back to life to show the power of the resurrection, but he still cried. He grieved at how sad Lazarus's sisters were.

So when you're at your saddest, remember that God is right there with you, sad with you, with his arms around you in comfort.

The Lord cares deeply when his loved ones die.
PSALM 116:15

Nearly all young mammals make cries when separated from their mothers. When a baby rat cries, its mother brings it back to the nest. Infant marmoset monkeys cry for attention, and when they're older, they cry to be picked up and carried. Chimps make all kinds of noises and whimpers when they lose their mothers.

• • •

TODAY: Thank God that he cares so much. And the next time you grieve, don't forget that God is grieving with you.

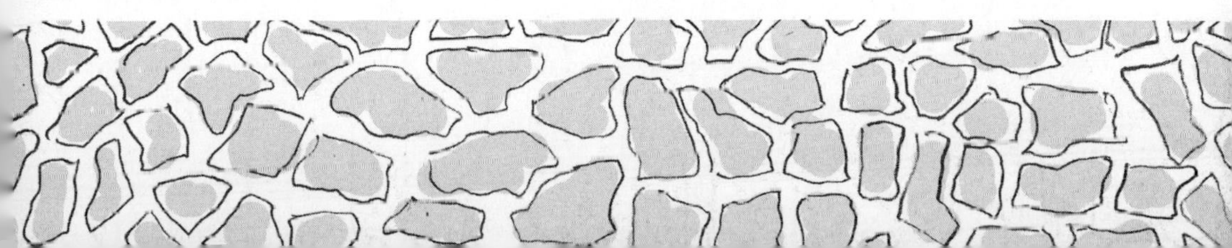

Some cats suffer from feline vestibular syndrome, which basically means dizziness. Symptoms range from a cat's tilting its head to falling down. A cat may roll around, lean on furniture, or stand still, looking completely out of it.

• • •

TODAY: The next time you feel your day slipping away from you, stop, talk to God, and imagine holding his hand and being steady again.

DIZZY DAYS

If a mouse twirls in circles, chasing its tail until it catches it, then bites the tip of its tail, it's probably trying to steady itself from extreme dizziness. If the dizziness is severe enough, the mouse will end up chewing off its entire tail, hoping to steady itself and stop the dizziness. Mice can suffer from Ménière's syndrome, a kind of extreme dizziness probably caused by inner ear problems or deafness.

You've probably seen dogs chase their tails. Some dogs do this regularly, getting themselves dizzy in the process. Vets don't agree on the reasons dogs chase their tails. Some say it's boredom, and the solution is to play with your pet. Other reasons offered are fleas lodged in the base or tip of the tail, or some other physical discomfort.

Do you ever have dizzy days? (Or dizzy years?) Times when you just can't seem to concentrate, when nothing goes right, and you keep making a fool of yourself?

Maybe things are changing too fast for you. You're in a new situation or a new school, or you get a new family member. There are big changes at home. You lose a friend. You get a big disappointment . . . or even some terrific news. You're changing too fast.

It's okay. When we're "dizzy," God is still our Rock. He's always steady. He never changes. And God never has a bad day.

So take a time-out and escape for a little while. Go where you can get alone with God and soak up that stability. He'll lead you on a smooth path, in a straight line. He'll keep you from running in circles.

God is our Rock.

He alone is my rock and my salvation, my fortress where I will never be shaken.

PSALM 62:2

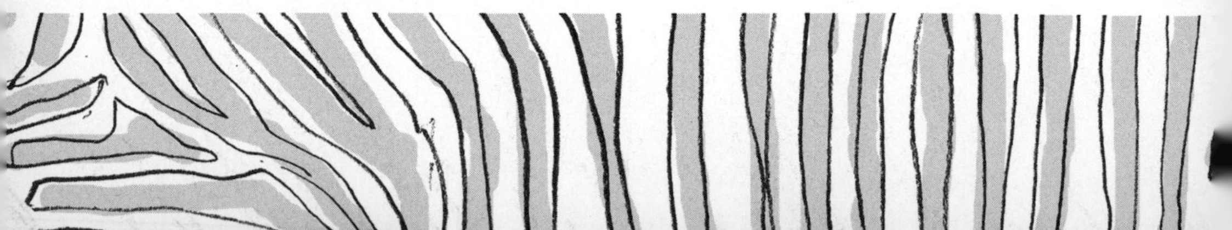

NO WAY!

Some things in the animal world seem impossible. How about a male giving birth?

The sea horse is a miracle of nature. A few weeks before sea horse babies are born, the mother lays her eggs in a pouch in the male's abdomen. There, the eggs fertilize and incubate. When the eggs are finally ready to hatch, the male gets labor pains—actual birth pangs. He hurries to get ready for the delivery. Using his tail, he fastens himself to an underwater plant.

Then he waits. After a while, tiny, quarter-inch baby sea horses explode from their father's brood pouch. A minute later, the sea fry can move on their own. And they swim off all by themselves.

Lots of things have looked impossible to humans over the years—landing on the moon, talking on a wireless telephone across continents, connecting in cyberspace—and on and on.

You probably run up against all kinds of seemingly impossible demands in school and at home. One year, getting a passing grade in history might seem impossible. Another year, giving a speech or report in front of the class looks out of the question. Being friendly to someone who's always mean could look impossible, and so could being nice to your little brother.

But God promises us that nothing—not one thing—is impossible with God. True, it would be impossible without God. But you're not without God.

> *Jesus looked at them intently and said, "Humanly speaking, it is impossible. But not with God. Everything is possible with God."*
> MARK 10:27

A bee can lift 300 times its own weight, which would be like you lifting thirty horses at the same time. Bees also shouldn't be able to fly. Their body weight is too high in comparison to their wing area. Bee flight goes against the principles of aerodynamics . . . and yet bees do fly.

• • •

TODAY: List 10 things you think are too hard for you to pull off. Talk to God about each one, and ask for faith to believe that with God's help, even these things are not impossible.

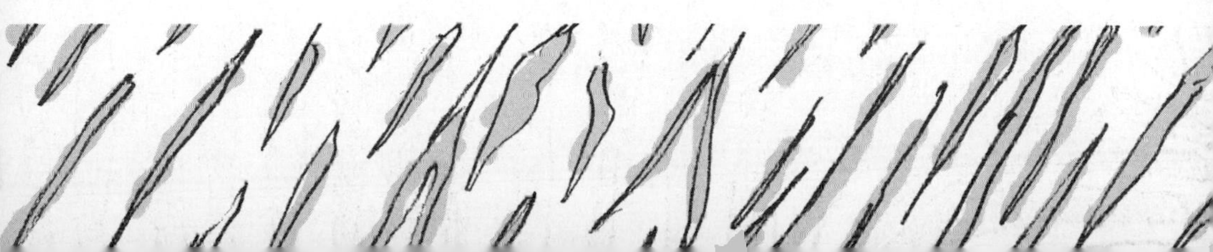

Lantern fish can be found in all the oceans of the world. One lantern fish can make enough light to let you read in bed at night.

• • •

TODAY: Carve out 30 minutes to read the Bible. (You might start with the Gospel of John and add a few psalms and a couple of proverbs.) Expect God to shine his flashlight directly on a problem you're having today.

LANTERN TO MY PATH

One of the coolest fish in the whole world is the lantern fish, a small fish that swims in the deep sea. There are at least 250 species of lantern fish, and almost all of them have tiny glowing lights along their bellies or sides. Some have lights around their eyes, like headlights, or on their tails. They create their own light as they swim and can make the light brighter or dimmer.

The *Diaphus* lantern fish has a big light on its head, like a coal miner's lamp. The light guides the fish and wards off enemies.

As amazing as it is that God chose to build in a light for this tiny fish to be able to survive in the depths of sea, it's even more amazing that we've been given all the light we'll ever need to be guided where we need go. We just need to look to God and to his Word.

In *The Message*, a paraphrased version of the Bible, Psalm 119:105-107 reads like this: "By your words I can see where I'm going; they throw a beam of light on my dark path. . . . Everything's falling apart on me, God; put me together again with your Word."

Picture a lantern fish with its miner's light leading it through an underwater maze. You have that kind of light to get you through the tricky paths of your day too. The Bible isn't just a book of rules and stories. It's light. Reading what God says is like shining a flashlight at your feet so you won't step into a black hole.

You might wish you had a floodlight instead of a flashlight, a lightning bolt instead of a lantern. But all you need to know is where to put that next step. And the next. You have all you need to stay on the path.

> *Your word is a lamp to guide my feet and a light for my path.*
>
> **PSALM 119:105**

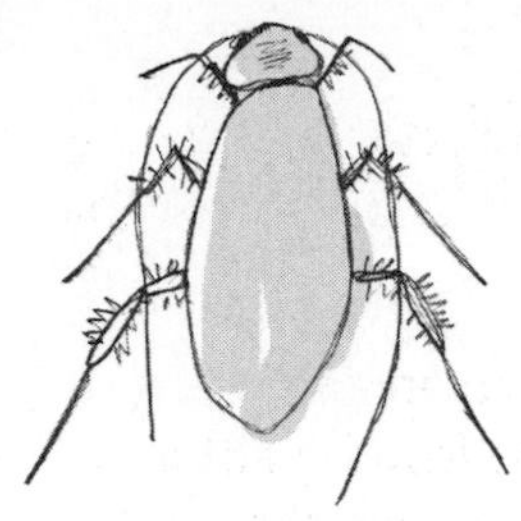

THEY'RE EVERYWHERE!

Cockroaches.

They've been known to pop out of silverware drawers, scurry across posh carpet in the dining rooms of million-dollar homes, work their way into bedroom mattresses, and take little midnight swims in the toilet.

And cockroaches don't just hang out in houses. In fact, they spread themselves into every corner of the world. Most cockroaches live in tropical climates, where they feed on living and dead plants and animals. Some roaches live a good part of their lives in water. Others live in the desert. And certain roaches live with termites, ants, or wasps in communities.

Cockroaches are everywhere.

No location is too hot or too cold for the roach . . . except the polar ice caps. Wherever you go, you can be fairly certain that a cockroach or two has gone before you.

If you think you can't get away from cockroaches, that's nothing. The one you really can't get away from is God. If you curl up in your closet, God surrounds you. If you run to your secret hideout in the woods, God is there, too. He's at every party you'll ever go to and in every car you'll ever ride in.

You can't escape from God . . . and you shouldn't want to!

God is everywhere!

> *I can never escape from your Spirit! I can never get away from your presence! If I go up to heaven, you are there; if I go down to the grave, you are there. If I ride the wings of the morning, if I dwell by the farthest oceans, even there your hand will guide me, and your strength will support me.*
> **PSALM 139:7-10**

Young cockroaches can sneak into a crack that's as thin as the edge of a dime. Adult male cockroaches only need a space that's as thick as the edge of a quarter. Pregnant female cockroaches need the most room to hide out—a space as big as two nickels stacked together.

• • •

TODAY: Ask God to help you remember all day long that he's right there with you. See how many places you can go and remember God's presence.

When a monkey opens its mouth wide and shows its teeth, it's not giving you a friendly smile. It's threatening to attack you. When a monkey wants to say a friendly hello, it smacks its lips together.

• • •

TODAY: Say one positive thing to someone you haven't complimented or encouraged lately.

BIG MOUTH

You don't want to mess with a crocodile. One look at that big, teeth-filled mouth, and you know the crocodile's bite is deadly. Its jaws can snap shut on you with the pressure of 3,000 pounds. Crocodile teeth are set all along its mouth, making a fierce weapon. And if the poor croc should break its teeth biting into your bone, no sweat. All 70 of its teeth can replace themselves over and over.

The five-pound marine toad of South America has a big mouth that is toothless but filled with poisonous spit. Farmers use the big-mouthed toad to protect their grain fields from mice and rats. The toad gulps down a rat, trapping the rodent in its mouth and poisoning it to death.

How's *your* mouth? Has anyone ever called you a "big mouth"? Or maybe you muttered that to yourself after something slipped out that you wish hadn't?

When someone else is talking, do you keep your mouth shut and really listen, or are you just waiting for a chance to interrupt with your own ideas? Do you ever find yourself with your foot in your mouth? How long do you really think before you speak?

The book of Proverbs is filled with advice for big mouths:

> *Those who control their tongue will have a long life;*
> *opening your mouth can ruin everything.*
> **PROVERBS 13:3**

> *The tongue of the wise makes knowledge appealing,*
> *but the mouth of a fool belches out foolishness.*
> **PROVERBS 15:2**

> *The heart of the godly thinks carefully before speaking;*
> *the mouth of the wicked overflows with evil words.*
> **PROVERBS 15:28**

> *Even fools are thought wise when they keep silent;*
> *with their mouths shut, they seem intelligent.*
> **PROVERBS 17:28**

Sometimes it's a good idea to be the strong, silent type. Check out your words with God before you let them out of your mouth.

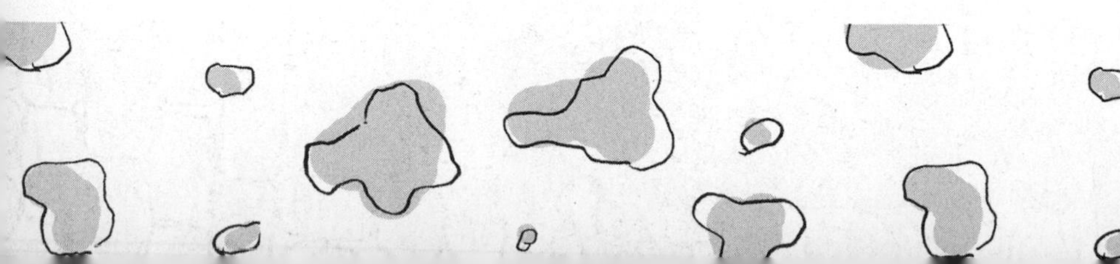

GIVE-AND-TAKE

Unlike the alligator, crocodiles don't have a good way to clean their teeth. A croc's tongue is stuck on the bottom of its mouth, so it can't help take out junk that sticks in its teeth.

Crocodiles can't floss. So they need help.

That's where the plover comes in. Crocodiles and plover have formed a strange partnership. The bird pecks at the particles of food stuck between the crocodile's teeth. The plover gets a nice meal out of the deal, and the crocodile gets clean teeth. It's an odd friendship, but it works. In fact, the plover is the only living thing that the crocodile has never been known to attack.

Good friendships work for both people—with give-and-take on both sides. If you're always giving, giving in, or trying to get the other person to like you as much as you like that person, that's not give-and-take.

On the other hand, if you have someone you're taking advantage of because you know that person wants to be in your group or wants to be your best friend—that's not give-and-take either.

The apostle Paul wrote to various churches and told them that when he came for a visit, he wanted to be encouraged and built up in his faith, just like he hoped to encourage them and build them up in theirs. He needed them as much as they needed him.

Try to have good relationships with everybody. But if God gives you one truly good friend, that's an enormous blessing.

When we get together, I want to encourage you in your faith, but I also want to be encouraged by yours.
ROMANS 1:12

Female crocodiles are surprisingly good mothers. Unlike other reptiles, the female crocodile doesn't take off after laying her eggs. She sticks with the eggs through the three-month incubation period, then stays with her baby crocs for several months, protecting and feeding them.

• • •

TODAY: Prayerfully examine your relationships. List the ones that you know are off kilter—with you taking too much or giving too much. Address one friendship today by talking honestly with your friend.

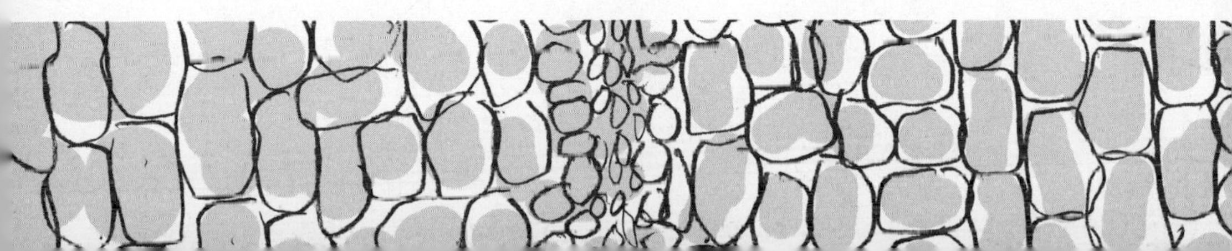

One way a bat can calm down quickly is by controlling its respiration—going from eight breaths a second down to one breath every eight minutes.

• • •

TODAY: What "storms" have you faced lately? Talk to God about the way you faced the last upsetting situation. The next time anything gets you riled or rattled, quickly hand it over to God, and calm down.

CALM DOWN

Bats have a life expectancy of about 20 years—longer than any other creature of their size. Why?

Scientists think the bat's long life has a lot to do with how fast bats can calm down. Bats can shift into rest mode almost instantly. They go to sleep quickly, and they hibernate. Almost immediately, a bat can slow its heart rate from 180 beats a minute to only three beats a minute.

How fast do you calm down when you're upset or scared or angry? Everybody gets upset. We can't help that initial reaction. But how long does it take before you're able to give your anger over to God? Do you stew for days? Are you a handwringer or a nail biter? Do you have to go over and over the incident in your head, replaying every insult or distressing detail?

Don't make things worse by playing the "What-if . . ." game. (What if I freeze on stage and forget my lines?) Don't play the "If only . . ." game either. (If only I hadn't tried to talk to her. . . . If only I'd told him to mind his own business. . . .)

Other people can upset us. Maybe your dad promised he'd come to your game, but he didn't show. We can get upset with ourselves, too. You strike out in the ninth and know you could have gotten a hit. Or you blow a test. Any of a hundred things can go wrong in a day. You're bound to get upset, but you don't have to stay upset. Talk to God, and turn things over to him.

Jesus calmed the storm when his best friends were freaking out and thinking they'd drown at sea. The sea calmed, and so did his friends. Trust Jesus with your storms, and he'll help you calm down too.

The disciples went and woke him up, shouting, "Master, Master, we're going to drown!" When Jesus woke up, he rebuked the wind and the raging waves. Suddenly the storm stopped and all was calm.
LUKE 8:24

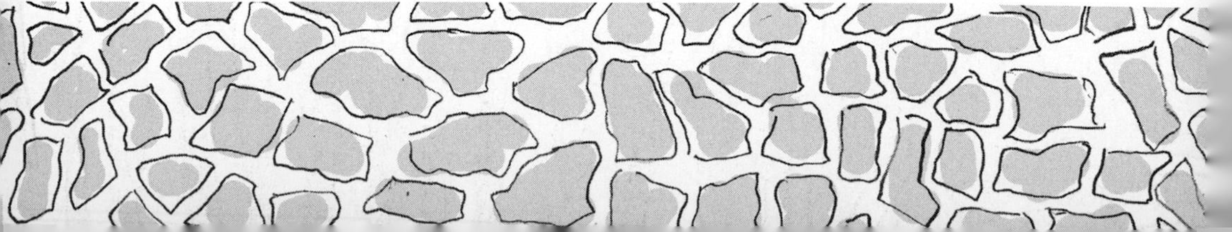

BAD VIBES

Rattlesnakes are good hunters, slithering through fields and deserts in search of prey. What's amazing is the fact that these great hunters are deaf. They can't even hear their own rattles rattle. They can't hear frogs and other prey scrambling to a hideout. But what they can do is sense a frog's vibrations. Rattlesnakes can pick up the slightest vibrations on the ground.

The blind subterranean mole rat gets along well without sight because it relies on making and receiving vibrations from friends and foes. In underground tunnels, the moles communicate with neighbors by head banging. They hit their heads on burrow walls to send messages. They lay their jaws against the same walls to increase conduction of vibrations through the jawbone, allowing them to pick up more vibes.

How sensitive are you to the good and bad vibes people send off every day? Are you paying close enough attention to your mom, for example, so you can tell she's had a rotten day, even though she plants a smile on her face and says things are fine? Do you know when your dad has something on his mind, even though he hasn't said anything?

If your friend suddenly becomes quiet and withdrawn, do you just take advantage of the situation and talk more? Or do you read the vibes and figure something must be wrong?

God's Spirit inside you can guide you into truth and give you insight that will help you help others. Pay attention.

Tune in to the vibes.

A prudent person foresees danger and takes precautions. The simpleton goes blindly on and suffers the consequences.
PROVERBS 27:12

Sharks (especially hammerheads) are great at detecting vibrations. They can tune in to even the tiniest ocean current caused by a prey's heart muscle contracting!

• • •

TODAY: Ask God to make you sensitive to other people's vibes today. Ask for guidance in how you can help.

BLOOMING MICE

Mice are everywhere.

House mice may be the most widespread and numerous mammals in the world. Scientists say that mice survive and thrive in so many climates because they have the ability to adapt. All that means is that mice do what it takes to adjust and to get along wherever they are.

Mice can walk, scurry, and run. But they can also jump and swim when necessary. They can vary their diets and living conditions. They "bloom where they're planted," if you can imagine a blooming mouse.

How do you handle change? Do you think you're adaptable, quick to adjust to new things? If you have to move and leave old friends, it isn't easy. If you have to switch schools, it can be traumatic. Changes in your family, or yourself, can make you feel like you don't belong anywhere.

But if we know God is in control of our lives, we know that he can make even unwanted changes work out for the best. You may not see how for a long time, but you can trust God to do what's right for you.

Sometimes a change in your circumstances requires a change in you. That's adapting. Maybe you were so secure with your best friend in your old school that you didn't have to worry about making new friends. In a new school, you might need to change and start introducing yourself and taking the first steps in making new friends.

Keep in mind that no matter what changes come along, God is there. He never changes. You can bloom and blossom, knowing that your relationship with God continues to be firm.

> *Be thankful in all circumstances, for this is God's will for you who belong to Christ Jesus.*
> **1 THESSALONIANS 5:18**

The edible dormice were farmed by Romans and fattened up to be eaten by Roman families and royalty. Until the little creatures were ready, they were kept in terra-cotta jars.

• • •

TODAY: List three changes you've had to adjust to this year. How did you do? Talk to God about any situation you don't think you're getting used to yet. Thank him for the change, even if you have to thank him by faith.

BORED?

Horse people sometimes talk about "problem horses," but most of a horse's problems are caused by people. Wild horses are born to run through fields of grass, drink from mountain streams, travel in the company of the herd, and sleep in the safety of a community of horses.

Horses kept in stables, especially if they're in small stalls without the companionship of other horses, frequently develop problems. It's not unusual to see a horse chewing on the wood of its stall door or the edge of its feed trough. In some stables you can see dips in stall doors, where horses have chewed.

If a horse discovers it can suck in air while chewing on the wood, the horse develops a more serious vice called wind sucking, or cribbing. The habit becomes an addiction, and you can end up with a very sick horse.

And each of these vices is brought on by boredom.

Do you get bored easily? Boredom may seem like a safe vice. You just sit around and sigh. You're the only victim, unless you're driving your parents crazy by complaining about being bored. But being bored opens you to getting into trouble just to put a little excitement into your life.

Being bored is also a slap in the face of God.

God's creation is all around you. Turn off the TV and computer games. Go outside and look around. Appreciate nature. Watch people. If you're stuck at home, try creating something yourself—a card for your grandma, a painting for your dad, a journal for yourself.

There's no such thing as a boring day—only bored and boring people.

You thrill me, Lord, *with all you have done for me! I sing for joy because of what you have done.*
PSALM 92:4

Horses aren't the only animals that get bored. Indoor cats are easily bored, and the result could be an overweight, unhappy, unhealthy, or aggressive and destructive feline. What's a cat owner to do? Here are some tips: Hide the cat toys and let Kitty seek. Place one thing (a sack, a shoe, a ball, a box) out of place when you leave the house. Try putting scratching posts and cat towers by windows. And play with your cat!

• • •

TODAY: Go on a short walk and find some excitement—by noticing what's around you. Make a list of 20 things you've never paid attention to before today.

I CAN'T STAND IT!

In most of the world, the ocean floor averages over 12,000 feet deep. Very few creatures can stand the pressure from all that water. Pressures may be over 100 times what we could be comfortable with.

Yet some animals do manage to survive the pressures of the deep. Besides the abundance of tiny flatworms, other animals at the bottom of the ocean include sea stars, sole, flounder, shrimp, corals, sponges, barnacles, oysters, mollusks, sea anemones, and even some crustaceans.

Thousands of creatures can stand the pressure of several tons per square inch.

How do you survive pressure? Do you ever feel like you just can't take one more thing going wrong? like the pressure is getting to you and you can't stand it?

It's true—life can come at you fast. But you can handle anything with God. Once you take a deep breath and step back, you can usually find ways to lessen the pressure.

If you're worried about several big tests falling on the same day next week, start studying for them right now. If you think your gym teacher or coach hates you and the pressure of performing gets you so wound up that you mess up every time, talk to your coach. And work harder.

Sometimes you can't really do anything about the outside pressures. But you can work from the inside out. Talk to God about everything that's making you crazy. Read the Psalms, and let God's Word take you away from life's pressures for a while. God is always next to you—all around you. Talk to him.

Remember that God has promised not to give you more than you can stand. So yeah—you can stand it.

As pressure and stress bear down on me, I find joy in your commands.
PSALM 119:143

On the bottom of the ocean floor, where scientists once believed no living creatures could survive, is a bizarre creature called the giant isopod. It feeds on dead whales, squid, and other fish (preferably dead ones). Although it's shaped like a wood louse or pill bug, the isopod is about a foot long and is related to shrimp and crabs.

• • •

TODAY: List five things in your life that are causing you to feel pressured. Write down concrete steps you can take to relieve some of those pressures, and turn everything over to God.

KEEP MOVING

Sharks are apparently the only animals that almost never get sick. They're immune to practically every disease, including cancer. Nobody's sure why, but it might have something to do with the fact that they're constantly in motion.

Sharks have to keep moving. If they don't, they'll sink. Besides, most sharks need to keep moving so they can breathe. They keep their mouths open and let water sweep across their gills, giving them oxygen. But if they stop or move backward, they'll die.

The cookiecutter shark cheats to keep moving. It uses a suction cup to grab onto a whale and get a free ride.

Sharks can rest, but they can't sleep. They have to keep moving.

How easy is it for you to stop instead of keeping moving? Say you start piano lessons and are pretty motivated at first. Then you realize that it's not always fun to practice every day, going over the same scales. You want to play songs you know, but you have to practice old tunes and ridiculous piano exercises. So you quit.

Maybe you start out with a great idea, like visiting people in the nursing home or working in the church nursery or helping an elderly neighbor. But if nobody appreciates your efforts or if the project gets too boring, it's so easy to quit.

Other good things are easy to quit too: tithing, calling or writing your grandparents regularly, trying to talk to friends about Christ. It takes a lot to keep moving.

God understands your struggles to keep moving. And he promises that if you don't give up, you won't be sorry. Good things will come out of your efforts.

> *I press on to reach the end of the race and receive the heavenly prize for which God, through Christ Jesus, is calling us.*
> **PHILIPPIANS 3:14**

SHARK TRIVIA:

Great white sharks have teeth that are as hard as nails.

Mako sharks can leap into the air.

Angel sharks bury themselves in the sandy sea bottom and wait for unsuspecting crabs to come by.

When cookiecutter sharks attach themselves to whales with a suction cup, they also bite out a chunk of flesh from their free ride.

• • •

TODAY: List three good things you've quit doing. Talk to God about each one and consider starting one thing again. Ask God to help you keep moving.

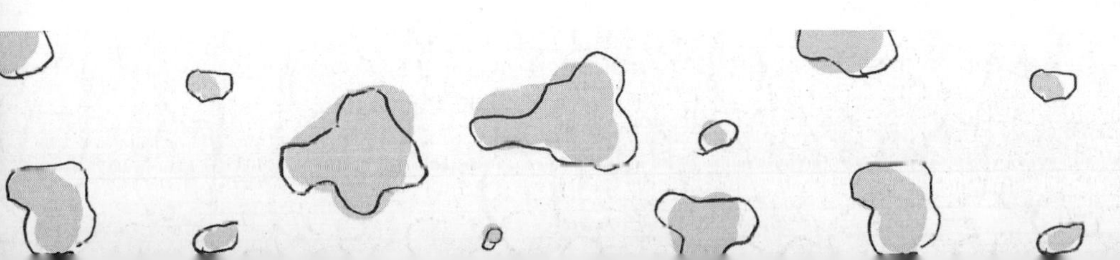

Flamingos may be the most social birds in the world. They hang out with other flamingos in groups of about 20, but on occasion, they like to gather in even bigger groups. (You can also find plastic versions on lawns from time to time.)

• • •

TODAY: Talk to God about the church you attend. (If you don't go to church, ask God to guide you into the right church, where you can have real fellowship with other Christians.) If there are any divisions, pray that the people in charge will remember to follow Christ and look out for one another.

FELLOWSHIP

Horses love hanging out with each other in the field . . . as long as they have a clearly defined leader. Without a leader, there may be chaos and fighting. And certainly no fellowship and friendships will be formed. But if the horses pay allegiance to the leader, all goes well with the herd.

The queen bee is the center of the hive. When all the bees are taking orders from the queen, the hive runs smoothly. And the bees work together as if they're one body with one purpose.

Dogs and wolves are good examples of social animals. In order to enjoy fellowship with one another, the pack needs a leader, an alpha dog.

Lions need a king, a leader of the pride. And so it goes with other social animals, like meerkats, chimpanzees, and gorillas.

Humans are social creatures too. Christians are commanded to fellowship with one another—to spend time getting to know one another and to work together for the good of the body of Christ. But if you're part of a church or youth group, you've probably seen divisions among Christians. Disagreements can get so heated that churches split and youth groups die out.

No matter what causes the division, the solution is the same: follow the leader.

Follow Christ. If everyone follows Christ, we'll all be going in the same direction. Our groups will run more smoothly, focused on the same purpose. And we'll be able to look out for each other and reach outside the group to be used by God.

Let us not neglect our meeting together, as some people do, but encourage one another, especially now that the day of his return is drawing near.
HEBREWS 10:25

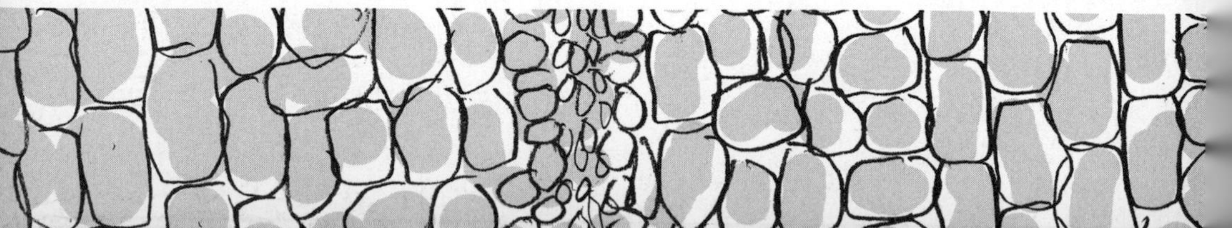

August 23

A HEDGEHOG'S SELF-DEFENSE

A hedgehog is a roly-poly creature with a pointy nose, tiny eyes, short legs, and sharp quills all over its body. It looks like a porcupine and has the same type of pointy spines. A male hedgehog has about 500 quills on its back.

When a hedgehog feels threatened, it curls up into a prickly ball and won't let anyone in. Sharp quills stick out everywhere, protecting the hedgehog's face, tail, legs, and feet, which are tucked safely inside.

Sometimes a rolled-up hedgehog gets rolled into the water by a sly fox. But for the most part, the hedgehog's defenses are fairly reliable, and predators learn to stay away.

Do you ever dodge people by pulling into yourself? Some people are shy by nature, and there's nothing wrong with that . . . as long as it doesn't keep you from having the relationships God wants for you. If you always avoid eye contact with other people, it won't be easy to get to know them.

God can help you open up. You could take a step toward friendship by admitting to others that you're shy but you'd really like to get to know them. If you don't know what to say, you can always ask people about themselves. You can be a good listener, and they'll believe you're the best conversationalist ever.

Shyness might not be your defense. Maybe being prickly is the way you keep from letting people in. Sarcasm and a sharp tongue can do the job, and soon people are afraid to talk to you. Being standoffish or snapping at people can do the same.

There's a better way. Ask God to show you how to let people in. It's hard to show people Christ if you always keep to yourself.

When I am afraid, I will put my trust in you.
PSALM 56:3

Wild hedgehogs can fend off most enemies by rolling into a spiny ball. But one creature that is not deterred is the flea. Hedgehogs are usually badly infested with fleas.

• • •

TODAY: Today, smile directly into the faces that pass you, and pray for each one as you smile. If you get the chance, ask one or more people a question about themselves.

Most insect fathers are worthless when it comes to looking after their kids. But the giant water bug allows the female to cement up to 150 eggs onto his back. She takes off, leaving him to carry the eggs with him wherever he goes for a whole month. Daddy Water Bug exercises to get oxygen to his eggs, suns himself to keep parasites away, and stops eating so that he won't accidentally eat his new babies.

• • •

TODAY: List 10 characteristics of a great dad. Then go through your list and thank your heavenly Father that he excels as a dad in every possible way.

REAL LOVE

Although not all animal fathers are great at the job, certain dads in the animal world give us a good example of what true love looks like.

A father emperor penguin makes big sacrifices to see that the single egg laid by the female will hatch and the chick will thrive. In Antarctica, where temperatures can fall to minus 80 degrees, Father Penguin uses the warmth from his body to incubate the egg, balancing it on his feet in a brood pouch of skin and feathers. For nine weeks, he doesn't eat. And when the chick hatches, the father still doesn't leave until the chick has grown enough to survive outside the pouch. At last, after having lost one-third of his body weight, Father Penguin has to travel about 60 miles to reach food.

Stickleback fish like to eat the eggs of other sticklebacks. So it's up to dear ol' dad to protect his fertilized eggs. He gives off a kind of glue from his kidneys to build a solid nest for the eggs. Every day he gets oxygen to the eggs by fanning water through his nest. When the eggs hatch, he gathers the fry who drift out of the nest, puts them into his mouth, and spits them back into the nest.

Other great dads, such as daddy deer mice and father foxes, hover over their young to protect and defend them. Male spotted sandpipers sit on the eggs for 21 days, then take care of the hatchlings for another 21 days.

Compared to the love of our heavenly Father, all human and animal fathers fail. God the Father's love is perfect, total, complete, and unconditional. He cares for us all the time, watches everything we do, protects us, and delights in us. We don't even realize a fraction of what God does for us every single day.

Don't take your Father's love for granted. He loved you first, and he loves you best.

> *God showed how much he loved us by sending his one and only Son into the world so that we might have eternal life through him. This is real love—not that we loved God, but that he loved us and sent his Son as a sacrifice to take away our sins.*
>
> **1 JOHN 4:9-10**

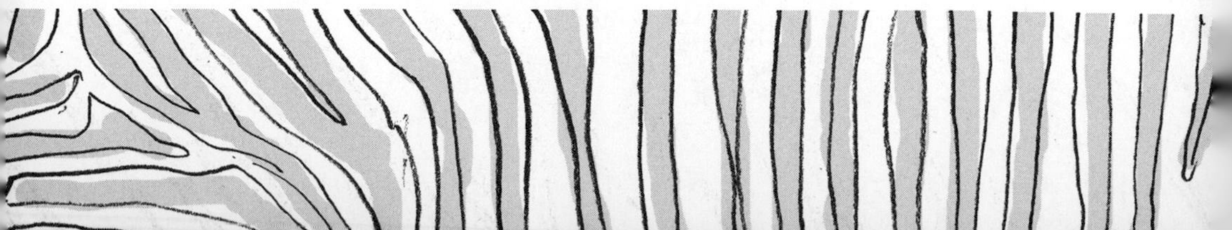

PRESS ON

God has placed amazing internal drives into some animals. Female sea turtles, for example, return to the beach where they were born, although no one knows how they can find that exact spot. They lay about 200 eggs in the sand, cover their nests, and then go back to the ocean.

When the eggs hatch, the baby turtles head for the water—a dangerous trip, with birds and other predators snatching some of them up along the way. Only one percent of baby turtles make it to adulthood. And when they do, they eventually find their way back to the beach where they were born.

Migrating animals press on over great distances. The Arctic tern flies 20,000 miles every year, about the circumference of the Earth, to reach its mating ground. Whales may migrate over 12,000 miles. The desert locust journeys 2,800 miles, and the monarch butterfly travels about 2,000 miles.

What drives you? What are you willing to press on toward? If you'd like to be the best basketball player in your school, are you willing to practice every night? ask for help? read everything you can about the sport? Or is it just a weak dream?

Maybe you're driven to play an instrument or make the top grades in your class or get a part in a school play.

The Bible talks about people who are driven to know the Lord. The prophet Hosea said, "Oh, that we might know the LORD! Let us press on to know him. He will respond to us as surely as the arrival of dawn or the coming of rains in early spring" (Hosea 6:3).

The apostle Paul was so driven to know Christ that he said he would gladly give up everything in exchange for knowing Jesus.

Press on to know Christ. Nothing else compares with that!

Everything else is worthless when compared with the infinite value of knowing Christ Jesus my Lord. For his sake I have discarded everything else, counting it all as garbage, so that I could gain Christ.
PHILIPPIANS 3:8

Elephant seals, in order to search for the food they need to stay alive, migrate from their homes out to sea and back. But male and female seals have different styles. Male seals travel the same route each migration, returning year after year to the identical spot. There they eat to their hearts' content, then return home. Female seals, on the other hand, stay away nearly twice as long and rarely take the same route twice.

• • •

TODAY: Make two changes in your regular schedule that will help you press on and get to know Christ better.

The lynx is a loner, keeping its distance from other animals and from humans. The endangered Iberian lynx goes out of its way to separate itself from other lynx. It lives in the mountains of Spain and refuses to mix with the other types of lynx living in forests below.

• • •

TODAY: If you're lonely, ask God to be your companion today. If you're not lonely or alone, consider taking some alone time to get away with God for a day.

LONERS

Remember the stories of the tortoise and the hare? The hare always comes out the villain. It looks snobbish and stuck up, right? But is that really true? Or is the hare simply a loner?

Hares are not the same as rabbits. Baby rabbits (kittens) are born blind, naked, and helpless. Baby hares (leverets) are born furry, able to see, and fairly independent. Hares are bigger than rabbits, with longer ears and longer hind legs. They like tougher food, like twigs and bark, while rabbits go for softer grass and veggies.

But the biggest difference between hares and rabbits is that rabbits are social animals, living in colonies and sharing burrows. Not hares. Hares spend most of their time alone. They only get together to mate. When the female has her babies, she stashes them in different locations and nurses them one at a time. She keeps them separated from each other and visits them at different times. Hares are loners from birth to death.

All of us go through periods when we're lonely, or at least alone. If a friend moves away or if you move to a new town, you'll probably feel lonely for a while. That's a good time to turn to God and let him fill the emptiness. If you have more time on your own, then you have time to read the Bible, pray, take walks, and think.

Just because you're alone, you don't have to be lonely. Everybody needs alone time. Even Jesus needed to get away from his friends and be alone with God. He went to the mountainside to pray by himself and to the desert to be alone with his Father.

It's okay to have times of aloneness. Sometimes it's a lot better to be a hare than a rabbit.

> *I am like an owl in the desert, like a little owl in a far-off wilderness. I lie awake, lonely as a solitary bird on the roof.*
>
> **PSALM 102:6-7**

I'VE HAD IT UP TO HERE!

How many times have you let your pet down? You walk into the house after school, and your dog jumps all over you because it's so happy to see you. But you push the pup away. You get so caught up with your friends that you forget to change the cat's litter or give it fresh water. Or you're too busy to go to the barn or stable to ride your horse, much less take care of it.

But your pets forgive you. Dogs especially seem ready and willing to forgive. Your dog will still be wagging its tail at the door when it hears you coming. It will still curl up next to you, as if you haven't done anything wrong. Your pet gives you a clean slate, a fresh start.

What about you? Is your general attitude quick-draw forgiveness? Or are you on the brink, ready to scream, "That's it! That's the last straw. I've had it up to here!"?

Your best friend acts like you don't exist as soon as that new, cool guy sits at your table. You're sick and tired of it, and you'll never speak to that friend again. That'll show her!

Your dad let you down—again. He promised to come to your parent-teacher meeting, but he didn't make it. He's sorry. He apologized, but no way. You've had it up to here!

The disciples must have had it up to here with people too. They asked Jesus how many times they had to forgive somebody who kept hurting them. They probably didn't like Jesus' answer: "Even if that person wrongs you seven times a day and each time turns again and asks forgiveness, you must forgive" (Luke 17:4).

Forgiveness is ongoing. Thankfully, God never has it "up to here" with us.

O Lord, you are so good, so ready to forgive, so full of unfailing love for all who ask for your help.
PSALM 86:5

The official Global Forgiveness Day is August 27 . . . but many dogs declare every day Forgiveness Day. They're pretty doggone smart!

• • •

TODAY: Think of three people that you've had it "up to here" with. Thank God that you're forgiven many times all day long. Ask God to help you overflow with forgiveness for the people on your fed-up-with list. What can you do to show them that all is forgiven?

Some people believe snakes can hypnotize people and prey, but there's no proof that they can. Snakes look like they're hypnotizing because they stare unblinkingly at a would-be victim. The truth is, snakes don't have eyelids, so they *can't* blink. Snakes probably don't sway to flute music either. When snake charmers play the flute, they sway back and forth, and the snake follows the swaying movement because that's what snakes do: track moving objects.

• • •

TODAY: Track your mind today and list your thoughts. What do you think about most during the day? Make an effort to think more about God and his gifts.

MIND CONTROL

Did you know chickens can be hypnotized? If you hold a chicken's head to the ground and draw a chalk line on the ground from the beak out, the chicken won't move. Some believe that the chicken thinks it's being held by the chalk line.

Another way to hypnotize a chicken is to hold it on its side against a tabletop or sidewalk for 30 seconds. After struggling a bit, the chicken will suddenly grow still, allowing you to position it any way you want. It should stay that way from a few minutes to a couple of hours.

Chickens aren't the only ones that give in to mind control. An octopus can be put into a trancelike state by having its tentacles stroked. Stroking the stomach of an alligator or crocodile is said to put it in a state of hypnosis. But don't try this one at home!

Our minds are up for grabs too. We don't have to undergo hypnosis to give in to the control of our thoughts. The things we think about night and day will work their way into our minds and attitudes.

If all you think about is cars, that's what you'll talk about all the time. You'll watch TV shows about cars. You'll notice every car that speeds past your house. You'll read about cars. Cars will, in a way, have control of your mind.

You can choose what gets first place in your head. You're the one who turns that TV show on or off. You're the one who keeps replaying the thought that flashed through your mind.

Choose thoughts that will make you a better person. Think about the things of God. Think about things that are good in the world, everything you admire about people you trust. Nobody can control your mind if you don't let them. So don't let them.

You will keep in perfect peace all who trust in you, all whose thoughts are fixed on you!
ISAIAH 26:3

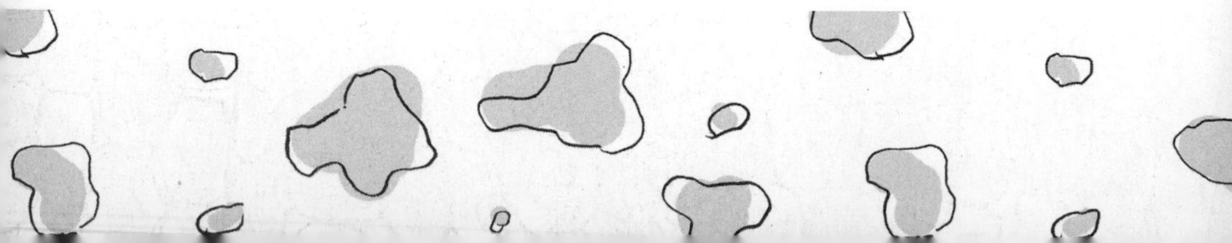

BELLY UP

Have you ever seen a dog roll over and go belly up? It might be playing with another dog, or it might be roughhousing with its human owner.

Belly up is a huge compliment from a dog. When a dog is on its back, it's in its least defensive position. It can't run away, and it can't fight very well. It can't dodge an attack or launch into one. The dog is leaving itself vulnerable because it trusts the other dog or the human.

If you watch two dogs playing and one of them goes onto its back, it may be submitting to the alpha dog, the leader of the pack. If a dog rolls over and lets you rub its tummy, that means it trusts you and may even consider you the alpha dog in your relationship. Be sure to say thanks for the compliment, and never take advantage of the trust.

Most of us don't even like the word *submission*. We don't like to be bossed around by anybody—not teachers, not parents, not siblings, not friends. We don't like to give in to other people. Not even to God.

God doesn't force us to go "belly up"—to submit to him and obey his commands. We have free will. We're not robots, and we can do what we want.

But refusing to follow God's lead isn't the route to happiness. Trusting God is. Submitting to God may be as simple as choosing to smile at somebody you can tell needs a smile. Or it may mean speaking up when a classmate is getting teased in a mean-spirited way. It's looking to God, praying, and asking for help when you're not sure what to do or say.

Dogs look the happiest when they're belly up, as if there's not a care in the world. Give it a try.

> *We keep looking to the* Lord *our God for his mercy, just as servants keep their eyes on their master, as a slave girl watches her mistress for the slightest signal.*
> **PSALM 123:2**

Although dogs will readily roll onto their backs and go belly up for a master they trust, cats aren't quite so willing. If a cat does roll over and lets you pet its belly, look out for those claws.

• • •

TODAY: Give in to God. Remember to talk to him throughout the day and ask for his direction. At the end of the day, talk to him about the decisions you made together.

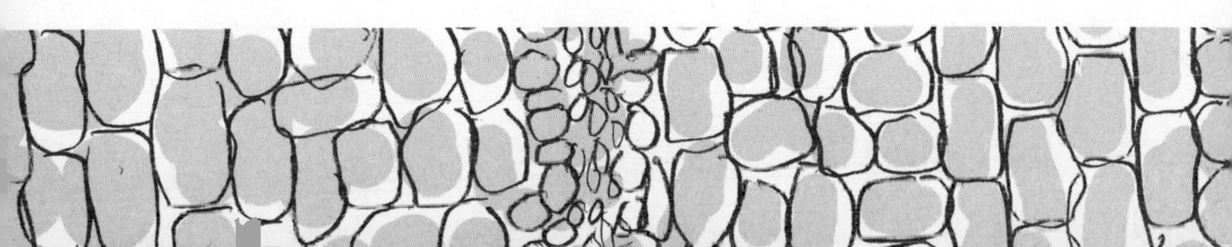

ANIMAL SLAVERY

Unfortunately some people do terrible things to animals. And sometimes animals do terrible things to animals.

Slave-making ants have one mission in life—to capture and oppress other ants and make them slaves. These slave-making ants can't do anything for themselves. They can't even get enough food to feed themselves without slaves. They can't take care of the queen or raise their young.

So they attack. They raid a colony of ants, steal the eggs, and bring them back to their own nest. When the ants grow up, they'll have to gather food, feed the slave-makers, groom and care for the queen and the larvae, defend this new colony, and carry the slave-makers if the colony moves. One colony might have 3,000 slave-making ants, with 6,000 slaves.

Slavery is an ugly thing, hated by God, and it's still going on in the human world too. We should do everything we can to help fight and end it.

But there's also another kind of slavery—one that reaches you and everyone you know. Peter wrote the early believers that people are slaves to whatever controls them (2 Peter 2:19).

If you care too much about what people think of you, you're a slave to their opinions. If all you think about is your weight or the shape of your body, then you're in danger of being a slave to how you look. If you live for weekend parties, you may be a slave to them.

Instead, let Christ control you. You're his servant, his friend. He's the only one you can be sure will always have your best interests in mind.

You have not received a spirit that makes you fearful slaves. Instead, you received God's Spirit when he adopted you as his own children.
ROMANS 8:15

South American slave-making ants take over a foreign colony by having workers give off a chemical that causes the other ants to evacuate their nest, leaving the pupae behind. The young ants are taken back to the slave-makers' nest and turned into slaves.

• • •

TODAY: Prayerfully and honestly think about what controls you. Food? Fun? Friends? Popularity? Start today to let Christ alone control you. Thank God that because of Christ you're not a slave to sin.

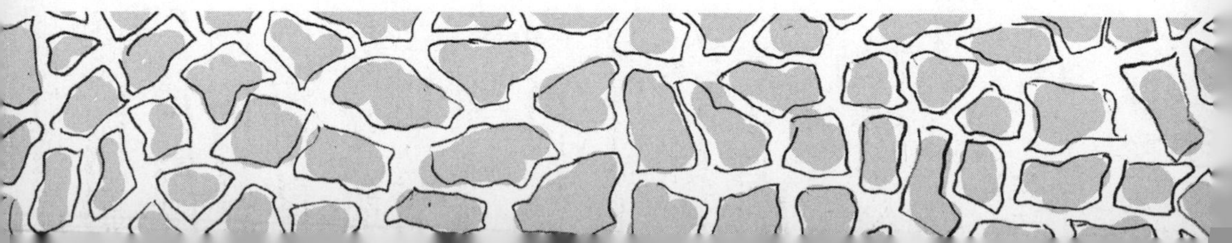

CAN A LEOPARD CHANGE ITS SPOTS?

Not all spots are created equal. Leopards in East Africa have spots, or rosettes, that are rough circles, while leopards in South Africa have squarish spots. But it's just too bad if a South African leopard wants East African–style spots, because a leopard can't change its spots.

It's not easy to get any animal to change a habit. Birds fly south in the winter and north in the summer. Spiders spin their webs in exactly the same way each time. If the web is destroyed, the spider will simply start over and construct the web exactly as it was before.

Dogs are creatures of habit too. Barking is a learned skill. A dog that hasn't been around barking dogs won't know how to bark. But a dog that has the habit of barking at every little thing is tough to turn into a nonbarking dog.

You've no doubt discovered how hard it is to break your own bad habits. All your friends exclaim, "Oh my God!" whenever you're together, and now you've started saying it too, even though you don't want to. Or maybe you and your friends are so used to gossiping that it seems impossible to stop.

Other habits are even harder to change—like envy, jealousy, or losing your temper. You can plant on a smile, but how do you get rid of jealousy?

The good news is that even though *you* might not be able to get rid of bad habits, Christ can change your spots. Don't believe the lie that you'll never change. All of Christ's power is living in you. You can change because nothing is too difficult for him.

> *Because you belong to him, the power of the life-giving Spirit has freed you from the power of sin that leads to death. The law of Moses was unable to save us because of the weakness of our sinful nature. So God did what the law could not do. He sent his own Son in a body like the bodies we sinners have. And in that body God declared an end to sin's control over us by giving his Son as a sacrifice for our sins.*
> **ROMANS 8:2-3**

Each songbird species has its own song, but the song patterns are learned. Birds aren't born with the tunes in their heads. Birds that were raised without parents or exposure to birds in their species can't sing the song of their brothers and sisters.

• • •

TODAY: List three things about yourself that you'd like to change. What have you done to bring about the change so far? Ask God to change you from the inside out.

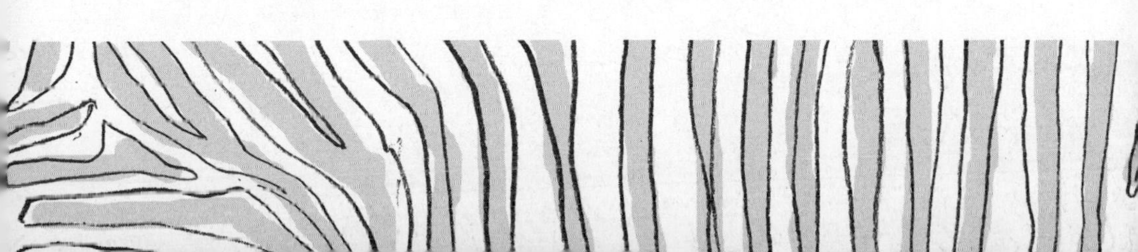

Chimpanzees share the less-than-desirable human trait of going to war consciously, with premeditation. One tribal group of chimps may hunt, capture, and kill another group.

• • •

TODAY: Are you "at war" with anyone, even in your heart? A sibling? Parent? A teacher or classmate? Is there one person in your life you just can't seem to get along with? Pray for that person. Take one step toward making peace today: smile, say hello, apologize.

EXTREME FIGHTERS

When you think about which animals are the best fighters, you might picture lion kings battling it out for the pride. Or longhorn sheep butting heads in life-and-death battles. Or bears wrestling or kangaroos boxing. . . . But those aren't the extreme fighters.

Some of the fiercest fighters have to be elephant seals, which use their giant tusks in face-to-face combat that leaves both animals beaten and bloody. Praying mantises are such good fighters that a kung fu style was named after their moves. Then there's the bombardier beetle that mixes chemicals in its rear end and squirts out boiling acid on its attacker.

The piranha, which loves the scent of blood, is a more ferocious fighter than the barracuda. Another fish, the wolf cichlid, delights in devouring the fellow inhabitants of its aquarium. The aggressive Jack Dempsey cichlid was named after the boxing heavyweight champion, who was known for his savage style of fighting.

How quick are you to fight? Fighting in schools has become a national problem, with girls as guilty as guys. When the fighters are pulled apart and taken to the office, these two questions are almost always asked: (1) What was the fight about? and (2) Why didn't you tell an authority (teachers, principal, dean) instead of fighting?

Answers don't vary much. Sometimes the fighters can't even say what the fight was about. "She called me a name." "He looked at me funny." "He can't talk to *me* that way." "She thinks she owns the lockers." Behind each answer is the feeble belief that fighting will make people respect you.

One day there may be a good reason to fight—to protect the life of someone else, for example. But most likely not at school or in your own house. That's not how you get respect. Respect yourself enough to walk away.

Turn away from evil and do good. Search for peace, and work to maintain it.

PSALM 34:14

ENOUGH ALREADY!

Horses love nothing better than eating grass all day with other horses. If you observe a pasture of cows and a pasture of horses, you'll probably notice that cows stop eating from time to time. Horses, on the other hand, rarely come up for air if the grass is good.

In early spring when the grass is thick and rich, horse owners have to limit the time their horses are allowed out to graze. If they don't, the horses will be in danger of eating too much. Horses don't have a shutoff valve when it comes to eating. That's why a horse that breaks into a feed bin can founder (eat itself sick and lame) or even eat itself to death.

Most of us go overboard on one thing or another. You're crazy about baseball, and it's all you can think about. You want to spend every spare minute playing or practicing. You watch countless games on TV and follow your team every day.

Or maybe your passion is becoming the best musician you can be. So you take lessons and practice your instrument so much that everything else suffers. Maybe your dream is to be a model or an actress, so you read all the fashion magazines and spend hours in front of the mirror. Or you may care so much about grades and school that all you do is study.

What's wrong with having a passion? Nothing.

Nothing . . . unless you don't know when to stop. Almost anything in excess can get you into trouble—even books, even studying, even over-churching yourself.

It's tough to balance homework, friends, hobbies, family, extracurricular activities, chores. Too much of a good thing isn't so good. But if you stay in touch with God, you can strike that balance. And when you tilt, God can help you get straightened out again.

> *My son, be warned: the writing of many books is endless, and excessive devotion to books is wearying to the body.*
>
> ECCLESIASTES 12:12, NASB

Colic in horses is damage or injury to the intestines, usually caused by eating too much or eating the wrong thing. Colic is the leading cause of sickness and death in horses.

• • •

TODAY: Make a chart of how you spend your spare time during the week. Ask God, and maybe your parents, to point out excesses—places where you're swerving out of balance.

STARE-DOWNS

When you were a kid—okay, maybe now—you might have had stare-downs with your friends. The one who dropped his or her eyes first, lost.

If somebody's staring at you, does it make you nervous? If you turn and look at the person, does he or she look away? If the person keeps staring, how do you take it?

Stares are meaningful in the animal world. Predators use stares to intimidate their prey and scare them. Alpha animals might reinforce their dominance with timely stares that had better not be returned . . . or else.

Most dogs get uncomfortable when you stare at them. Dog handlers advise against staring down a dog unless you're using it as a training technique.

One of the tools of a good horse handler is eye contact. Staring at a horse signals your displeasure with her behavior, and dropping your eyes from the stare can be a reward. If you want to catch a horse, pretend it's the last one you want to catch. Look at all the other horses instead. Eye contact is a powerful weapon.

How do you feel about the fact that God keeps his eyes on you? You can pull the wool over everyone's eyes . . . but not God's. God sees you even more clearly than you see yourself. But God's stare is motivated by love, not aggression. Because of God's love for you, you're always watched over and cared for. God's stare-down should make you run *to* God, not away from him.

> *Nothing in all creation is hidden from God. Everything is naked and exposed before his eyes, and he is the one to whom we are accountable.*
>
> **HEBREWS 4:13**

We all know we're not supposed to feed the animals at the zoo (unless the zookeeper says we can). But a sign in the Antwerp Zoo in Belgium (open since 1843) asks visitors not to stare at the chimpanzees.

• • •

TODAY: As you go through your regular routine, try to imagine God watching you . . . with love and concern. Talk to God about everything you're doing or any thoughts you're having.

MEAN BEAUTIES

Some of the most beautiful creatures in the animal world are also the meanest. Their beauty seems to be only skin deep.

Remember the story about the ugly duckling that turned into a beautiful swan? Swans *are* beautiful, but you don't want to get chased by one, or you'll soon see that the beauty ends with those gorgeous white feathers and long, graceful neck.

Trumpeter swans are very aggressive, even toward humans. If they believe you've crossed into their territory, look out! Swans have been known to challenge the equally aggressive Canada geese. And if the geese aren't smart enough to take off, they can end up injured or even killed.

Peacocks strut around the yard displaying their elegant colors, but they're not above chasing and pecking anyone who gets in their way.

God cares more about inner beauty than outer beauty. Sure, you want to look your best. But compared with the amount of time you spend physically primping, how much time do you spend getting yourself ready spiritually? What are you doing to become a more beautiful person on the inside—kinder, more sincere, more like Christ?

You probably think about the new clothes you want before school starts in the fall. Maybe you plan to get a new haircut or hairstyle. Nothing wrong with that.

But give the same kind of thought and consideration to your spiritual beauty. How can you make this your best year spiritually?

That's beauty that will last.

Don't be concerned about the outward beauty of fancy hairstyles, expensive jewelry, or beautiful clothes.
1 PETER 3:3

Peafowl is the general name for both the male and female of their species. A male is called a peacock, a female is a peahen, and their babies are pea chicks. A family of peafowl is known as a bevy, and a group is referred to as an ostentation or a pride.

• • •

TODAY: Time yourself today and tomorrow to see how much time you spend on outward beauty—your hair, face, clothes—and inward beauty—praying, reading the Bible, talking about God. Keep timing yourself until you spend more time on your inside than you do on your outside.

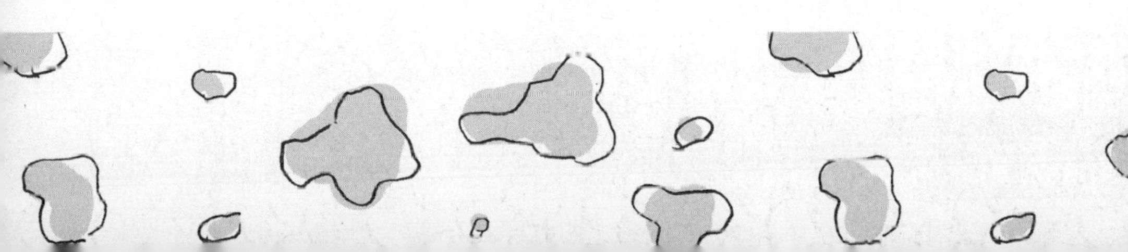

The walrus has small eyes and lousy eyesight, which would make it tough to find food . . . if it weren't for all those whiskers. Although the walrus's whiskers (between 400 and 700) aren't that attractive, they're extremely sensitive. They send information to the brain to help the walrus find food.

• • •

TODAY: Try to remember at least 10 things you thought were seriously bad breaks for you. See if you can find the gold in the garbage yet. Thank God for being smarter than you are and for giving you what you need rather than what you thought you wanted.

FROM GARBAGE TO GOLD

At first, having worms in your nice front lawn may not seem like such a good thing. Gross worms crawling around in your mom's flower garden or digging in the rows of the vegetable garden may not seem like something that would make the family happy.

But it should. Earthworms turn over the soil, breaking it up and making it richer. They eat their weight in food every day, and their food is dirt and organic garbage. Worms leave behind waste, or "casts," but that's a good thing too, because the casts are rich in fertilizer. When soil passes through a worm, it comes out with seven times the nitrogen, mixing in organic and mineral materials—all good things that return to the ground.

Earthworms are the most beneficial of all living creatures for garden soil. They make for the best, all-natural fertilizer factories in the world. One ton of worms can turn one ton of organic garbage into gold.

Remember Joseph with the coat of many colors? What looked like "garbage" in his life—being sold into slavery, falsely accused, and thrown into prison—turned into gold—rising to power in Egypt, where he was able to save many lives.

Sometimes the things in our lives that we've considered garbage turn out to be gold. You get the teacher you *really* didn't want, but she turns out to be the best teacher you've ever had. You didn't make the cheerleading squad, so you join the band. And you realize you love it more than you would have loved cheering. You thought you'd hate getting a little brother, but you discover you were wrong about that.

It might take years for you to see the good in what you thought was so bad—and you may never see it. But you can trust that God's in control. He doesn't make mistakes.

If we'll let him, he'll turn the garbage in our lives into gold.

You intended to harm me, but God intended it all for good. He brought me to this position so I could save the lives of many people.

GENESIS 50:20

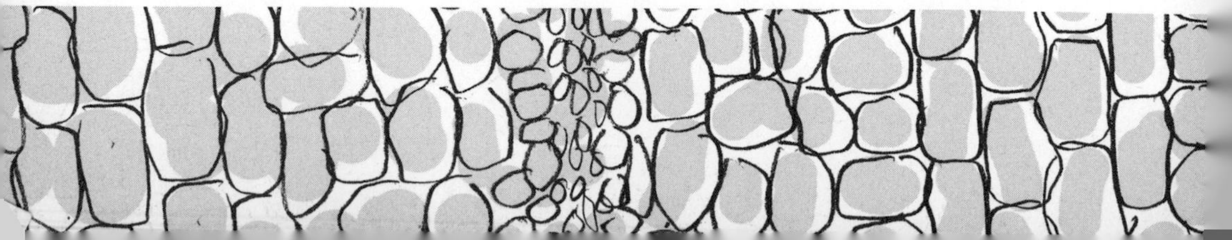

BRAINY IS AS BRAINY DOES

Most scientists agree that the human brain is the most amazing material on the planet. This twisty-turny, soft and mushy piece of flesh allows you to walk, talk, think, make friends, feel sad or happy or angry or scared, dream, create, and whistle.

Whales have the biggest brains—seven times bigger than yours. An elephant's brain is bigger than yours too. But neither of those animal brains has the complex folds and grooves that your brain has.

Some people believe that birds and ants have the largest brains compared to their size. Others say humans win the big-brain award in terms of brain to body weight, with bottlenose dolphins and chimps a close second and third.

And don't forget magpies, whose brains are almost as big as yours, when you consider their size. Birds are capable of learning complex songs and memory patterns.

Having a big brain isn't the same as being intelligent. Intelligence involves being able to make connections and to learn and apply knowledge, not just having information stored between your ears.

And intelligence and wisdom aren't the same either. Wisdom comes from listening with good judgment and learning from experience and from the advice of trustworthy people. Few fail in life because they didn't get a big enough brain. Most failures come from not using the brains God gave us.

Wise up. The best source of wisdom is God.

The Lord grants wisdom! From his mouth come knowledge and understanding.
PROVERBS 2:6

Some birds really are "birdbrains." A few birds build three nests because they can't find the first two. Other birds simply won't learn, no matter how many times they bang their brains into that picture window. And the Hawaiian goose is totally clueless about the dangers of the Hawaiian goose–eating mongoose and will walk right up to the waiting mongoose.

• • •

TODAY: Ask God for wisdom and the mind of Christ so that you will understand God's will in everything you decide today.

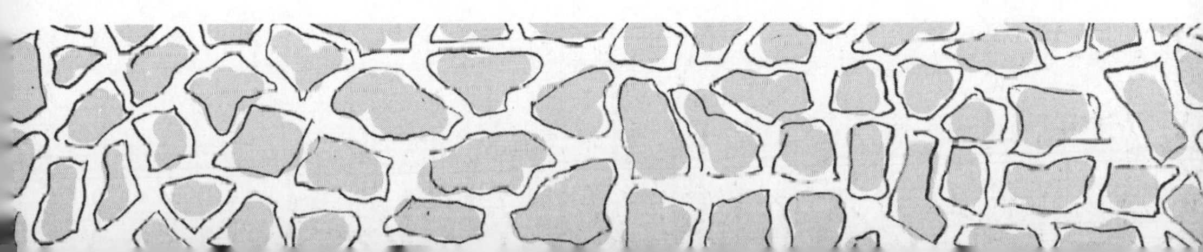

WHAT DID THESE ANIMALS DO TO DESERVE THE NAME-CALLING ASSOCIATIONS?

"You're chicken!"

"Silly goose!"

"Lazy dog."

"Messy pig."

"Scaredy-cat."

"Are you a man or a mouse?"

• • •

TODAY: Talk to God about a specific time when you were teased or looked down on because of your faith. If you are given a hard time, make sure it's truly because you're following Jesus, not because of a judgmental spirit, a holier-than-thou attitude, or an I'm-better-than-you personality.

ASKING FOR TROUBLE

Not all problems are created equal.

Let's say you take your dog on a morning walk. If you're running late or running short on patience, and if you constantly jerk the poor pooch's leash, don't blame your dog for a bad walk. The dog didn't bring it on—you did.

If your cat is minding its own business when the neighbor's dog leaps the fence and launches into an all-out chase, you can't blame your cat for running away. But if your cat steals food from the dog's dish and ends up running for her life, your cat asked for it, right?

Right. But even when your pet is asking for trouble, you know you're not going to stand by and watch it suffer. You'll be there to comfort and help that cat through its distress, just like you would have if the cat had been totally innocent.

God is there to help you, too. Whether your problems are your own fault or not, God is there to help and comfort you.

Nobody asks for persecution in any form. Yet throughout the ages, people have been mistreated and oppressed for their faith. You're blessed to live in a nation where you can worship openly. But even here, if you stand up for Christ, you might get teased or talked about behind your back. If you do, you can feel better knowing that Jesus and his friends went through the same kind of ridicule and endured much worse persecution.

> *Be happy when you are insulted for being a Christian, for then the glorious Spirit of God rests upon you. If you suffer, however, it must not be for murder, stealing, making trouble, or prying into other people's affairs.*
>
> **1 PETER 4:14-15**

STUCK ON YOU

Most animal babies are attached to their parents to some degree, but some animals are totally stuck on their parents.

The Holy Cross toad has special glands in its skin that release a gooey substance whenever the toad is upset. The gooey secretion turns into a glue that's five times stronger than the glue we use.

When a male and female Eastern narrow-mouthed toad get together, the male hops onto the female's back and hugs her. Meanwhile, he lets out a gooey substance from his belly, effectively gluing himself to the toad he loves. After a time, his fair lady lays up to 800 eggs that float on the water's surface for a few days until they hatch.

Then there are the famous barnacles (small, crusty, spineless shellfish, cousins to crabs), which glue themselves to a boat or a piece of wood and stay there, glued tight, for their entire lives.

Christ is our anchor, our rock, the one we can count on to always be there. Whenever you feel unsettled or unsure of where you stand with your friends—when people are trying to get you to try new things, dress a certain way, or talk a certain way—remember that you're "glued" to Christ, who never changes.

Throughout your whole life, you'll need to deal with change. You may go away to school. You'll probably have different friends. The world will change.

But you have an unchanging anchor. You're glued to the Rock. The storm can't wash you away.

Evil people try to drag me into sin, but I am firmly anchored to your instructions.
PSALM 119:61

The orb weaver begins building its web with the sticky end of one silk string that has to be attached to both sides of the web. The spider waits until the wind can carry the line to the right branch or structure, and then it reinforces the web with a second string. Next comes a Y, followed by all the radii extending from the center. Finally the circles are spun. After the hunt, the spider eats its web, but it saves that first string. And construction begins all over again.

• • •

TODAY: Thank God for being your anchor. Be specific—how is God your anchor when things are rough at home? at school?

Any animal clueless enough to attack the sharp-ribbed newt of eastern Asia will get what it deserves. When a predator bites into the newt, the little salamander's spiked ribs pierce the attacker's skin and shoot a painful poison directly into the attacker's mouth. Usually the predator spits out the newt as it realizes—too late—it has bitten off more than it can chew.

• • •

TODAY: List five good deeds nobody has thanked you for or praised you for. Now list 20 great deeds you forgot to thank God for.

GETTING WHAT YOU DESERVE

A greedy shark that bites into a spine-covered sea hedgehog gets what it deserves. Inside the shark's stomach, a nightmare begins. First, the sea hedgehog blows up like a spike-covered balloon. Next, the sharp spines rip a hole in the shark's side. Finally, the hedgehog escapes through the hole, but the shark is fatally wounded and eventually dies.

Any animal that launches an attack on a bombardier beetle will have a similar ghastly fate. First, the beetle pops, and a spray explodes on the attacker. At best, the spray irritates the predator's skin and eyes. At worst, the spray burns as a boiling chemical, eating away everything it touches. It sounds like the attacker gets what it deserves.

All of us struggle to get the good things we think we deserve, although few of us try to make sure we get the bad things we deserve. We don't want people talking about our failures, but we sure like to get credit for all the good things we do.

Sometimes it seems like the same people get all the glory. Teachers praise their work. Coaches give them recognition awards. They get the good parts in plays. Even your youth pastor favors them and holds them up as examples.

But nobody notices that you're the one emptying the wastebaskets at church. You have your hands full at home, taking care of a younger sibling or possibly a grandparent. Or maybe you're working as hard as you can to get those okay grades that nobody praises.

God sees it all. He notices and knows everything you do. If you're not given honor and rewards on earth, you've got some waiting for you in heaven.

And besides, even here on earth, there are lots of not-so-good deeds that go unnoticed. Maybe the next time you feel bad about not getting what you deserve, you can thank God that you haven't been given some of those bad consequences you've deserved at times. Thank him for his grace.

It's not good to eat too much honey, and it's not good to seek honors for yourself.
PROVERBS 25:27

CHOOSING A LEADER

Some animals are better than others when choosing a leader. A pride of lions usually follows the victorious male, the best fighter. A herd of wild mustangs will follow a stallion or the bossiest mare.

The honeybee that finds nectar just has to perform its special waggle dance, and the hive members will follow it anywhere.

But when bigger groups get together, it can be harder to end up with the best leader. The perfect school of fish allows a fish length between each individual fish. Members of the school are able to select a leader based on the fish's experience and gifts (mostly knowing where to go). But when the school is overcrowded, most of the fish lose sight of the leader and end up following the crowd.

Every three to four years, Norwegian lemmings get overpopulated. Food runs low, and it's time for them to migrate. Unlike many creatures who have mass migrations, the Norwegian lemmings don't have much of a plan. Their lack of leadership explains why, in 1532, people watched in horror as hundreds of lemmings plunged to their death from a high cliff in the first reported mass migration.

It's dangerous to follow the wrong leader—whether as a world or nation we choose the wrong head or as a church we follow the wrong pastor. It's true that you need to respect those in authority, but it's not okay to follow someone who is doing the wrong thing. At school, it's risky for you to follow the wrong person too. You need to separate yourself from the "mass migration" and make up your own mind.

Ultimately, the only one we can safely follow 100 percent of the time is Christ. Even if another leader does his or her best, that person is going to be wrong some of the time.

Follow Christ. Check out all decisions with him.

Putting confidence in an unreliable person in times of trouble is like chewing with a broken tooth or walking on a lame foot.

PROVERBS 25:19

Female Norwegian lemmings can get pregnant when they're only about a month old. In 16 to 21 days, a lemming may have 12 babies.

• • •

TODAY: List two people your age you think of as leaders. Why do you think other people are willing to follow them? Are those reasons good qualifications for leadership? Ask God for help in following Christ.

A group of researchers led by Michael Beran documented self-control in chimps and orangutans, which were each offered a glass bowl with a piece of chocolate in it. If they ate the chocolate, that's all they got. But if they left it in the bowl, they got more. They learned to wait until their bowls were full of chocolate. Their self-control paid off.

• • •

TODAY: List five things you do that show you're disciplined. List five things that show you need more self-control. What can you do to build self-control?

CONTROL YOURSELF!

Animals show varying degrees of self-control. Some animals, like squirrels, birds, ants, and termites, save up food for the winter. But horses will eat themselves sick, saving nothing for later. Other animals, like the father emperor penguin, will stop eating for months in order to raise his young.

We value discipline and control in our pets. A good dog is the one who sits on cue, doesn't jump up on people, and holds it until it's time to go outside.

Do we value self-control in people? If you admire someone, you might tell a friend, "Gracie is so funny" or "Ben's smart and outgoing." But have you ever said, "She's so self-controlled" or "He's really got self-discipline"?

God values self-control, and so should you. Not having it can get you into serious trouble. Some of the biggest mistakes you'll ever make will happen fast—and all because you wouldn't, or couldn't, stop yourself. It doesn't take long to say something you'll regret.

To feel like punching somebody's lights out is bad enough. To actually do it because you couldn't control yourself—that's even worse.

Some of the most long-lasting problems are a result of no self-control. Addictions, weight problems, and poor grades could reflect a lack of daily discipline. If you keep forgetting to read your Bible and pray, that lack of discipline will show itself in a stagnant spiritual life.

But according to King Solomon, if you can control yourself, it's better than conquering a city.

> *Better to be patient than powerful; better to have self-control than to conquer a city.*
> **PROVERBS 16:32**

> *A person without self-control is like a city with broken-down walls.*
> **PROVERBS 25:28**

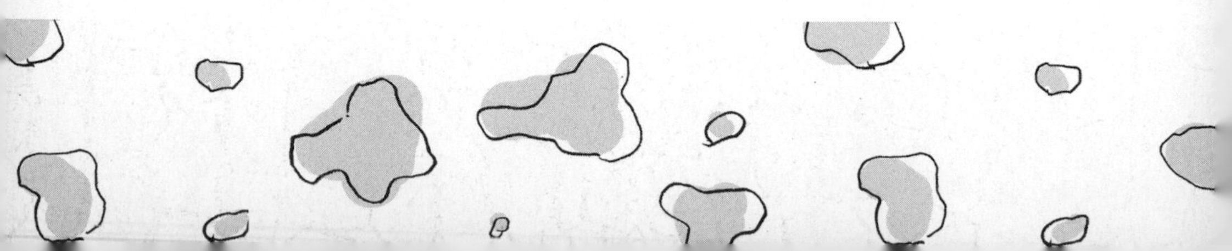

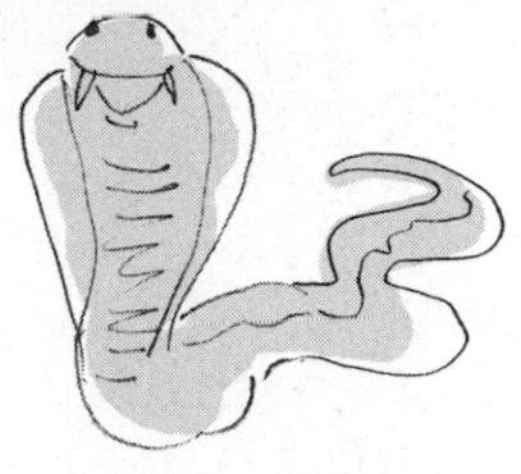

MIMICS

There's a lot of deceit going on in the animal kingdom. Certain creatures pretend they're something they're not. Some animals mimic or imitate other animals.

One reason an animal tries to pass itself off as a different species is for protection. Several creatures mimic the wasp to keep other creatures away. The wasp stings, but its mimic, the ash borer moth, can't sting. Still, because the moth looks so much like a wasp, predators keep their distance.

Tiger moths taste lousy to bats, and they make a clicking sound to ward off these predators. Other moths have learned how to click too, successfully keeping away bats, which might find them to be a yummy snack.

Maybe it's easy for you to pretend to be someone you're not. You might not be imitating another person exactly, but you're not free to be yourself, either. If your friends don't think it's cool to run track instead of play football, you go out for football, even though you'd rather run. Or if you'd rather play the clarinet than be a cheerleader, are you brave enough to do it?

If you waste your energy making sure you fit in at school—dressing right, talking the way everybody else does—you may never discover what God has for *you* to do.

Nobody else in the whole world can be you . . . except you. Don't waste God's creation trying to be somebody else.

> *[Christ] is your example, and you must follow in his steps. He never sinned, nor ever deceived anyone.*
> **1 PETER 2:21-22**

The false cobra can spread out its neck to resemble the deadly Indian cobra, and the milk snake looks enough like the deadly coral snake to keep predators away from it, too. The mimic octopus can change its shape and color to resemble deadly lionfish or sea snakes.

• • •

TODAY: Ask God to show you if you're deceiving yourself or others. Ask for Christ's help in being the unique individual he created you to be.

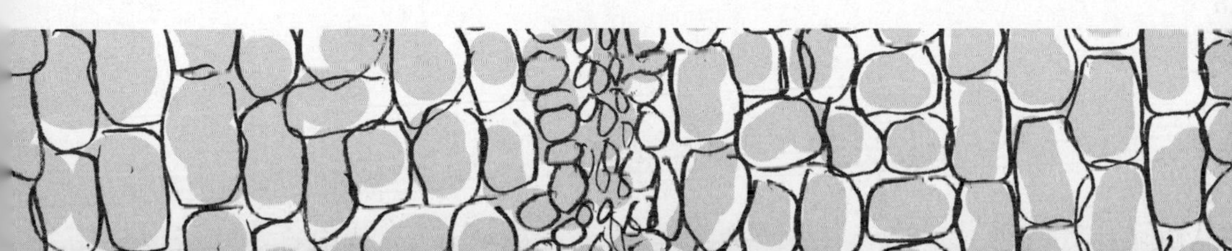

The tongue of a blue whale is as big as, and weighs as much as, a small elephant.

• • •

TODAY: Be on guard against your tongue this week. Account to God for each word you say about other people or to other people.

SPEAKING WITH FORKED TONGUE

Tongues can be used for good . . . or for not-so-good.

By flicking its forked tongue, a snake can pick up scent particles in the air and sense an enemy or its next meal.

When threatened, the blue-tongued lizard opens its mouth and sticks out its tongue (just like some people you know?). The blue tongue inside the pink mouth freaks out most enemies and scares off would-be attackers. Then the lizard flattens it body to look bigger and lets out a fantastic hiss. But it's not all for show. The blue-tongued lizards bite. They latch onto your finger and don't let go.

Frogs have long, sticky tongues that are attached in the front of their mouths. The tongue can curl back then shoot out and capture an unsuspecting bug or fly.

The archerfish has an unusual tongue that serves as a water gun. It can knock off a beetle from a leaf by shooting water at it.

But the human tongue may be the deadliest of all. It's easy to let fly a juicy piece of "news" or to repeat gossip and rumors. It's a surefire way to get attention. But rumors and gossip are destructive, and they're hard to stop.

James describes the tongue as a restless and evil thing, full of poison—a spark that sets off a forest fire.

The military and the CIA have a phrase for limiting information: "need to know." The next time you feel like spreading "information," ask yourself if the person you're about to tell really needs to know or if you're just talking to get attention.

> *The tongue is a small thing that makes grand speeches. But a tiny spark can set a great forest on fire. And the tongue is a flame of fire. It is a whole world of wickedness, corrupting your entire body. It can set your whole life on fire, for it is set on fire by hell itself. People can tame all kinds of animals, birds, reptiles, and fish, but no one can tame the tongue. It is restless and evil, full of deadly poison.*
>
> **JAMES 3:5-8**

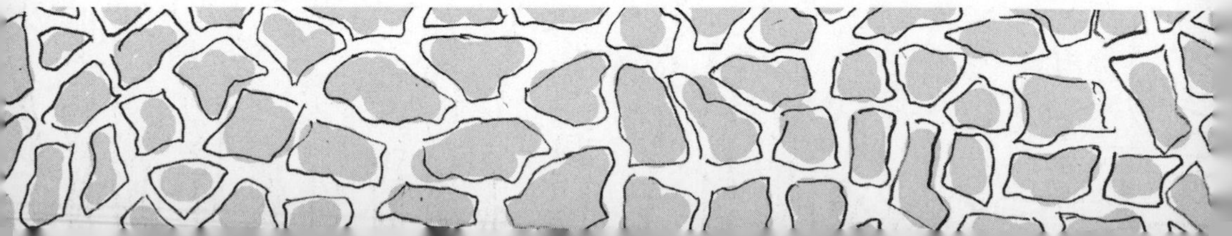

MOTH-EATEN

There are many kinds of moths, but you probably don't want to invite any of them into your clothes closet. Even though most adult moths don't eat, they can have as many as 10 broods of caterpillars, or larvae. And larvae love your fabric.

Clothing moths feed on wool, silk, cashmere, and fur—sweaters, gloves, socks, shirts, boots, you name it. They love stains, as well as perfume and cologne, on clothes.

Some dark closets provide such welcome shelter to caterpillars that as more and more join in on the feeding frenzy, you may be able to hear them munching away on your favorite outfit.

Jesus used moths as an example of what can happen to our "treasures here on earth"—the material things we value. He warned against caring so much about *things*, which can be easily destroyed—by moths or rust or thieves.

What possessions are your personal treasures? What do you care the most about? That new computer game system? Your music? Clothes? Shoes?

Everything you can see, touch, or hear now will be gone one day. Games and clothes wear out. Think about that gift you just had to have a couple of Christmases ago. Do you still love it? Do you still have it? Do you even remember what it was?

On the other hand, Jesus said that we should think more about getting "treasures in heaven." Love, joy, peace, patience, kindness, goodness, self-control . . . those are the things that are valued in heaven. Store up those qualities, and you won't have to worry about losing them. There are no moths in heaven.

> *Don't store up treasures here on earth, where moths eat them and rust destroys them, and where thieves break in and steal. Store your treasures in heaven, where moths and rust cannot destroy, and thieves do not break in and steal.*
>
> **MATTHEW 6:19-20**

Most moths get a bad rap about eating clothes. The truth is, most adult moths don't eat at all. And those that do get hungry simply drink nectar. Species like the luna moth and the atlas moth don't even have mouths. And only one species of moth eats wool.

• • •

TODAY: Name five things you own that you consider really valuable. Then estimate how long you think each item will last. Then write down five to ten treasures that can be stored up in heaven. Put a check mark next to each one you see in yourself now.

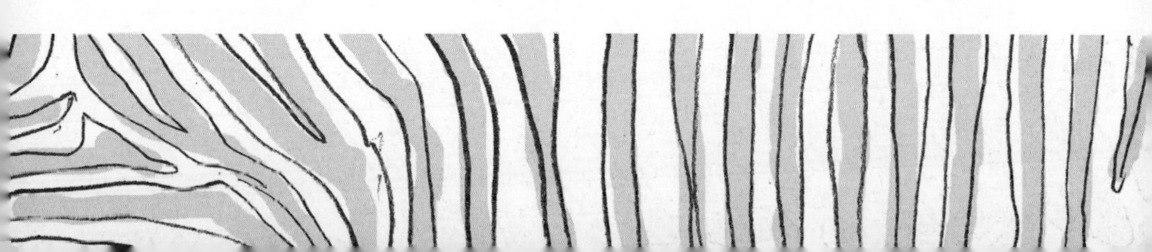

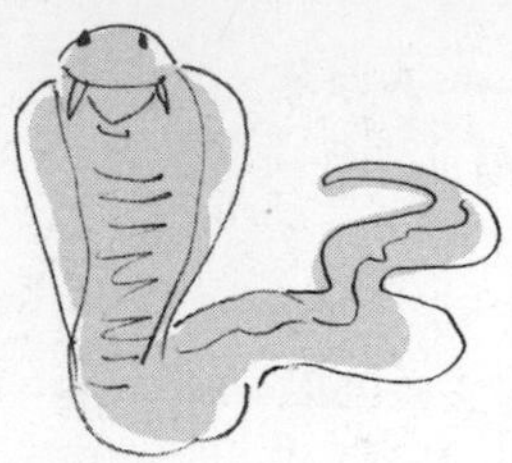

King cobras feed on other snakes, but when they run up against a thick-skinned elephant, getting a good meal isn't so easy. Still, a cobra can kill a full-grown elephant by biting the edge of its toenail or by getting a good bite out of the tip of the elephant's trunk.

• • •

TODAY: Be on the lookout for examples of people trying to get ahead at someone else's expense. Ask God to make you a giver, not a taker; a team player, not somebody always out for him- or herself.

DOG-EAT-DOG WORLD

Nobody's really sure who came up with the phrase *It's a dog-eat-dog world*, but it means that the world is tough and everybody's out for him- or herself.

Although dogs don't normally eat each other, there are exceptions. Dogs that have been cruelly trained will at least fight each other to the death. On rare occasions when a mother dog senses that one of her pups will die or that it was born too soon to live, she may eat her underdeveloped puppy.

Mother cats might do the same and eat a sick or deformed kitten just after birth.

Maybe the expression should be about a "gull-eat-gull" world. Seagulls steal eggs from other birds and have no problem stealing babies from other gulls. The great skua can pounce on seagulls, drown them, and steal *their* chicks. Meanwhile, herring gulls watch ducks dive for fish and then steal the fish as soon as the ducks resurface.

When somebody does something mean to you, do you try to get the person back as soon as you can? If you figure that fair is fair, and this person has it coming, you might be playing by the rules of the dog-eat-dog world.

The world's rules say take what you can. So if you're working on a class project and get the chance to look good—better than your teammates—you should go for it. Do what it takes to get ahead.

But the rules of God's Kingdom are way different. In God's economy, the last will be first. If somebody takes your coat, you give him your shirt, too. If she slaps you, instead of slapping her back harder, you turn the other cheek.

It may be a dog-eat-dog world, but it doesn't have to be. Play by God's rules.

> *If someone slaps you on one cheek, offer the other cheek also. If someone demands your coat, offer your shirt also. Give to anyone who asks; and when things are taken away from you, don't try to get them back.*
> **LUKE 6:29-30**

OPEN YOUR EYES

Many animals are born blind. Kittens can't open their eyes until they're about 8 to 14 days old. And they can't see as well as an adult cat until they're several months old.

Puppies are born with their eyes closed. When they open their eyes depends on the breed of dog, but usually it's around 10 to 15 days after birth.

Flying squirrels can't see until around four weeks, and gray squirrels are blind until they're nearly five weeks old.

Other animals, like deer and horses, are born with their eyes wide open. You probably already know that human babies are born with their eyes open. But even though those eyes are open, babies don't see very well immediately. Objects and faces are blurry to a newborn baby. Later, everything will come into better focus.

When we're born spiritually, our eyes are open too. We've come to understand that we need Christ's payment for our sin and his presence in our lives. But so many things in the spiritual world are still out of focus. We need to grow spiritually, just like we grow physically.

Stretch your spiritual muscles. You can't see God, but the closer you grow to him, the better you'll get to know him and the more you'll love him.

Open your eyes of faith.

You love him even though you have never seen him. Though you do not see him now, you trust him; and you rejoice with a glorious, inexpressible joy.

1 PETER 1:8

It's really important for wild horses to be able to see soon after birth. If they couldn't, they'd have trouble keeping up with the ever-moving herd.

• • •

TODAY: Take a long walk with God and think over your spiritual growth. What do you "see" now that you didn't understand before? What things do you still need to see more clearly?

Most birds, especially birds of prey, are born with hard bills that can tear their prey to shreds. Vultures, however, have weak bills. Yet the weak bill of the vulture is exactly what it needs, because it's perfect for devouring the rotten flesh of roadkill. And where would our roads and highways be without the vulture cleanup patrol?

• • •

TODAY: Ask a parent or grandparent to tell you about something that looked pretty bad at first but turned out to be good in the long run. Tell that person about something in your life that worked the same way.

THE GOOD, THE BAD, AND THE JOYFUL

Imagine you're a baby giraffe about to be born. You've been waiting patiently inside your mother for the big day to arrive. And finally it does. Your mother gives birth to a bouncing baby giraffe—you! You tumble through the air, flailing those long legs and that long neck, until you crash to the ground, about a five-foot drop.

Shocked and dismayed, you do the only thing that comes naturally. You cry. And suddenly, with the help of that soulful cry, your lungs open and you start breathing. In a split second, your mother is at your side, loving you and making you feel better. A baby giraffe moves from unhappy to joyful because its mother loves it through the process.

God can do the same thing with us when we get stuck in a bad or unhappy phase. If we let God in, he will love us through the toughest times and bring us to a stronger faith. We can end up with more joy than we thought possible—a joy based on God.

Look back over some of the bad things that have happened to you. A friend moved away. You didn't get a game or a bike or something you thought you had to have. A class at school was really hard for you. You had to start over in a new town.

How did you get through your hard times? Times like those can be opportunities to turn to God and discover that he is really all that matters. And if you can grab onto that idea and make it your own, then the end is pure joy.

Be truly glad. There is wonderful joy ahead, even though you have to endure many trials for a little while.

1 PETER 1:6

PATIENCE—NOW!

A lion's roar can be heard from five miles away. The jungle quakes, and so do the creatures of the jungle. But that lion wasn't born with a great roar. In fact, there was no roar at all until the lion reached two years old. It took practice and patience to learn to roar.

Monkeys (like humans) tend to be creatures of impulse. We see something we want, and we grab for it. So do most monkeys, although some species of monkeys are more patient than others. Scientists studied the common marmoset and the cotton-top tamarin to see how long the monkeys could wait to eat if waiting meant they got a bigger reward. The marmosets, who were used to waiting on slow-moving sap from trees, waited twice as long as the tamarins, who were used to relying on their quickness to snatch insects.

Are you a patient marmoset or a grabby tamarin?

When you take what you want right away, it's called *gratification*. Most Americans are used to instant gratification. We have cell phones to call friends the second we want to talk, and we don't like it when we don't get an answer immediately. High-speed Internet still isn't fast enough. We want that new download the day it's released. We can't believe it when the supermarket runs out of chocolate peanut butter jelly marshmallow ice cream. We want it now—even though it isn't good for us.

Stop. Delay gratification. Not everything has to happen *now*. Be patient and wait for what you want. Remember how patient God has always been with you.

> *Finishing is better than starting. Patience is better than pride.*
> **ECCLESIASTES 7:8**

Dogs vary in the amount of patience they can muster. Golden retrievers are considered to be one of the most patient dogs. Originally trained as hunting dogs, they had to learn to wait for the hunter to get a shot off, hit a bird, and then send the dog on its mission to retrieve the prize. Finally, the dog had to resist chowing down on the bird while it waited patiently for a treat or an "Attaboy!"

• • •

TODAY: List three areas where you're usually impatient. Why do you think it's so hard for you to be patient in each case? Ask God to give you the strength to choose delayed gratification instead of instant gratification.

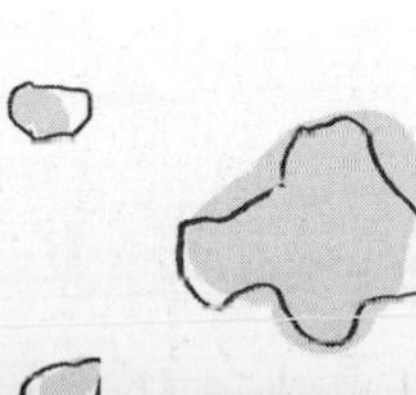
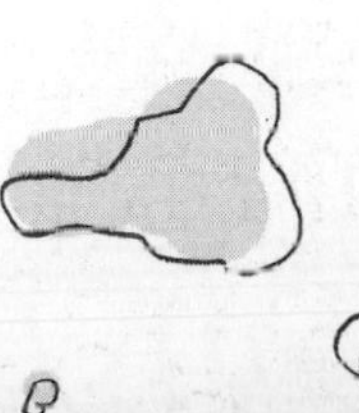

The toughest animal in the world is probably the teeny tiny tardigrade. It can live in deep oceans or on Himalayan mountaintops. The tardigrade can survive radiation, starvation, dehydration, enormous pressure, or a vacuum. It needs water to live, but if there's no water around, it can drop its metabolism to 1/100th of its normal rate and wait as long as 10 years for a little rain. Now that's tough!

• • •

TODAY: Think about the things you tend to complain about. Be honest—when aren't you very tough? Ask God to help you be tougher when you need to be and to complain less.

TOUGHEN UP!

Cockroaches are tough. You can freeze a roach then thaw it out, and it will be just fine. Cut off a roach's head, and it will survive for weeks until it starves or dies of thirst. These insects can live off their own body fat (the white junk that squirts out when you squash them).

Cockroaches can stand 100 times the radiation that a human can endure. And although astronauts are pretty tough, roaches can survive 10 times the gravitational pull an astronaut can. Cockroaches have managed to infiltrate every part of the world, and they can live happily ever after in any environment, with the possible exception of polar ice caps and the deep blue sea.

African bull elephants are pretty tough too. A bull elephant can kill a full-grown rhino and suffer little or no damage itself. The only real threats to the bull elephant (not counting humans) are prides of lions or groups of poisonous snakes.

Sometimes we all need to toughen up a bit. If you get a scratch or a blister, do you whine and complain about it? Do you make it a big deal so you'll get more attention? Everybody gets bumped and scraped. That's part of living. Save the complaints for when you're really hurt. That's when you don't want to play tough guy.

Riding in the backseat between your two little brothers might not be so great. But just because you're cramped or hot or thirsty, you don't have to announce your misery every two minutes. Chances are everyone in that car feels the same way you do.

Just because you may need to toughen up doesn't mean you have to pretend all is well. If you're scared of a bully or if you can't stop grieving over the loss of your friend or if you're depressed and unhappy, don't keep things bottled up. Ask someone close to you for help. And let God know exactly how you feel about everything, but mix it with gratitude.

> *We patiently endure troubles and hardships and calamities of every kind. We have been beaten, been put in prison, faced angry mobs, worked to exhaustion, endured sleepless nights, and gone without food.*
> **2 CORINTHIANS 6:4-5**

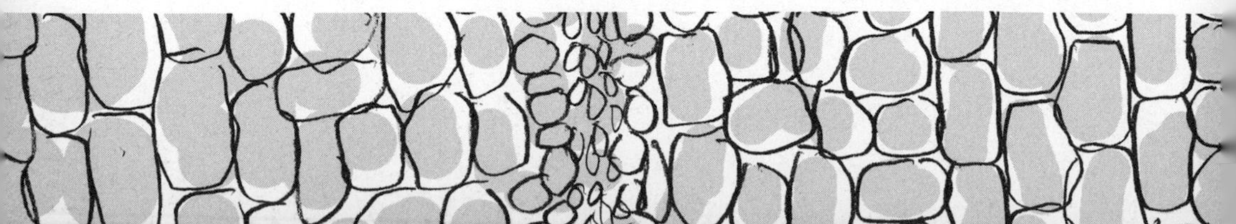

THE UGLY CONTEST

Every year at the coliseum in Petaluma, California, people hold the World's Ugliest Dog contest. The winner gets $1,000 and the title of "World's Ugliest Dog." A truly ugly dog named Sam won three years in a row and became known as "the Grim Reaper of the Animal World."

The naked mole rat is an East African rodent that makes rats look like beauty queens. In addition to having only a few tufts of stray, coarse hair on its scrawny body, the mole rat is blind, nearly cold-blooded, and cursed with buck teeth.

Some say the Matamata turtle is uglier still, covered with warts and ridges all over its weird face, with small eyes and a long snout. The warthog may be the ugliest of all—300 pounds, with a piglike body, giant tusks, facial warts, and a wide head.

Wherever you think you fall on the beauty/ugliness scale, you probably have definite ideas about what makes a person beautiful or ugly. But these are just ideas that have been formed by other people or by the culture in general.

Have you ever seen paintings from the Renaissance, with pleasingly plump females? Those chubby women were considered much more beautiful than the skinny model types we call beautiful today.

You've probably laughed at the clothes and hairstyles of your parents and their classmates in old yearbooks. But guess what—your kids will be chuckling at your clothes and hairstyles when they get a look at your yearbook someday.

Styles change, and so does beauty—at least what people consider beauty. But what doesn't change is true beauty—beauty on the inside.

People are like grass; their beauty is like a flower in the field. The grass withers and the flower fades.
1 PETER 1:24

Charm is deceptive, and beauty does not last.
PROVERBS 31:30

One of the worst laws ever was nicknamed the "Chicago Ugly Law," a municipal code that said no person who was diseased, maimed, mutilated, or deformed was allowed to be in public places in the city, or that person would be fined no less than one dollar and no more than $50. Similar laws were on the books in Omaha, Nebraska; Columbus, Ohio; and other cities. The laws weren't repealed until 1973 or 1974.

• • •

TODAY: List 10 qualities you think make a person beautiful on the outside and 10 qualities that make a person beautiful on the inside. Circle the qualities you have. Ask God to make you beautiful on the inside.

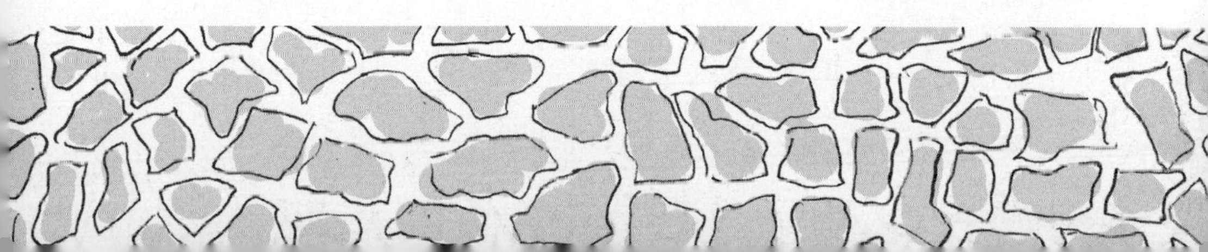

The palm-nut vulture is the only bird of prey that lives primarily as a vegetarian. It fills up on nuts and oils, but will also eat fish, crabs, and even dead meat on occasion.

• • •

TODAY: Talk to God about two "neighbors" you've been putting in the vulture category. Start praying that God will give you his love for them. Show that love (by faith) and do or say one nice thing to them.

"LOVE THY VULTURE AS THYSELF"

People cringe at the sight of vultures circling around a tasty bit of roadkill. Most vultures don't care if the kill has been dead for minutes or days. And if there's still life in the victim, some vultures will dive-bomb into the poor creature to finish it off.

Vultures don't have many predators, which is a good thing for the vulture because it wouldn't do well in a fight. The vulture's best defense is projectile vomiting at an enemy so it will fly away.

Turkey vultures are the mildest of the vultures. Their feet look more like chicken claws than the strong claws of hawks. They could never kill prey. They float in the air on drafts of wind. If they're mobbed by ravens or jays, they simply speed up to 60 miles per hour to get away from the little guys. The scientific name for turkey vulture is *Cathartes aura*, which means "cleansing breeze." Nobody should fear the cleansing breeze.

Know any vultures at your school? Some people earn their reputations by being mean and greedy. They're ruthless, inflicting pain and cruelty on their victims.

But they're also our neighbors. And Jesus taught that we should love our neighbors as ourselves. How do you love someone who bullies you and makes your life miserable? How can you love somebody you don't even like? You'll never feel love for this person!

Jesus gives part of the solution when he says you're supposed to love your neighbor as you love yourself. How do you love yourself? You probably have days when you don't like yourself much. But no matter how down you are on yourself, you always want the best for yourself, don't you? You wish yourself well. And that's a start to love.

Wish those "vultures" well. God made them in his image. You may not like them, but you must love them. You can pray the best for them and let Jesus love them through you.

Love your neighbor as yourself.
MATTHEW 22:39

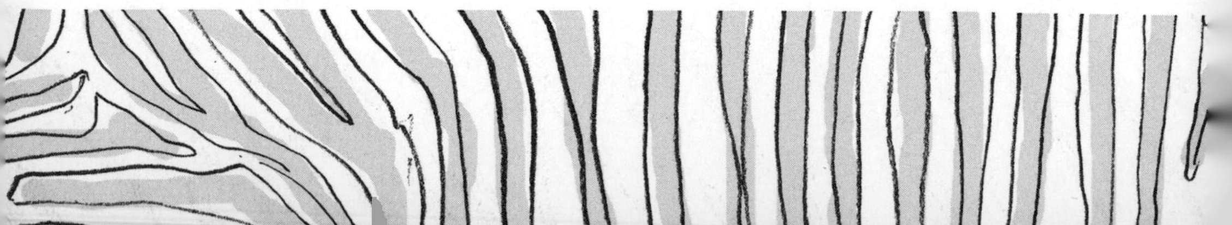

SPEAKING SOFTLY

Animals like a soft voice. Horses can be calmed with soothing, softly spoken words, even if all you're saying is gibberish. There's a reason great horse gentlers like Monty Roberts are called "horse whisperers" and not horse shouters. They understand the value of a gentle tone.

Some dog trainers (sometimes called "dog whisperers") believe dogs respond to voice attitudes rather than word commands. They advise family members to analyze the tone and levels of voice used when talking to the family pet. Whining at a dog doesn't promote learning, and neither does shouting or "barking" at the dog. A soft, steady, firm voice is the best for teaching a dog and ending up with a happy, well-adjusted pet.

You probably have more tones of voice than you realize. And you may be using those tones automatically, without even realizing it. When your mom tells you to take out the trash, does she get the *why-me?* groan from you in response? When your dad asks where you were last night and what you were doing, is your answer short and harsh?

When you get into an argument with your best friend—and disagreements will come sooner or later with a friend—does your voice get louder and louder until you're shouting and being shouted at?

Listen to your voice, and pay attention to your tone. Even when you totally disagree with someone, you can keep your voice soft and gentle. You'll be amazed what speaking softly can accomplish.

Gentle words are a tree of life.
PROVERBS 15:4

Most animal trainers agree that the tone of a trainer's voice command carries more impact than the words themselves. "Horse whisperers," trainers who gentle horses rather than break them with force, use soft, controlled tones to calm down their horses. Dog trainers speak in a low voice when they want their dogs to sit or stay, but they rely on a higher tone of voice to get the dogs to come or run.

• • •

TODAY: Take an inventory of your tone of voice. Write down every attitude you convey through volume and tone: calm, angry, snarky, sarcastic, mocking, harsh, sassy, etc. Ask God to help you with gentle answers.

Lovebirds are small parrots. They got their name because it's common to find them snuggled up and sitting in pairs, looking pretty lovey dovey.

• • •

TODAY: List five ways you can show love today. Pray that God will make your love sincere and help you follow through with actions.

LOVEBIRDS

Many animals openly show love and affection for each other and for humans.

When two dogs sleep side by side, with one dog's head on the other's neck, it's a good indication that the dogs like each other. If one dog dies and another one grieves, refusing to eat, we can assume those two dogs loved each other.

In a pasture filled with horses, certain ones may pair up. You'll see them regularly grazing side by side, standing under a shade tree together, and possibly scratching each other's backs. Is it love? It has to be "like," at the very least.

We can't always tell what a pet is feeling, but we can make a good guess by observing its actions.

That's all people have to go on with us, too. It's a trite saying, but it's true: Actions speak louder than words.

You can claim that you love your brothers and sisters in Christ. But if you gossip about other people in your youth group, nobody's going to believe you love them.

How will people know we're Christians? Because we say so? Nope. They'll know we're Christians by our love. And how will they know that we love? Because we say so? Not likely. They need to see love in action.

What actions prove that we love people? When you go out of your way to say hi or to help someone, that's showing love. When you make a sacrifice, even if it's sacrificing a fun time with your buddies so that you can listen to someone else's problems, that's a demonstration of love too. Volunteering for Habitat for Humanity or at a homeless shelter, helping a friend find a lost pet, visiting someone in the hospital—those are actions of love.

Nobody can see your heart except God. But what people can see are your actions.

> *You were cleansed from your sins when you obeyed the truth, so now you must show sincere love to each other as brothers and sisters. Love each other deeply with all your heart.*
>
> **1 PETER 1:22**

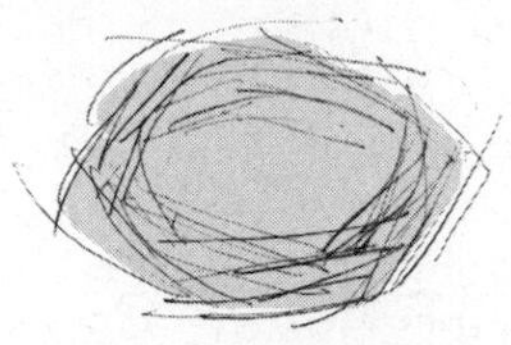

A MASTERPIECE

A nest can be as simple as a dent in the ground or as complex as a multistory mansion of clay, glue, feathers, and engineering expertise.

Scrape nests are small indentations in the ground, used by gulls, penguins, vultures, terns, and nighthawks. Horned larks use rocks or tufts of grass and build their nests to the north of the object.

Kingfishers and bank swallows build burrow nests that aren't fancy but do protect their eggs and babies from predators. Other birds use bushes, tree limbs, or rock ledges for simple nests.

Weaver finches create intricate woven nests that hang from branches and offer multiple rooms inside. Some weavers build nests in colonies of 30 pairs. Flamingo mud nests are built on lakes like sand castles sticking out of the water, while ovenbirds construct nests that look like Old World domed ovens.

So what do these birds use to construct their masterpieces? Stuff! Ordinary, everyday material: sticks, straw, leaves, grass, fibers, feathers, mud, and saliva. Birds gladly make hundreds of trips searching for ordinary building materials. They use discarded stuff too: wire, candy wrappers, napkins, old tissues.

God has called us his masterpieces. We're examples of his workmanship. And the best part is that—like the birds—God prefers to use whatever material is on hand. God doesn't need royal genes or genius DNA to make you exactly the person he created you to be. You contain everything you need.

Don't ever get down on yourself and wish you were someone else. God had you—exactly you—in mind from the creation of the universe. You are God's masterpiece!

> *We are God's masterpiece. He has created us anew in Christ Jesus, so we can do the good things he planned for us long ago.*
> **EPHESIANS 2:10**

The nest of a bald eagle may look messy, like a stack of random sticks, but that nest has been crafted strong enough to hold a 200-pound human. Sticks that are several feet long are first placed in a triangle, with another triangle on top of that, and another, and another.

• • •

TODAY: All day today, praise God for his creative masterpieces all around you, including *you*!

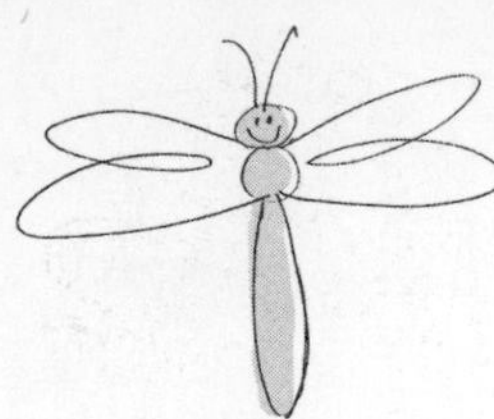

IT'S HOW YOU LOOK AT IT

If you could see life the way bugs and spiders do, you'd envision a whole new world. Insects and arthropods (like spiders and lobsters) have compound eyes with lots of individual lenses that produce a multitude of pictures.

Dragonflies have two big eyes, each with 30,000 tinier eyes that send individual images. If you could look through the eyes of the dragonfly, you'd probably see broken-up images and repeat pictures arranged in a honeycomb pattern.

Pretty crazy. But the dragonfly's brain can pull the mosaic images together into a great vision. And the dragonfly can see all around its body, in a complete circle. It can distinguish color, and it has no problem hunting in the hazy dusk of evening.

The way a dragonfly sees its world is radically different from the way you see yours. But the way God sees the world is even more different than that.

Most of our problems would go away if we could see the world as God sees it. God sees the good in people. Yet he also sees the sin . . . and loves us anyway. He sees what we can be—what we will be with his Spirit leading us. God sees possibilities where we've already given up. He sees beauty in places we wouldn't even look.

God sees that grouchy teacher and understands her deep sadness. He looks at the most popular guy in school and sees the way he treats people. God sees that the people who end up last will be first in his Kingdom. He sees that we're weak when we think we're so strong and strongest in him when we think we're weak. And where we see nothing but disappointment, God sees hope.

The eyes are the doorway opening to the world. Try seeing it the way God does. It's all how you look at it.

Your eye is a lamp that provides light for your body. When your eye is good, your whole body is filled with light.

MATTHEW 6:22

DRAGONFLIES HAVE STACKED UP QUITE A FEW NICKNAMES:

Snake doctors: People used to believe that dragonflies warned snakes of danger.

Horse stingers: Dragonflies can't actually sting or bite, but don't tell that to a horse.

Mosquito hawks: Hunting at night, dragonflies make a dent in the mosquito population.

• • •

TODAY: Pick two people you see today and try to see them the way God sees them. Ask God to give you his vision and hope for them—and for yourself.

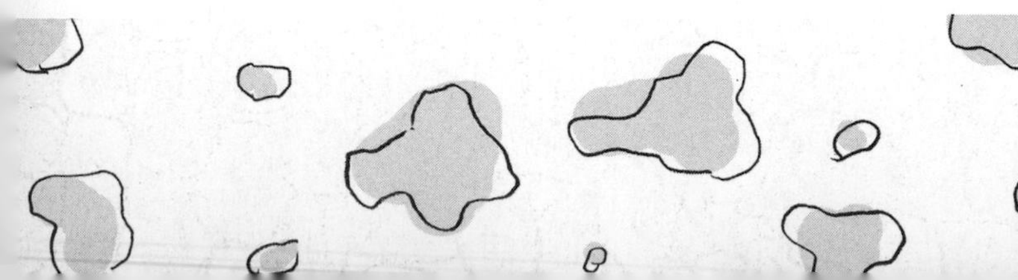

HEART-TO-HEART

Scientists at the Institute for Amphibian Biology at Hiroshima University in Japan have developed a see-through frog. They bred frogs that lacked pigment in their skin until they got a mutation: a nearly transparent frog. The researchers wanted to be able to observe the way the organs of a living frog work. Besides the fact that it's cool to see a heart beating, to watch the eggs developing, and to see through a frog, scientists are hoping to be able to monitor organ growth and do cancer studies on these frogs.

God thought of this idea first, though. In Central and South America, there's a see-through frog called the glass frog, which is only an inch or two long. Sadly, the glass frog is almost extinct because its habitat is being destroyed and a fungal disease is killing off many amphibians in the areas glass frogs inhabit.

Imagine if people could see through to your heart—not just the organ of the heart, but deeper, into your real motives. If your best friend knew half of the thoughts you've had about him, he probably wouldn't be your best friend any longer, right?

God sees through you. When God selected a king for Israel, he chose little David over his big brother Eliab because David's heart was purer.

Jesus shook up his listeners by telling them God cares about motives—not just keeping the law. It's not enough that you don't murder someone, he taught. If you're angry with someone, then you're guilty. Don't commit adultery. But don't even look at someone with lust. Motives matter.

Maybe you're feeling good about yourself because you don't get into trouble at school. You go to church, and you're a "good kid." But God sees through to your motives. Is your heart in the right spot?

You alone know each human heart.
1 KINGS 8:39

You look deep within the mind and heart, O righteous God.
PSALM 7:9

Frog hearts aren't all that similar to human hearts since a frog's heart only has three chambers and we have four. So how come science classes make you dissect living frogs? Because the heart will keep beating, even after you take it out of the poor frog. (So wrong, in so many ways. . . .)

• • •

TODAY: Have a heart-to-heart talk with God and be more honest than you've ever been with anybody, even yourself. God already knows your motives. Ask him to change your heart.

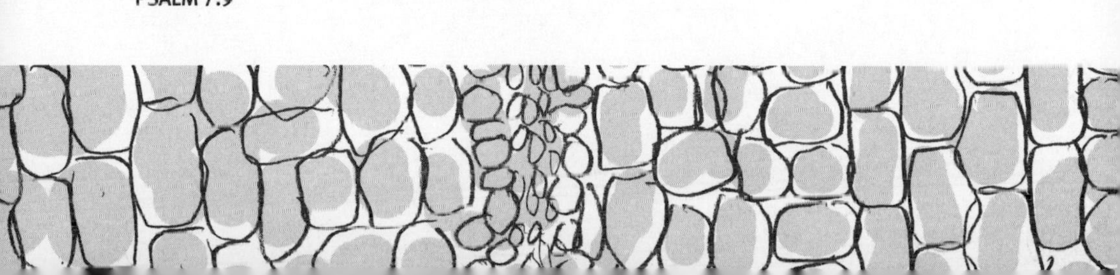

ALL PUFFED UP AND NO PLACE TO GO

When some fish get scared, instead of running or fighting, they puff up. The Porcupine fish swallows air or water until its spines stick out. Then it looks fierce enough to scare off other fish.

When the puffer fish is threatened, it inhales water until it puffs up to twice its normal size. Some puffer fish—also called swellfish, globefish, fugu, or blowfish—swell to four times their size, making it impossible for them to swim fast and even shortening their life spans.

So although puffing up can sometimes be a good thing since it scares off mean fish, puffing up can also be a bad thing, shortening the fish's life.

People get "puffed up" too. When pride takes over and makes you feel like you deserve people's praise, you could be in danger of getting puffed up. You score the highest on a test and want everyone to know about it. Or you're the player with the best defensive skills on your team, and everybody had better agree.

Instead of getting puffed up with your own success, remember that every good thing—including every talent or skill you have—comes from God. He gives it, and he can take it away.

Some people get puffed up as a defense for being insecure. You might brag about how much money your family has because you don't think there's any other way to get people to like you. But "puffed" isn't a good look on anybody.

Be real. Be genuine. Be humble. Don't just say things that you think make you look good. Give credit where credit is due—to God.

> *See, he is puffed up; his desires are not upright—but the righteous will live by his faith.*
> **HABAKKUK 2:4, NIV**

The skin, muscles, liver, and other parts of most puffer fish contain a poison that's a thousand times deadlier than cyanide, and it has no antidote. And yet the Japanese puffer fish, called fugu, is eaten in Japan, cooked by specially trained chefs who know how to get rid of most of the poison. Still, many Japanese diners have died from eating this poisonous dish.

• • •

TODAY: Ask God to show you if you've been "puffed up" over anything. Thank God for this gift, and start basing your self-image on the humbling fact that you belong to him.

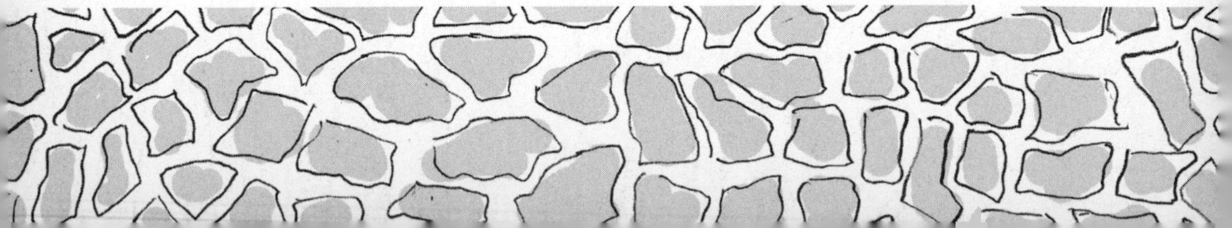

SHOW-AND-TELL

Have you ever taken a pet to show-and-tell? You're so proud. You can't wait to tell everything you know about your pet.

Although there are more dog owners in the United States than cat owners (and it's close), more cat owners tend to have more than one pet, making pet cats more numerous than pet dogs. Next in line are fish, ferrets, guinea pigs, hamsters, and birds.

Different pet owners favor different pets. Imagine someone showing up with a Madagascar hissing cockroach for show and tell. Maybe the owner loves that spine-tingling hiss. And watch out for the kid with the man-eating piranha.

Tarantulas are kept as pets in some countries, where the hairy spiders are thought of as beautiful, not dangerous. Other people keep crickets in cages to hear them sing. Potbellied pigs were popular over a dozen years ago, until many owners in the United States overfed their cute little piggies and ended up with big, fat pigs.

We're God's children, not God's pets. But just as we're proud of our pets, we want God to look at us and be proud of us. Imagine being taken to a heavenly version of show-and-tell, where God gets to point to you proudly. That's what God did when he talked about Job: "The LORD asked Satan, 'Have you noticed my servant Job? He is the finest man in all the earth. He is blameless—a man of complete integrity. He fears God and stays away from evil'" (Job 1:8).

What would God say about you at show-and-tell? "See how kind and honest my child is? See how much this person loves me?" Now's the time to get ready for heaven's show-and-tell.

> *You are a chosen people. You are royal priests, a holy nation, God's very own possession. As a result, you can show others the goodness of God, for he called you out of the darkness into his wonderful light.*
> **1 PETER 2:9**

PRESIDENTS WHO HAVE HAD UNUSUAL "FIRST PETS":

John Quincy Adams owned an alligator, and his wife raised silkworms.

James Buchanan had a pet elephant.

Teddy Roosevelt owned a guinea pig named Father O'Grady and a snake named Emily Spinach, not to mention his zebra, coyote, hyena, and lion.

Calvin Coolidge had a pygmy hippopotamus, an antelope, a bear, a wallaby, a lion, and a cat.

• • •

TODAY: Imagine that God is taking you to show-and-tell. At the end of the day, list five things he could point out about you.

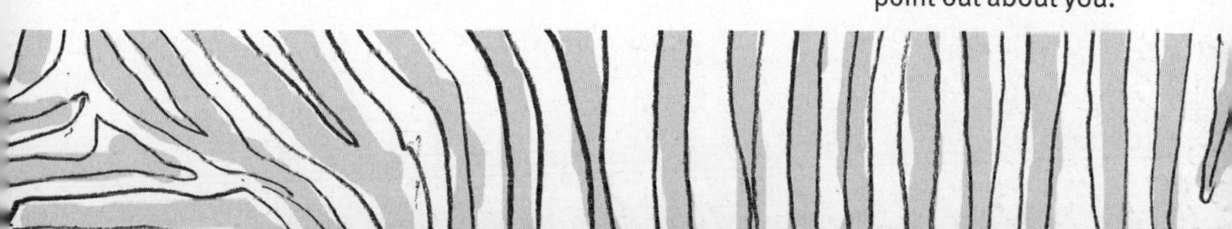

A polydactyl cat is one with more than the normal number of toes. Ernest Hemingway, the Nobel Prize–winning author, loved his six-toed cats. When Hemingway died, his home in Key West, Florida, was turned into a home for his cats—most of them with extra toes.

• • •

TODAY: Thank God for all the ways you think you're not "normal." Look for ways to appreciate people around you who may not be what others consider cool or acceptable. Make an effort to get to know one "not normal" person.

FANTASTIC FELINES

God could have settled for one breed of cat, but that's not God's style. Not only did God create variety, but in his creations God shows an appreciation for what others might think of as odd, different, or "not normal."

The Scottish fold cat has flat ears and a face like an otter. The levkoy is hairless, with wrinkled skin and folded ears. The Oriental shorthair has a skinny, triangular face, framed by gigantic ears, and this unusual cat comes in more than 300 colors.

The Maine coon is a cat that looks so much like a raccoon that people used to think it was the offspring of a cat and a coon. People say the Cornish Rex looks more like an alien than a cat, with a pointy face and huge, batlike ears.

God obviously appreciates diversity in humans, too—and not just in terms of race, culture, and nationality. The world is a richer place because it includes people who are considered "not normal." We attach names to these "different" people: "handicapped" or "challenged" or "special needs." Or we give them much worse names and maybe even think it's funny.

But if you've ever taken the time to get to know one of God's "special" children, you may understand how genuinely special they are. We may never know why some people are born with disabilities, but we know that everything in creation brings glory to God if we don't get in the way.

It would be a pretty dull world if we were all alike.

God chose things despised by the world, things counted as nothing at all, and used them to bring to nothing what the world considers important.
1 CORINTHIANS 1:28

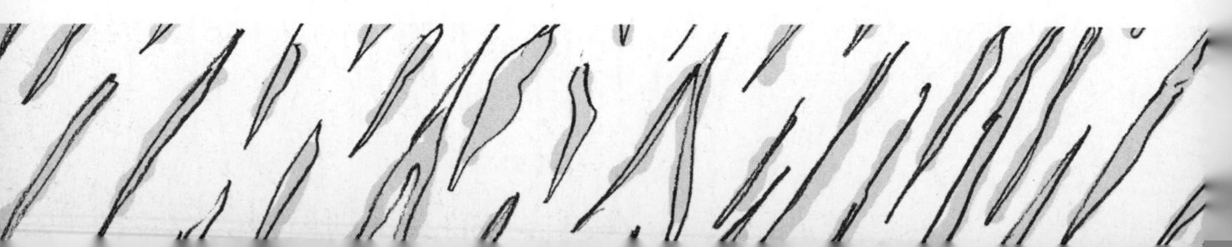

September 30

DON'T BITE MY HEAD OFF

The animal world can be dangerous. Moles bite off the heads of earthworms and store them underground. But those earthworms are pretty tough (and the moles aren't so smart). If the mole forgets where it stored the worm, the earthworm grows a new head and escapes.

Foxes bite off the heads of dozens of chickens in a henhouse and leave them or bury them. People think it's the fox's way of storing food, although it's not a very good one.

You've probably heard the expression "Don't bite my head off!" If anyone has ever said it to you, then you've probably been guilty of an outburst of anger. How often do you lose your temper? What does it take for you to bite someone's head off?

The answer to that question might tell you what you're too attached to. Do you bite off your little brother's head when he touches your stuff? Or do you bite off your parents' heads when they ask you to do your chores?

If you're flaring up all the time, there's a bigger problem than the incident itself. It should be a signal to you that you're not walking in the Spirit. If Christ were in your shoes, he wouldn't be getting upset over every little thing.

Stop and talk to God about whatever upsets you. It's only God's power that can keep you from biting heads off.

> *When you follow the desires of your sinful nature, the results are very clear: sexual immorality, impurity, lustful pleasures, idolatry, sorcery, hostility, quarreling, jealousy, outbursts of anger, selfish ambition, dissension, division.*
> **GALATIANS 5:19-20**

A shark can grow a new set of teeth in a week. The teeth of rabbits and guinea pigs never stop growing, like our fingernails. Walrus, elephants, and wild boars have teeth that keep growing too.

• • •

TODAY: Think back over the past year and try to remember any times when you "bit off somebody's head." Talk to God about each one and thank him for his forgiveness. Ask for help the next time you sense the anger building up.

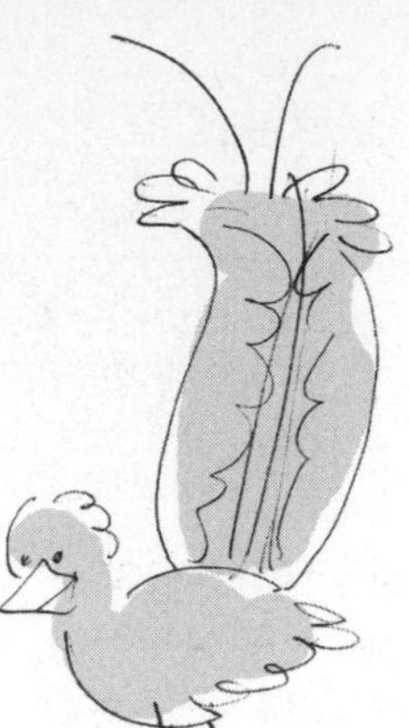

The lyrebird of Southeast Australia —a close relative of the mynah bird—can imitate car sirens and chain saws, as well as carry off a pretty good imitation of most other birds indigenous to the area.

• • •

TODAY: List 10 things you know are true about you. Then list three things other people probably believe to be true about you, but they're not. Talk to God about what it will take for you to get real with yourself, with him, and with other people.

MISTAKEN IDENTITY

Mockingbirds get their name from a Latin phrase that means "many-tongued mimic." It's a good name for this North American bird that can sing the songs of at least 39 different species of birds, mimic another 50 birdcalls, cackle like a hen, bark like a dog, and imitate a police siren. Mockingbirds are so famous for mimicking the songs and sounds of others that most people forget that the mockingbird has its own hauntingly beautiful song.

Everybody pretends, at least some of the time. You stand in front of the mirror before heading to a new school for the first day, and you're not that crazy about what you see. You change clothes half a dozen times until you have to get on the bus. But when you get to school, you act as if you're not nervous, right? Or at least you try to act cool.

All day you could be tempted to act like that popular girl in the front row or the cool guy in back. Maybe you'll style your hair like that tomorrow. Nobody looks interested in what the teacher's saying about the Civil War. So even though you love learning about the Civil War, you act uninterested too. At lunch, you laugh when everybody else does, even when you don't think the joke is that funny. You start to take home books for homework, but nobody else is, so you shove your books back into your locker and act like homework is no big deal.

If you act like other people long enough, you forget where they leave off and you begin. Some people go through life never forming their own opinions because they're too worried about what other people think.

Don't go through life with a case of mistaken identity. Be honest with God, honest with yourself, and honest with other people.

Keep me from lying to myself; give me the privilege of knowing your instructions.
PSALM 119:29

MAKING ALLOWANCES

A good family dog makes allowances for the youngest members of the family. When your two-year-old brother pulls the old dog's hair, Lassie lets it happen. Now, if your 14-year-old sister did the same thing, Lassie might at least growl in protest. But good dogs make allowances and show patience and love.

In the same way, lots of horses are kind and well mannered to children riders. They'll walk instead of gallop, even when the young rider gives mixed signals in the saddle. The horse might show spunk and feistiness with a skilled rider, but it's willing to make allowances for the younger kid.

We need to make allowances too—with animals. Your old dog learned to come to you right away, but you need patience with the new puppy, which still doesn't get it. The stable horse you rode last year was a grand jumper. This year's mount doesn't seem to understand what those jumps are for.

People require our patience too. Nobody can be as annoying as a little brother or sister who wants to butt in on everything you do, who won't leave you alone or respect your privacy. But you need to try to understand and then make allowances.

Why should you be patient with annoying people? Good question. But here's a better one: why should God be patient and make allowances for you? The answer is the same: love. A lack of patience is a lack of love.

Imagine how annoyed God could get with you for making the same mistakes over and over. Or for not doing what you said you'd do or for doing what you said you wouldn't do. Or for going so long without talking to him.

But God loves you. Thank goodness for those allowances!

Always be humble and gentle. Be patient with each other, making allowance for each other's faults because of your love.
EPHESIANS 4:2

Some of the dog breeds that show up on lists of the best family dogs include golden retrievers, bichons frises, German shepherds, cocker spaniels, terriers, boxers, schnauzers, Labs, beagles, and poodles. And don't forget mutts! But any dog might end up being good—or bad—for your family. Dogs have personalities, just like people do.

• • •

TODAY: Every time you get annoyed with someone today, take a deep breath and remember how patient God is with you. Then let that patience carry over to the way you treat "annoying" people.

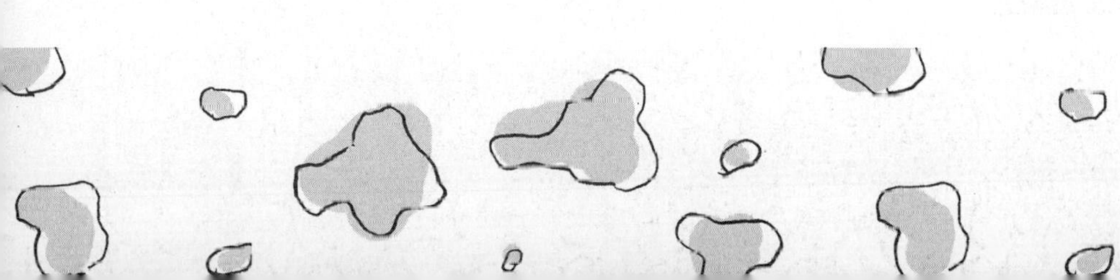

Fish are mostly cold-blooded, so their temperature is about the same as the water they're swimming in, which is why they're in trouble when the aquarium water changes temperature too fast. But tuna and sharks are exceptions. They're warm-blooded fish and can raise their temperatures as much as 20 degrees above the water they swim in.

• • •

TODAY: Is there anything lukewarm about your spiritual temperature? Confess your lack of passion to God and ask him to help you "fire up."

NOT TOO HOT, NOT TOO COLD

Alligators are temperature conscious. They bury their eggs in a mound of vegetation and keep them warm under the pile of garbage. Mama Alligator swims off but continually checks on the eggs. And she does more than that.

She adjusts the temperature of her eggs by adding on more trash and junk or by taking some away. Alligator eggs that are incubated below 86 degrees will hatch as females, and eggs kept above 93 degrees will hatch as males. In between the two temperatures, it's anybody's guess. The eggs hatched at lukewarm temperatures will be a mix of male and female hatchlings. Alligators do their best to keep each litter balanced, with half males and half females. Temperature is all important.

Spiritual growth can be thought of in terms of temperature too. Have you ever heard the expression that somebody is "on fire" for God? Or that somebody used to be "all fired up," but now they've grown "cold"?

In Revelation, God warns believers against being "lukewarm"—neither hot nor cold. You'd think God would at least appreciate someone being lukewarm over somebody who has grown cold. But what God wants from us is honesty, and at least someone who's cold spiritually isn't pretending to be religious.

A lukewarm person goes through the motions of going to church but never gets anything out of the sermon. That person may even pray, but the prayers are rote and empty.

Someone on fire for God is excited, grateful, and eager to fellowship with other Christians and to talk to people about Jesus. Don't settle for warm when "on fire" is so much . . . cooler.

> *I know all the things you do, that you are neither hot nor cold. I wish that you were one or the other! But since you are like lukewarm water, neither hot nor cold, I will spit you out of my mouth!*
> REVELATION 3:15-16

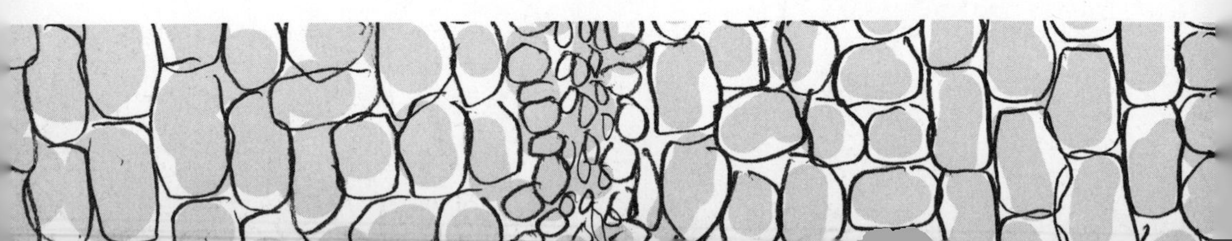

October 4

FRIENDS

Many pet owners will tell you that their dog or cat or horse is their best friend. They don't speak the same language, eat the same food, or even like the same activities . . . and yet they're friends.

It's remarkable that a horse would let you be its friend. Why would a thousand-pound creature of muscle and strength let you sit on its back and tell it where to go and what to do?

And what about dogs? You know why you like dogs as friends. They're loyal and forgiving. When you walk in the door, they're always glad to see you, even when you're grumpy. But why would a dog want you as a friend? Surely another dog would make a better companion.

As amazing as it is that animals agree to be your friends, it's infinitely more amazing that God wants to be your friend. The God of the universe longs to be your best friend!

Before the creation of the world, God knew you and he should be best buddies. God knew you'd sin, and he couldn't have a deep friendship with sin. So he sent Jesus to die to bridge that gap between you and him.

Maybe you've wished you could be friends with somebody at your school, and that person is obviously not interested. But if you *could* have your pick of friends—that classmate, a movie star, an athlete—you'd never come close to the Friend who already longs to be your best friend.

Take God up on the offer.

Since our friendship with God was restored by the death of his Son while we were still his enemies, we will certainly be saved through the life of his Son. So now we can rejoice in our wonderful new relationship with God because our Lord Jesus Christ has made us friends of God.

ROMANS 5:10-11

Starlings value the friendship of other starlings and like to gather in huge flocks to feed and roost together. Like about 60 percent of birds, starlings are passerines, or perching birds, with three toes pointing forward and one toe back so they can cling to a perch.

• • •

TODAY: Make a list of the qualities you value in a best friend. Thank God that he surpasses everything you can imagine. Why do you think God wants your friendship?

The Swahili word for *lion* means "strong," "king," and "aggressive." Lions hunt and take down buffalo, antelope, crocodiles, wild dogs, leopards, rhinos, and more.

• • •

TODAY: Talk to God and together imagine three great things that just might happen today. Ask God to direct you and give you the boldness to make good things happen.

LION FEVER!

Lions have to be ready to fight. Male lions that are head of a pride of lions have to be ready to defend their position against a stronger, younger male lion or a coalition of males who want to throw out the king.

Male lions weigh over 400 pounds, and females weigh just under 300. Even if you're fast, you can't outrun a lion. They reach up to 50 miles per hour.

If you want to keep a roomful of people from going outside, all you have to do is yell, "There's a lion out there!" If they believe you, they won't go anywhere, right?

What if you're all alone in the house, but you start thinking, *Hmm . . . you know, there could be a lion outside*. Before you know it, you've convinced yourself that there really is a lion outside. So, of course, you won't leave. You'll stay where you are. And when that happens, there might as well be a lion outside.

You probably couldn't convince yourself that there's a lion outside or a lion at school. But you *could* make yourself believe that there's a bully waiting to beat you up. Or you might have yourself convinced that most of your classmates and teachers sit around dreaming up ways to embarrass you and laugh behind your back.

If you worry about things long enough, you could make your own fear come true. Believing that people are against you will change the way you treat them, which will affect the way they treat you.

Instead, give people the benefit of the doubt. If they know the real you, the you who reflects Jesus, of course they'll like you! They're probably as anxious about making friends as you are. Maybe you can help put *them* at ease.

The lazy person claims, "There's a lion on the road!
Yes, I'm sure there's a lion out there!"
PROVERBS 26:13

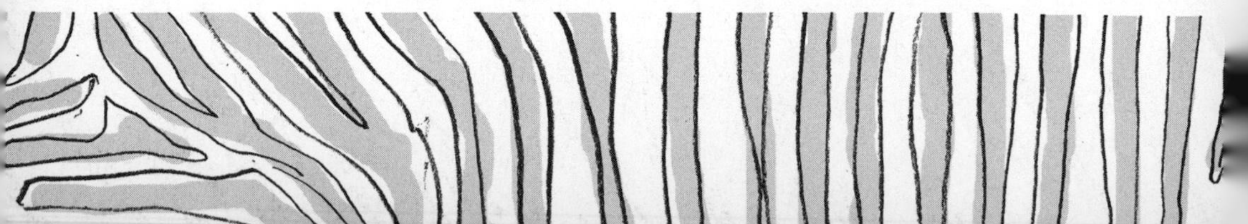

BREAK OUT OF YOUR SHELL

Animals that lay eggs rather than have live births present their young with a challenge right from the start. How is the baby supposed to break out of its shell?

God has it all worked out. Many hatchlings, including most birds and reptiles, begin life with an "egg tooth," a sharp, toothlike structure sticking out of the head that's ready for action. The egg tooth can break or tear through the egg's surface as the bird or reptile hatches.

Other lizards and snakes inside the egg have a true tooth that easily breaks the egg. After hatching, the baby sheds the tooth.

Still other reptiles and birds develop a horn, rather than a tooth. It falls off or gets pulled back in after hatching.

Baby birds have a special pipping muscle on the back of their necks to help them break open the eggshell. All they have to do is peck, and the strong muscles help them do the rest.

God thought of everything so birds and reptiles could break out of their shells.

And God thought of everything for you, too—even before you were born. You may not always feel like you have all you need to succeed, or even survive, in life. But you do. If you use what God has built into you and given you in his Word, you can break out of any shell and do whatever God has put you here to do.

You have everything you need.

All Scripture is inspired by God and profitable for teaching, for reproof, for correction, for training in righteousness; so that the man of God may be adequate, equipped for every good work.
2 TIMOTHY 3:16-17, NASB

Kiwi birds don't have an egg tooth. So when a kiwi wants to break out of the eggshell, it uses its beak and its legs to break through the thin shell.

• • •

TODAY: List 10 ways you feel inadequate or poorly equipped—not ready to do the things you'd like to do. Memorize today's verses, 2 Timothy 3:16-17. If you're not reading the Bible regularly, work out a plan and follow it.

There are about 5,000 different species of songbirds. Although mainly it's the males who sing, female cardinals, Baltimore orioles, and grosbeaks sing too.

• • •

TODAY: For seven days in a row, sing a happy song or a hymn as soon as you wake up. See if it gets your day off to a good start.

GOOD MORNING!

Most songbirds prefer to sing in the early morning. A male will stake out the highest branch he can find and sing out to claim the territory and attract a mate with his beautiful song.

Birds like to come back to their favorite singing branch each day or each season. But they don't usually sing around their own nests because they don't want to advertise to predators where home is. Some birds, however, will sing softly from the nest, a "whisper song" that can only be heard a few yards away.

Other birds, like bobolinks, buntings, and larks, sing while they're flying.

Songbirds have a double voice box with two sets of muscles at the bottom of the windpipe. A songbird can take turns exhaling between its two lungs and actually sing harmony with itself.

We can't say for sure why birds sing in the morning, but the songs usually sound happy. So singing must be a good way to start the day.

How do you start your mornings? Do you wake up and groan? Does your alarm get thrown across the room? Is your mom afraid to get too close when she wakes you for school?

Waking up grumpy is a big waste of time. If you can't sing in the morning, you can at least say "Good morning" to your family and to God. Talk to God before your feet hit the floor.

Mornings can be the best part of the day. Just ask one of those annoying "morning people." Or better yet, see if you can turn into one yourself.

This is the day the Lord has made. We will rejoice and be glad in it.
PSALM 118:24

Praise the Lord! How good to sing praises to our God! How delightful and how fitting!
PSALM 147:1

Listen to my voice in the morning, Lord. Each morning I bring my requests to you and wait expectantly.
PSALM 5:3

KEEP ON KEEPING ON

Animals aren't quitters. Their stick-to-itiveness can make them annoying to humans, but that persistence is what keeps them alive.

Squirrels are clever and persistent in getting what they want to eat. If you want proof, check out a catalog of dozens of bird feeders designed to keep out pesky squirrels. (Most of them don't work.)

Squirrels sneak into attics and basements. They take over flower beds and bury seeds and nuts. They won't quit until they have plenty to get them through the winter.

Ants are even more persistent. Step on an anthill, and the ants immediately begin rebuilding.

Persistence can accomplish a lot. Quitting doesn't even give you a fighting chance.

Jesus had a lot to say about not giving up. Once he saw Simon Peter, James, and John cleaning their nets after an unsuccessful night of fishing. Jesus asked them to let down their nets one more time. Simon could have said no. They'd already tried countless times, and now the nets were in and clean. Besides, who catches fish in the day? But they did what Jesus asked, and so many fish were caught that the boats began to sink (Luke 5:1-11).

Jesus also told a story about a widow who knocked on a judge's door and demanded justice. The judge ignored her at first but finally gave her what she wanted because of her persistence (Luke 18:1-8).

Keep at it. Whether it's prayer, or a dream, or a need, don't give up. The more you struggle, the more your faith will grow as you trust in God.

> *We give great honor to those who endure under suffering. For instance, you know about Job, a man of great endurance. You can see how the Lord was kind to him at the end, for the Lord is full of tenderness and mercy.*
>
> **JAMES 5:11**

The North American silkworm, the cecropia moth, hangs in its cocoon on a bush or a tree during the winter. Finally, when spring comes, the top of the cocoon breaks open, but just a crack. A long struggle begins for the moth to get out of its cocoon. That struggle is essential for its muscles to develop and to push blood to the wings. If the struggle is shortened at all, the wings will never develop, and the moth won't fly.

• • •

TODAY: Think of two things you used to pray for but have given up on. If you believe those things are God's will for you, start praying again!

If ants were bigger, they would be our most efficient "beasts of burden." An ant can lift a minimum of 20 times its own body weight (which would be like you lifting two horses). Ants have strong legs and can run fast over long distances. One drawback is that ants only live between 45 and 60 days.

• • •

TODAY: Give your worries and "load" to Jesus when you pray today. Then take *his* load, which will be much lighter. And thank him for pulling the load with you.

CARRYING YOUR LOAD

Animal power is still used all over the world. Oxen plow fields, and so do draft horses and draft mules.

Water buffalo help in rice paddies in the wet tropics. And elephants are used for logging in Southeast Asia.

In the Arctic, the Nordic countries, and Siberia, reindeer are used for heavy work. The Bactrian camel carries loads in Central Asia, and the Arabian camel is a pack animal in deserts. Dromedaries, or one-humped camels, carry loads in Australia, North Africa, and the Middle East. In the Andes, llamas transport materials, and in the Himalayas, people use yaks.

People still depend on animals to carry their burdens.

What kind of burdens are you carrying these days? School can pile up on you. Classes can move too fast and be too hard. There's always a test hanging over your head and more homework than you think you could ever do. And that's just the schoolwork.

Friends can be a burden. Some people get hurt feelings if you don't call or text them every night. It takes a lot of energy just to keep up with your circle of friends. You don't want to miss out on anything.

Home can add to the burden. You have chores and rules. Sometimes your parents think they're helping, but they're really adding to your stress when they worry about your test scores and whether you're fitting in with classmates.

No matter what's weighing down your load, Christ promises that he can make it lighter. You're not in this alone. Talk to him. Ask him to take your load. Then you're free to share his.

My yoke is easy to bear, and the burden I give you is light.
MATTHEW 11:30

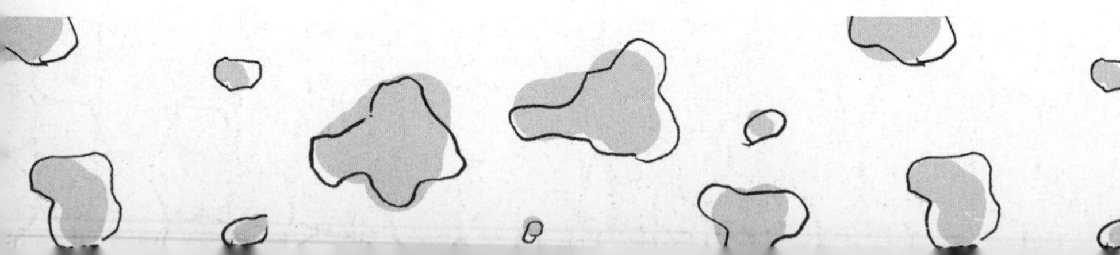

HEADS UP!

The vervet monkey is one of more than 80 kinds of African monkeys. One of the most common types of monkey in Africa, the vervet spends half of its time on the ground and half in trees. All day long, vervets give the heads-up to warn one another of dangers lurking.

Vervet monkeys have special calls for each danger:

Snake alarm: When the monkeys hear the snake alarm, they stand straight up and are on guard. As many as 50 monkeys will scan the grass for the python.

Leopard alarm: At the sound of the leopard alarm, the monkeys race into the trees and watch for the leopard.

Eagle alarm: At the call of the eagle alarm, vervet monkeys duck and hide deep in the canopy of the trees.

These monkeys have learned how to be sensitive to the various alarm calls. When they obey the warnings, they make life easier for themselves.

God's Spirit and God's Word, the Bible, give us all kinds of warnings and advice. Each day we get to choose dozens of times whether we'll follow the advice or not. You have a strong sense that you shouldn't get into that car with that group of guys. You can choose to ignore the warning or to follow it.

You're sitting by the new kid at school, and you know she doesn't have a lunch or lunch money. A verse about sharing and giving pops into your head. You can ignore it, or you can offer to share your lunch.

Doing the right thing is an ongoing process. You don't just do something good and then take it easy for a while. You have to keep choosing, making one right choice after the other. As you learn to walk in the Spirit and listen to God's warnings, life gets better.

The commands of the Lord are clear, giving insight for living. . . . They are a warning to your servant, a great reward for those who obey them.

PSALM 19:8, 11

Vervet monkey disease is a deadly infection the monkeys can pass on to humans. People in zoos and in experimental laboratories can get the disease from handling monkey tissue.

• • •

TODAY: Ask God to make you supersensitive to his little warnings today. Go with them!

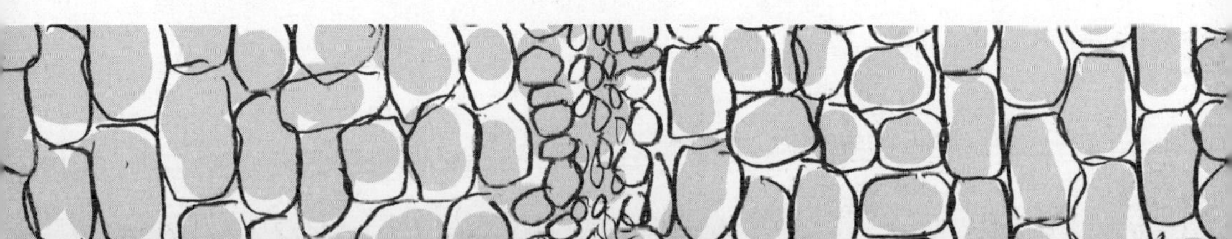

Orphaned penguin chicks have to band together in a group called a crèche in hopes of protecting themselves from predators. The chicks inside the circle are relatively safe and can catch a few winks of sleep. But the chicks on the outside perimeter never fully go to sleep.

• • •

TODAY: Thank God that he's watching over you all the time. See how many times you can think about him today. And when you do, take a deep breath and rest, knowing he's in control and looking out for you.

THE GIFT OF REST

All animals need rest. Horses can rest and sleep standing up, but even they need a good night's sleep lying down. Dogs and cats rest and sleep most of the day.

Clown fish are pretty amazing. They manage to sleep right inside the poisonous tentacles of sea anemones.

Baby koalas sleep holding on to their mothers' fur as the mothers sleep on tree branches.

Ostriches sleep, but only when they're in a group with one bird, the designated guard, assigned to stay awake all night.

Sleeping penguins have what's called a "vigilant sleep." They close their eyes for a short period of time, then peek out, staying on guard.

Many animals appoint lookouts—guards responsible for keeping watch on behalf of the whole group.

If you've ever spent a night in new surroundings, you know that it's comforting to have people you trust with you. You have confidence that they'll look out for you and protect you. And knowing that makes it easier for you to rest.

God promises that he'll always watch over us and protect us. He never sleeps and never slumbers. So you can rest, knowing he's on guard duty.

Jesus promised that if we come to him, he will give us rest: "Come to me, all of you who are weary and carry heavy burdens, and I will give you rest" (Matthew 11:28).

Rest is an awesome gift—both the kind of rest that lets you relax when you're awake and the kind of rest that lets you sleep soundly when you want to sleep.

He who watches over Israel never slumbers or sleeps.
PSALM 121:4

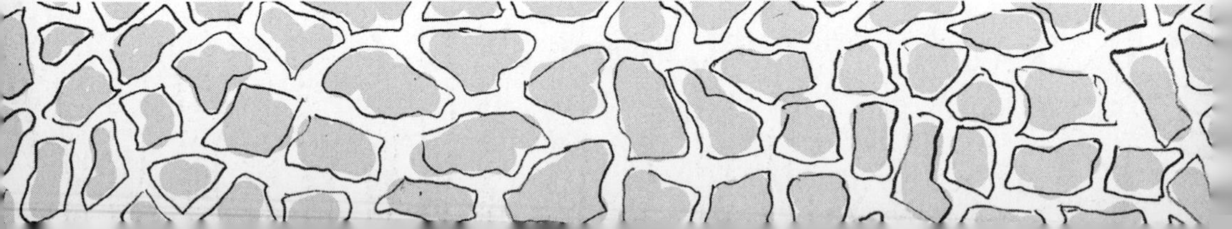

TEAM UP

Working animals are usually teamed up. Farmers who use oxen to plow their fields claim that oxen are stronger and calmer than horses. Oxen can haul logs, dig up stumps, and pull wagons, as they did for the pioneers who moved across the country several hundred years ago.

When the Pilgrims came to America in 1620, they had to plow their fields themselves, with no teams of animals to help. But when they sent Edward Winslow back to England for supplies in 1623, he returned with three Devon heifers and a Devon bull. Milking Devons are still the best farm oxen in the world.

Oxen work in teams by pushing against a yoke, or wooden beam placed behind the animals' horns or on the back of their necks. The other end of the yoke is attached to the load to be hauled. Oxen were the main animals used to haul heavy loads in America until mules caught on in the 1930s. Oxen are still favorites for toting logs from forests without ruining the environment. Plus, oxen don't need gas, they don't break down, and you can pet them.

People should be able to work well in teams too—to share burdens and help carry the load. Even in your own house, there are opportunities to partner up. Can you imagine how your big brother would handle it if he came home from a late practice at school and saw that you'd swept the porch for him? Or what would your little sister say if you set the table for her because you knew she had a big test the next day?

Maybe you get a chance to work with a partner on a school project. If you do, remember Jesus' offer to help you with your burden and to teach you because he is "humble and gentle at heart." If you're humble and gentle, everybody will want to be on your team.

> *Take my yoke upon you. Let me teach you, because I am humble and gentle at heart, and you will find rest for your souls.*
> **MATTHEW 11:29**

An ox is a mature (at least four years old) working bull that has been neutered. *Oxen* is the plural of *ox*. A pair of steers is called a yoke of steers, and four or more make a team of steers.

• • •

TODAY: Think about the last team you were a part of (or the one you're on now). What kind of teammate were you? Ask God to teach you humility and gentleness.

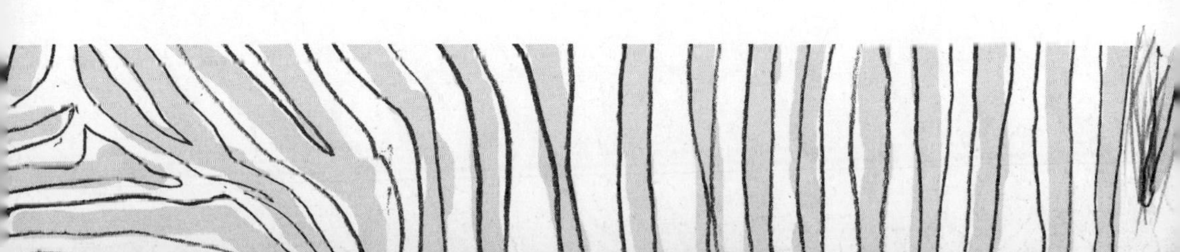

Pet personalities vary within any breed, but here are a few breeds of dogs that tend to get along with cats: Cardigan Welsh corgis, Pembroke Wesh corgis, Saint Bernards, spaniels, and retrievers. Here are a couple of breeds that usually don't like cats: hounds and terriers.

• • •

TODAY: Name three people you have trouble getting along with. Every day this week, pray for them all and ask God to bless them in specific ways.

CAN'T WE JUST GET ALONG?!

Have you ever had a dog and cat that didn't get along? If so, you understand that old expression "fighting like cats and dogs." Nobody's sure where the saying originated, but it implies some pretty fierce fighting.

There's another expression about cats and fighting: "Fight like Kilkenny cats." Unfortunately, we do know where that expression began. In the ancient town of Kilkenny in Ireland, bored soldiers were said to have tied two cats together for sport and watched until one cat killed the other. It's a horrible thought, but somebody turned it into a popular limerick:

> There once were two cats of Kilkenny.
> Each thought there was one cat too many.
> So they fought and they fit
> And they scratched and they bit
> 'Til instead of two cats, there weren't any.

As a pet owner, don't you hate it when the two animals you love can't get along? It's so easy for you to see how their lives would be better if they were friends, but they don't seem to get it.

On the other hand, it's wonderful when you have two pets that cuddle up, keep each other company, and truly love one another.

That's the way God feels about us. It hurts him when we fight. God longs to see us love one another and live in harmony. That doesn't mean we have to be the same. In harmony, different notes—not the same note—are brought together in beautiful ways.

Work at getting along with other people. Always do your part and more. Ask God to help you do what it takes to get along.

> *How wonderful and pleasant it is when brothers live together in harmony!*
> **PSALM 133:1**

GARBAGE IN, GARBAGE OUT

Healthy animals get that way from healthy eating. Dogs have shinier coats and exhibit more pep and energy when they're eating the right food. On the other hand, more dogs get sick and die from obesity than from any other problem.

Cats have glossier fur when they eat right, and fat cats simply aren't healthy cats.

Horses have shinier coats when they're on the right feed and getting vitamins. Racehorses have special dieticians to make sure what goes into the horses' stomachs can translate into energy.

It's important for us to eat right, to have healthy diets, and to be in the best shape we can be in—for all the right reasons. God lives in your "temple" (your body), so you should keep it in tip-top shape, never putting anything into it that could be harmful.

But you need to think about your spiritual diet too. What are you sending into your mental, emotional, and spiritual being? There's an old adage that holds true: "Garbage in, garbage out." If you feed junk into your mind all day, that's what will become part of your thoughts and come out of your mouth.

What images bombard you when you watch TV? What messages come at you when you listen to certain music? What words do you hear over and over from the friends you hang out with?

God isn't legalistic. There's no command that says, "Thou shalt not watch rated-R movies or stupid TV programs." But garbage flowing into your head can take the place of pure thoughts and lovely ideas. Fill your mind with thoughts that draw you closer to God and make you joyfully in tune with Jesus.

You're the one who gets to choose what you'll fill your "tank" with. Don't go for the garbage.

Fix your thoughts on what is true, and honorable, and right, and pure, and lovely, and admirable. Think about things that are excellent and worthy of praise.
PHILIPPIANS 4:8

Even snakes have to watch what they eat. Snakes that eat right grow faster and shed their skins more often than snakes that will eat anything. When healthy snakes shed their skins, the skins come off in one complete piece instead of flaking off in fragments.

• • •

TODAY: Every time you get a "garbage thought" today, imagine throwing it where it belongs—into the garbage. Then replace it with one pure and lovely thought.

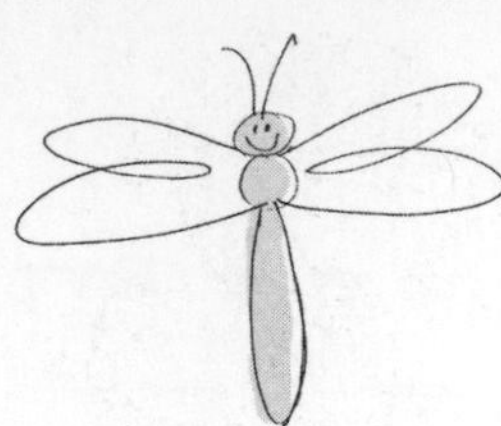

Dragonflies can fly between 30 and 60 miles per hour. They don't hurt people—they don't bite or sting. And they eat mosquitoes, ants, termites, spiders, and gnats.

• • •

TODAY: Think over the last victory and the last loss you experienced. Thank God for both.

VICTORY

In Japan, dragonflies are a symbol of victory on the battlefield. The fossil dragonfly meganeura was probably the largest insect that ever lived, with a wingspan of over two feet. It's not hard to imagine the creature's victory over rival insects.

Some countries choose fierce-looking birds of prey to put on their nation's flag, like the flags of Albania, Ecuador, Kazakhstan, Mexico, Moldova, Montenegro, Zambia, and Zimbabwe.

Sports teams rarely pick sweet mascots, like kitties, wooly worms, or puppies. Instead, we cheer for Tigers and Lions, Bears and Eagles, Hornets and Wolverines.

"V-I-C-T-O-R-Y! That's our great school's battle cry!"

Nearly every school across the United States has a victory cheer or two. Our teams are all about winning. That makes sense, but there's a lot more to true victory than simply winning. And there's a lot more to losing than being defeated.

Some people can't stand to lose. They'll do just about anything to win—even cheat. They cheat at solitaire and get angry if they don't win. They knock over the checkerboard if they can see they're losing. They get too rough on the field if they smell defeat. They're sore losers.

If you're a sore loser, the chances are good that you're also a sore winner. You like to rub it in. Victory is yours, and victory is everything.

Only it's not. Even when you win, your victory belongs to God. Who do you think gave you the skills you're so proud of? Be a good and gracious winner . . . and loser.

> *They did not conquer the land with their swords; it was not their own strong arm that gave them victory. It was your right hand and strong arm and the blinding light from your face that helped them, for you loved them.*
> **PSALM 44:3**

> *I wait quietly before God, for my victory comes from him.*
> **PSALM 62:1**

> *The horse is prepared for the day of battle, but the victory belongs to the LORD.*
> **PROVERBS 21:31**

MY MISTAKE

Dogs make fantastic pets. They aim to please. They're ace companions.

Only they do have one universal fault: dogs eat their own vomit.

Why? Why would an otherwise delightful canine eat something nasty, hurl it up, then eat the gross thing all over again? That's just disgusting.

Some dog lovers insist dogs scarf up vomit so they won't leave traces of themselves for predators. Others say dogs eat their vomit so a would-be prey won't realize that they're stepping into dog territory. Still others claim the charming practice is a way to exert dominance, in the same way the dog will rush to pick up anything that has been dropped.

The truth is, nobody knows why dogs eat their vomit. Maybe they just forgot how bad the food was the first time around.

That's the way it is with mistakes. Proverbs 26 compares a dog eating its vomit to a fool repeating his foolishness. So the question is, Why do *we* keep repeating the same mistakes?

You tried to get into the popular group last year, and for a week all went well. Then they dropped you, and they've snubbed you ever since. This year you watch the same group in action, and there you go, trying to worm your way in again.

You almost flunked last chapter's test because you didn't study. And yet the next test is tomorrow, and you haven't even started studying.

You broke the no-texting-after-midnight rule again or told another white lie. Didn't you learn anything from your past mistakes?

Wise up! Don't be like a dog returning to its own vomit.

As a dog returns to its vomit, so a fool repeats his foolishness.
PROVERBS 26:11

Dogs are in more American homes than any other pet. But in many Arab countries, dogs are considered unclean and are unheard of as pets.

• • •

TODAY: List five mistakes you don't want to repeat. Ask God to help you see the same situations coming up again so you can respond differently from now on.

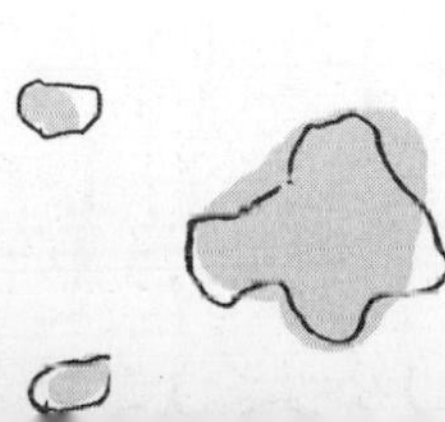
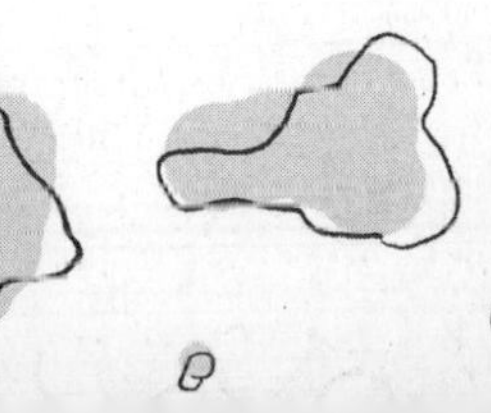

The breed of dog with the biggest ears is the basset hound, one of the few dog breeds that can't swim well.

• • •

TODAY: Think about any arguments going on at home or at school. Pray for the people on both sides of the argument.

STAY OUT OF IT

Yanking a dog's ears won't win you any friends. President Lyndon Baines Johnson had two White House pet beagles named Him and Her. The president was known to be an animal lover, and his friends teased him about how much he loved his dogs.

But in 1964, President Johnson made a big mistake as far as animal lovers were concerned. While talking with reporters and photographers on the White House lawn, the president leaned down and scratched Him's ears. Then he lifted the dog off the ground by his ears. Outraged dog lovers phoned in to radio talk shows. They wrote letters condemning President Johnson's mistreatment of his dogs. They vowed not to vote for him again, ever—even as dogcatcher.

Proverbs 26:17 says that getting in the way of somebody else's argument is as foolish as yanking a dog's ear. And that's pretty foolish. Even if the dog doesn't snap at you, other people might, as President Johnson learned the hard way.

You don't always have to take sides when two friends get into an argument. If you do, one of them will probably feel like you're being unfair and siding against that person just because you like the other friend better. And that will only make things worse.

It's hard enough to settle your own arguments peacefully, right? And the more people who get involved, the more likely it is that the argument will escalate. People will start taking sides, even though they have no idea what the original argument was about.

There may be times when God will use you to help settle an argument or a quarrel between friends. But that's not the same thing as jumping into an argument that really has nothing to do with you.

Avoid those secondhand arguments. And never pull a dog's ears.

Interfering in someone else's argument is as foolish as yanking a dog's ears.
PROVERBS 26:17

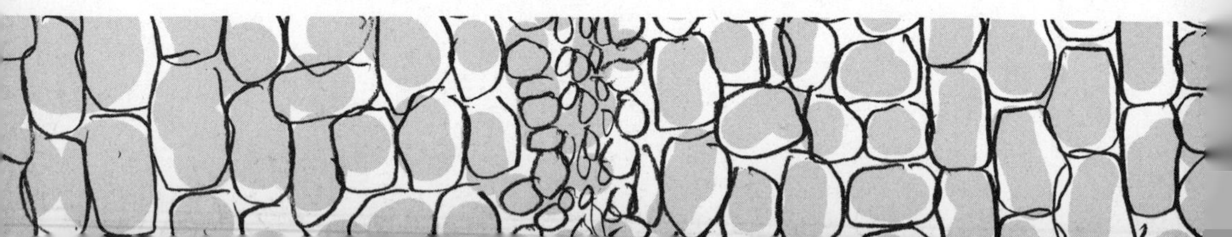

MISSING THE MARK

Many animal lovers claim that mistakes made by a pet are actually mistakes made by the owner. They believe that if a dog or horse knows what you want it to do, it will do it. Animals aim to please.

If your new puppy goofs and does its business inside the house instead of outside on the lawn, it's a mistake. Maybe you weren't quick enough getting your pet outside. Or maybe you fed the poor thing and forgot to walk it. So if you punish the dog by swatting it with a rolled-up newspaper (as some wrongly advise), it will have no idea why you're hitting it.

If your horse keeps taking the wrong lead when you break into a canter, it's not doing it on purpose. Why would it? Again, you're the one making the mistake. You might be giving mixed signals or shifting your weight without realizing it.

Mistakes aren't the same thing as sin. Usually you can tell the difference. Sin is falling short of God's standard for you. It's an archery term for "missing the mark." When an archer aims for the bull's-eye and misses by three inches, that's a three-inch "sin."

You love your pet and wouldn't do anything to hurt it. But how many times do you *not* do the things you know you should for your pet? Clean the cage, provide fresh water, make sure it gets exercise and attention?

Sometimes it's easier to identify sin when you do something that's all-out wrong—steal, lie, cheat. It may not be as easy to realize you've sinned when you do nothing at all. But God calls that sin too—knowing what you should do and not doing it.

Ask God to help you to be a person other people (and pets) can depend on. And when God tells you to do something, do it!

> *Remember, it is sin to know what you ought to do and then not do it.*
>
> **JAMES 4:17**

Most veterinarians agree that your most important chore is to give your pet clean water. Dogs and cats taste a big difference between fresh and day-old water. Fish need a clean aquarium. Horses need fresh water, and plenty of it.

• • •

TODAY: If you own a pet, make a list of the jobs you should do every day to take care of your pet. If someone has been covering for you, thank that person but ask to take over the responsibility. Keep a checklist all week to see how you do.

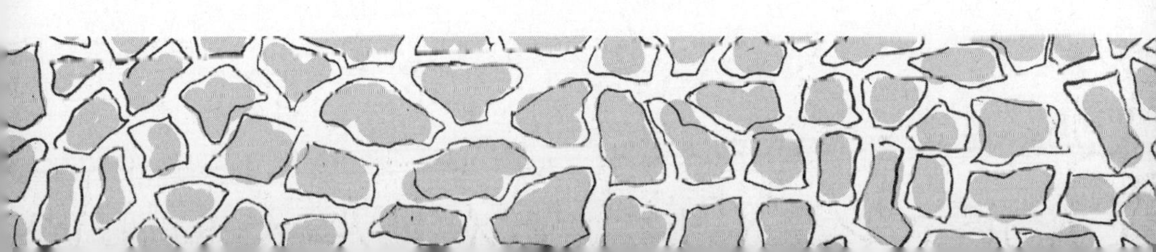

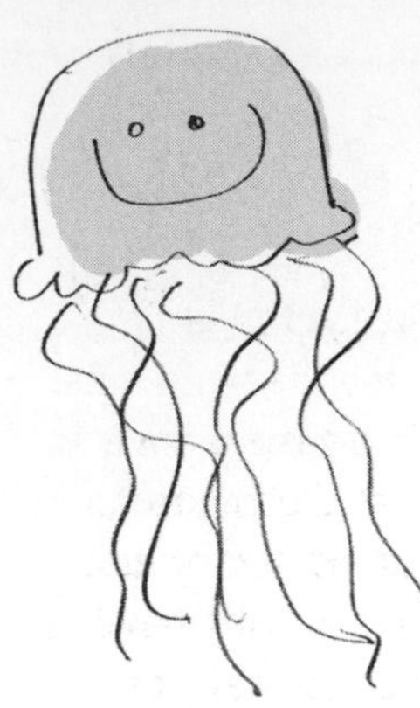

DUH!

We don't know a fraction of what there is to know about the animals God has created. Every year more creatures are discovered and scientists uncover even deeper mysteries of the animal world.

After the Vietnam War, soldiers talked about a strange-looking deer that had been spotted by various troops. A new species of muntjac deer was "discovered," described, and named.

The International Commission on Zoological Nomenclature (the organization that names new animal species) expects that more than 20,000 new animal species will be named each year. Some recent discoveries were four new types of lemurs from Madagascar, a strange rodent from Vietnam, a new monkey from Tanzania, and a vampire fish from the Amazon. Who knew?

Is it any wonder that there's so much we don't understand about God? Jesus told his disciples that there were things he wanted to tell them but knew they wouldn't understand. God knows our limits too.

Do you ever feel like the smartest kid in your class? Or the cleverest person in your family? You shouldn't. Even if you get the highest test scores and the best grades, there's not much difference between the highest and lowest in your class—not when you consider how little we all know compared to God.

Since even the most intelligent humans on earth don't know that much, nobody should ever be a know-it-all.

Is it your wisdom that makes the hawk soar and spread its wings toward the south? Is it at your command that the eagle rises to the heights to make its nest?

JOB 39:26-27

About a mile below the surface of the sea around the Farallon Islands, near Hawaii, scientists have discovered a brand-new species of jellyfish in recent years. Instead of tentacles, it has a group of fleshy arms, and it sports a yard-wide red bell, unlike any other known jellyfish.

• • •

TODAY: List 10 things that you wonder about but don't understand or know.

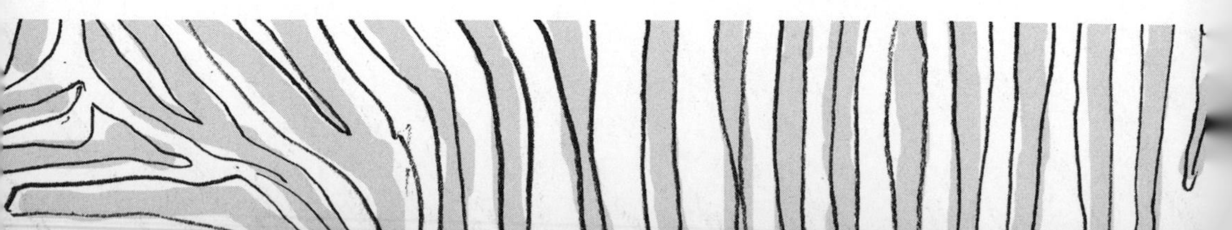

DO YOU TRUST ME?

Animals are quick studies—at least, most of them. Even domesticated horses seem to be able to size up humans in a short visit or on a short ride. Dogs and cats can sense whether or not a would-be predator is out to get them—and to most animals, we look like would-be predators.

Horses have been known to hang on to their distrust of certain individuals for a lifetime, even though the offense was done when the horse was just a colt.

All puppies are born trusting. They have to learn to distrust. Mean dogs are made, not born.

For most of us, trust is something we struggle with. On the one hand, you'll never have deep friendships if you don't develop trust. On the other hand, people can let you down.

Have you ever told a secret to someone, only to have them tell your secret to someone else—someone you didn't want to know about it? Have you ever spilled someone else's secret or betrayed a confidence? Most of us have—at least once, probably more.

Jesus had close friends he loved so much that he died for them. But he didn't entrust himself to anybody but God. And in the end, he *was* betrayed by people, but he was resurrected by God.

God is the only one who can be trusted totally, all the time. We can forgive people when they let us down because they're weak, like we are. We should get that.

And we should be even more grateful that the God of the universe is 100 percent trustworthy and will never let us down.

> *It is better to take refuge in the Lord than to trust in princes.*
>
> **PSALM 118:9**

Wild animals have some pretty good reasons not to trust humans, who have made so many of them endangered. In parts of Africa, hunters have killed many rhinos for their horns. Some other Africans are trying to save the rhinos by sawing their horns so short that hunters will leave the animals alone.

• • •

TODAY: Talk to God about the person you trust most in the world. Thank God for that person. Then thank God that you can trust him infinitely more than the most trustworthy person in your life.

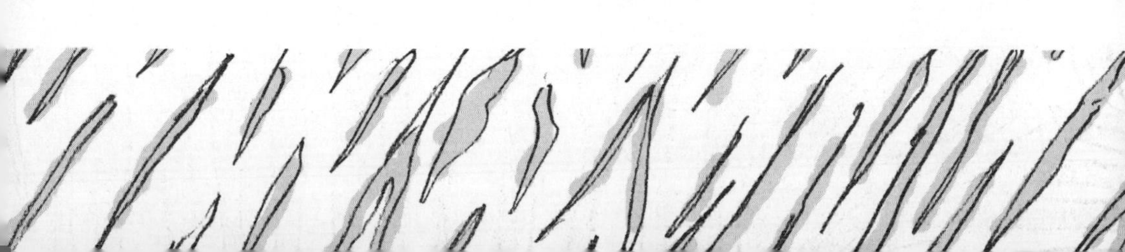

Orangutan mothers stay with their babies the first six or seven years after birth. Meanwhile, Father Orangutan does his job by burping to warn other males to keep away from his territory.

• • •

TODAY: List 10 ways you are dependent on God. Talk to God about anything you think you may be trying to do without him.

IT ALL DEPENDS

Most baby animals are born fairly helpless. They instinctively know that they need their parents in order to survive. Baby birds open their mouths, and parents drop in worms. Their needs are big, obvious, and fulfilled by Mom or Dad.

Baby ducklings are extra vulnerable and needy because they can't fly away from a predator. Sea otters are completely dependent on Mom for over a year. For the first four weeks, she feeds, grooms, and carries the babies on her belly as she swims or lies on her back. Then she spends her time teaching the otter pups how to hunt, groom themselves, and dive for food.

After 22 months in its mother's womb, a 250-pound baby elephant calf is born—with fewer survival skills than most baby animals. Not only Mom but also a number of the "elders" from the herd will be called on to teach the elephant during its long childhood.

Jesus told his disciples that they needed to get their strength and power from him. He compared the relationship to a vine and its branches, with God the Father as the gardener, Jesus as the grapevine, and his followers as the branches. On their own, the branches of a grapevine are worthless. You can't build with them. They don't burn well. You can't make anything, even a pencil, out of a branch from the vine.

But when the branch is connected to the vine, power flows through it, and it can help produce grapes. In the same way, when we're not connected to Jesus, nothing we do counts for eternity. We're a waste of space. Even if you helped an old lady across the street, it would be a selfish gesture, done just to look good.

But when we depend on Christ and let his power flow through us, we can do great things.

> *Remain in me, and I will remain in you. For a branch cannot produce fruit if it is severed from the vine, and you cannot be fruitful unless you remain in me. Yes, I am the vine; you are the branches. Those who remain in me, and I in them, will produce much fruit. For apart from me you can do nothing.*
>
> **JOHN 15:4-5**

PLAYING FAVORITES

What happens when you have two cats and you favor one over the other? Or two dogs and you give more attention to one? Chances are they fight over you.

Playing favorites is never fair. But we see it in nature sometimes. In a large litter in the wild, if a mother sees she doesn't have enough food to feed all her newborns, she'll generally favor the biggest and strongest in the litter.

Everybody knows what if feels like to be on the wrong end of favoritism. But we never know what's in the other person's mind. In the wild, the mother instinctively pays more attention to the strongest in her litter, in hopes that at least some will survive and carry on the family.

Your parents might seem like they're playing favorites, but it's usually not that simple. You might be right—they might not be treating you and your siblings fairly. Even parents make mistakes.

But if you're honest, you may see another explanation. If your sister gets extra privileges, maybe it's because she's older. Or it might be because she doesn't get into as much trouble. Your parents have learned they can trust her. Maybe your dad and brother love football, so they spend more time together tossing the ball around and talking sports. They don't mean to leave you out.

Maybe you have two good friends at school, but you get the feeling that they like each other better than they like you. They talk on the phone and text more than you do. It sure seems like you're the third favorite in your group of three. And whether they really are playing favorites or not, it hurts to be left out.

God never leaves anyone out. He never plays favorites.

And you shouldn't play favorites either.

God will never love anyone more than he loves you. He'll never think about anyone more than he thinks about you.

The wisdom from above is first of all pure. It is also peace loving, gentle at all times, and willing to yield to others. It is full of mercy and good deeds. It shows no favoritism and is always sincere.

JAMES 3:17

In Italy, the favorite pet is a cat. Cats are also favored in China and Hong Kong, where they're considered lucky, and people keep cats in shops and homes. The Inuit Eskimos of Northern Canada might take in a bird, a fox, or a seal cub as a pet. But in Africa, virtually no one has pets.

• • •

TODAY: Talk to God about every feeling you have of not being the favorite or of anyone not playing fair with you. Thank God that he doesn't play favorites.

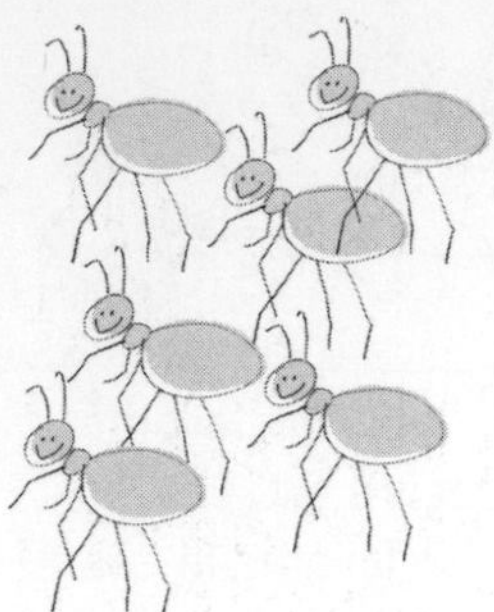

For every human, there are one million ants. And the total weight of ants on earth is greater than the total weight of humans.

• • •

TODAY: Choose one activity, one hobby, or one homework assignment, and work at it harder than you've ever done. Talk to God while you work.

LAZYBONES

Whenever Solomon wanted to make a point about working hard, he turned to the ant. In Proverbs 6:6, he wrote: "Take a lesson from the ants, you lazybones. Learn from their ways and become wise!"

What are their ways? Ants work hard all summer so they bring in enough food to last all winter. Worker ants never stop as they care for the young, look for food, bring back food, store it, and still have time to defend the colony. When winter comes, worker ants do double shifts, carrying the larvae inside so they won't freeze.

Ants are clean, too. They clean their rooms . . . *and* the rooms of other ants. Some ants even take out the trash to a special dumping ground—without being asked.

Hard work is . . . well, hard. It's much easier to leave that writing assignment in your backpack and lie down after a hard day at school, right? It's so much easier to pick up that game controller and get lost in a game until dinner. What fun is there in helping with dinner?

But work is part of the package of being human. Don't shy away from hard jobs. If your lawn needs mowing, mow it. If the dishes need to be washed, do it. Don't stretch chores into the absolute longest time period just so you won't be given another chore.

When your homework gets tough, don't throw up your hands and declare it's just too hard. Work at it, asking God to help you understand, and maybe asking a parent or an older sibling to help you out.

Don't let anyone call you "lazybones." Don't deserve the name.

Take a lesson from the ants, you lazybones. Learn from their ways and become wise!
PROVERBS 6:6

October 24

TAME THE TONGUE

Any mammal can be tamed if you take it from its mother and give it a human protector for the first year or years. But so-called "tamed" animals don't always stay tamed. The wildness may burst out when you least expect it.

Modern horse whisperers have had tremendous success in taming, or gentling, wild mustangs. They observe horses in the wild and imitate their herd behavior, establishing themselves as a leader in the horses' hierarchy. Yet even though the "tamed" horse may perform beautifully 99 percent of the time, the wildness is there and may come out on occasion.

Our tongues are like that. We might say nice things to everyone nearly all the time. Then there's that one mean comment that just pops out, as if we had no control over what we were saying.

It seems like the New Testament author James sounds almost baffled when he writes about the tongue. How can the same tongue praise God, then in the next moment curse people who are made in God's image?

You can't control everything you say by sheer force of will any more than a tamed horse can stay 100 percent tame. But the more control you yield to Christ, the better off you'll be. If you're thinking of people the way Christ does, then you won't have mean thoughts that will show themselves, sooner or later, in words. If you love with Christ's love, you'll care too much to say hurtful things.

And if you blow it, the tongue can also apologize.

> *Sometimes [the tongue] praises our Lord and Father, and sometimes it curses those who have been made in the image of God. And so blessing and cursing come pouring out of the same mouth. Surely, my brothers and sisters, this is not right!*
> JAMES 3:9-10

There are about 30 kinds of "untamed" dogs, including coyotes, foxes, dingoes, and jackals. Jackals can't even get along with one another. They hunt alone and only meet in packs to grab leftovers from a lion kill.

• • •

TODAY: Confess to God the last out-of-control thing your tongue said. (Apologize if you haven't yet.) Be on guard the whole day and see if you can let Christ control what you say.

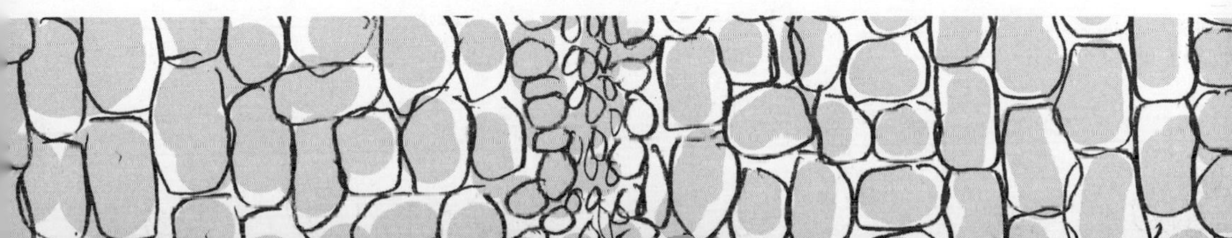

In New Zealand, the male and female kiwi birds have a great, lifelong relationship. They live together their entire lives, maybe 20 years. From June to March they can be heard calling to each other every night. And they get together in their nesting burrow every three days.

• • •

TODAY: Ask God to help you develop good friendships with classmates of the opposite sex. If you're not sure where to begin, start by saying hi at school.

ONE DAY IN YOUR DISTANT FUTURE . . .

Don't you just love lovebirds? Lovebirds are a type of small parrot. They live in pairs and like to scoot close on a perch or branch and touch noses, looking like they're madly in love.

But lovebirds aren't the only ones that mate for life. Owls, geese, swans, eagles, and doves make the list too.

Only 3 percent of about 4,000 species of mammals are monogamous—exclusively one guy and one girl.

Wolves mate for life. Other lifelong mates include gibbon apes, termites, anglerfish, coyotes, and beavers. Black vultures must have passed a law against adultery. Whenever one of them tries to stray, the others attack the offender.

A male anglerfish grabs his female and never lets go . . . literally. As he holds on and time passes, both of their vascular systems mesh into one so that the male becomes totally dependent on the female.

You're a long way from finding a marriage partner, but it's never too early to deepen the conviction that a union with one person is worth waiting for. God calls it "one flesh" (Genesis 2:24, NIV) when two people give all they have to God and to each other. Marriage is meant to be forever, and you don't want to mess it up by rushing things, right?

Until then, it's good to have a bunch of friends of both genders. Don't be like that anglerfish that grabs on and won't let go. Enjoy friendships with many of those "fish in the sea."

> *"At last!" the man [Adam] exclaimed. "This one is bone from my bone, and flesh from my flesh! She will be called 'woman,' because she was taken from 'man.'" This explains why a man leaves his father and mother and is joined to his wife, and the two are united into one.*
>
> **GENESIS 2:23-24**

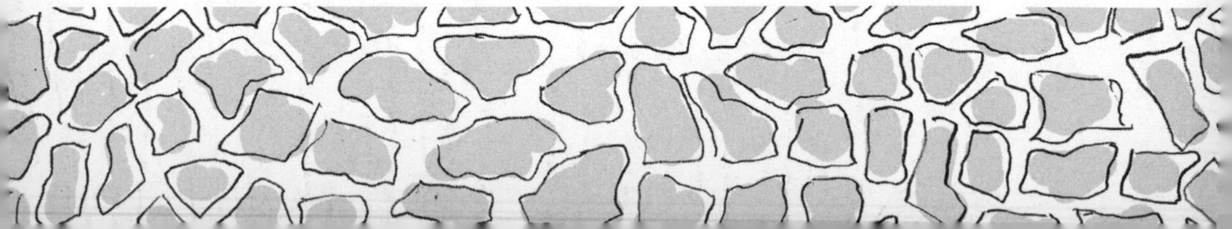

GET SHARP

If you turn out an old horse and a new horse into the veteran horse's pasture, you'll probably see sparks fly. But eventually the two could become friends. And they'll learn from each other. The young horse could take its cues from the old pro on feeding and behaving calmly. And the old horse might get new life from having a spry youngster around.

The same thing happens when a one-dog family adds a second dog. At first the older dog resents the new dog, and vice versa. But if things work out right, they'll both be better and happier dogs once they work out their differences.

Have you ever had to be around someone who rubs you the wrong way? Siblings have a special art for annoying each other. Even good friends can get on each other's nerves sometimes. You're different people, and those differences can cause friction: You like the Browns, but he's a Steelers fan. Yankees or Red Sox? Country or hip-hop? And what about TV shows, movies, favorite fast-food places, and on and on?

We have to learn to deal with differences and resolve conflicts, especially with friends and family. If we do, God says we'll end up sharper, as iron sharpens iron. That's the way knives used to be sharpened—by rubbing them against each other until the edges wore down to a point.

That's what we may have to do when dealing with some of our own conflicts. If we let our edges wear down, we'll end up sharper.

As iron sharpens iron, so a friend sharpens a friend.
PROVERBS 27:17

Frogs have many natural enemies that not only rub them the wrong way but eat them: snakes, birds, lizards, hedgehogs, fish, diving birds, water shrews, and other frogs. But their biggest enemy is humans. There's a worldwide decline in the number of frogs. Frogs are so sensitive to pollution and changes in the ozone that many scientists use frog statistics for signs of a well-balanced ecosystem.

• • •

TODAY: Think of one friend who sometimes rubs you the wrong way. Can you see how you've been sharpened by that friend? Thank God for that person, and thank God for the differences between you and your friend.

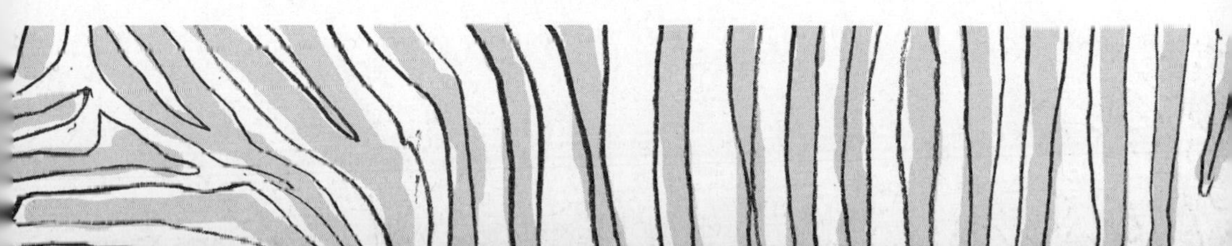

Instead of having four feet, like most animals, monkeys have four hands, with a palm, long fingers, and a three-jointed thumb for grasping. Add in the tail, which can wrap around branches, and you have an acrobat—a bit like Blondin the tightrope walker—that can dangle, climb, perch, cling, and swing.

• • •

TODAY: Talk to God about three specific actions you can take to demonstrate your trust in him. Step out in faith.

TRUST IS ACTION

It isn't all that hard to tell whether or not a pet trusts you. You don't have to read your pet's mind. You can tell by its actions.

Actions that prove your horse trusts you:

It eats from your hand. (This isn't always a good idea though.)
It lets you groom it and pick up its hooves.
It will follow you into a trailer.
It allows you to treat its wounds.
It nickers when you enter the barn.

Actions that prove your dog trusts you:

It eats when you're around.
It doesn't cower when you pet it.
It responds to your commands to come, sit, stay.
It hands over its favorite toy to you for a game of fetch.

Actions speak louder than words when it comes to demonstrating trust. A tightrope walker called Blondin used to amaze audiences by crossing the gorge beneath Niagara Falls. The crowd cheered when he pushed a wheelbarrow across the tightrope. They said they knew he could do it again. But when he asked for a volunteer to get into the wheelbarrow for the next walk, nobody came forward.

It's easy to say that we trust Christ. But it's our actions that demonstrate true faith. If you stay joyful even when things go against you, people will see your faith. If you volunteer and help the homeless in your community, that's faith in action.

What good is it, dear brothers and sisters, if you say you have faith but don't show it by your actions?
JAMES 2:14

FRESH WATER, PLEASE

With nearly three-quarters of the earth covered by water, you'd think animals wouldn't have to worry about getting a nice drink. But 98 percent of the earth's water is salty, and most animals need fresh water.

All animals need water, but they don't all drink, exactly. A kangaroo rat in the Southwest gets its water from plants, and groundhogs get most of their water from food. Certain lizards absorb through their pores the little moisture they run across. The darkling beetle stands on its head to squeeze out moisture in the desert.

Female mosquitoes have their own method of getting the water they need. Since they also need protein, they drink the blood of birds, reptiles, mammals, or humans. Hummingbirds are the biggest drinkers for their size, drinking five times their body weight in water every day. If we drank that much, we'd die.

Jesus called himself the "living water." One day in the heat of Samaria, Jesus met a woman who was drawing water from a well, and he asked her for a drink. Surprised that he, a Jew, would even be speaking to a Samaritan woman, she wondered why he'd asked her for a drink.

Jesus offered her water that would quench her thirst forever: "If you only knew the gift God has for you and who you are speaking to, you would ask me, and I would give you living water" (John 4:10).

Jesus is still offering living water that lasts through eternity. Make sure you've accepted his offer.

> *Jesus stood and shouted to the crowds, "Anyone who is thirsty may come to me! Anyone who believes in me may come and drink! For the Scriptures declare, 'Rivers of living water will flow from his heart.'" (When he said "living water," he was speaking of the Spirit, who would be given to everyone believing in him.)*
> **JOHN 7:37-39**

The expression that someone "drinks like a fish" misses the boat. Saltwater fish don't drink much. Freshwater fish don't drink, period. They absorb water through their skin.

• • •

TODAY: If you have any doubt about whether or not you've tapped into the living water of Jesus and eternal life, talk to someone—a parent, a good friend, a pastor. The offer is open to you, and the promise is eternal.

SUPER NANNIES

Some animals team up to raise their kids. Elephant moms rely on other females to help teach daughters of the herd all they'll need to know to survive in the jungle. A "super nanny," or primary female elder, is placed in charge. One of the young female elephants that Nanny teaches will end up taking over for her when she dies.

Dolphins are raised in families, but all the grown-ups help raise all the young. And groups may stay together for life.

Ants have actual nurseries, where nannies take care of the young. Other nannies are found among giraffes, certain kinds of penguins, crocodiles, lions, and meerkats.

A generation ago in the United States, most neighborhood adults felt responsible for the neighbors' kids, as well as their own. Anybody's mom was everybody's mom. A buddy's mother had as much power to boss him as his own mother did. If a kid didn't obey her friend's parents, hers would hear about it, and they wouldn't like it.

Times have changed. Your parents may not even know your best friend's parents. Still, you owe the adults respect.

God calls us to honor our own parents, but the command gives a dignity to all parents. Be polite, honest, and helpful. You don't help your friends by laughing when they mock their parents behind their backs.

Respect other kids' parents. After all, it takes a village to raise you.

> *"Honor your father and mother." This is the first commandment with a promise: If you honor your father and mother, "things will go well for you, and you will have a long life on the earth."*
> **EPHESIANS 6:2-3**

Flamingos are social animals. They like to lay eggs at the same time and in the same location, in huge colonies. Moms and dads take turns incubating their eggs for 26 to 31 days. For 4 to 7 days, each parent will care for only his or her own chick, identifying it out of hundreds of chicks by vocalizations alone. After a week, the chicks become fledglings, leave the nest, and form a crèche—a big nursery school headed up by a few adults.

• • •

TODAY: Pray for two friends' moms—one you like and one you like . . . not so much.

CUD CHEWERS

Check out any cow in the pasture, and you'll probably see a lot of chewing going on. Cows are notorious for chewing their cud, an activity that makes your worst dinner habits look like Miss Manners.

Here's how it works. Cows have four chambers, or compartments, in their stomachs. A cow takes a mouthful of grass, and the process begins: (1) Chew. (2) Swallow. (3) Food passes through two stomach chambers. (4) Food is brought back up to the mouth to be chewed again. (5) Swallow a second time. (6) Food passes through the third and fourth chambers. (7) The mess is slowly digested at last.

If only we would learn to chew our "spiritual cud" the way cows chew their cud! Meditation is dwelling on God. You can memorize a passage of Scripture and go over and over the meaning in your head. Pray about it. Put it into your own words. Think about it. Call it up again and again during the day—just like cud.

Or meditate on God himself, going over and over who God is and what he does for you. You know how your mind automatically replays cool things that happen to you—your winning shot at the end of the game, the applause you got when you spelled the winning word in the spelling bee? Meditation helps you get your mind to replay God's actions and focus on him. Why not give it a try?

> *I remember the days of old. I ponder all your great works and think about what you have done.*
> **PSALM 143:5**

> *I will meditate on your majestic, glorious splendor and your wonderful miracles.*
> **PSALM 145:5**

Antelope and deer chew cud just like cows do. They digest food the first round in special stomachs, cough it up again, chew it some more, swallow, and on and on.

• • •

TODAY: Pick one thing about God that you can meditate on each day this week. Start today with goodness. How is God good to you? to animals? to others? Tomorrow think about love. List the evidence of God's love around you.

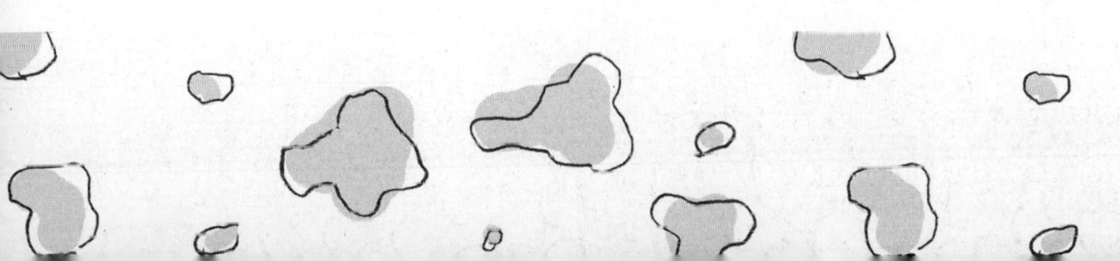

The name *chameleon* means "ground lion." This may refer to the tuft around the chameleon's neck, which looks a little like a lion's mane. Chameleons aren't the only creatures that can change colors. So can some fish, frogs, and other lizards.

• • •

TODAY: Talk to God about one person at school you're afraid doesn't know Christ. Ask God to build a bridge between that person and you—some common ground where you can meet that person and talk naturally and freely about your faith in Christ.

BECOMING ALL THINGS

Most chameleons change to match their surroundings. Different varieties can change from green to yellow, blue, red, orange, black, brown, or pink.

Some scientists say that chameleons change colors because of surrounding light and temperature. Others attribute the change to a chameleon's mood—especially anger . . . or love.

But recent research offers another reason for the changes. Chameleons may change color as a way to communicate with other chameleons.

It's true that we have to be careful not to become like everyone else. You shouldn't change who you are or what you believe just so you'll fit in. And you do need to pick your friends wisely because there's a good chance you'll end up becoming more like them.

But it's also true that when you're strong in the Lord, you can venture out prayerfully, fully aware of what you're doing. You can do what needs to be done to connect with people and draw them to Christ.

The apostle Paul said that he became all things to all people. He searched for what he might have in common with other people so that he'd have a point of connection. Becoming all things to all people means identifying with them while keeping your true self.

If it means you can connect and have a platform to share Christ with someone, why not learn chess or play football or listen to someone else's favorite music or take up jogging? It doesn't hurt to wear the costume now and then—just don't wear the mask.

> *When I am with those who are weak, I share their weakness, for I want to bring the weak to Christ. Yes, I try to find common ground with everyone, doing everything I can to save some.*
> **1 CORINTHIANS 9:22**

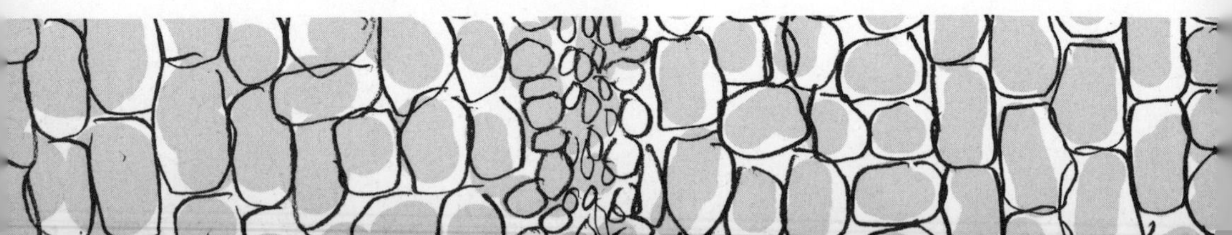

TRAINING TIPS

Animals and people are happier when pets are well trained. Dogs that are housebroken and don't have to get screamed at are happier dogs. Cats that don't jump up on the dinner table don't get shooed away. Horses that can neck-rein and follow a rider's slightest signals can enjoy the ride as much as the rider.

Training pays off.

Without trainers, there wouldn't be racehorses. And racehorses without good, solid physical training suffer more injuries than other racehorses with better muscle development. The right kind of training can protect the horse.

Your gym teacher will tell you how important it is for you to be in good physical condition. And the way to get in good shape is to train. Walk, jog, run, lift weights, exercise. It's amazing what people will do to get in shape or to stay in shape. They want to be strong and healthy. Even people who rarely organize other areas of their lives may discipline themselves when it comes to exercise.

Yet even more important than physical discipline is spiritual disciple and the shape of our spiritual lives.

In the same way we have to kick ourselves into gear to get disciplined physically, sometimes we have to kick ourselves into gear spiritually. It's easier to be lazy than to ride a bike or run a mile. And it's easier to be lazy than to get up early and read a chapter in the Bible or go to youth group or talk to a friend about Christ.

But the payoff is well worth it—not just on earth, but forever.

> *Physical training is good, but training for godliness is much better, promising benefits in this life and in the life to come.*
> **1 TIMOTHY 4:8**

Most scientists agree that the easiest animal to train is the dolphin. Dolphins have a friendly disposition and don't get mad at their trainers. Petmedsonline.org lists the following 10 breeds as the easiest-to-train dogs: border collies, Labrador retrievers, papillons, beaucerons, Pyrenean shepherds, Australian shepherds, Doberman pinschers, Belgian sheepdogs, toy poodles, and Australian cattle dogs.

• • •

TODAY: Start your spiritual training. Pick a favorite verse and memorize it. Start and end your day with prayer.

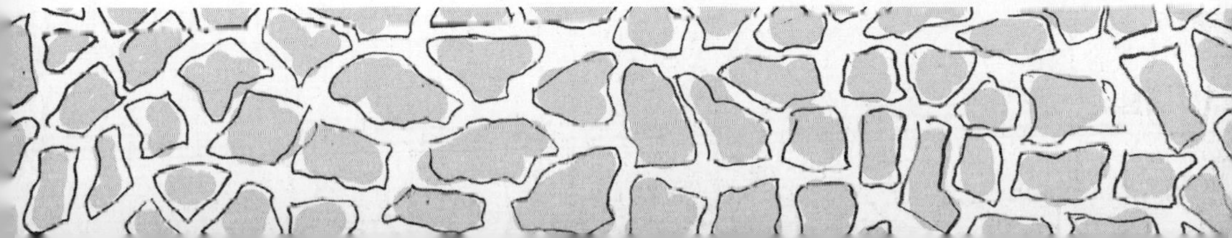

THE SWEET SCENT OF YOU

Australian koalas are also known as koolabuns, koolewongs, and boorabees. We usually call them koala bears, but koala bears are not bears. They're marsupial mammals, like kangaroos.

The koala is a fussy eater and will only eat leaves from the eucalyptus tree. First, it pulls down the leaf, sniffs it, then eats it. Eucalyptus leaves contain aromatic oils, so koalas smell like eucalyptus.

Many animals have a distinctive scent, which some people love and others hate. There's no denying a fishy smell from the docks or from a fish fry. If you handle the fish, you'll smell like fish too.

For horse lovers, there's nothing better than the smell of a horse.

Smell is a powerful sense. More than any of the other senses, a smell can trigger a buried memory, bringing back an event or a person in full detail.

We don't all love the same smells. You may love the scent of wet leaves, but your dad hates it. You may love a perfume your friend can't stand.

You have an aroma too—a smell that rises to God. Thankfully, it's not that smell you get after gym class or when you forget to take a bath. Instead, your smell can be a sweet perfume when your life imitates Christ's life on earth.

It's important that the scent of who you are pleases God.

> *[God] uses us to spread the knowledge of Christ everywhere, like a sweet perfume. Our lives are a Christ-like fragrance rising up to God. But this fragrance is perceived differently by those who are being saved and by those who are perishing. To those who are perishing, we are a dreadful smell of death and doom. But to those who are being saved, we are a life-giving perfume.*
>
> **2 CORINTHIANS 2:14-16**

Most mammals have a good sense of smell, but the toothed whale has none. It may not be surprising that the lower invertebrates (like worms and sponges) have no sense of smell since they don't have much going for them. But birds? With few exceptions, birds have no sense of smell either. Maybe that explains how vultures can dine on disgusting roadkill.

• • •

TODAY: Ask God to point out anything "stinky" about you that keeps your life from smelling great.

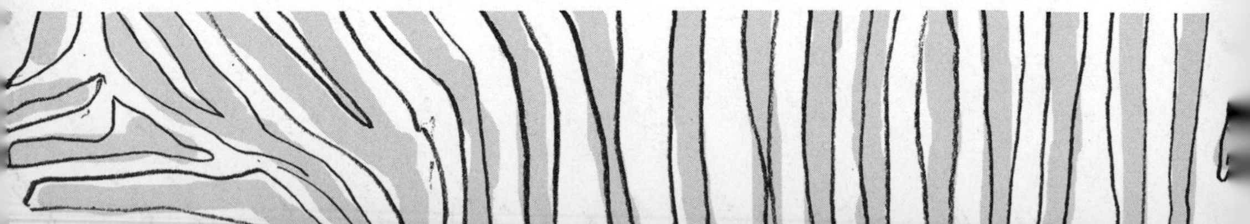

REMINDERS

You've probably heard a chickadee calling its name: *chick-a-dee-dee*. Chickadees don't migrate but stick it out through the winter, when they may need 20 times more food to fend off the cold.

During warmer months, chickadees hide seeds and insects in secret hiding places. Then about six months later, with snow piled on the ground, they have to remember where they've hidden thousands of seeds.

Birds with the best recall have a bigger hippocampus than other birds. The hippocampus is the part of the brain that stores information. Once a year, these nonmigrating birds grow whole new areas of the brain to help them remember.

God wants us to remember too. We need to remember his promises to us and the words he has given us in Scripture. We need reminders to think about what Christ did when he died for us and what it means that he was raised from the dead. When we're scared and trouble comes, we need to be reminded of the ways we've seen God come through for us before.

To help us remember, God has given us his Spirit to live inside us. When you read the Bible or memorize Scripture, the Spirit can call it to mind at the exact time you need it. You're tempted to tell off your teacher, but you remember that verse in James about keeping your mouth shut. Or you get depressed because you don't think anyone likes you. Then suddenly you remember how God has shown his love for you over and over again.

We have the best Reminder living inside of us. Listen to God's Spirit and remember.

> *I am telling you these things now while I am still with you. But when the Father sends the Advocate as my representative—that is, the Holy Spirit—he will teach you everything and will remind you of everything I have told you.*
>
> JOHN 14:25-26

Birds like the chickadee have amazing memories to recall all their secret hiding places for seeds—under bark, in the ground, among pine needle clusters, even in moth cocoons. They can locate everything they've hidden. Squirrels, on the other hand, don't have great memories, but they have a great sense of smell that helps them find acorns buried under snow.

• • •

TODAY: Go on a walk with God or find a quiet place to talk to him. Reminisce. Ask God to help you recall "God moments" from your past.

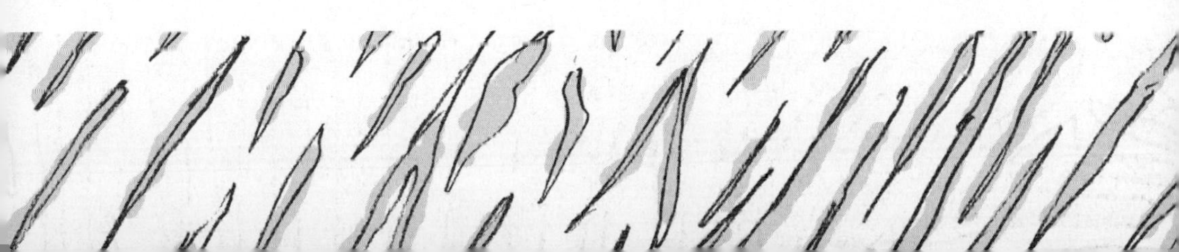

AND THE INSECT CHAMPIONS ARE:

Fastest running insect: tiger beetle

Insect that can eat the largest blood meal: Asian blood-sucking tick

Insect with the most toxic venom: harvester ant

Loudest insect: African cicada

Insect most tolerant to heat: desert scavenging ant

• • •

TODAY: Pray for your friends. Ask God to show you any records you're keeping against them. Erase the entries. And thank God that he's erased your own record.

KEEPING SCORE

Americans love keeping score and keeping records. With the help of computers, baseball announcers can come up with some kind of record being broken nearly every game.

Each racetrack keeps race records. Whether you're into horse racing, harness racing, dog racing, ostrich racing, or cockroach racing, you can find thousands of records.

We even keep score of insects. The University of Florida keeps an official book of insect records. Here are some of the vital categories for record keeping: fastest running insect, largest blood meal, most toxic venom, loudest insect, most tolerant to cold, longest life cycle, smallest eggs, fastest wing beat, longest insect migration, most tolerant to heat, and most parental sharing of brood care.

It's fun to keep score and records, but not when we're keeping score of the mean things people do to us. There's a time to forget. Some of us hold on to things people did to us years ago. We'll never forget, we tell ourselves.

Even between friends, old problems can come back. You get into an argument, and before you know it, you're both letting past wrongs creep into the conversation. "I should have known not to trust you! You wouldn't even sit by me back in first grade!" "Here you go again. You never stand up for me. Remember two years ago when we were at the pool and you laughed, just like everybody else? Some friend you are!"

God doesn't want you to keep a record of other people's wrongs. What if God kept a record of yours? He'd have a long list, and he could use it against you. But he chooses to forgive and forget. You should do the same.

LORD, if you kept a record of our sins, who, O Lord, could ever survive? But you offer forgiveness, that we might learn to fear you.

PSALM 130:3-4

BIG APPETITES

The shrew is related to the mole but has a mouselike body with a pointed nose and tiny, sharp teeth. Shrews are only two to six inches long, but they have the biggest appetites for their size. A shrew eats several times its own weight each day.

Because shrews are so active and nervous, they burn up calories from food faster than any other mammal. The heart of the masked shrew beats 800 times a minute, faster than a hummingbird's heartbeat. Shrews are so nervous that they're easily startled and may jump, faint, or even drop dead at a sudden noise.

Yet shrews are no wimps when it comes to getting what they want. They'll eat anything, but they prefer small animals and will viciously kill mice and other shrews to meet that huge appetite.

What are you hungry for? Are you always thinking about the latest computer game, new shoes like your friend's, a better bike, a new computer, new jeans, more stuff?

It's hard not to want things. Ads bombard us with images. Maybe it seems like other kids get more than you do. And the more you have, the more you want.

In most parts of the world, whole families could survive on what the average U.S. student owns. We lose perspective. We can't tell a need from a want or a desire.

How do we stop desiring more and more stuff? It doesn't usually work to pretend you don't want that latest thing everybody else has. You *do* desire it. But if you can stay tuned in to God, he can replace your desires with his.

Walk with God. Think and pray outside of your own little world. Let God satisfy you.

> *Just as Death and Destruction are never satisfied, so human desire is never satisfied.*
> **PROVERBS 27:20**

Shrews have to eat constantly in order to stay alive, and most will starve to death if they have to go without food for half a day. But they're not the only ones who have to eat nonstop. An eight-ton blue whale has to constantly fill up on little krill and shrimp. Elephants weigh between three and a half and eight tons, but they only eat nonfattening leaves, branches, and grass, so they have to eat all the time.

• • •

TODAY: Make a list of 10 things you really want. Talk to God about your desire for these things and whether they're needs or wants. Ask God to give you *his* desires.

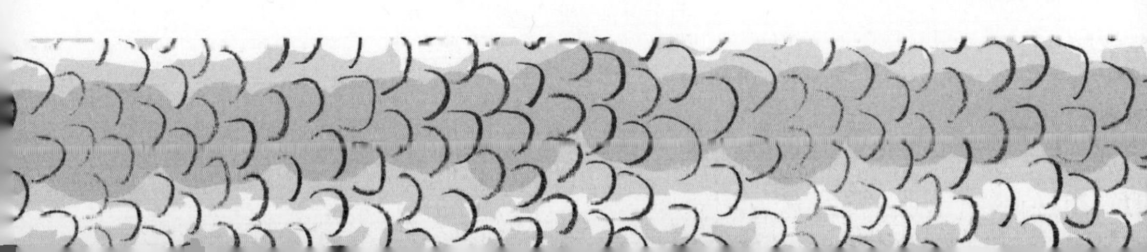

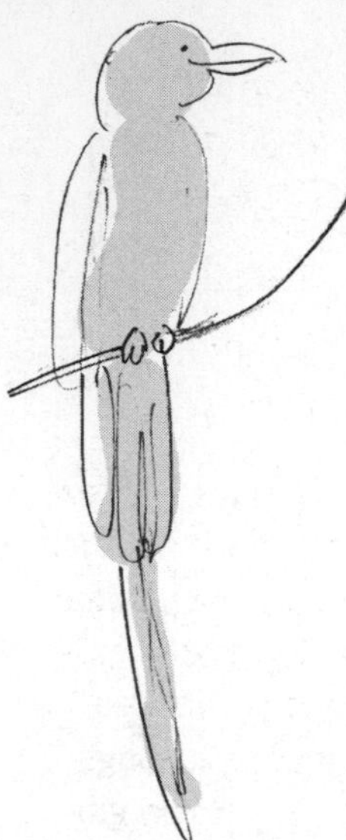

The carmine bee-eater, an unusual type of bird, has a curious way of building its shelter. It flies headfirst into the dirt to make a dent in the earth and start its nest. Then it eats a bunch of insects, pukes up their remains, and uses that to line its nest hole. The smell keeps rodents away.

• • •

TODAY: At least five times during your normal day, "escape" to your shelter and thank God that he's always there waiting for you.

OUR SHELTER

Animals build all kinds of homes, but the homes have this in common: they shelter the animals from the weather and protect them from enemies.

Beavers are master builders, felling trees with their strong teeth and using logs to construct dams up to a half-mile long. Chimpanzees seek shelter in treetops and build nests by bending branches and weaving twigs. The harvest mouse builds a nest in the tall grasses to hide from enemies. Badgers seek the shelter of an underground sett, a home with tunnels and many decorated rooms, lined with grass, straw, sticks, or leaves.

In the desert, where it seems like no creature could survive the intense heat, animals still find shelter. They lie in the dust and burrow under the scorching hot sand to find cool shelter beneath the desert's surface. In the Arctic, creatures survive buried under snow and ice.

God is our shelter. He will protect us from everything around us, if we let him. No matter where you are, you can escape to your shelter. God is there waiting. If things are tough at school, you can slip into that quiet place with him until you get yourself together. Then you and God can face whatever needs to be faced.

You don't even realize it, but God's shelter keeps you from being hurt countless times each day. He's a shelter, even when we don't appreciate it. He's always protecting and defending us.

With God as our shelter, we should always be able to rest.

Those who live in the shelter of the Most High will find rest in the shadow of the Almighty. This I declare about the Lord: He alone is my refuge, my place of safety; he is my God, and I trust him.

PSALM 91:1-2

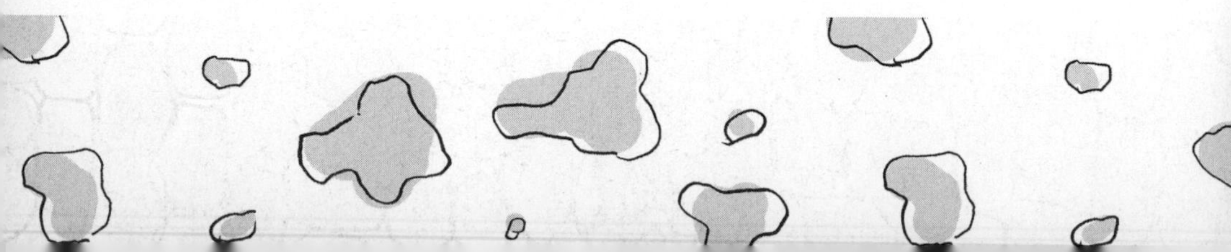

INSTANT OBEDIENCE

Animals in the wild depend on the ability to react instantly to the threat of an enemy. When a musk ox gives a signal that a predator is approaching, other male oxen respond immediately and join that musk ox to stand shoulder to shoulder in front of their calves and females, with their horns facing the attacker.

You'll never see a naked mole rat because these creatures live underground and would die if exposed to sunlight. But when one mole rat gives a warning, the rest—up to 300 in a colony—start tunneling in a chain gang line, with each mole digging into the tunnel and passing the freshly dug dirt or sand to the one behind.

In our society, we like instant service. If we have to wait three minutes for fast food, we act like we're going to starve. We want instant snacks from a vending machine, instant oatmeal, instant pudding, and instant downloads. We think just about everything should be instant . . . except obedience.

Does this conversation ever go on in your house?

Mom: "Did you get your homework done?"

You: "No."

Mom: "You've had all afternoon to work on it. And you still need to walk the dogs and empty the dishwasher."

You: "Why do I have to do everything?"

Mom: "Those are your chores, and you know it."

You: "I'm watching TV. I'll do it later."

Mom: "Do it now!"

You: "In a minute!"

Five heated minutes of arguing later, you do it.

Wouldn't it have been easier to play out the conversation like this?

Mom: "Walk the dogs. Then empty the dishwasher and finish your homework."

You: "Okay." Or better yet: "Already did it."

Mom: "Thanks."

It's healthy to honestly wrestle with your faith in order to better understand God. But when delayed obedience—whether to your parents or to God—is really just laziness or selfishness, that's sin. And you make your life, and the lives of everyone around you, miserable for no reason.

Young people who obey the law are wise.
PROVERBS 28:7

Only in the last few years have researchers discovered that white-handed gibbons in Thailand forests use songs to warn fellow gibbons. As soon as one sings the warning, others pick it up. And everybody gets out of there!

• • •

TODAY: List all the things you know you're supposed to do without being asked. Do them without being told. If your parents ask you to do more, just say, "Okay" (and be ready to catch them when they faint).

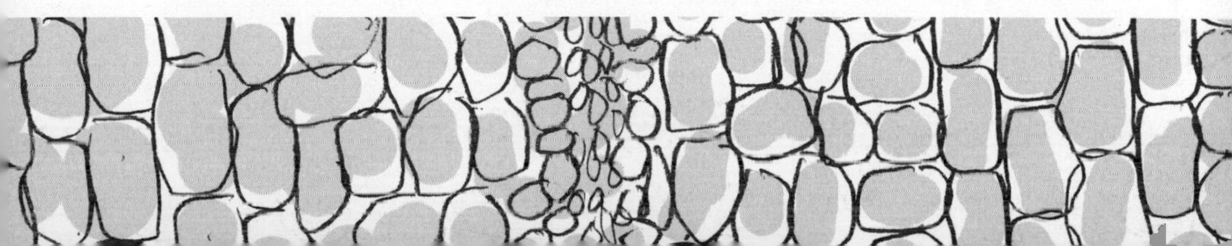

WING IT

Birds have between 1,000 and 25,000 feathers, with five to six different kinds of feathers, each crafted for a special job. Contour feathers cover the wing, the tail, and the body. Next to the bird's body are down feathers that trap air and create a layer of insulation (and make down comforters so warm). Between the down and the contour feathers, semiplumes fill in spaces. Filoplumes are hairlike feathers that can sense the location of other feathers and adjust. Bristles are the scruffy barbs around the eyes and bill.

Each type of feather has a purpose in protecting the bird. The feathers insulate or fluff up for warmth, or squeeze down when the weather gets warm. Some birds use certain feathers to line their nests. Each feather fulfills its purpose.

If feathers were created for a purpose, it makes sense that you were created for a purpose too.

No one has exactly the combination of gifts, talents, desires, abilities, skills, and experiences that you do. Nobody ever has, and nobody ever will. Only you. And if you don't fulfill the purpose God has for you, no one else can do it.

You weren't created in an assembly line. Pay attention to the gifts God has woven into you. Do you like certain things other people really aren't interested in—writing, reading, taking things apart, working with numbers, designing, building things? Pay attention to those inborn signs of God's craftsmanship. Ask your friends what they think you're good at. Try new things, and be open to discovering God's gifts in you.

One day, you'll spread your wings . . . and God's design will help you fly.

God has given each of you a gift from his great variety of spiritual gifts. Use them well to serve one another.
1 PETER 4:10

Feathers are made of tough, flexible material called keratin. They look solid, but they're not. Vanes on each side of the feather attach to the hollow middle shaft. Each vane is made up of thousands of barbs, or branches, with spaces between barbs. When you put the whole thing together, a feather has as much air as it does matter. Which makes it . . . as light as a feather.

• • •

TODAY: Every time you see a bird, watch where it goes and what it does. Then take a second to thank God for the way he has uniquely designed you for a specific purpose.

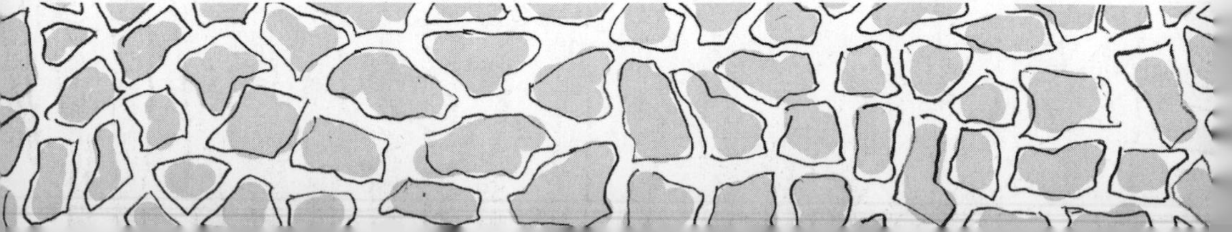

KISS, KISS

When prairie dogs meet in burrows, they "kiss." Apparently the first kiss is to see if they really know each other or not. If they don't, the intruder is kicked out. But if they agree that they actually do know each other, they kiss again. After that, they'll probably start grooming each other.

Chimpanzees freely show how glad they are to see a buddy or a relative. A chimp may smile, make a happy face, shake hands, or even hug. Some chimpanzees will touch each other's faces.

Horses sometimes blow into one another's nostrils and exchange warm greetings that way.

Elephants touch trunks and rub shoulders. Sometimes they touch trunk tips and hold it in an elephant "kiss."

Friendliness should start at home. If you're a family of sleepyheads who drag yourselves to the kitchen bleary-eyed and silent every morning, shake it up a bit. Give your mom and dad a good-morning hug. You can at least say hey to your siblings, right?

At school, you might greet your friends when you see them. But what about the "invisible people"—the kids you walk past because everyone else does? You know Jesus wouldn't. He'd give them a high five or ask how they're doing today. He might stop and talk awhile. Maybe you can make it a point to say hello to these overlooked people, too.

Be prepared. Your newfound friendliness might not be appreciated at first. It might not be returned. You might get mocked or razzed.

So what? You're not responsible for other people's reactions. You're just responsible for your own actions. Don't let anyone rob you of your friendliness.

Greet each other in Christian love. All the churches of Christ send you their greetings.
ROMANS 16:16

When ducks meet for the first time, they take a nice, long drink of water together. Bonobo apes greet each other with a kiss—to seal peace after a disagreement, to reassure one another that all is well, or for no reason at all.

• • •

TODAY: Try treating your parents and siblings like best friends all week. You might even try a nice hug or kiss every morning.

When a cat rubs up against your leg, it's a compliment. It's claiming you as part of its space and marking you as part of its territory. Congratulations.

• • •

TODAY: Ask God to show you people who are left out because you and others have been claiming your space. Make an effort to include at least one new person this week.

MY SPACE

Animals are extremely touchy when it comes to having their own space. Wild animals, especially, are territorial. They do what it takes to make sure other animals know which space is already taken.

Some animals mark their territories with urine (enough said). Antelope have their own method of claiming space. An antelope has two glands on its head—one in front of each eye—that produce a scent. All it has to do is rub the sticky gland juice over branches and twigs to mark its territory.

A rhinoceros needs its space too. One way it will mark its territory is by stamping the ground and wiping off oils from the glands on its feet in order to leave its scent.

Hyenas rub their backsides along the ground to spread scent from small glands on their bottoms.

How territorial are you? At home, do you demand your space, ordering parents and siblings out as if it's your royal right to be left alone? Maybe it's a privilege given to you by your parents, but most of the world's population wouldn't even dream of that kind of privacy as a right.

School cafeterias are scenes of spoken and unspoken demands for "my space." If you sit down uninvited at certain tables, do you think you'll get some territorial glares warding you off the space?

Even church, Sunday school, and youth group can be territorial. Ask a new person if he or she really felt like one of the insiders on the first and second visits to your youth group. Do you always plop down with your friends and jump into conversation with them? What about the guy who doesn't know anybody there? In church, most regularly attending families have the prime example of "my space" in the family pew.

Try to be aware of territorial claims that shut out people who aren't on the inside. It's really all God's space anyway.

Don't forget to show hospitality to strangers, for some who have done this have entertained angels without realizing it!

HEBREWS 13:2

FEEDING THE POOR

On the Galápagos Islands of Ecuador is a poor bird that ranks as one of the rarest birds surviving in the world: the flightless cormorant. With wings too small to support its body, the bird can't fly. It dives for food off the rocky ocean shores, but its feathers aren't waterproof, so it spends much of the day drying in the sun. It has to look out for hurricanes and natural disasters from weather patterns like El Niño, which killed half of the cormorant population in 1983, reducing the number of birds to 400.

Thankfully, the male cormorant looks after the female as she sits on her nest. She waits for him to return and take his turn incubating the eggs. But before he comes, he has to find just the right gift for her. He usually brings seaweed. But on occasion he manages a special gift—a piece of rope or a bottle cap—presented as if it were diamonds.

Chances are, you've had little exposure to true poverty. You might not really know what it feels like to be honestly hungry (having gone without food for days, rather than hours). You might have trouble telling a *want* from a *need*.

If you have all your physical needs met, that's something to be grateful for. And it gives you an added responsibility to let God use you to help meet the needs of people who are poor and hungry. God loves the poorest person on earth every bit as much as he cares for you. We're called to share, to give, to love.

One person can help. You can start by praying. Then find out how you can help in your community—volunteer at a donation center, a shelter, or a food pantry. Ask at your church how you can get involved. Save part of every dollar you get or earn, and give some to international food organizations. Maybe one day God will call you to be a missionary or an aid worker.

> *Blessed are those who are generous, because they feed the poor.*
> **PROVERBS 22:9**

The flightless cormorant birds on the Galápagos Islands are endangered, with only about 1,500 birds remaining. Long ago, the cormorants settled on the islands with no natural enemies. Then humans settled there, and the dogs, cats, rats, and pigs that came with them became enemies of the cormorants. So did the nets used by fishermen. Yet the cormorants have no fear of humans.

• • •

TODAY: Begin praying for the poor and for an opportunity to help. Talk to your parents or pastor about ways to meet the needs. Give a percentage of everything you get or earn.

When people see a baby bird on the ground, they often think it needs rescuing. But if they try to help, most of the time they're interfering with the learning process. Fledglings (partially feathered birds) fall or jump out of the tree to learn to fly. Mom Bird will feed her baby on the ground for a day or two, until it can fly. The best thing you can do for the bird is to keep your cat away.

• • •

TODAY: List three of the best influences in your spiritual life—people you want to be more like. Make plans to spend more time with them, and thank God for them.

BORN TO FOLLOW

When a baby duckling or gosling hatches, the first thing it sees will become its leader. Somehow that person, animal, or moving object is imprinted on the animal's brain. Usually the first thing a baby duck sees is its mother, so it will follow Mom and learn the ropes on how to survive in the world.

But if the first thing a duckling sees isn't its mother, then that baby may be in big trouble. It may be in over its duck bill trying to follow a big dog around—or a horse or even a human. Those first few hours after coming into the world are crucial.

The early years of a human baby are crucial too. Children under four are in what's called a "critical learning period." They can learn language easily. They can even pick up two or more languages. Later, languages become harder to learn, and it is almost impossible to speak as a native (which you know if you've studied a foreign language in school).

When we come to know Christ, we're born spiritually. And just like newborn babies, we have a lot to learn. It's important to get off to a good start. If you've only recently found Christ, you may be eager to learn all you can. That's great! Just be sure that the one you're following is Christ. Find a good church—one where you'll be taught more about Jesus and how you can live your life of faith following him. Make sure the Bible is taught there and that members are reaching out to others.

If you've been a Christian most of your life, it's still a critical learning period for you. Make sure you're growing spiritually and still following the Leader.

> *Dear friend, don't let this bad example influence you. Follow only what is good. Remember that those who do good prove that they are God's children, and those who do evil prove that they do not know God.*
>
> **3 JOHN 1:11**

DAILY DELIGHT

We delight in our pets. A good dog doesn't have to sit up, fetch, beg, or do much of anything to get us to exclaim, "Good dog!" We love our pet, and to us, it's absolutely the greatest.

Cat lovers admire and delight in their cats. If you love your cat, you're proud that it's so independent. You think its purr is the best gift you could get.

A guinea pig's owner can laugh out loud with joy at that clever pet twitching its nose. The owner of a hamster could watch that pet running on the wheel all day and never get tired (the owner, not the hamster).

And our pets delight in us too. Dogs bark, wag their tails, and jump up on us. Horses nicker. They might even kick up their heels in delight. Cats sweep their tails with subdued joy.

And all that fuss is simply because they get to see us, to be with us.

What kind of delight and joy do you show when you get to be with God?

God says that he delights in *you*. He can't wait until you talk to him or smile inside about something he has given you. He's thrilled when you shake your head in wonder at how much he loves you.

How about you? Do you look forward to praying? Is your heart pounding as you imagine God listening to you?

You can't get in to see a doctor or a dentist without an appointment. You're not allowed backstage or in the dugout. But the God of the universe delights in the few minutes you give him, and he's always waiting for more.

> *He led me to a place of safety; he rescued me because he delights in me.*
> **2 SAMUEL 22:20**

Some people delight in exotic animals and are willing to pay for the pleasure of owning one. White lion cubs sell for about $138,000. The Bengal house cat and the Ashera are among the most expensive cat breeds (from $1,000 to $40,000). And in 2009, a Tibetan mastiff was bought for $582,000, the most anyone has ever spent on a dog.

• • •

TODAY: The next time you go to church, think about it as meeting the most famous person in the universe. How can you best prepare for that? Then thank God that he's always ready for a visit—anytime, anywhere.

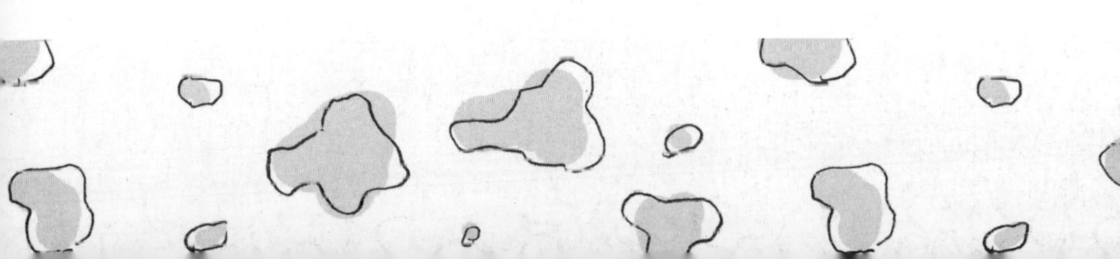

The great-tailed grackle seems like a joyful bird, singing its slightly weird song. These birds nest together in groups of thousands. The males get along well, even in close quarters. But the females envy other nesting sites, squabble back and forth, and steal nesting materials right out of the other gal's nest.

• • •

TODAY: List 10 things that rob you of your joy (worries, jealousy, greed). Be specific. What can you do to protect your joy?

JOY THIEVES

Dogs must be born joyful. But even dogs can get low. Steal a dog's favorite toy, and you steal a piece of its joy. If you're in a bad mood and ignore your pet, which is probably dancing around because you're home, you rob that dog of joy.

Horses that have to stand in a small stall all day instead of romping and grazing in the pasture have a piece of joy taken from them.

Sometimes animals steal joy from one another. Kleptoparasitism is when one animal takes food from another animal. Gulls, for example, snatch fish away from diving birds. Herring gulls wait until unsuspecting ducks dive for fish and come up joyfully with their prizes, only to have them stolen by the gulls. Seagulls even steal eggs and young from other birds.

We should be joyful all the time because Christ lives in us and we have all God's promises for eternity. Yet most of us aren't joyful all the time. Some days you start out joyful. But by the time you get home from school, you're close to depression.

What steals your joy? If somebody says something mean, does it shoot you down? You're wearing a new outfit and feel great . . . until a "friend" asks if you do all your shopping at the thrift store.

You were feeling pretty confident about classes until you got that essay back with your teacher's notes telling you to rewrite the paper. What if you can't make it any better?

Keep your focus on God, where your lasting joy is. There are a million potential thieves out there waiting to steal your joy. But the truth is that none of them can. Not unless you let it happen.

> *You have sorrow now, but I will see you again; then you will rejoice, and no one can rob you of that joy.*
> **JOHN 16:22**

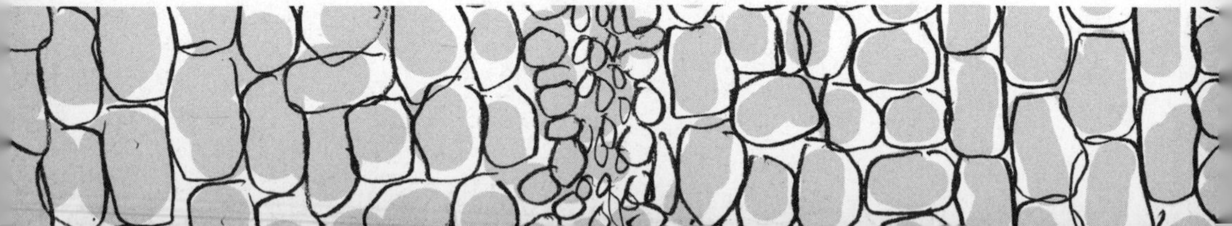

STEALING SQUIRRELS

Squirrels steal.

They may look cute to you, with their fluffy tails and twitchy noses. But squirrels are master thieves when it comes to breaking into birdhouses and stealing birdseed. Squirrels will even steal acorns from other squirrels. And if they could talk our language, they'd probably say it wasn't really stealing, just eating.

Birds steal too.

If a bird sees the opportunity to get food without working for it, it's there. Crows that take berries from a strawberry patch probably wouldn't call it stealing. They figure the patch has plenty to go around.

Spotted hyenas steal the kills of lions. But they'd be the first to tell you that lions steal from them, too. Jackals steal from everybody, and they wouldn't waste their breath coming up with an excuse.

There are lots of ways people steal, and most people don't think of it as stealing. Adults may not report all of their income on the tax form, or they might not return an overpayment from a big company.

You may know kids who shoplift for fun. If you're with them, even if you don't take anything yourself, you're a part of the stealing. Other kids raid Mom's purse when she's not around. Or they sneak into a sibling's closet to "borrow" something without asking. They'd probably never call it stealing, but it is. And they know it because they're doing it in secret.

"Thou shalt not steal." It's an oldie but a goodie—as true now as it was when God wrote it on stone tablets.

You know the commandments: "You must not commit adultery. You must not murder. You must not steal. You must not testify falsely. Honor your father and mother."

LUKE 18:20

Milichiid flies are small, nasty flies that like to hang around manure, dead animals, and decay . . . and they steal. Adult milichiids sneak into spiderwebs and scavenge half-eaten stinkbugs. Then there are "robber flies," which steal food and pupae carried by ants back to their ant homes.

• • •

TODAY: Be honest with yourself and write down anything you may have stolen, even if you rationalized that you weren't actually stealing. Confess any wrong to God, and prayerfully consider how you can make it up to the person you stole from.

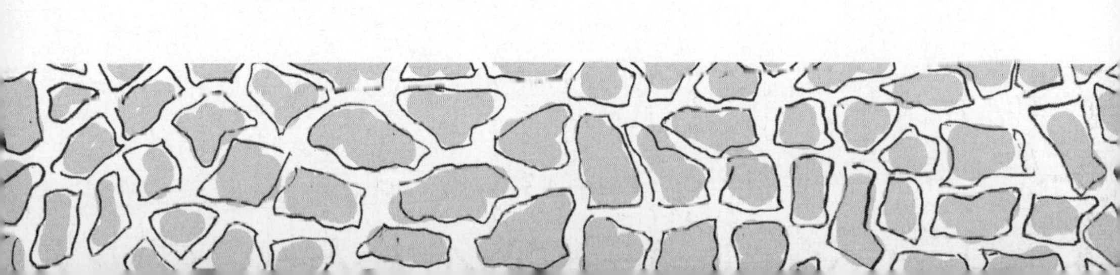

GOD'S STYLE

One stroll through any zoo should convince you that God has a sense a humor and that he delights in strange and wonderful creations. The more you learn about the animal world, the odder and more amazing it is.

Clown fish aren't particularly funny or weird-looking. Their orange and white bodies are actually gorgeous. But what's odd about this fish is that it chooses to hang out with the sea anemone, a creature whose many poisonous tentacles would kill most fish. Just like a rodeo clown dancing around a fiery bull, the clown fish swims around the anemone, eating leftovers stuck to the creature and sleeping on top of its tentacles. Who would have thought? God. That's his style!

Flying foxes aren't foxes. They're bats that can hang upside down on one foot, fan themselves with their wings, and fly on average 18 to 25 miles a night to find food, but their legs are too weak to walk. Flying lemurs aren't lemurs, and they don't fly. They glide as if on a flying trapeze and live upside down in trees, their skin matching the look of bark. Who would have thought? God. That's his style!

Learn to see and love God's style in the world around you . . . and in you. Don't hate your hair that won't lie flat or your crooked smile or the nose you got from Gramps's side of the family. Embrace your individuality. God has built in a little lovable weirdness in all of us.

Who would have thought? God. That's his style!

"My thoughts are nothing like your thoughts," says the Lord. "And my ways are far beyond anything you could imagine."
ISAIAH 55:8

Dung beetles are gross, but we need them. They love cattle dung. They eat it, roll it into a ball, and toss it down their burrow homes. Then the beetles lay their eggs in the dung balls so when the babies hatch, their meal is right there. Gross, but dung beetles can clean a pasture of dung, and they help prevent disease in many parts of the world.

• • •

TODAY: List three "strange" things about your best friend—traits you really like. List three of your own quirky traits, and thank God for each one.

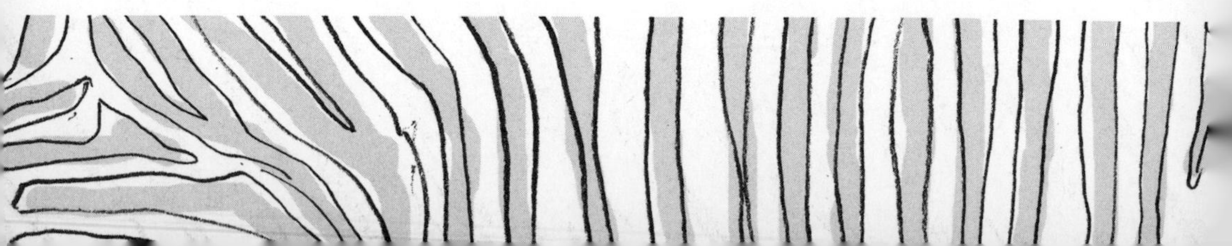

USE YOUR BRAIN

Starfish have no brains. They have the biggest heads of any animal for their size, up to one-third of their body length. But they are brainless. Big head, no brain. Sound like anyone you know?

Sperm whales have the biggest brains, which weigh in at about 20 pounds, but nobody claims whales are the brainiest animal. Elephants have brains that are a hefty 16 to 17 pounds. Yours is maybe 3.3 pounds on a good day. The bottlenose dolphin's is about 25 percent bigger than yours, and it even has folds and twists and turns like yours, something elephant brains don't have.

The squirrel monkey's brain weighs about 5 percent of its body weight. Yours is maybe 2.3 percent of your body weight. The animal with the largest brain compared to the size of its body is probably the ant. But nobody says, "She's smart as an ant!"

Sometimes kids at school get labeled as "brainy" or "slow" or "dumb"—or worse. That label can stick with you for the rest of your life, even though it's not accurate or fair. The "brainiest" kid in college wasn't necessarily all that "brainy" in high school or middle school. And the brainy college student may not be the most successful out in the real world.

You have all the brain you'll ever need . . . and more. Scientists used to believe that humans used less than 10 percent of their brains. Recent studies have challenged that percentage, but it's still true that we don't use all of our brains. An even bigger tragedy is that we don't allow God to give us the wisdom that would save us so much grief.

There's a difference between knowledge and wisdom. Wisdom comes from applying what we learn about life to the truth God gives us. Ask God for it.

If you need wisdom, ask our generous God, and he will give it to you. He will not rebuke you for asking.
JAMES 1:5

A sperm whale's brain is the largest brain in the universe (at least, the biggest we know about). Echinoderms—marine animals that include over 7,000 species, like starfish, sand dollars, and sea urchins—have no brains.

• • •

TODAY: Right now, ask God for wisdom in general and wisdom concerning one specific problem you're facing.

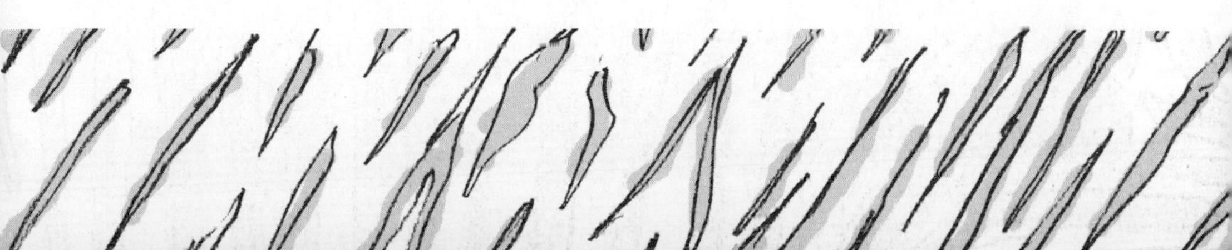

Humans have tricolor vision, since every color we see can be mixed with variations of red, blue, and green. Scientists have recently discovered that birds not only see ultraviolet light (which we can't), but they may have four- or even five-color vision. Birds—and some turtles and fish—see colors we've never even imagined.

• • •

TODAY: Ask God to help you really see. Pray that God will lead you to help one other person today.

THE WAY I SEE IT

People used to think sharks had terrible vision because they didn't seem to see things that were right in front of them. Now we know that sharks see great. They're just farsighted—able to see better than we can from a distance. And they're 10 times more sensitive to light than we are.

If you gazed out at a beautiful meadow, you'd see green grass in several shades, a blue sky, maybe an apple tree with bright red apples. But a prairie dog sticking its head out of its burrow would only see the blue sky, a gray pasture, and yellowish gray fruit on the tree. Prairie dogs have a form of color blindness.

Bees see a whole different world than we do. A honeybee has two compound eyes, with three simple eyes between them. Each compound eye has 7,000 hexagonal "mini-eyes," each with its own lens. Plus, bees see ultraviolet light, which we can't see.

Things are not always as they appear. It's easy to be shortsighted and miss the whole picture.

Things go on all around us without our seeing. A friend is going through a rough time, or the kid next to you in class is thinking about running away. But we don't see because we're looking for the wrong things—appearance, success, popularity. Sometimes we don't see because our vision is limited, like the prairie dog that can't see reds and greens.

But God sees everything.

God sees all and knows all. And the more we can come to see the world as God sees it, the better our world will be.

Jesus told him, "You believe because you have seen me. Blessed are those who believe without seeing me."
JOHN 20:29

HAND-HOLDING

Animals, especially when they're together in families or herds, look out for one another. When one elephant is injured, the others in the herd will lag back and go at the pace of the injured.

Wild horses usually keep moving. But when one gives birth or needs help, the herd will risk attack and stay in the same place longer.

As for otters, chimps, and apes, they actually hold hands for long periods of time. Otters may float on their backs while holding hands.

Have you ever watched a little kid walking with his dad? The kid wants to keep up with Daddy's big strides. Dad walks steadily ahead, getting them where they need to go, but he never lets go of his child's hand, which reaches up to his. If the kid stumbles, he doesn't fall because his hand is in his father's hand. Eventually he gets his feet on the ground again and the walk keeps going.

In Psalm 37, David gives us this picture—only it's God holding our hands. God directs our steps and holds us by the hand. So it's okay if we stumble. We won't fall.

If you do lousy on a test this week, you can still do great next week. If you say the wrong thing today, the world won't end. Say the right thing tomorrow.

You're going to stumble. But you'll land on your feet because God's got you by the hand.

> *The Lord directs the steps of the godly. He delights in every detail of their lives. Though they stumble, they will never fall, for the Lord holds them by the hand.*
> **PSALM 37:23-24**

When a sperm whale is hurt, the other members of the pod circle around it and join in to support the injured whale. Together they lift it near the surface of the water so it can breathe. This circle formation is called marguerite, after a kind of daisy.

• • •

TODAY: Whenever you "stumble" this week—in class, at home, on the phone—imagine God reaching down to hold your hand.

One female fly lays several hundred eggs (usually in garbage or manure). The larvae (maggots) only need about a week to grow, followed by five days in the pupae stage. More than six generations of flies (great-great-great-grandflies) can be born and live in a single summer.

• • •

TODAY: Talk to God about a couple of things people have said that hurt your feelings. Then write down five things God says about you.

BE HARD TO SWAT

Flies are hard to swat, which is why there are dozens of fly-swatters to choose from.

A fly might not look sensitive to you, but it is. Its body is covered with tiny hairs that are sensitive to air pressure. Flies feel you coming, and they feel the flyswatter before you get close enough to swat them. That's why most flyswatters have little holes in them to reduce the air pressure. And it's why you're even worse at swatting when you grab something like a rolled-up newspaper.

The average housefly lives about two to three weeks, even when we wish it didn't. Flies are tougher than they look . . . and much harder to swat.

Hopefully you're not worried about anyone at school swatting you with a rolled-up newspaper. But people verbally swat each other every day. Is it easy for people to get your goat—to razz you and get you upset by teasing you? If it's easy, they'll probably keep doing it.

Being sensitive is a good thing . . . if you're sensitive about the right things. Flies are sensitive to air pressure, and it saves their lives over and over. You should want to be sensitive to God—to God's calling, his leading, his still, small voice inside you. It's good to be sensitive to situations that just don't feel right too. Listen to that.

But don't be too sensitive to what people say to you or about you. Don't be easy to "swat." Remember that people don't know you as well as God does. Listen to him. Only what God says about you is true.

If the world hates you, remember that it hated me first.
JOHN 15:18

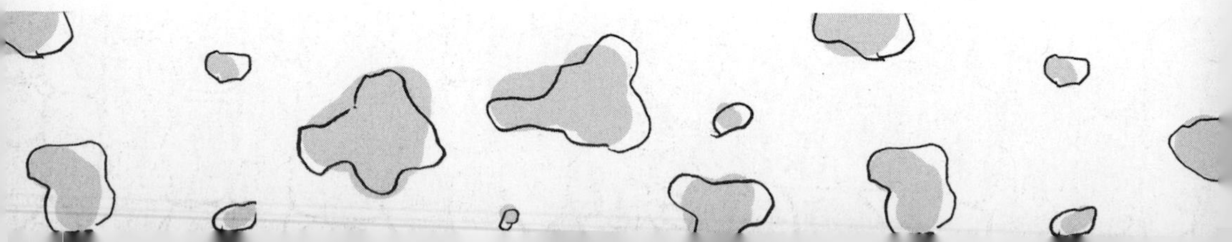

CAREFUL BUILDERS

Beavers may be the most careful builders on the planet. First, they select the body of water they want to build a home in. Next, they select their trees carefully and chew through the trunks. They build dams out of stones and plant matter and weave branches into a giant triangle, filling gaps with mud and branches.

Beavers construct their nests, or lodges, with a new selection of building materials: sticks, twigs, and mud. They need the best materials that will hold the lodge secure in the water—keep the sleeping chamber and air shaft dry—and make sure the two underwater exits stay free and clear. Every crack in the home is filled so that the temperature inside stays above freezing, even when the outside temperature drops to minus 31 degrees Fahrenheit. Building materials matter!

God calls your body a temple, a building. We all get the same foundation: Jesus. Then each Christian needs to grow, to be "built up" in Christ.

You're building every time you go to church, pray, talk to someone about Christ, listen to a friend with a problem, carry in your mom's groceries, do your chores. But it's not like you can score points for the good works you're building with.

Paul told new believers that they needed to continue to build on grace with grace. You could do the same act—go to youth group, for example—and it might be golden or worthless, depending on your motivation. Is it something you're doing to go deeper with God, or are you just doing it so people think you're a good kid? The materials you're building with depend on the quality and condition of your heart—something only God sees.

> *No one can lay any foundation other than the one we already have—Jesus Christ. Anyone who builds on that foundation may use a variety of materials—gold, silver, jewels, wood, hay, or straw. But on the judgment day, fire will reveal what kind of work each builder has done. The fire will show if a person's work has any value. If the work survives, that builder will receive a reward. But if the work is burned up, the builder will suffer great loss. The builder will be saved, but like someone barely escaping through a wall of flames.*
>
> **1 CORINTHIANS 3:11-15**

Beavers are such great engineers that before they start gnawing down trees for a dam, they check the wind to make sure it's blowing toward the water. When the trees fall, they'll fall toward the water, making it easier for the beavers to transport their logs.

• • •

TODAY: Prayerfully make a list with two columns, marked "Gold" and "Straw." Then put your deeds from today into one column or the other (gold for the things that will last and straw for the things that were done with the wrong motives). Ask God to show you *his* building plans for your life.

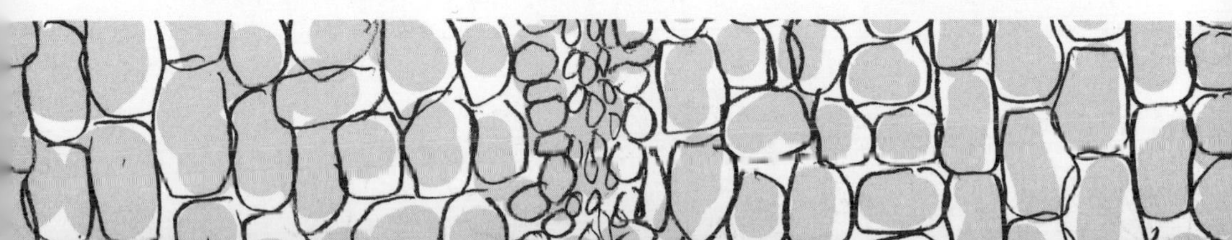

There's a reason for expressions like "a bird's-eye view," "eagle eye," and "eyes like a hawk." Scientists believe that birds have the best eyesight on earth. Sometimes a bird's eyes weigh more than two times as much as its brain (which explains another expression: "You birdbrain!").

• • •

TODAY: Every time someone bugs you today or you feel like being critical of anyone, pray. Ask God to show you the log in your own eye.

FISH EYE

Goldfish owners will assure you that their pets watch them move around the room. Aquarium owners who stare in at their fish are sure those eyes are staring back. And they may be right. Most fish have okay eyesight, although bug-eyed fish have worse sight than fish with regular eyes.

Flatfish have the weirdest eyes in the fish world. If you look at a very young flatfish, the eyes look normal, with an eye on each side of the head. Soon one eye begins to move, to migrate toward the other eye. By the time the fish is an adult, that eye has shifted all the way to the other side of the fish's head. Old flatfish have both eyes on the same side of the head.

We'll probably never fully understand what the world looks like through the eyes of a fish or a bird or any other animal. So it shouldn't surprise us to hear that we'll never fully understand how anything looks to another human being, either.

Your friend just doesn't get why school is so important to you, but you'll never understand why your friend goes overboard when it comes to who wins the Super Bowl.

Why is it so easy to see what's wrong with someone else? He talks too much. She cares too much what people think. He's selfish, she's jealous, they're stuck up. . . . But it's much harder to see what's wrong with yourself.

Jesus said we're hypocrites when we try to take out a "speck" in someone else's eye but we can't see the "log" in our own eye.

You can't do much about that speck anyway. That's the other guy's problem. Besides, with the log, how could you see well enough to help?

Time to pay attention to the log.

Why worry about a speck in your friend's eye when you have a log in your own? How can you think of saying to your friend, "Let me help you get rid of that speck in your eye," when you can't see past the log in your own eye? Hypocrite! First get rid of the log in your own eye; then you will see well enough to deal with the speck in your friend's eye.

MATTHEW 7:3-5

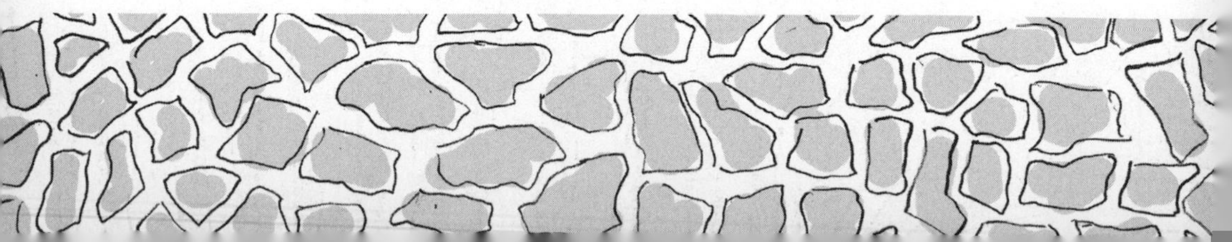

GIVE PARENTS A BREAK

Not all animals make great parents. A guinea hen has no patience for poky offspring as she leads them on a walk. She's likely to lose half of her brood if they're stragglers.

If a mother panda has two babies, she only takes care of one, leaving the other baby panda to die.

Even when the African black eagle mother has food to spare, she feeds only one of her two babies. Then that fat eaglet pecks its starving sibling to death while Mom looks on.

A mother penguin lays two eggs a season and rolls the first and smaller egg out of her nest to make room for the bigger egg. Magellanic penguin mothers, however, let both eggs hatch, then feed most of the fish to the bigger chick, while the littler guy starves to death.

Your parents probably aren't that bad, right? Maybe you can give them a break . . . or at least the benefit of the doubt. You might think you deserve to stay up later—your friends stay up late (at least that's what they're telling you). But your parents care more about making sure you get the sleep you need.

Your parents may disappoint you. They might have gotten a divorce. They might argue. They might not always keep their promises. They're no way near as cool as your "dream parents" or your friend's parents. Still, God gave you your parents.

Give your parents a break.

And if it's true that your imperfect parents are not being the parents they should be, God can fill the gap. Sometimes you have to look past your earthly parents, to God.

Grandchildren are the crowning glory of the aged; parents are the pride of their children.
PROVERBS 17:6

Hunting wasps think about their babies even before birth. A female wasp catches a juicy spider or caterpillar, paralyzes it, and carries it, still alive, to the wasp burrow. The wasp then lays her egg on top of the prey and leaves. When the lava hatches, it has fresh meat right there. (Adults are vegetarians.)

• • •

TODAY: Pray for your parents every morning for a week. Ask them how you can pray for them. At the end of each day, tell your parents one thing about them that you're grateful for.

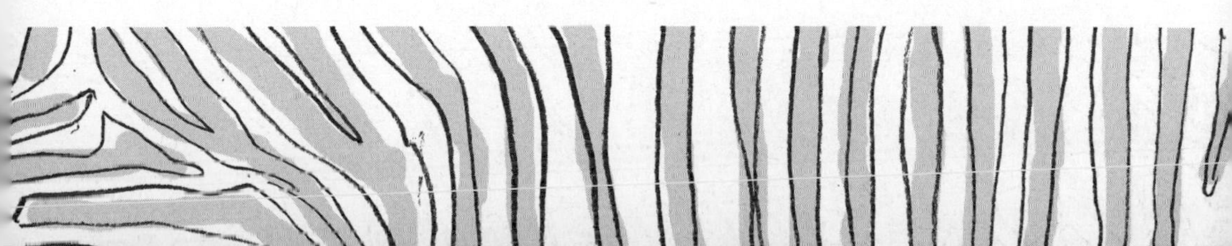

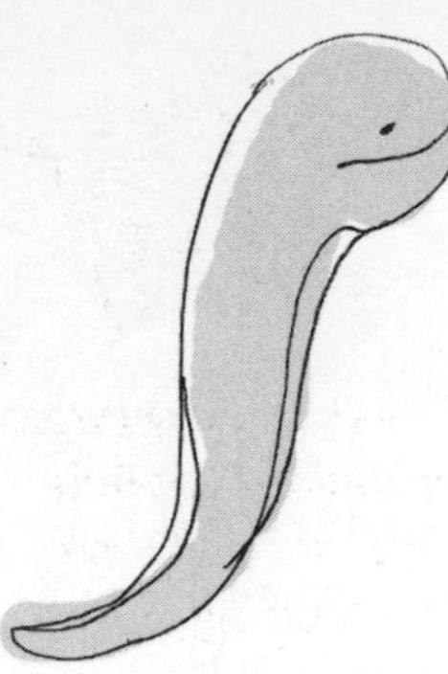

One of the biggest predators of leeches is other leeches, which drink their friends' blood and leave them to die. A note about animal blood: the blood of mammals is red, the blood of insects is yellow, and the blood of lobsters is blue.

• • •

TODAY: List 10 things you wish you had more of. Then talk with God about each one and honestly try to figure out your motives. Turn your list into thanksgiving for what you do have.

I'M SATISFIED

All leech species are meat eaters. They snack on worms, snails, insect larvae, and crustaceans. But a few are bloodsucking leeches, preferring to feed on the blood of reptiles, amphibians, fish, and mammals. And that includes humans.

A hungry leech will attach to a human with a sucker or two and about 100 sharp teeth. The victim won't feel it because the leech releases an anesthetic into the bloodstream. The leech also releases an anticlotting agent into the blood so the blood will keep flowing. Leeches drink so much that they have to use mucus and suction to stay attached to their victims until the leeches decide they're full. Then they simply fall off and digest their meal, totally satisfied . . . until they're ready to eat again.

What does it take to satisfy you? Some people are never satisfied, and they're almost never happy, either. They ask for an allowance, get it, then wish they'd asked for more. They get a great sound system for a birthday gift, but by the next month they're already wishing for something else.

Proverbs 30 makes a comparison between someone who is never satisfied and a bloodsucking leech. The leech keeps wanting more and more and can't seem to get enough to satisfy it.

Satisfaction in life has much less to do with what you have than with who you are. People with much less than you have may be satisfied. People with much more than you may not be satisfied.

There's a joy in knowing you have Christ now and all of heaven later. If that doesn't satisfy you, nothing will.

The leech has two suckers that cry out, "More, more!"
PROVERBS 30:15

SIBLING RIVALRY

If you have a brother or a sister, you're probably an expert on sibling rivalry. Brothers and sisters don't always get along.

And neither do animal brothers and sisters. For sharks, sibling rivalry starts *before* birth. Sand sharks eat each other in the womb, usually leaving only one or two little sharks to be born and live happily ever after.

Animal siblings don't just fight behind their mothers' backs either. When it comes to cranes, pelicans, and other seabirds, Mom supervises. But instead of breaking up the unfair fight as the bigger baby pecks at and kills the runt, the mother watches.

Hopefully it never gets that bad at your house, but sibling rivalry is everywhere, including the Bible. David was Jesse's youngest son. When the prophet came to anoint one of Jesse's sons as king, Jesse didn't even bother to call David in from watching the sheep because he figured one of the older, stronger brothers would be chosen. No doubt David's brothers didn't appreciate it when God chose David instead of them.

Joseph's brothers were so jealous of Joseph (and his many-colored robe) that they sold him into slavery.

Some sisters had the same kind of rivalry, like Leah and Rachel, when Jacob fell in love with the younger sister instead of the older sister.

If you have siblings, it's no accident that you've ended up in the same family. You may wish you had your friend for a sibling instead, but God knows best. Friendships will probably change as you get older, but your brothers and sisters will always be your siblings.

So you might as well start getting along with them now.

As for me and my family, we will serve the L*ORD*.
JOSHUA 24:15

"This little piggy went to market. This little piggy stayed home. This little piggy had roast beef. This little piggy had none." No kidding! In a large litter of piglets, the big ones not only push the runt away from Mother Pig and her milk, they use their tiny eyeteeth to cut up the little guy. No wonder this little piggy cried all the way home. . . .

• • •

TODAY: Say one kind, encouraging thing to each of your siblings this week. (If you don't have siblings, try it on a cousin or another family member.) Thank God for the people he has placed closest to you in your life.

If an animal (or a person) threatens the hive, a honeybee will sting, leaving its stinger in the victim. But it's not just the stinger that's lost. It's the bee's lower abdomen and some of its internal organs—which means the bee may save the hive, but it will die in the process.

• • •

TODAY: Plan three unselfish things you can do for someone today: (1) at home; (2) at school or in your community; (3) in the world.

GRUMBLE-BEES

Bumblebees are cousins to honeybees. They don't swarm like honeybees, but they buzz loudly enough for you to hear them coming. And if you're trying to doze in your backyard hammock, the *buzz-buzz-buzz* could drive you crazy.

Bumblebees aren't as sociable as their cousins, and they don't collect as much pollen or make as much honey. The queen is the biggest bee, followed by the female workers. Males, or drones, are the smallest, and they don't even have a stinger.

But on occasion, a bumblebee, like its close cousin the honeybee, is capable of great unselfishness. When a bumblebee stings an enemy to protect the bee's young or when a honeybee stings to save the hive from sure destruction, the bee dies. It sacrifices itself for its young or for the other bees.

Are you a "grumble-bee," a complainer? Or do you fall in the category of the unselfish, even sacrificial, bumblebee?

It's easy to grumble about life. You don't like your parents' rules at home. You think school rules are unfair. Church is boring, and the youth group kids aren't cool enough for you. You grumble when you have to do chores and homework. And on and on . . .

But grumbling doesn't get you anywhere. In the Bible, Jude writes that grumblers and complainers are living for only one thing—to satisfy their desires. *Ouch.*

Selfishness hits just about all of us. Few people grumble on behalf of others. We're too busy looking out for number one.

Let God's Spirit convict you of grumbling and selfishness and change your heart and actions. You might not be called to sacrifice your life for someone else, but maybe you could sacrifice your time, your treasure, or your gifts.

> *These people are grumblers and complainers, living only to satisfy their desires. They brag loudly about themselves, and they flatter others to get what they want.*
>
> **JUDE 1:16**

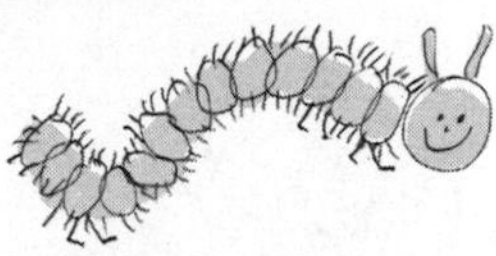

EATING MACHINES

Some animals are so greedy about food, they put pigs to shame.

The Tasmanian devil, a weird mammal in Tasmania, Australia, growls when it hunts for food, then screeches and screams as it gorges itself on gross carcasses, no matter how old and rotten they are. Taz can down 40 percent of its body weight in 30 minutes.

Glutton is actually another name for the wolverine, a big, bearlike weasel from the Arctic. It will gobble down just about anything, from a frog to a moose.

Hyenas scratch and bite each other as they devour a wildebeest or a zebra in no time flat. If the male kills the prey and a female hyena happens by, the lady will take over the meal and drive away the gent, which waits nearby for any leftovers. A hyena can eat one-third of its weight in minutes.

How are your eating habits? Do you watch what you eat? And do you control your eating for the right reasons, not just because you're obsessed with your looks?

There are plenty of reasons to curb eating. Gluttony is a sin we don't talk much about, especially at church potlucks. But overeating says to the world, "I don't have self-control, even though I claim to be walking with Christ."

Bad eating habits can wear down the body God has given you. You won't have the energy you would if you were eating right and exercising. First Corinthians 6:19 says, "Don't you realize that your body is the temple of the Holy Spirit, who lives in you and was given to you by God? You do not belong to yourself."

Take good care of that temple, and watch what goes into it.

> *Sodom's sins were pride, gluttony, and laziness, while the poor and needy suffered outside her door.*
> **EZEKIEL 16:49**

> *Do you like honey? Don't eat too much, or it will make you sick!*
> **PROVERBS 25:16**

Caterpillars are hefty eaters and can eat 1,000 times their weight in a month or two. Hummingbirds are constantly hungry and have to eat about every 10 minutes.

• • •

TODAY: Are there any foods that you eat too much of? Talk to your parents about your eating habits at school and at home. What can you do to change any unhealthy eating habits?

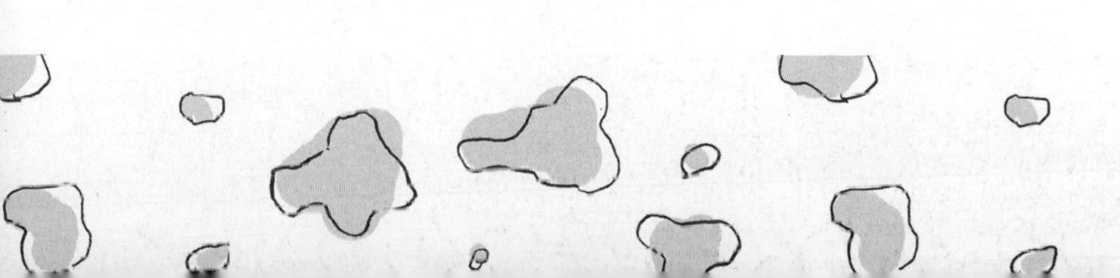

28 November

Male elephant seals fight over girls. The seals hit the beaches in December, and 5,000-pound males battle it out to win the gals.

• • •

TODAY: Every time you feel the slightest twinge of jealousy, thank God for something specific—something about yourself, your family, or God himself.

AN UGLY EMOTION

Jealousy can be an ugly thing. The spotted hyena is aggressive by nature. But when it's jealous, look out! Females battling over a male will tear each other to pieces. And it's not just males that bring on jealousy. Female hyenas hunt together and catch the prey, often crushing the animal's skull and disemboweling it. When the hyenas are really hungry, they demand their fair share of the food . . . or else. They'll scream and howl and turn on their fellow hyenas.

Our house pets aren't usually that extreme, but they get jealous too. A cat that gets jealous of the new cat may wait until the family sleeps—and then attack the newcomer. If the cat's jealousy continues, it may have other ways of showing it, including neglecting to use the litter box.

Dogs can be like kids. In a room full of chew toys, two dogs will both want the same one.

Any family that adds a baby after owning a dog or cat has to keep an eye on that potentially jealous pet.

Jealousy is a natural emotion. It's also a sin that often leads to more sin. Every day you run into people who are better looking than you, live in nicer homes, have more friends, dress better.

Some people seem to get it all. And maybe you're not one of them.

But that's okay. God made you like you are and put you exactly where you need to be. You're still growing and changing. Don't waste your energy on jealousy.

If you have Christ, you have it all. You've been given life, love, and more blessings than you can count. You have everything you need.

Wherever there is jealousy and selfish ambition, there you will find disorder and evil of every kind.

JAMES 3:16

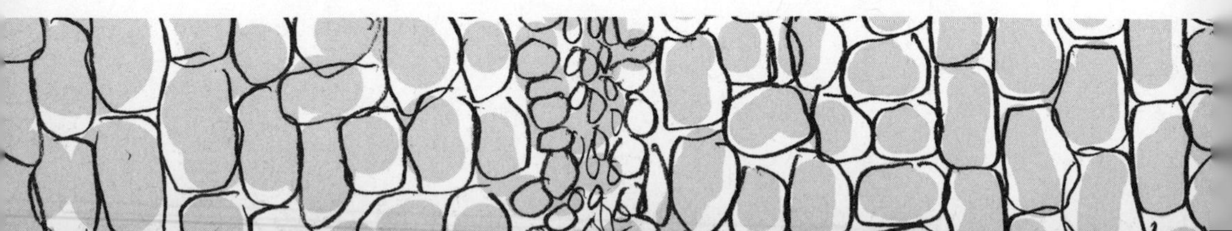

SOME BIRDS NEVER LEARN

Glass windows kill more birds in the United States each year than any other human factor. Estimates for the number of dead birds resulting from flying into windowpanes range from 100 million to a billion. Worldwide, the total is in the billions.

The swift parrots in Tasmania face a severe problem from too-clean window glass. One and a half percent of the total swift parrot population is wiped out every year by crashing into windows. And many of the parrots survive the first crash, only to rebound, take to the air, and smash into the same window again and again.

Some birds never learn.

And neither do some people. Most of us repeat the same mistakes over and over again. Why? Because we can.

Say, for example, you lie to your parents about where you went after school. Later you feel rotten about it. But the next week, you do it again. Maybe this time you get caught in your lie. And still, the following week you lie again.

Christianity isn't a set of laws that God will grade you on. God won't zap you (like a bird into a windowpane) when you sin. He doesn't reject you if you keep blowing it. You suffer consequences over and over, but God doesn't boot you out of heaven. You won't be living the joyful Christian life, but that's your choice too. God won't force you away from that window. You're not his slave.

Instead, in Christ, you're free . . . as a bird. And you can choose to repeat your sins, to bang your head into the glass over and over again. Or you can fly with God's Spirit, letting God guide you away from trouble and into his light.

> *You have been called to live in freedom, my brothers and sisters. But don't use your freedom to satisfy your sinful nature. Instead, use your freedom to serve one another in love.*
> **GALATIANS 5:13**

In ancient Rome, flamingo tongues were considered a delicacy for dinner. Songbirds used to be prime gourmet delicacies in France, Cyprus, and Italy. And we all know about blackbirds baked in pies.

• • •

TODAY: Thank God for the freedom you have in Christ. Ask God to make you more sensitive to the invisible dangers in front of you and to help you learn from experience.

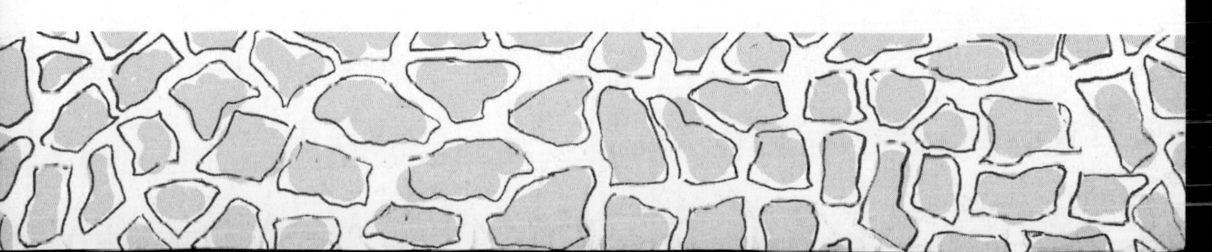

KNOCK, KNOCK

Knock, knock.
Who's there?
Cockadoodle.
Cockadoodle who?
Go back to bed, Rooster.

• • •

Knock, knock.
Who's there?
Thumping.
Thumping who?
Thumping is knocking on your door.

• • •

Knock, knock.
Who's there?
Bug spray.
Bug spray who?
Bugs pray that woodpeckers can't find them.

• • •

You've probably heard, or told, knock-knock jokes. You may have heard woodpeckers knocking on your tree. And you might have seen a painting that hangs in a lot of churches—Jesus is standing at a big, wooden door with no handle, and he's knocking, waiting for someone to open the door.

Many have felt as if Jesus were standing at a door to their lives. People who turn to Christ, confess their sins, and gratefully accept Christ's payment on the cross and his resurrection "open the door." They open to Christ for a variety of reasons. Some people want to be sure they're headed for heaven. Some are more concerned about their lives now.

Whatever the reason, Christ promises to come in and to be our friend.

Look! I stand at the door and knock. If you hear my voice and open the door, I will come in, and we will share a meal together as friends.
REVELATION 3:20

Pileated woodpeckers are the largest woodpeckers in North America, growing to 15 to 20 inches long. A pileated woodpecker will make about 16 holes in its tree to be sure it has plenty of escape routes. And it pecks away the bark from the entrance holes so that sap runs down and keeps snakes away (it's too sticky for them).

• • •

TODAY: If you're not sure that you're going to heaven, admit that you can't make it there on your own—you need Jesus to pay for your sin. Answer the door. Let Jesus come inside. Talk to a parent or a pastor about it.

MAKE ROOM

Red foxes are loners, living alone until their mating season in December. Then Mr. and Mrs. Fox settle into a couple of dens, perhaps burrows taken over from an armadillo or a woodchuck. That way, the foxes can outfox predators and move the baby foxes (usually five) from one den to the other.

There's always room for the kits, or baby foxes, which are born blind and helpless. Their mother, the vixen, stays in the den with them night and day for six weeks, relying on Dad to bring food. It's not until the following October that the kits will venture out on their own. And even then, the daughters might stay with their mother and help raise the next litter of babies.

As you're moving into the Christmas season, what kind of room are you leaving for Jesus? Most of us are pretty quick to nail the heartless innkeepers in Bethlehem. How could they have looked at Mary, who was so close to having her baby, and turned her away? Surely someone could have found a room, even a tiny room, for this poor woman who had traveled so far!

But no one did. Maybe they really didn't have a room. Maybe they knew they could get more money from a wealthier person. Maybe they were too busy with their own lives to think about the new life that was on the way.

Unfortunately, it's easy to lose Christ in the busy Christmas season. If we don't carve out time to read Scripture and think about what it means that Jesus left heaven, was born on earth, died, and was resurrected, we'll breeze right through Christmas without him. Shopping, wrapping, parties, and presents will fill any extra rooms.

Don't let it happen to you.

Dear children, keep away from anything that might take God's place in your hearts.
1 JOHN 5:21

The worst enemies of the red fox used to be wolves, panthers, bobcats, and lynx. Now the worst enemy of the red fox is humans. Foxes are in danger of being shot by hunters for sport, killed by farmers protecting their livestock, trapped for their fur coats, or hit by cars.

• • •

TODAY: List five things that compete with your thoughts about Jesus this month. Prayerfully come up with a plan to make more room for Christ this Christmas. Here are some ideas to get you started: read all four Gospels, get up early to pray, get your family together to read the Christmas story.

G. I. Joe was a homing pigeon used by the Allies in World War II. The British needed to cancel a bombing planned in Italy, but communication lines were down. So the British officers released the pigeon with a message to stop the bombing. It reached the air base in time to stop the bombs and to save the lives of about 1,000 British allies.

• • •

TODAY: If you've wandered away from "home"—from the nearness of God—come back. Thank God that he's always near, even when you don't feel him. Talk to God about things and people who draw you away.

HOMING PIGEONS

Homing pigeons have amazed people for centuries. They have the ability to travel thousands of miles to reach home. Some pigeons seem to follow highways or railways to get home, but others veer off the main paths and follow a more direct route.

A few researchers insist a pigeon's sense of smell guides it home. But for the last few years, most researchers agree that the earth's magnetic field plays a big role in the journey of a homing pigeon. Pigeons sense the strong pull of home.

Salmon migrate thousands of miles to get back to the place they were born. Even though the fish have drifted far away, they're drawn back when they're grown up and it's time for them to deposit their eggs in the water. The pull is so strong that they'll swim upstream, against the currents, and up and over waterfalls.

It's easy for us to wander from Christ, almost without realizing what's happening. Maybe you felt the "high" of a church camp or a terrific meeting at your youth group once. Or on a walk at sunset one day you sensed God's nearness. But life got in the way, and you got wrapped up in friends, school, and surviving day to day.

Come home.

If you've drifted from Christ, then God is drawing you back. Don't ignore the tugs. God built into you a new heart, a "magnet" that longs to be close to him. That longing you feel inside isn't for anything or anyone else. Only God can fill it.

God wants you home.

I long, yes, I faint with longing to enter the courts of the Lord. With my whole being, body and soul, I will shout joyfully to the living God.

PSALM 84:2

PLAYING FAVORITES

If you could observe mustangs in the wild, you'd see the way horses stick together. They hang in tightly knit groups that graze together and move out as one.

Herd behavior is intriguing because herds of wild horses function so much like social cliques at school. And it's not just the stampede in the halls when the bell rings.

Most herds have a dominant mare in charge. She's the leader of the pack, and the rest of the herd pretty much does what she tells them to. If a horse bucks the system, it will be ostracized from the group. On the dominant mare's cue, all the horses will ignore the one that dared challenge the leader.

What happens when a new horse is introduced into the herd? Usually it's not a pretty sight. The horses already in the group will do whatever it takes to make sure that new horse doesn't join in their reindeer games.

Most schools have cliques—groups that hang together and exclude everyone else. You might be part of the "popular group," or your group might have a much less flattering name. Maybe you're not in any group at all. You feel like you're on the outside looking in at kids who are enjoying school a lot more than you are.

Imagine Jesus walking into your school at lunchtime. He'd treat everyone the same. If he were sitting with you and your friends at the "cool kids" table, don't you think he'd go out of his way to invite kids who were sitting alone to come and join you?

If you're one of the "insiders," you need to look out for the stragglers and new kids. Don't exclude anyone because of the way he dresses or where she lives. If you're the one on the outside, it's okay. Jesus is the head of your herd. Keep being friendly to everyone, including the insiders. And find other loners who could use someone to talk to.

> *Suppose someone comes into your meeting dressed in fancy clothes and expensive jewelry, and another comes in who is poor and dressed in dirty clothes. If you give special attention and a good seat to the rich person, but you say to the poor one, "You can stand over there, or else sit on the floor"—well, doesn't this discrimination show that your judgments are guided by evil motives?*
>
> **JAMES 2:2-4**

"Wild" mustangs aren't really wild; they're "feral," descended from domesticated horses. Most of the mustangs in the United States were brought to Mexico by the Spanish. They escaped or were taken by Native Americans, who brought them to the Wild West.

• • •

TODAY: Prayerfully pick out one person you never talk to—someone you suspect of being an "outsider"—and talk to that person.

If someone calls you "camel breath," it's no compliment. Camels have the most absolutely awful breath in the entire animal kingdom.

• • •

TODAY: Make a packing list of "God moments," memory kernels of kindness you can carry with you into any desert.

ONE HUMP OR TWO?

Arabian camels, or dromedaries, have one hump and hang out in the Sahara Desert or in the Middle East. Bactrian camels live in central Asia and have two humps.

Camels are designed for the desert, with hooves that can walk on sand, a steady body temperature so they won't get too hot, nostrils that close off sand, and a double row of eyelashes to keep sand out of their eyes. Camels barely sweat, so they hang on to the water they do have. And they store energy in those humps.

Know what's in those humps? Not water, like you might think. Fat! One hump has 80 pounds of fat. In the summer, a camel can go five days without water. In the winter, a Saharan camel might go six to seven months without water. The fat in the humps is converted to water and energy when the camel needs it.

We can learn a lot from the camel. We know we'll have deserts of our own to cross—dry spells when it feels like God is far away and nobody likes us. Bad things do happen. This is earth, not heaven. But we can help ourselves get through the roughest times by storing what we need.

Think about it. God has given you so much. Christ died for you. You have his Spirit living inside you. God has already brought you through a lot.

If you're paying attention, there are "God moments," those extraordinary times when you know God took care of you. Maybe you heard a line from a hymn, and you knew it was for you. Or you were lying in bed and were overwhelmed by God's forgiveness. Maybe you glimpsed a sunrise, a smile, or your favorite flower.

Store those moments. Keep them. Remember them. Bring them out when you need them. They'll get you through the desert.

> *When our fathers were in Egypt, they gave no thought to your miracles; they did not remember your many kindnesses, and they rebelled by the sea, the Red Sea.*
> **PSALM 106:7, NIV**

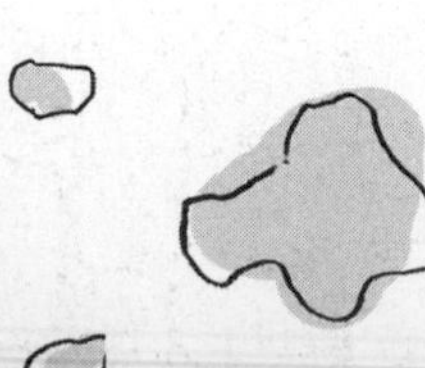
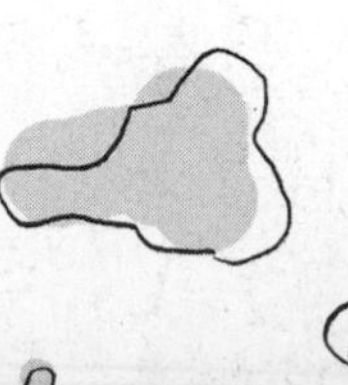

GIFT GIVING

Animals know how to give gifts, although some are better at it than others.

The male tern, a small migratory bird, offers a fish as a gift to the female he left behind or to a female he'd like to share a nest with. If she likes that fish, the guy's in business.

Roadrunners do more than speed down highways escaping from wily coyotes. A male roadrunner will catch just the right lizard and proudly present it to the girl of his dreams.

Even spiders try gift giving, usually a fly or an insect. The male spider wraps his gift in silk and carefully presents it to his dream spider . . . so that, with any luck, she won't eat him.

What's your own gift-giving style? Do you put it off until the last minute and then hate the rush? Do you try to find out what someone is giving you so you can give them something that costs the same amount? Do you think more about what you want for Christmas than what you want to give people for Christmas?

Gift giving can be a blessing or a curse. Most Americans spend too much on gifts we won't remember by the time next Christmas rolls around. We don't take enough time thinking about the person we're shopping for. We don't have time to make anything.

But this Christmas could be different. You're the one in charge, you know. Start now. Take your time. Think about a gift that says what you want to say to each person. It doesn't have to cost a fortune. Instead, it should show that you're paying attention to what this person likes—the right mystery novel, gloves for batting practice, a favorite flower.

God is the perfect gift giver, and Jesus is the perfect gift. Ask for divine guidance in your gift giving this Christmas.

> *If you sinful people know how to give good gifts to your children, how much more will your heavenly Father give good gifts to those who ask him.*
> **MATTHEW 7:11**

More rejected pets turn up in animal shelters after Christmas than at any other time of the year. Pets can make the best gifts, but only if the owner realizes that ownership comes with a commitment.

• • •

TODAY: Prayerfully think about, or rethink, the gifts you plan to give to your family. Every time you see a gift or an ad for a gift, thank God for his perfect gift, Christ.

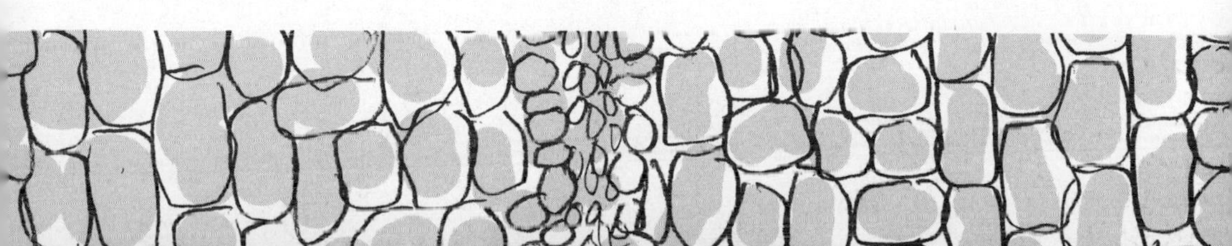

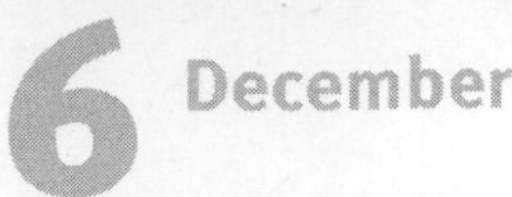

Although lions prefer eating zebras and gazelles that other animals have killed, they will eat people. The Chicago Field Museum houses the two Tsavo lions (stuffed) of Kenya, which stalked and killed about 30 Ugandan railway workers in 1898. In the 1930s in southern Tanzania, lions attacked and killed 1,500 people.

• • •

TODAY: Between you and God, make a plan to read and study the Bible daily. Start today!

BREAD ALONE

There's no accounting for the appetite of certain animals. What do pandas, elephants, squirrels, and giraffes have in common? Plants—that's what they all eat. Although most herbivores, or plant eaters, will try different plants, pandas stick to bamboo, even though it's not great nutritionally. Pandas have to eat 10 to 12 hours a day, downing about 40 pounds of bamboo just to stay alive.

Sharks, polar bears, woodpeckers, bald eagles, and anteaters: what binds the odd bunch together? They're carnivores, or meat eaters. Eagles will settle for rabbits, fish, or even roadkill, while anteaters stick to ants and termites.

Omnivores, like raccoons, grizzly bears, turtles, and monkeys, eat both meat and plants.

Mormon crickets eat other Mormon crickets, and snakes eat snakes. On occasion, certain snakes will digest their own hearts.

Humans have some weird diets too. But no matter what you eat, it can't keep you going spiritually. We're physical *and* spiritual beings.

When Jesus was tempted by the devil in the wilderness, Satan tried to get him to turn a stone into bread. Jesus must have been awfully hungry after 40 days in the desert without food. Satan had to think food was a pretty good temptation, as temptations go. And so what if Jesus had turned the stone to bread and had a slice?

Jesus rejected food to make a spiritual point. He said that people don't live by bread alone, but by hearing what God says. How do we hear God? Through prayer, through paying attention, and through the Word of God, the Bible.

Jesus is the Bread of Life. He's all the nourishment we'll ever need.

Jesus told him, "No! The Scriptures say, 'People do not live by bread alone.'"
LUKE 4:4

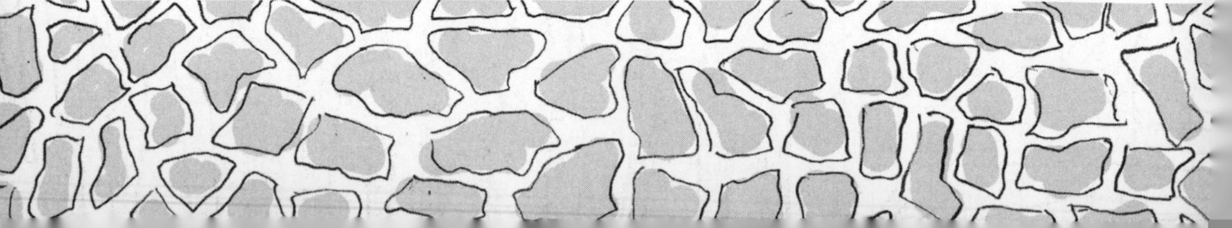

FAITHFUL FEW

Imagine this. You need to hide away from the world for a while, so your buddy says to trust him. He'll take care of everything. He has you climb inside a hole in a cement wall . . . and he cements you in with some food and a promise to be back with more later and to get you out . . . in about three months. You'd better hope he's one of the faithful few—one of the people you can always depend on.

That's the plight of the female hornbill, a weird-looking bird from Asia, Africa, and Australia. When it's time to nest, the male hornbill finds a hole in a tree, and the female lays one to five eggs inside it. She stays in the nest with the eggs, sealed in the hole by a wall she makes out of mud, sticky goo, and leaves. Mom Hornbill leaves a small slit so Dad Hornbill can give her food. The female hornbill stays in the hole until her eggs hatch and then for 100 days afterward. Finally the male helps Mom and babies peck their way out.

If you have a faithful friend, you can count yourself blessed. Are you one? Do friends and family know they can always count on you? If you say you'll walk the dog, is it as good as done? Or do you forget until someone asks you again? If you've promised to call Granny every week, do you do it? Calling Granny and walking the dog may sound like little things, but they make a big difference. Faithfulness starts with "little things." Jesus said, "If you are faithful in little things, you will be faithful in large ones. But if you are dishonest in little things, you won't be honest with greater responsibilities" (Luke 16:10).

Now is the time to start being faithful in the little things. The apostle Paul surrounded himself with faithful people:

Epaphras, our beloved co-worker . . . is Christ's faithful servant, and he is helping us on your behalf.
COLOSSIANS 1:7

Tychicus . . . is a beloved brother and faithful helper who serves with me in the Lord's work.
COLOSSIANS 4:7

I am also sending Onesimus, a faithful and beloved brother.
COLOSSIANS 4:9

Two male helmeted hornbills defending their territories put on quite a sky show as they fly straight toward each other, cackling all the way, and ram their bald red heads into each other like battering rams.

• • •

TODAY: List three people you know you can count on. Thank God for them, and thank them, too. Ask God to make you someone who would appear on other people's "top three most faithful" Hall of Fame lists.

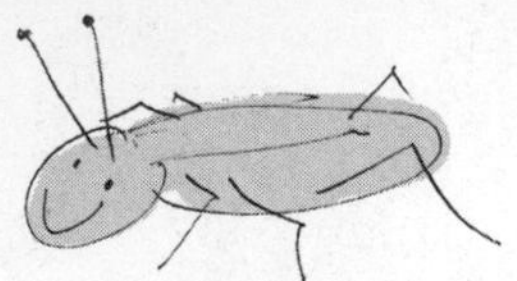

Fleas and crickets have different jumping styles, which makes it hard to compare which are better leapers. A cricket takes off from a dead start and jumps straight up. A flea has a rubberlike construction that squeezes its body together, then pushes the flea up and into a cartwheel spin.

• • •

TODAY: Ask God to make you kinder, more honest, more like Christ, and freer to talk about Jesus. At the end of the week, compare yourself this week to yourself last week.

I CAN JUMP HIGHER THAN YOU CAN!

A kangaroo can jump 10 feet straight up and hop 40 feet in a broad jump. Not bad. But a grasshopper can jump 10 to 20 times its length, which would be like a kangaroo jumping 120 feet.

And the winner is . . . Fleas can jump 13 inches in a broad jump and a foot into the air. That's 300 times a flea's length, which would be like the kangaroo jumping six football fields.

If you weren't born competitive, you probably started competing, or at least comparing, when you were pretty young. As soon as you start getting grades, you try to find out who's the smartest in the class, the best reader, the best writer. At recess, you have races to see who's the fastest. Soon you find out who's the best batter or the best at shooting hoops.

It doesn't take long to start comparing your clothes to someone else's. You go home with a friend, and you can't help seeing that her house is nicer than yours.

Comparing and competing may be natural, but those habits can also be destructive. Even if you come out on top now because you're a big fish in a little pond, it's a big world out there. There will always be someone faster, smarter, better looking than you. So what?

If you have to compare and compete, try being your own competition. Do better in math this year than you did last. That's success—not that you're better than your buddies. Have fun playing sports, even if you'll never score the winning goal. If you love music, join the band. You don't have to be the best tuba player around.

Measure yourself by yourself, and leave the judging to God.

Pay careful attention to your own work, for then you will get the satisfaction of a job well done, and you won't need to compare yourself to anyone else.
GALATIANS 6:4

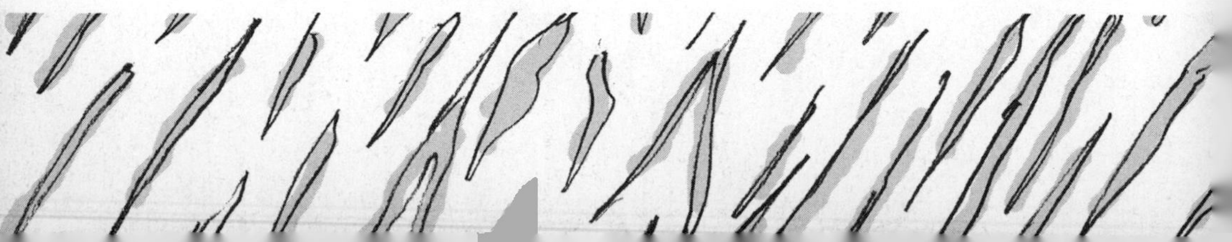

KNOWING WHAT'S GOOD FOR YOU

Sometimes even animals don't know what's good for them. Cubs stray too far from their dens. Puppies trot out onto the highway. Kittens climb up trees they can't climb down.

Other animals seem to know what's coming, but they self-destruct just the same. Certain male bees get ripped open by the queen during mating. Male praying mantises are often eaten by their mates. Both Mother and Father Octopus look after their babies so diligently that some have neglected to feed themselves . . . and starved to death.

Why do we do things we know aren't good for us? Maybe you don't abuse drugs or drink alcohol or smoke cigarettes. Maybe your self-destructive behaviors aren't that obvious. You don't get enough sleep, or you eat too much or eat the wrong things. You feed your mind junk by watching TV night and day.

Do you cheat, lie, or refuse to ask for help? Do you hang on to bitterness and let it eat away at you? Or maybe you keep repeating the same destructive actions, like chasing after someone who keeps hurting you or getting in your teacher's face.

Take better care of yourself. You are extraordinarily valuable. You've been created by God, who didn't have to make you but chose to anyway. God has given you a purpose in life that nobody else can fulfill. If you'd been the only person on earth, Jesus would have gone through the Crucifixion and Resurrection just for you. That's how much he loves you.

God's Spirit lives inside you. You are God's temple. When you mistreat yourself, you're mistreating God. Do the things you know are good for you.

> *Don't you realize that your body is the temple of the Holy Spirit, who lives in you and was given to you by God? You do not belong to yourself, for God bought you with a high price. So you must honor God with your body.*
>
> **1 CORINTHIANS 6:19-20**

Some parasites make their host animals commit suicide. Certain bumblebee parasites make the bee dive into ponds and drown. Some shrimp parasites make shrimp swim at the surface of the water until they are eaten. Ribbon worms don't need a parasite to drive them to destruction. If they're hungry enough, they'll eat themselves.

• • •

TODAY: Talk to God about anything self-destructive going on in your life. With Christ's help, you can change that behavior. Talk to someone you trust.

Many people used to believe horses were swaybacked because they'd been ridden too early. Even though we now know the cause could be due to genetics, age, copper deficiency, or other problems, it's still a bad idea to ride a horse too early. Horses under the age of three can develop leg and back problems since their bones aren't fully matured yet.

• • •

TODAY: Pray for any new Christians you know. Do one thing to encourage a new believer this week.

SWAYBACKS

Have you ever seen an animal with a swayback? In horses, goats, and cud-chewing animals, sometimes the back dips, making it look like a piece of the animal's back is missing.

Older horses may get swaybacked because the tissue on their backs softens. If younger horses become swaybacked, it's usually because they have a genetic weakness.

Horses can also have their backs weakened by overeager riders. Sometimes horse owners are so excited to ride their new horses that they don't wait until the horses are ready. They don't mean to harm the horse, but that's what can happen. The young horse's skeletal system is too weak to carry the weight of a rider, and the animal may develop back and leg problems for the rest of its life.

Young animals need special consideration.

So do young Christians. If you've ever had a friend come to Christ, you know how exciting that is. Right away you want the best for this new believer. You want to make sure this person doesn't mess things up the way you did. So you try to let the new Christian know as much as you can right away.

This person has to go to church, right? And Sunday school. And your youth group and Bible study. Plus, prayer! Maybe you could meet with your friend every day before school and pray. On top of that there's Scripture memorization—you could make a list of verses.

And then there are the things this new believer should stop doing. Maybe she needs to dress more conservatively so she's not sending out the wrong message. Or he should stop hanging out with those friends of his. And . . .

Be careful. All those things may be great, but the timing is up to God. And conviction of sin is up to the Holy Spirit. Jesus put off telling the disciples certain things until they could handle it. He scolded the Pharisees (religious leaders) for putting heavy burdens on people.

Don't overload your new Christian friends. Don't make them spiritually swaybacked.

> *What sorrow also awaits you experts in religious law! For you crush people with unbearable religious demands, and you never lift a finger to ease the burden.*
>
> **LUKE 11:46**

IMMUNE

What if a scorpion stings itself? Will it die? Nope. Most animals are at least partly immune to their own poison. To kill itself, the scorpion would have to get a dose 200 times as strong as the dose it delivers to kill a guinea pig.

Gila monsters are immune to their own poison. One Gila monster can bite another without feeling the effects of the poison. Komodo dragons are immune to their own poison too.

Cobras can't poison other cobras. In India, some people keep a pet mongoose because the mongoose can fight and kill that deadly snake without being poisoned itself.

Christians can become immune to the truths of Christianity. You're blessed if you come from a good Christian home and a solid church background. But you need to keep your faith fresh. Even if you could go through the motions at church blindfolded and sing the hymns without looking, don't take your faith for granted. Even if you've heard those verses hundreds of times, dig deeper for their power.

Christianity isn't inherited. You need to have your own personal relationship with Jesus. Sometimes you have to work to keep that relationship fresh. If you always pray in bed at night, try taking a prayer walk in the morning sometimes.

Don't let yourself grow immune to God's Spirit. Sing those hymns as if you mean every word to go straight to God. Listen to the verses as if they're written to you . . . because they are.

> *For God loved the world so much that he gave his one and only Son, so that everyone who believes in him will not perish but have eternal life.*
> **JOHN 3:16**

The meerkat can eat scorpions without being poisoned. It pounces on the scorpion, bites off the tail including the stinger, brushes off the remaining poison into the sand, and chows down. Meerkats pass along this art to their kids too.

• • •

TODAY: Read John 3:16 as if you've never heard the verse before. Read it over and over until God gives you fresh appreciation and gratitude.

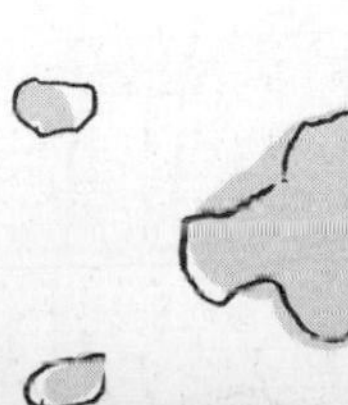
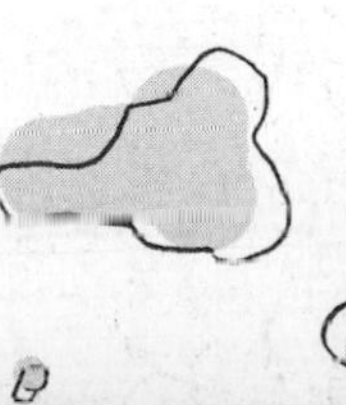
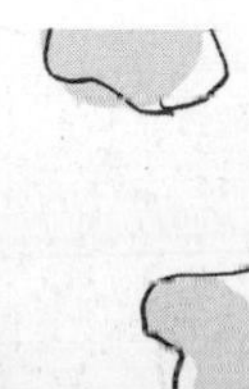

The Alaskan malamute dog is so in tune with its master that the malamute's ears face backward when it's running. That way the dog can hear its master's voice back in the sled.

• • •

TODAY: List three things you did "at first"—when you felt closer to God than you do now. Do all three things today.

FIRST LOVE

Do you remember the first time you got a pet? Even if you've never had a pet, as an animal lover, you've at least dreamed about it. Before you bring the pet home, you get ready for it. You buy a bowl, food, toys, a bed. You might even have a name all picked out. You have so many plans for that pet and you.

At first, your pet can do no wrong. All you want to do is hold it or play with it. Your friends are sick of hearing about your new best friend because you can't seem to stop talking about it or thinking about it.

But pets aren't all fun and games. You have to keep taking the puppy outside. You can't forget to change the kitty's litter.

Besides, you can't put the rest of your life on hold. So you play ball after school instead of coming home to play with your pet. You talk on the phone at night and almost forget you have a pet.

What happened to that first love?

That's what Jesus asked in a message sent to the early church in Ephesus. He had some great things to say about the people there. But Jesus held one thing against them: they didn't love him the way they had at first.

How about you? Do you remember a time when you first understood what Christ did for you? Or maybe you remember a time when you felt so close to God that you talked freely about him with your friends. Did you used to be into the Bible and prayer more than you are now? Have you lost that first love of Jesus?

If you're nodding your head, the good news is that Jesus told that church at Ephesus what they needed to do: "Turn back to me and do the works you did at first."

Recapture your first love for God.

I have this complaint against you. You don't love me or each other as you did at first! Look how far you have fallen! Turn back to me and do the works you did at first.
REVELATION 2:4-5

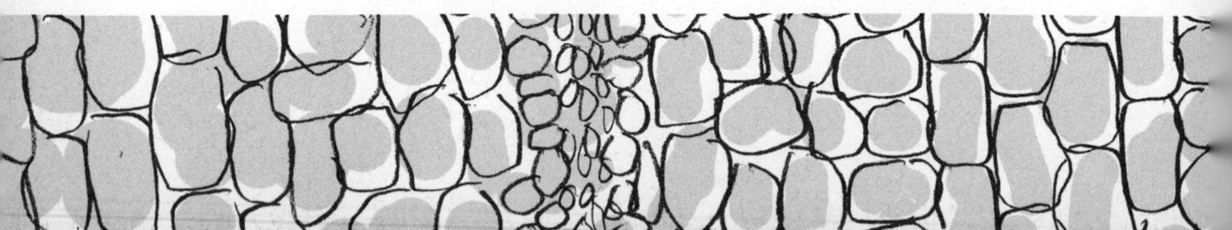

GET YOUR HOPES UP

Imagine you're a squirrel monkey and you're wishing you could catch those flying insects taunting you from the trees. You'd sure love an insect sandwich. But when you climb the tree, they buzz off to the next tree. So you sit on your branch and complain that life is so unfair.

But another squirrel monkey gets its hopes up. Why couldn't it catch those insects in midair? The monkey combines hope with its dream of an insect sandwich. And *whoosh*! Suddenly it leaps from its branch (squirrel monkeys can leap eight feet into the air) and catches its dream.

Reindeer must hope for survival as they prepare for the frigid winter and long migration to come. They have nothing but yucky moss to eat. Yet the ones that get their hopes up for toughing it out until spring eat the moss. It turns out the moss contains a chemical that helps the hopeful reindeer keep its body fluids warm, like reindeer antifreeze. The moss eaters make it through the Arctic winter.

Are you afraid to dream big? Can't stand the disappointment? What if you dream of being a veterinarian and can't come up with the grades or the money to make your dream come true? Do you decide you'd better not get your hopes up, just in case?

Think again. If God wants you to be a vet—or anything else—it's a done deal. Not that you won't have to work like crazy to bring that dream to pass. Even squirrel monkeys have to practice jumping. But don't be afraid to hope.

God wants you to have hopes and dreams. The sky's the limit when you share your dreams with God. He can do anything. And when your hope is in God, so can you.

> *Hope deferred makes the heart sick, but a dream fulfilled is a tree of life.*
> **PROVERBS 13:12**

What do these things have in common: dead leaf, paper kite, great eggfly, American snout, comma, question mark, sailor, blue morpho, and striped blue crow? They're all names of butterflies.

• • •

TODAY: If you didn't have to think about money, talent, limitations, or problems, what would you hope for and dream of? Tell God your dreams and hopes today.

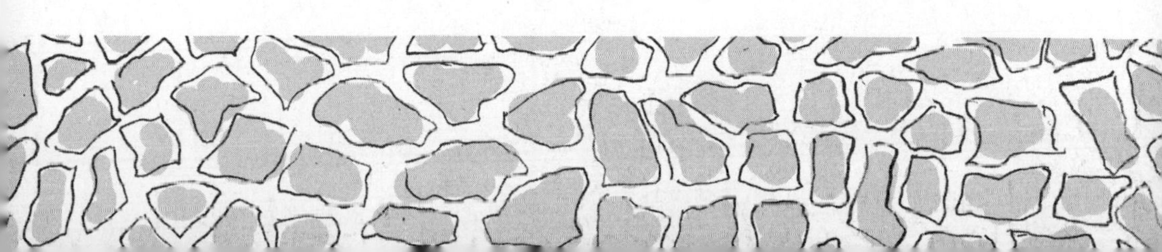

SAY WHAT?

When dogs are young, they hear frequencies up to 40,000 vibrations per second—twice as high as you can hear. Both cats and dogs hear soft sounds better than you can. They prick their ears and rotate each ear for sound. Dogs have 17 muscles that move their ears, and they can adjust each ear to bring in sound from two different directions at once. Cats have over 30 muscles per ear. Humans only have 6 ear muscles.

As our pets get older, like our grandparents, their hearing gets worse. Sometimes hearing loss seems to happen overnight. That's possible, if an infection or a disease is the cause. But usually the loss of hearing is gradual as the pet ages. We just don't notice until one day it's obvious the animal doesn't hear us anymore.

Physically, we should do all we can to protect our hearing. Listen to what your parents and doctors say about loud noises, headphones, and other habits that take a toll on your eardrums.

Spiritually, we can suffer the same kind of loss—with even worse outcomes. We can grow spiritually deaf. Maybe you've heard those Ten Commandments so often that they don't mean anything to you anymore. Honor your parents? *Yawn.* No other god before him? *Whatever.*

How can you be expected to get excited about John 3:16 when you've heard your whole life that God so loved the world. . . ?

The Good News of John 3:16 is as exciting as it was over 2,000 years ago, much less a decade or so ago. Join a new Bible study. Volunteer to teach little kids in Sunday school. Talk to someone about Christ—someone who may never have heard how much God loves the world and why he sent his only Son.

Don't let your hearing grow old.

Concerning him we have much to say, and it is hard to explain, since you have become dull of hearing.
HEBREWS 5:11, NASB

Most older dogs suffer hearing loss, and a wise owner will try to make life easier for the old family friend. Stomp on the floor when you approach your dog from out of its sight so you don't scare the poor guy. Don't let your dog run wild outside, where it can't hear danger coming. Try out a high-pitched dog whistle and see if it can still hear that.

• • •

TODAY: Think about two "hearing aids" you can start using to buck up your spiritual hearing. Volunteer for something that will help you put what you've heard into action.

SERIOUSLY, I'M HAPPY FOR YOU!

Like rats, marmots are rodents. But they don't act much like rats. They weigh up to 20 pounds and look like they enjoy each other and life. Marmots hang out in colonies and know how to have a good time with their friends. They lie in the sun, play-chase each other, and good-naturedly wrestle with their friends, with no signs of competition. They appear to have empathy for one another.

Empathy is the ability to identify with or in some way feel for another person—to be happy when they're happy and sad when they're sad.

Many pets seem to have empathy. If you dash home from school, excited about making the team or getting the teacher you wanted, your tail-wagging dog will probably bound along with you through the house. But if you trudge through the door and disappear into your room for a good cry, that same dog might curl up quietly beside you.

How's your empathy? When someone at school or in your family is going through a tough time, are you able to identify with that person? Do you listen and try to understand? Can you share what your friend is going through?

You'd think sharing happiness would be easier than sharing somebody's sadness, but that's not always the case. If your buddy makes the team, are you sincerely happy for your friend? Or do you have to fake it because you're thinking you should have gotten on the team instead? Can you share the joy of a friend who gets a horse? Or a friend who is singled out for great work at school?

God tells us to rejoice with people who rejoice and weep with people who are weeping. That's true empathy.

> *Rejoice with those who rejoice, and weep with those who weep.*
> **ROMANS 12:15, NASB**

As a tribute to his sheepdog, Paul McCartney, one of the famous Beatles, recorded a high-pitched whistle at the end of the song "A Day in the Life."

• • •

TODAY: Thank God for 10 great things that have happened . . . to other people. Ask God to change your heart so you can be completely happy for others.

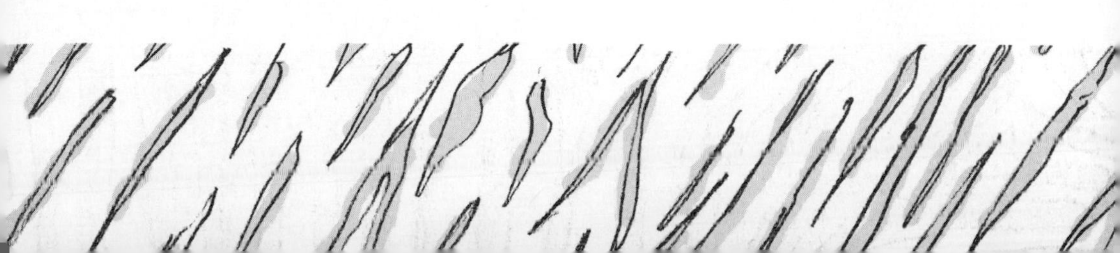

The most popular name for a dog in the United States for six years in a row was Max. And the most popular name for a cat in the United States for six years in a row was also Max.

• • •

TODAY: Thank God all day long for your family, including your pets, and for all the animals he has placed in your world (birds, squirrels, geese, cows, horses, dogs).

THANK YOU, GOD, FOR ANIMALS!

If you have a pet, you don't need to be convinced how great pets are and how thankful we should be for our animals. You've experienced firsthand the joy of having a dog curl up beside you or the feeling of riding and moving as if you're part of your horse. Maybe you've watched your guinea pig grow or your fish swim. Or you've smiled at the peaceful sensation of hearing your cat purr.

Some of the biggest animal lovers don't have pets . . . yet. If that's you, then you're no doubt just as thankful for every contact you do have with the animals God has created for you to enjoy and care for. He loves the fact that you have a special gratitude for all the animals.

There are around 163 million cats and dogs in the United States today. Type in *dog* into a search engine and see how many hits you get (417 million, according to one search engine). Type in *cat*, and you get even more (around 847 million!).

Animals offer companionship and give owners a sense of well-being. They can lower blood pressure in adults and teach responsibility to children. They can help people develop compassion and love.

Animals give us countless reasons to thank God every day.

God made all the animals, even though he didn't have to. But he loves giving gifts to his children. Every good gift comes straight from God, and animals are definitely good gifts.

> *Whatever is good and perfect comes down to us from God our Father, who created all the lights in the heavens. He never changes or casts a shifting shadow.*
>
> **JAMES 1:17**

FAKE!

The praying mantis is a fake. The insect doesn't pray, despite its pious look with arms raised in an attitude of prayer. And even worse, it's a hypocrite, going to great lengths to pretend it's something it isn't.

Lots of animals use camouflage to hide from enemies. Grasshoppers are green, like the grass. Bark beetles look like bark. But a praying mantis takes "fake" to a whole new level. It doesn't just blend in. The mantis mimics. It changes to fit its surroundings. Different species of the mantis can look like a stick, then a stone. One type of Australian mantis actually turns black after a forest fire so it will look charred like its surroundings.

Okay, it's not the mantis's fault that it looks like it's praying when it's not. But what about you? When you're in church and saying the Lord's Prayer, do you mean it? Or are you noticing what somebody's wearing? Or thinking about what you'll say to that friend who made you mad? Or replaying in your head the TV show you saw last night?

When you're saying prayers at night or praying out loud in youth group, is it for show, or is it for real? You can fool a lot of people, but you can't fool God.

God doesn't care if your hands are folded or if you're on your knees, standing up, or running to catch the bus. Prayer, real prayer, will connect you with the Creator of the universe. And you have an open invitation! Don't waste the privilege.

When you pray, go away by yourself, shut the door behind you, and pray to your Father in private. Then your Father, who sees everything, will reward you.
MATTHEW 6:6

The lovely praying mantis is a cannibal, quite ready and willing to eat other mantises.

• • •

TODAY: Go someplace private—your closet or another secret spot—and talk to God. Three times during the day, while others are watching, pray—but in a way that no one will notice except God. Keep it between you and God.

18 December

A male deer (the one with antlers) is a buck or hart. A female is a doe or a hind. Females have one to three fawns in May or June. The deer's white tail is used to communicate with other deer. When a deer raises that white tail, it's saying, "Run for your life!"

• • •

TODAY: Talk to God about any path you're taking that you're not sure about—a friendship, something at school, a role in your church or youth group. Ask God to put you on the right path and keep you there.

DEER YOU . . .

If somebody tells you that you have deer feet, that's a compliment. Deer, like mountain goats, are sure-footed climbers and runners, thanks to those hooves and legs. Most mountain goats can climb a 90-degree cliff. Deer can jump up to nine feet and run 40 miles per hour without stumbling.

Deer generally travel on trails. When a deer runs along the trail, it doesn't even have to look down to stay in the precise center because it has the ability to place its back feet exactly where its front feet were. That lets the deer run like crazy, without looking down.

When God promises to make us as sure-footed as a deer and to set our feet on the right paths, he means that he'll lead us and stay with us. God doesn't just give us a rule and tell us to keep it. He gives us his Spirit inside of us to keep on guiding us. And if we do slip or take a wrong turn, he forgives us and welcomes us back onto the right path.

You don't have to worry about the answer to that classic (and often dreaded) question, What do you want to be when you grow up? Why? Because God has already set you on the right path. You don't have to check each footstep. God's Spirit will show you if you step off the path, and Jesus will lead you back.

You don't have to worry and struggle to stay in God's will—in the center of his path for you. You have to struggle to get out of his will. God's will might not always be the easiest path, but it's the best one.

Keep running on the right path. You'll get there. . . .

The Sovereign Lord is my strength! He makes me as surefooted as a deer, able to tread upon the heights.
HABAKKUK 3:19

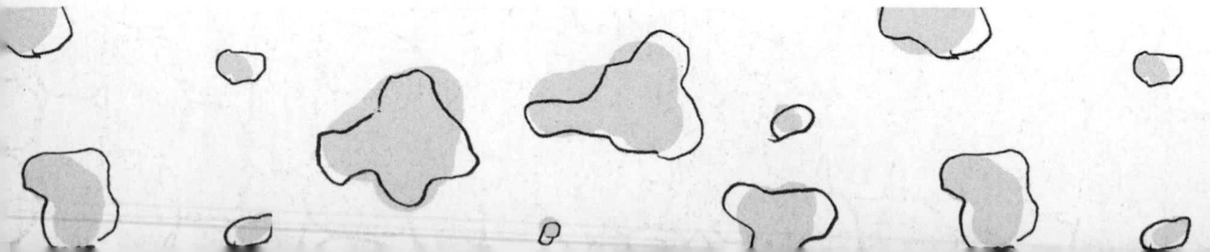

SHOWING LOVE

If you own an indoor-outdoor cat, you may have received an unusual "gift" from your pet. You opened your front door to find a poor dead bird on your step.

Or if you're really lucky, you might have awakened to sunshine streaming through your bedroom window with your cat standing on your chest. In its mouth is a dead mouse, which it sweetly drops onto your pillow. Merry Christmas.

Why do cats bring home dead critters that they have no intention of eating themselves? Because they love you, that's why. Bringing you a gift they'd like themselves is how they choose to show you love. It's their way.

What's your way of showing love to other people? Take your parents, for example. How much thought do you give to showing them that you love them?

When you were little, maybe you colored pictures that your parents proudly put on the fridge. What have you made for them lately? When your mom kisses you good-bye and says, "I love you, honey," is she lucky to get a quick, "Yeah, me too"?

Sometimes words don't cut it. A strong show of love requires action. Do your chores without being told. Volunteer to do chores your mom or dad normally do. Carry in groceries when you see Mom needs help. Those actions scream, "I love you!"

Christmas is a time to remember Christ's sacrifice, as well as Jesus' birth. Take the time to make something for your parents and siblings. Make homemade cards that say what you really want to say.

This year, give gifts that communicate your love. God proved his love by sending us the greatest gift of all, Jesus.

Thank God for this gift too wonderful for words!
2 CORINTHIANS 9:15

CHRISTMAS SAFETY TIPS FOR PETS:

1. Keep chewers (dogs, cats) away from all Christmas lights and cords.
2. Skip the tinsel, especially if you have a cat.
3. Guard your pets from that real tree! Pine needles can get lodged in a pet's throat. And drinking the tree water can make them sick.
4. Holly, mistletoe, and yew can poison pets.

• • •

TODAY: Start making something for your parents—something that requires a sacrifice on your part. You can probably come up with something even better than a dead mouse or bird.

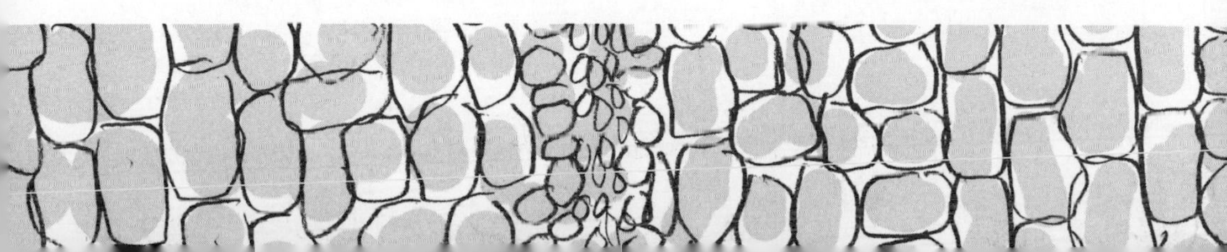

Plant-eating animals, like deer, giraffes, cows, and horses, need to keep a lookout for enemies while they graze. Their eyes are to the sides of their heads so they can see sideways and in front of them. Hunters like cats, dogs, lions, and bears need to focus on the prey ahead of them, so their eyes are on the front of their heads.

• • •

TODAY: Try to think of Jesus 20 times throughout the day, and ask for guidance.

EYES ON THE PRIZE

Riding horses is all about balance and focus. Horse people will tell you to guide your mount by looking through the space between your horse's ears. That focus will communicate to your horse. There's an old adage about jumping horses: Throw yourself over the fence first, and your horse will follow. If you focus on where you want to be, it's much easier to get there.

Cougars and tigers do the same thing. They focus on the prey, then lunge, crossing fields and arriving exactly on target.

There's a legend about a Native American chief who knew he was nearing death and needed to choose the tribe's next chief. He selected three possible leaders and took them deep into the woods, where he pointed to a narrow tree 100 yards away. "Walk from here to there in the shortest distance," he instructed.

The first warrior watched his feet, careful to place each foot directly in front of the other. But when he looked up, he was yards to the left of the tree. The second warrior alternated his gaze from tree to path, tree to path. He arrived at the tree. But his footsteps zigzagged along the path. The final warrior kept his gaze on the tree as he walked directly to it and became the new chief.

We need to keep our eyes on Jesus. How? Talk to him all day long. Practice remembering that he's with you wherever you go. Start and end each day thinking about all God has done for you. Thank him continually.

Take this time before celebrating Christ's birth and focus on Jesus throughout the Christmas season.

> *[Keep your] eyes on Jesus, the champion who initiates and perfects our faith. Because of the joy awaiting him, he endured the cross, disregarding its shame. Now he is seated in the place of honor beside God's throne.*
>
> **HEBREWS 12:2**

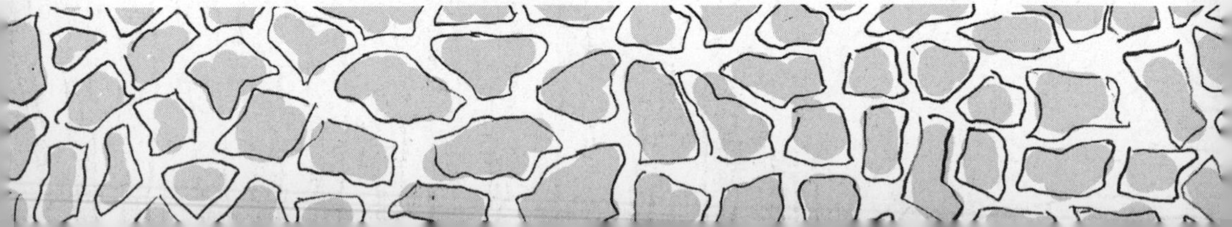

FLY AWAY HOME

You've probably seen abandoned bird nests in trees, on window ledges, nestled inside drainage pipes, and on roofs. The most common nest is the cup nest, which looks like a bowl made of twigs. Some birds live in their nests all year, but most leave the nest when the babies leave, a process called fledging.

Although most birds never return to their home nests after they fledge, some do. Many of the big platform nests of ospreys, hawks, storks, and eagles are reused year after year. Crows may build a new nest right next to their original homes, using the old materials, while weavers just repair the old nests.

Cup nests aren't reused by the same birds very often because the materials harden and may get parasites. Yet starlings return to their old nests and line them with other plants that are toxic to insects and parasites that could infect their babies.

No matter what building you call home, your real home is your family. When you were younger, you depended on your parents for survival. Now that you can look after yourself in so many ways, you and your family have to seek a balance between keeping you safe and letting you stretch your wings and fly. And that's tricky.

You probably sleep and eat at your house, at least most of the time. But home is much more than the "nest." Your major influences should still come from your home, rather than your friends.

It's easy to pull away from your family. But God gave you your parents, and he can use them to help teach you how to fly. Don't turn your back on family. Keep coming back to the nest.

The trees of the Lord are well cared for—the cedars of Lebanon that he planted. There the birds make their nests, and the storks make their homes in the cypresses.

PSALM 104:16-17

A male wren knows he'll need a great home to snag a female wren. As the potential Mrs. Wren watches, the hopeful Father Wren finds a few nests that have been used by other birds in other seasons. Mrs. Wren inspects the homes while Mr. Wren sings and flits about, adding twigs to the houses until she finally selects one. She adds her own feathers to the nest and settles in to lay her eggs.

• • •

TODAY: Thank God for your home base. Find one way to promote family time: Rally everybody for church or a community activity. Suggest a game of football. Declare a board game night.

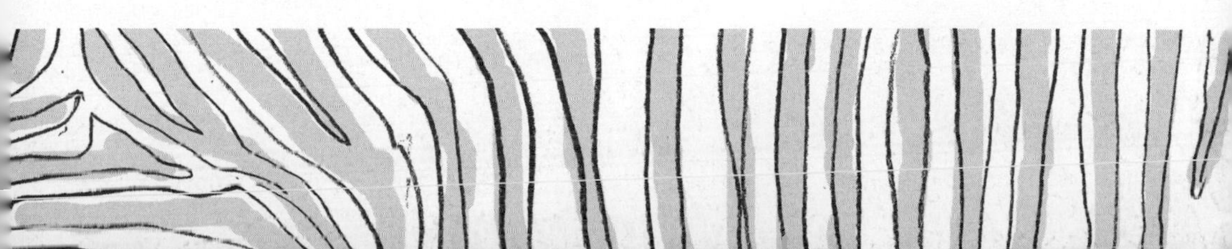

According to the New York Veterinarians' annual list of Dogs Most Likely to Bite, the biting-est award goes to the German shepherd.

• • •

TODAY: Try to think of God watching you all day, every minute. Smile back at God. Thank him for always wanting the best for you and for forgiving the rest.

BETTER WATCH OUT

Not all watchdogs are created equal. And not all dogs—even the big ones—make good watchdogs.

A good watchdog has to bark when it sees or hears something out of the ordinary. A bad watchdog sleeps through the home invasion.

Here are some of the dogs you don't want watching out for you because they sleep with an invisible Can't Be Disturbed sign around their necks: Bloodhounds can track your intruder, but don't expect them to wake up for the big event. Saint Bernards would rescue you if you were dumped in the snow somewhere, but they would probably sleep through an entire kidnapping. So would American bulldogs, huskies, Irish wolfhounds, and sheepdogs.

If you want a dog that will bark like crazy (whether there's an intruder or not), consider these potential watchdogs: rottweilers, German shepherds, Chihuahuas, miniature schnauzers, poodles, and most terriers.

This time of year you've probably heard that song about how Santa Claus sees you when you're sleeping and knows when you're awake. The idea of somebody watching you all the time can creep you out, especially when you add the part about knowing if you've been bad or good. "Be good, for goodness' sake!"

So what about the fact that God watches over us all the time? God sees us when we're sleeping, waking, and in between. He knows better than we do when we've been naughty or nice. But there's nothing creepy or threatening about God's watching over us. God isn't waiting for you to make a wrong move. He's helping you make the right ones. He watches you to protect you. And he loves you no matter what he sees.

The eyes of the Lord watch over those who do right, and his ears are open to their prayers.
1 PETER 3:12

DON'T BUG RUDOLPH

Did you know there really are such things as reindeer? Wild reindeer roam the cold climates of Siberia, Greenland, Alaska, and Canada. Both males and females sport antlers.

Reindeer populations have dwindled dramatically in the last century. They have some pretty big and powerful predators to worry about. Bears hunt caribou and reindeer. Wolves hunt in packs, cornering the reindeer for a communal meal. Then there's the eagle, which swoops down and attacks from above.

But the worst enemies of the reindeer aren't the giant hunters, but insects. In the summer, mosquitoes swarm onto the poor reindeer. Each mosquito can suck up to four ounces of a reindeer's blood in one day.

In the fall, warble flies lay eggs on an unsuspecting reindeer's leg hairs, and the larvae drill into the animal's flesh. Nose botflies lay eggs in the reindeer's nostrils and work their way into the nose and throat, making the poor thing cough and sneeze. In the spring, full-grown botflies crawl out of the reindeer's nose and mouth. Insects bug the reindeer its whole life.

What "bugs" you in your relationship with God? If you're taking care of the big sins and confessing them but you still feel far away from God, maybe it's the "little" sins that are getting in the way.

Say, for example, you take money from your mother's purse. That's stealing, and you know it's way wrong. Hopefully, you won't be able to rest until you confess to God and your mom.

But if you're just rude to your little sister, or if you mouth off to a parent or skip a chore because you don't feel like doing it, you might not feel the same internal pressure to confess. And the problem is, those "little" unconfessed sins will end up distancing you from God.

Don't let that happen. Take care of what's bugging you.

People who conceal their sins will not prosper, but if they confess and turn from them, they will receive mercy.
PROVERBS 28:13

Reindeer travel farther than any other land mammal. Moving at speeds of 50 miles per hour, large herds of reindeer migrate about 3,000 miles a year.

• • •

TODAY: Prayerfully replay last week in your head and ask God to point out every "little" unconfessed sin. Talk to God about each one, and thank him for his forgiveness.

Goldfish have been kept as pets longer than any other fish. Indoor goldfish usually range in size from one to four inches. They may have fringe tails, fantails, or veil tails, with double or triple fins. And they don't just come in gold. You can get them in red, white, silver, or black. Some of the rarest, "scaleless" goldfish, can look bright red, blue, purple, and even calico.

• • •

TODAY: Get off by yourself and spend 30 minutes alone, pondering why Jesus had to be born and what Christ's resurrection really means to you.

LIFE IN A FISHBOWL

Many people choose a goldfish as a pet because a fish appears easy to take care of. They dump the goldfish out of the water-filled plastic bag and into a small globe fishbowl. And that's where the goldfish will spend the rest of its not-so-long life.

A goldfish isn't a great choice for a tiny fishbowl. Goldfish need more oxygen than most other fish, and they make more messes—which means yucky water all the time.

If you have to have a fish in a little bowl, a better choice is the betta, also known as the Siamese fighting fish. But don't put another fish in there, or you'll see where the fighting fish got its name. If there's nothing cool going on in the betta's bowl—no plants, nothing to play with—it'll jump out of the bowl. Even bettas can get bored in a fishbowl.

How long can you last when you're by yourself—no TV, no games, no phone, no iPod, no computer? What if you were thrown into a tiny prison cell, as small as a fishbowl to a goldfish? The one thing you could still do there is ponder. You could still think and pray and connect with God.

Mary "pondered" everything about Jesus. She was getting flak from nearly everyone around her, but she knew how to survive by connecting with God in her mind. She pondered, or thought deeply, about the things of God.

Most of us are rotten at pondering. Give us a list of 25 things to rush around and do to get ready for Christmas, and we can check off the list—no problem. But tell us to sit and be still and think about what it means that Christ was born, what it really means to us, that's hard work.

This Christmas, take time out to ponder.

Mary treasured up all these things and pondered them in her heart.

LUKE 2:19, NIV

AMAZING BIRTHS

Some pretty amazing births take place in the animal world. Some take longer in the pregnancy stage than others. Opossums only carry their babies 12 days. Mice carry their babies about 20 days; skunks, 31; dogs, 60; cats, 63; and horses about 336 days.

But that's nothing. Camels take 400 days; giraffes, 425; rhinos, 450 to 540; and the African elephant 700 days, give or take a couple of months. Yet the winner is the spiny dogfish shark, which just might be pregnant for up to two years.

Some animals, like rhinos and horses, almost always have one baby at a time. And then there's the tailless tenrec, which has been known to have as many as 31 babies at once.

Some babies, like kangaroo joeys, need to stay close to their moms after birth. But a kiwi baby hatches in time to wave good-bye to its mother as Dad takes over. Baby fish swim as soon as they hatch. Antelope can run with the herd within an hour after birth.

When your mom had you, she probably carried you for close to 266 days (eight days shy of nine months). And that's about the amount of time Mary carried Jesus in her womb.

When God sent his Son Jesus to earth, every care was taken for Jesus to be born fully human (and fully God). Jesus was born like other babies. He experienced everything the way we do so he can fully understand everything we go through.

The God of the universe, the one who created wombs, let himself be closed into a womb for nine months and then be born as a baby.

Talk about an amazing birth!

Look! The virgin will conceive a child! She will give birth to a son, and they will call him Immanuel, which means "God is with us."
MATTHEW 1:23

The blue whale's baby grows inside her for 10 months, until it weighs about three tons. The birthing is so hard that most whales have a whale "midwife" that helps the mother push out the big baby and swim with it to the surface of the water so Baby Blue Whale can get its first breath.

• • •

TODAY: As part of your Christmas celebration, talk with your family about how each of you got here. What was it like for your grandparents to give birth to your parents? For your parents to have you and your siblings? What do you think it was like for Mary and Joseph?

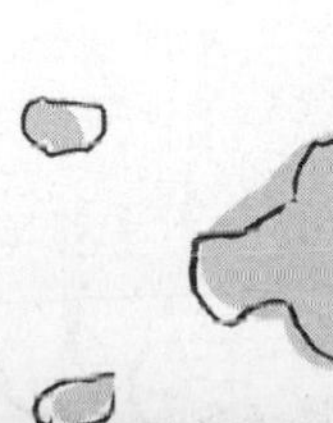
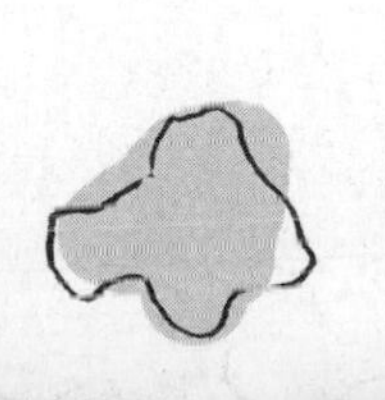

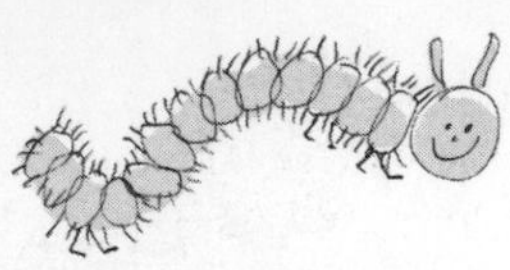

26 December

JUST A FLUKE?

Some of the definitions for *fluke* are "an accidental advantage," "a chance happening," or "a stroke of good luck." If you're usually a crummy speller but you score 100 percent on your spelling test without studying, you could say it was a fluke.

The liver fluke looks like an odd worm, and its life cycle is one of the oddest (and grossest) in the animal kingdom.

For the liver fluke, life begins when Mom lays her eggs in sheep dung. A snail crawls by and eats some of the eggs, and eventually the eggs hatch inside the snail. Out come thousands of little flukes. Only they gather together into a slimy ball, and the snail can't take it anymore. So the snail shoots out the slimy fluke ball.

Ants happen along and munch on that slimy ball. Not a good move. Inside the ant's stomach, flukes eat into the ant's stomach wall and grow into adults.

But one fluke gets a super-duper, special job—to brainwash the ant. It burrows into the ant's brain and somehow convinces the poor ant to climb to the top of a blade of grass and stay there for hours, until one of the grazing sheep ambles by and eats the grass, brainwashed ant and all.

Success! The fluke is now in the sheep's liver, where it matures and lays eggs. Eventually the sheep will get rid of it, and it will end up in sheep dung. Then along comes a snail, and . . .

What a plan! Yet the amazing life of a fluke is nothing compared to the plan God has for *your* life! God is so in control! You may never get a clear picture of the way God orchestrates events in your life to get you where you need to be. But this much is sure: it's no fluke.

> *We may throw the dice, but the LORD determines how they fall.*
>
> **PROVERBS 16:33**

A type of silk caterpillar doesn't like dangling in plain sight for caterpillar-loving birds. Instead of hanging in its cocoon all alone, the caterpillar first prepares five or six other cocoons just like the real one it will be entering. The others become decoys, making it tougher on a bird to choose which leaf has the caterpillar.

• • •

TODAY: Look back at some of the "accidents" or "flukes" in your life. Then thank God that he's in control of everything.

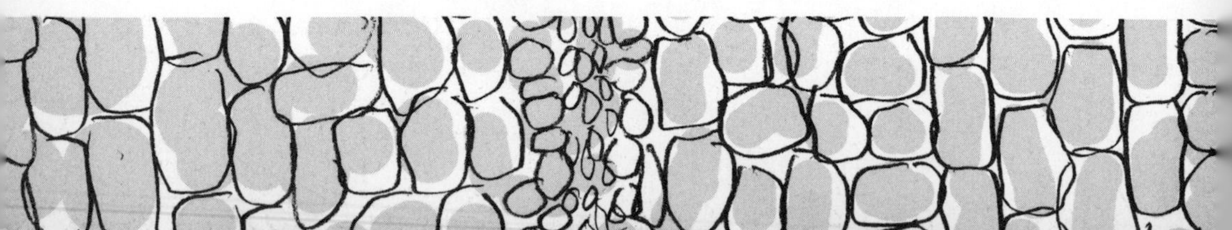

CROCODILE TEARS

There was an ancient belief that crocodiles cried real tears while eating their victims. Then someone noticed that only saltwater crocodiles cry. And the way they go after their victims makes you wonder how sincere those saltwater crocs really are.

The truth is, saltwater crocodiles "cry" to get rid of the salt. They're not sorry at all. And that's why crying crocodile tears has come to mean pretending to be sorry when you're really not.

It's so important for us to be honest with God and with other people. Insincere tears might fool your mom, but God knows your heart.

The prophet Hosea delivered God's messages to the religious leaders of his day. Many of those leaders at least pretended to take the message to heart. They made a big show of being sorry for all they'd done wrong. But they didn't try to make up for their wrongs. They didn't return to God. God said they cried on their beds, but they weren't crying out to him. They were just crying for themselves.

When are you truly sorry? Is it only when you're caught? God knows the answer. He's the absolute lie detector, and he can tell when you say you're sorry but you really aren't.

We all have a lot to be sorry about. Let God's Spirit convict you so that your sorrow will be real.

> *They do not cry out to me with sincere hearts. Instead, they sit on their couches and wail.*
> **HOSEA 7:14**

The female Nile crocodile lays her eggs in nests on sandy riverbanks, then buries the eggs in the sand. When the eggs hatch, the crocodile babies cry. Mama Croc digs them out of the sand and carries them in her mouth, one by one, to the river.

• • •

TODAY: Talk to God about the last few times you said, "I'm sorry" and the last few times you cried. Ask God to nail you when you're insincere. Try putting your "sorrow" into action and doing whatever you can to make things better for the people you wronged. Tell God how sorry you are—for real this time.

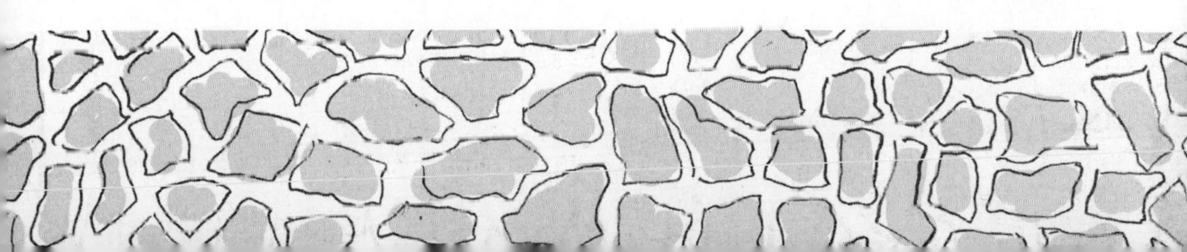

IS THAT A THREAT?

Some animals do the weirdest things when they feel threatened, even if the threat isn't real.

When the puss moth caterpillar feels threatened, the little worm stands up tall (as tall as it can), wags its tail forward, and squirts acid at the enemy.

Ladybugs have the same idea. They release not-so-pleasant chemicals from their knees. When a lubber grasshopper feels threatened, it oozes gross goo from its mouth, while the horned lizard simply squirts a jet of blood from its eyes.

Tiger moths let out high-pitched warning clicks to a would-be threat, alerting the predator that it won't get away with anything: "I taste yucky. You'll be so sorry if you eat me."

If you feel threatened, what do you do? Do you decide you'd better not take any chances? Hit them before they hit you? Get some buddies to back you up?

What if you think kids are making fun of you but you're not positive? Do you launch into a verbal war, just in case?

If you're really physically threatened, you need to tell an adult who can help. But there are a lot of possible ways to react to people you only think are threatening you. Maybe you can come up with the right thing to say to defuse the whole threat. Maybe you can laugh or joke your way out of it.

But the first thing you need to do is turn to God. God can help calm you so you can think clearly.

Let God show you what to do when you feel threatened. Go to him first.

> *When evil people come to devour me, when my enemies and foes attack me, they will stumble and fall. Though a mighty army surrounds me, my heart will not be afraid. Even if I am attacked, I will remain confident.*
>
> **PSALM 27:2-3**

When a porcupine is threatened by a snake, the porcupine stands its ground but doesn't fight back. It doesn't have to. It lets the snake attack those spiky quills until it gives up and slithers away, all worn out. Then the porcupine continues on its way.

• • •

TODAY: Think back over the last three times you felt threatened. Talk to God about the way you reacted to the threat and how you should handle it if there is a next time.

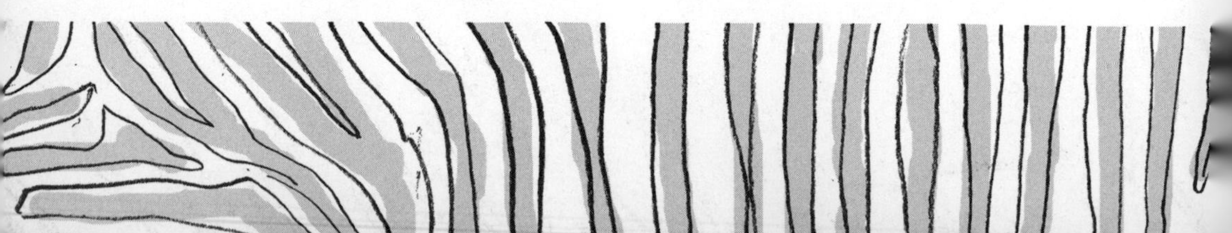

COLOR-BLIND

In a bullfight, when a matador waves his red cape to taunt the charging bull, why does the bull get all fired up? Do bulls hate the color red?

The answer is no. Bulls don't even see red. They're color-blind. At a bullfight, it's the motion of the cape that drives the bull to charge.

When animals or people are color-blind, it means they can't see the range of colors most of us see. For most people who are color-blind, the world appears in blues, yellows, grays, and other shades, but reds and greens are missing (which makes stoplights interesting).

Dogs, cats, mice, rats, and rabbits have poor color vision. Monkeys, squirrels, and certain fish, birds, and insects see fairly well in color. Butterflies and bees see more colors than we do. Some birds see a wider range of color, which explains why some birds are so brightly colored. The colors are appreciated!

Do you ever feel like you see certain things totally differently than your parents see them? Your mom thinks you're turning into a punk, but you think you're finally cool. Your dad wonders where his little girl is, but you believe you've discovered your true self.

Yet when you're honest, you have to admit that even you see things differently on any given day. Yesterday you felt great. Today you don't think you have a friend in the world. How do you know which view is for real?

God's viewpoint is the only true one. We all need to try to see the world through his eyes and to see ourselves as God sees us.

Ezekiel warned Pharaoh that he had no idea what the truth was about himself: "You think of yourself as a strong young lion among the nations, but you are really just a sea monster, heaving around in your own rivers, stirring up mud with your feet"(Ezekiel 32:2).

Ask God to keep you from being "color-blind" about yourself.

> *You say, "I am rich. I have everything I want. I don't need a thing!" And you don't realize that you are wretched and miserable and poor and blind and naked.*
>
> **REVELATION 3:17**

When a Florida man's Seeing Eye Dog, a German shepherd, went blind, the man couldn't stand the thought of retiring his beloved guide dog. So he got Howdy, a boxer, as his Seeing Eye Dog's Seeing Eye Dog.

• • •

TODAY: Take time to see your world through God's eyes. Ask him to search your heart and to show you if you're lying to yourself in any areas of your life.

ANIMAL RESCUE

Every second, eight companion animals are killed because no one wants them. Animal shelters are overflowing with pets people decided were too much trouble. Pet owners who don't neuter or spay their pets get puppies and kittens they can't give away. So off to a shelter they go. Out of sight, out of mind.

There are so many unwanted dogs that it would take every person in the world to own seven dogs apiece (and to neuter or spay those dogs) for the euthanasia of dogs to stop.

But it wasn't supposed to be like that.

When God created the world, he delighted in fashioning every creature on earth. Animals didn't just happen. God reveals something about himself in every living creature. After he made animals, he created human beings in his own image. And one of the first duties God mentioned was that humans would reign over the fish, birds, livestock, wild animals, and small animals.

When we think about God reigning over us, we don't think of him cracking a whip and demanding things from us. Instead, he cares for us, leads us, and loves us.

We have a responsibility to care for animals. So how can you do that? First, before you get a pet, make sure your family can handle it. Talk to pet owners and see what's involved in raising that dog, horse, iguana, or cat. Read about the animal. Contact several local and online animal agencies to learn more.

Then consider adopting a pet from a good shelter or adoption site. You'll be rescuing one animal, and that's a great place to start.

> *God said, "Let us make human beings in our image, to be like us. They will reign over the fish in the sea, the birds in the sky, the livestock, all the wild animals on the earth, and the small animals that scurry along the ground."*
>
> **GENESIS 1:26**

GREAT RESCUE SITES

Adopt a Pet: www.adoptapet.com

Pets 911: www.pets911.com

The Animal Rescue Site: www.animalrescuesite.com

Petfinder: www.petfinder.com

• • •

TODAY: Enlist the help of a friend, and check out some of the animal rescue sites listed here. Many of the sites give ways you can help.

Humane Society: www.humanesociety.org

Local shelters: check your phone book or look online

Society for the Prevention of Cruelty to Animals: www.spcai.org

TAKING CARE OF GOD'S CREATURES

Proverbs 12:10 says, "The godly care for their animals."

Even before Adam and Eve sinned in the Garden of Eden, God put us in charge of caring for the animals he created. And animals have never needed us more desperately than they do now.

By early 2009, the list of endangered and threatened animal species was well over 1,000. (Check out the U.S. Fish and Wildlife Web site at www.fws.gov/endangered for daily updates.)

Endangered animals include beavers, bears, and bats; seals, sea lions, and sea turtles; whales and wolves. One-third of the world's amphibians are headed for extinction.

How would you like to lose the kangaroo, mountain gorilla, Siberian tiger, snow leopard, Komodo dragon, blue whale, California condor, prairie dog, and on and on? They'll all be gone eventually, if people don't take on the responsibility of caring for the animals.

What can you do? Plenty! Here are a few ideas that start close to home:

Adopt your pets from the pet shelter. Then take great care of your pets, and encourage your friends to do the same.

Put decals on picture windows if birds fly into the glass. Spread the word—and the decals.

Do school reports on endangered animals and animal care.

Write letters to the editor in various newspapers, alerting people about abuses to animals, encouraging people to adopt pets from shelters, or giving tips on how to care for pets.

Volunteer to help with animals at a local shelter.

Check out Web sites that offer specific ways you can help endangered animals all over the world, such as www.fws.gov/educators/students.html.

You care for people and animals alike, O Lord.
PSALM 36:6

Most dictionaries begin and end with the names of animals: *aardvark* (an anteater) to *zyzzyva* (a tropical American weevil).

• • •

TODAY: Write out a plan to help care for the animals God has put on earth. Get your friends to help too. Ask God to use you to make a difference.

COOL VERSES
ABOUT ANIMALS

Use this space to write some of your favorite animal verses you found in this book.

max is agood name Becawse

itsad. it isagood name Beagle Bear

it wonasix year ind row

Dog eat Dog world

COOL FACTS
ABOUT ANIMALS

Use this space to write some of your favorite animal facts you found in this book.

I love animuls Beause

it isagood animule

FAVORITE
ANIMALS
Snack's
Lions
chins
alugader li on's
wals Pig frogs
fox hipopotamis
caterpiller
parits cat
nemons rando are
wort hog grona hag
dog and a at
Birds. BaBBll Pinds
pupenfish I love
animals rabits
wals inons Drafl

MY STYLE
ANIMAL DRAWINGS

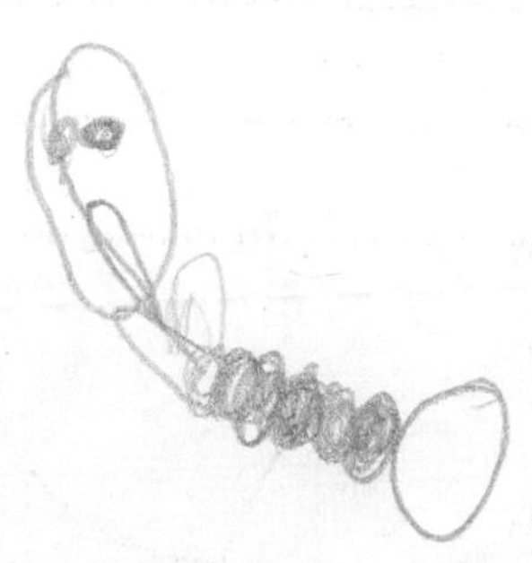

Dandi Daley Mackall grew up riding horses, taking her first solo bareback ride when she was three. Her best friends were Sugar, a Pinto; Misty, probably a Morgan; and Towaco, an Appaloosa. Dandi and her husband, Joe; daughters, Jen and Katy; and son, Dan, (when forced) enjoy riding Cheyenne, their Paint. Dandi has written books for all ages, including Little Blessings books, *Degrees of Guilt: Kyra's Story*, *Degrees of Betrayal: Sierra's Story*, *Love Rules*, *Maggie's Story*, the Starlight Animal Rescue series, and the best-selling series Winnie the Horse Gentler. Her books (about 450 titles) have sold more than 4 million copies. She writes and rides from rural Ohio.

Visit Dandi's Web site at
www.dandibooks.com

Winnie
The Horse Gentler